Makers
and Manners

Makers
and Manners

Politics and Morality in Postwar Britain

ANDREW HOLDEN

POLITICO'S

First published in Great Britain 2004 by
Politico's Publishing, an imprint of
Methuen Publishing Limited
215 Vauxhall Bridge Road
London SW1V 1EJ

10 9 8 7 6 5 4 3 2 1

A CIP catalogue record for this book is available from the British Library

ISBN 1 84275 115 8

Printed and bound in Great Britain by
Mackays of Chatham

Contents

Preface

A recent BBC Four programme entitled *I Hate the Sixties*, 'documentary' would be dignifying it undeservedly, presented a comprehensive demolition of the political, social and cultural currents of the decade, from abortion, homosexual and divorce law reform to architectural modernism, transport, urban planning and pop and youth culture. No opinion, whether uttered from right or left, was too outrageous to go unchallenged, like Anne Atkins' favourite line that abortion since 1967 was as bad as the Holocaust, as if the 1960s had invented abortion. There was not even a passing mention of the extent and horror of abortion before then – so much for BBC Four being 'a place to think' as it claims. What this exemplifies, which *Makers and Manners* seeks to challenge, is the 'tyranny of decades' which imprisons debate about postwar Britain. This phenomenon manifests itself in two ways. The first is a monochrome picture of history. The 1960s are, still, the black sheep of the family, as Tony Blair's most recent attack on a supposed '1960s liberal consensus on law and order' shows, but the 1950s and the 1980s are equally prone to lazy caricature from critics on the liberal left as well as nostalgic conservatives. The second is the ahistorical compartmentalisation of history. This enables commentators to ignore underlying trends and fix responsibility on totemic political actions which may or may not have had significant long-term effects. Recent books like Arthur Marwick's monumental history of the 'long' cultural revolution of 1957–1974 have begun to chip away at some of these artificial walls preventing a more nuanced understanding of historical trends. This book takes the same approach to the political reaction to social and economic change in postwar Britain.

As yet there have been few accounts to take this story through the eventful first years of New Labour. As one political scientist, Philip Cowley, accurately predicted at the beginning of the Blair administration, the most profound effects on the political handling of issues of morality would come through Labour's implementation of devolution and incorporation of the European Convention on Human Rights into UK law. *Makers and Manners* charts this process, and it accounts for the rather leisurely approach taken in the last chapter of what is supposed to be a history of the whole postwar period. Inevitably the printer-cartridge runs out before the material.

With organised religion virtually dead as an inculcating moral force in Britain, the postwar uncertainty among politicians about the framework on which individual moral choices and public policy should be based has reached a new height. This is greatest where politics and sex collide, but recent controversy about binge-drinking and other anti-social behaviour show that concern about an insidious individualism, driven by the intertwined pressures of the commercial market, individual freedom and social deprivation, goes far wider. *Makers and Manners* charts the course of the political chasing of a new moral rainbow from the ruins of a Victorian Christian morality, through the utilitarianism embodied by Wolfenden and Warnock, to the language of equality and human rights under New Labour which, so far, has proved inadequate to fill the void.

While many of the protagonists are inevitably, sadly, dying off, there are still rich seams of untapped source material available to the contemporary historian. If interviews should be used sparingly, the national archives are rich in documents rolling off the Kew conveyor belt. More surprising are archives which have been totally neglected in the past, notably the Lambeth Palace Library, which holds the papers of successive Archbishops of Canterbury. Reading the papers of Geoffrey Fisher and Michael Ramsey can only make one empathise, and sympathise, with Rowan Williams. Even more remarkably, given the fact that they have been in the public domain for so long, little use has been made of much of the biographical material of the period, including the diarists – Crossman, Castle, Benn. What these and other biographical sources give, that has often been absent from writing on this subject, is any sense of what politicians were actually trying to do, or how difficult it was to achieve anything, in such a controversial area.

I have, of course, incurred many debts on the road, although all mistakes, of course, remain mine alone. Peter Hennessy continues to be both a guiding light and unfailing support. I hope his fulsome praise is at least partially justified. Few academics combine such talents as a scholar, teacher, recruitment consultant, friend, and gossip par excellence. The late Ben Pimlott was an inspiration. His biography of Harold Wilson first drew me to the study of the 1960s, and from there to one of the few aspects of that period that bore significant fruit, whether sweet or rotten, depending on your perspective. History, biography and Labour politics continue to be the poorer for his untimely passing.

Stuart Proffitt gave generously of his time and advice in the early stages of the project. Lorraine Harding, Pat Thane and Gabrielle Holden read early drafts and made myriad helpful suggestions for improvement, and Chris Lawrence-Pietroni helped with the proofs. Mark Jarvis allowed me to have a sneak preview of his excellent book on the Conservative administration of the 1950s. Simon Fanshawe, Jonathan Altaras and Paul Jozefowski were among those who helped enrich the tapestry of anecdote.

The following people were good enough to allow me time to bombard them with questions in writing or in person: Leo Abse, Baroness Boothroyd, Sir Brian Cubbon, Lord Deedes, Lord Dubs, Gwynneth Dunwoody MP, Lord Fowler, Stanley Henig, Anne Perkins, Alistair Service, Gillian Shephard MP, Baroness Williams, the late Lord Jenkins of Hillhead and the late Baroness Serota. Thanks also to staff at the National Archives in Kew, the British Library, the National Museum of Labour History in Manchester, Lambeth Palace Library, particularly Clare Brown.

Profound gratitude also goes to Joyce Quin MP and future political star Emily Bird. Fellow Marian Andrew Blick also always seemed to be on hand for moral support around Westminster. Sean Magee, my editor at Politico's, was a consistent champion and Martin Rowson's wonderful cartoon is a joy. Dominic Sweeney ironed out all the creases.

The unstinting support of my parents, Alan and Gabrielle, and their gastronomic refuge, provides the security one can only get at home. Finally, Alessandro is an example to us all, repeatedly showing what a determined creative mind can achieve, even in the harsh climate in which artists work. Without him I would have given up long ago, and this book is dedicated to him.

1. Introduction

'Dear Kate, you and I cannot be confined within the weak list of a country's fashion: we are the makers of manners, Kate; and the liberty that follows our places stops the mouth of all find-faults, – as I will do yours for upholding the nice fashion of your country in denying me a kiss: therefore, patiently and yielding.'

William Shakespeare, *Henry V*

'As our history only too clearly shows, it is comparatively easy to make criminal law and exceedingly difficult to unmake it.'

H. L. A. Hart, *Law, Liberty and Morality*[1]

'The only purpose for which power can rightfully be exercised over any member of a civilised community against his will is to prevent harm to others. His own good either physical or moral is not a sufficient warrant. He cannot rightfully be compelled to do or forbear because it will be better for him to do so, because it will make him happier, because in the opinions of others, to do so would be wise or even right.'

J. S. Mill, *On Liberty*[2]

'The Jains of India say that it is a sin to kill mosquitoes; the Jews think it wrong to eat pork; in England it is indecent to describe the sexual act in one syllable instead of three.'

Sir Edmund Leach, *A Runaway World?*[3]

'Now, of course, if any considerable body of Englishmen are arranging to marry their mothers, whether by accident or design, it must be stopped at once. But it is not a frequent occurrence in any class of English society. Throughout the course of my life I have not met more than six men who were anxious to do it.'

Dramatist Henry Arthur Jones on the banning of Sophocles' *Oedipus Rex* by the Lord Chamberlain[4]

Makers and Manners is the story of how successive governments since the Second World War coped with the social changes wrought by rising affluence and the decline of religion. In the six decades since 1945 Britain has changed from a society where public morality and the criminal law were firmly rooted in Christian doctrine and the sensibilities of late-Victorian England to one where the very existence of a public morality is questioned, and the laws governing the behaviour of individuals are affected more by a European human-rights document than by religious doctrine directly. This has not been an easy journey for many, either on the right or on the left. As affluence opened up new avenues to the British people from the mid-1950s onwards, the bonds of social cohesion began to be strained by the economic liberalism which Conservative governments espoused and encouraged. For the left, power in the 1960s and 1970s posed comparable dilemmas when greater social liberalism was added to the deprivation of many working-class communities. Politicians have also seemed caught by a profound naïveté about the effect of reforming laws governing individual behaviour and morality – on the one hand that changing the law will have precise effects, and on the other that these will be measurable. Years down the line, when the results are far from what was predicted, they express astonishment and disclaim responsibility. In 2004 a number of issues made headline news which demonstrated that politicians' perverse and contradictory attitudes toward issues of morality, at once obsessive and fearful, had not dimmed under New Labour. In fact, the role of government and politicians in shaping the moral climate is as controversial as ever.

The symbolic concatenation of these issues came with Tony Blair's pointed condemnation of the '1960s liberal, social consensus on law and order', when launching a new five-year strategy for the Home Office in July 2004. Displaying his unrivalled skill at kicking those of a liberal persuasion, while at the same time infuriating conservatives who believe he has encouraged dangerous liberal trends, the Prime Minister declared:

Today's strategy is the culmination of a journey of change both for progressive politics and for the country. It marks the end of the 1960s liberal, social consensus on law and order.

The 1960s saw a huge breakthrough in terms of freedom of expression, of lifestyle, of the individual's right to live their own personal life in the way they choose. It was the beginning of a consensus against discrimination, in favour of women's equality, and the end of any sense of respectability in racism or homophobia. Not that discrimination didn't any longer exist – or doesn't now

– but the gradual acceptance that it was contrary to the spirit of a new time. Deference, too, was on the way out and rightly. It spoke to an increasing rejection of rigid class divisions.

All of this has survived and strengthened in today's generation. But with this change in the 1960s came something else, not necessarily because of it but alongside it. It was John Stuart Mill who articulated the modern concept that with freedom comes responsibility. But in the 1960s revolution, that didn't always happen. Law and order policy still focused on the offender's rights, protecting the innocent, understanding the social causes of their criminality. All through the 1970s and 1980s, under Labour and Conservative govern-ments, a key theme of legislation was around the prevention of miscarriages of justice. Meanwhile some took the freedom without the responsibility. The worst criminals became better organised and more violent. The petty criminals were no longer the bungling but wrong-headed villains of old; but drug pushers and drug-abusers, desperate and without any residual moral sense. And a society of different lifestyles spawned a group of young people who were brought up without parental discipline, without proper role models and without any sense of responsibility to or for others. All of this was then multiplied, in effect, by the economic and social changes that altered the established pattern of community life in cities, towns and villages throughout Britain and throughout the developed world.

Here, now, today, people have had enough of this part of the 1960s consensus. People do not want a return to old prejudices and ugly discrimina-tion. But they do want rules, order and proper behaviour. They know there is such a thing as society. They want a society of respect. They want a society of responsibility. They want a community where the decent law-abiding majority are in charge; where those that play by the rules do well; and those that don't, get punished.'[5]

Of course, the quality of the prose wasn't as important to the Prime Minister as the spinning of the soundbite. Commentators were quick to pull apart some of the absurdities. What about the 1950s, when economic affluence began to loosen the bonds of the nuclear family and encourage individualism? What about the 1980s, when, according to the left, Thatcherism wrought havoc on the social fabric of Britain? What was this 1960s consensus on law and order anyway – the decriminalisation of suicide, the abolition of flogging in prisons and capital punishment? Was he suggesting Britain needed more miscarriages of justice? What about the attention gradually paid to victims of crimes previously largely ignored by conservatives, such as domestic violence and child abuse? Home Secretary David Blunkett was seen to distance himself from this absurdly extreme caricature of the 1960s and focus on the socially destructive effects of economic liberalism under Margaret Thatcher in the 1980s.

Whatever the historical illiteracy of Blair's speechwriters, there was a growing sense that politicians were grappling urgently with some of the unwelcome results of changes in postwar British society, and revisiting some of the solutions first fashioned in the 1960s. A growing focus of New Labour's health and criminal justice policies was the seemingly uncontrollable rise of 'binge drinking' among young people, the threat it posed to their long-term health, and its role in fuelling crime and anti-social behaviour. For the second year in a row, reports and research highlighting the continuing rise in the level of sexually transmitted diseases among young people also spoke to some of the unhappy consequences of greater individual freedom since the war. As the sociologist A. H. Halsey has concluded, 'these trends suggest that important sections of Britain's population have experienced the sexual revolution in a less responsible or educated fashion than the teenagers on the continent.'[6]

Just days before his '1960s' speech, Blair conceded in the House of Commons that the law on abortion might need reviewing in the light of scientific advances enabling more babies born before the twenty-four-week limit for terminations to survive. Most dramatically, Blair was pelted with purple flour bombs in the House of Commons by two members of the extremist Fathers4Justice pressure group, which had staged progressively more headline-grabbing stunts and successfully created an impression in the media that, in a large number of cases, fathers were being ruthlessly banned after divorce from contact with their children by mothers of almost Medean cruelty and family courts wholly biased against them. Both the Conservative Party and the government soon adopted new policies in an attempt to address these concerns. Any suggestion that the dominance of New Labour meant that feminism had triumphed in the politics of Blair's New Britain was further banished by the comments of Godfrey Bloom, Yorkshire MEP for the UK Independence Party who, on being nominated to sit on the Women's Rights Committee of the European Parliament (the UKIP contingent of MEPs comprised a total of twelve men and no women), railed against the modern woman:

> *I just think they don't clean behind the fridge enough. I am here to represent*
> *Yorkshire women, who always have the dinner on the table when you get home.*
> *I am going to promote men's rights … The more women's rights you have, it's*
> *actually a bar to their employment. No self-respecting small businessman with*
> *a brain in the right place would ever employ a lady of child-bearing age.*[7]

If political soul-searching about the changes in society's mores and the laws and regulations which govern them reached a new level at the beginning of the new century, the way in which politics discussed moral issues would seem very familiar to the politicians allegedly complicit in the 1960s liberal consensus. Unlike many continental countries, where the existence (and electoral success) of postwar Christian Democrat parties saw religious values manifest in the policies of those parties, the British party system has not neatly coincided with religious affiliation in society since parties coalesced in the nineteenth century.[8] The split in 1886 of the Liberal Party, and the subsequent defection of the 'Liberal Unionists' to the Conservatives, started the confusion. The rooting of the Labour Party, famously, in Methodism as much as in Marx reinforced the disorder as the Liberal Party declined. Labour has traditionally been the repository of most working-class Catholic voters, as well as the home of most non-religious political liberals and radicals. As non-Christian religious communities grew in late-twentieth-century Britain, the religious and moral perspective of Islam, Hinduism, Sikhism and other faiths gradually made their presence felt in political debate. Although Labour has historically been the repository for the vast majority of the votes of black people, many Asian voters felt more at home in the Conservative Party. An increasing tension between the traditional moral teaching of the evangelical black churches and the liberal human-rights-based policy of the Labour Party after 1997 has yet to make itself felt on the voting patterns of black Christians, but that tension is undoubtedly there.

The philosophical and practical difficulties of handling moral issues within the political parties has led to the convention, even political cliché, in Britain since the 1960s that issues of 'conscience' which touch on questions of morality should usually be dealt with by backbenchers in Parliament, or at least should be subject to free votes, without the discipline of the party whips. In 1945 such legislation was considered an anachronism of the Victorian pre-party age. It was particularly frowned upon by some Labour figures such as Harold Laski of the London School of Economics, who thought that once a majority Labour government was elected, it was the duty of that government, and all its members and backbench supporters, to concentrate on implementing its socialist programme. This exhortation, unlike other advice Laski gave Clement Attlee, was heeded, and no time for private members' legislation was allowed in 1945. Winston Churchill, before the war, had also commented that it should be made difficult for 'all sorts of happy thoughts to be carried on to the statute book'. But, by the end of the parliament, with all the main pillars of the new welfare state on the statute book and in operation, and the energy of the Attlee Government flagging, dying on its feet in fact, the procedure was reintroduced.[9]

By 1957 the foremost parliamentary historian of the period, Ivor Jennings, was noting approvingly that 'the fact that much government legislation is either vote-catching or of a departmental character renders desirable the provision of time for other measures'.[10] Yet although the procedure flourished during the 1950s, MPs were rarely actually able to effect significant social reform through their own legislation. Labour MP Eirene White's attempts to mitigate some of the harshness of divorce proceedings were deflected by a Royal Commission. Sydney Silverman was frustrated by the resistance of the Churchill and Eden Governments, and the House of Lords, to abolishing capital punishment, despite MPs voting for it in 1948 and 1956. Only a quick hit on prostitution by Barbara Castle in 1951, with backing from all sides, stands out. Roy Jenkins and Norman St John Stevas eventually forced the Macmillan Government to accept reform of the obscenity laws but had to fight hard to keep the provisions in the bill which were designed to protect literary works from censorship in a meaningful condition.

However, in 1964 Harold Wilson signalled a change of policy. Knowing that the majority of the Labour Party supported the abolition of capital punishment, he pledged to give the Commons time to come to a decision. More significantly, once in government he gradually appointed an array of Labour MPs and peers who had been active in promoting such liberalising legislation before 1964 to ministerial posts most relevant to law reform, including Jenkins, Dick Crossman, Gerald Gardiner, Douglas Houghton, Kenneth Robinson and John Silkin. It was just as well for the reformers that some of them, like Welsh maverick Leo Abse, were not offered jobs, otherwise there would have been even fewer people left on the back benches to perform the Sisyphean task of sponsoring such bills. Wilson attempted to enforce a vow of *omertà* on his ministers towards the substance of the moral issues involved. This was always something of a charade, but it was the price to be paid for the benevolence by which some bills were afforded extra parliamentary time. However, it elevated a tradition into almost a constitutional principle, which future governments, less generous with parliamentary time, would exploit to avoid their discussion. Wilson attempted to stick to this policy of neutrality on issues of conscience right until his retirement in 1976, shortly before which he balled out Castle, the social services secretary, about the damage she would do to party unity if she let it be known what her personal views on debating an abortion bill were.

At the beginning of the Blair era a new book, edited by Philip Cowley, tested three elements of the private-members cliché against the experience since 1970 – the theory that issues of 'conscience' were normally dealt with by private members' bills, that MPs normally had a free vote on such issues, and that Parliament, rather than the Government, controlled the agenda. Since 1997 private members' bills have continued to be an important vehicle for discussing moral issues which the main parties are not willing to sponsor within their manifestos, even where the balance of support for such issues within the main parties has been clear, for example the homosexual age of consent or fox-hunting. Interestingly, Peter Richards mused in 1970 about what the consequences would be if the House of Lords refused to accept a private members' bill which had passed the Commons. He now has the answer. The refusal of the House of Lords to pass these measures has meant that the Government has had to make the decision whether or not to use the Parliament Act to enforce the twice thwarted will of MPs. The private member's procedure has fallen into desuetude, with the time available, and the attendance at debate, falling even further as MPs' time becomes more pressured. Private members' bills are still a crucial way for new or marginal subjects of moral concern to be aired, for example religious discrimination or female genital mutilation. However, the number of private members' bills being passed has fallen considerably since 1997. Within this number there have been only a handful which have dealt with issues of 'conscience' as normally understood. Not surprisingly the largest number deal with animal welfare, and almost all are extremely limited in their scope compared to those issues which have been taken over by government legislation. Governments eat further into this private members' time by helpfully providing a list of 'off the peg' handout bills, which consist of small, technical measures which the government has not had time to implement. This is not a new practice. As David Steel recalls in his memoirs, if he had been so obliging, he could have gone down in history as the instigator of the Plumbers Registration Act, rather than relaxed abortion legislation.[11] Another alternative tactic which has been on the rise again since 1970 has been the practice of MPs piggy-backing their own reforms on to government measures as amendments during the passage of a bill. The first time MPs voted to abolish capital punishment in 1948 was an early postwar example. This was how the controversial Section 28 became law in 1988, banning the promotion of homosexuality as a 'pretended family relationship' by local authorities. Appropriately this was also the vehicle for its repeal in 2003. As ye sow, so shall ye reap.

The period in the late 1960s was, to the extent that private members' bills dealt with so many significant issues, atypical. After 1970 'conscience issues', defined as ones where MPs are allowed a free vote, tended more to be subsumed within government legislation either as government bills or amendments to them. However, it is important to set all these measures throughout the postwar period within a wider context. During the first Wilson administration private members' bills were complemented by government policies aimed at extending personal freedom and softening the harshness of Victorian public morality. Race relations and equal pay legislation began to remove the social disabilities facing the growing ethnic minority population and women. Incredibly, neither the Commons nor the Lords ever debated the introduction of the oral contraceptive pill. Some parliamentarians began to raise concerns about the long-term health risks, including possible cancers and thrombosis, from about 1962. But there was no discussion of the potential benefits of the Pill, or the wider question of its implications for control of women's fertility or the separation of sexual intercourse from reproduction. Only when family-planning services were extended under the NHS Family Planning Act 1967 did Parliament systematically consider this fundamental development in individuals' control over their fertility.

The role of the House of Lords in debating issues of morality in the postwar period has been highly significant, acting at different times as both a stimulus to, and brake on, reform. In the Commons, the chances of a private members' bill even being debated are slim, and are dependent either on the pot-luck of the annual ballot, in which only the first dozen or so can expect this, or securing a debate under the ten-minute rule procedure, as Barbara Castle's Prostitution Bill did in 1950. Such motions can easily be objected to by opponents. In the Lords private members' bills are accorded much greater respect. They are more usually given a second reading, often without a vote, though when the Earl of Arran attempted to reduce the age of consent for homosexuality from twenty-one to eighteen in 1977 (which had originally been the recommendation of the Wolfenden Committee in 1957), opponents led by the Earl of Halsbury massively defeated the Bill at second reading, and peers similarly refused to give further consideration to the repeal of Section 28 in 2000. The importance of the Lords as a forum for moral debates was raised precisely because it was more willing, from the late 1950s onwards, to contemplate reform which the executive-dominated Commons shied away from. The introduction of life peers in 1958 was an important watershed. Significantly, among the first people to be given life peerages was former Conservative MP Bob Boothby, the (allegedly bisexual) lover of Dorothy Macmillan, wife of his friend, the Prime Minister, Harold Macmillan. Boothby, who was to skirt round sexual scandal towards the end of that Conservative administration when it was suggested he had some association with Ronnie Kray, consistently supported homosexual law reform, being one of the first MPs to champion the cause in the early 1950s, and was responsible for one failed attempt to bring Scottish law into line with that in England and Wales in 1978. Another of the 1958 trailblazers was the economist and social scientist Barbara Wootton. Her part in debates on moral issues over the following thirty years was more controversial. Although a strong liberal, she questioned some of the social and medical effects on women of contraception and divorce. In 1966 she was asked to chair a Royal Commission on drugs. Its report, which recommended a more liberal approach to soft drugs, was repudiated by Jim Callaghan as Home Secretary and caused him to make his oft-quoted condemnation of the excesses of the permissive society. Life peerages were successful in gradually re-energising (and legitimising) the House of Lords, not least by the introduction of women and people from an increasingly wide range of social backgrounds including, eventually, members of ethnic minorities.

However, it would be wrong to characterise the body of hereditary peers as wholly conservative in its approach to issues of morality. In fact, as the number of life peers did not reach 100 until 1964, their numerical effect was limited, even if their personal advocacy punched about their numerical weight.[12] The leading sponsor of homosexual law reform during the 1960s in the House of Lords was the Earl of Arran. His dogged determination to remove what he saw as the humiliating persecution of unfortunate homosexuals sprang from the personal tragedy of the suicide of his older, homosexual, brother – a tragedy which led to his succeeding to the earldom. Yet it continued to be the hereditary peers who produced some of the stoutest defences of traditional moral values. The Earl of Halsbury, who led resistance to the lowering of the age of consent for homosexuality in the late 1970s, returned to the fray for a spectacular swansong, just before the majority of the hereditary peers were excluded from the House in 1999. What Lord Halsbury attempted to do had eluded conservatives for four decades. Since Roy Jenkins' Obscene Publications Act in 1959 it had become almost impossible to gain a conviction from a jury for publishing obscene material – the definition of what constituted 'obscenity' seemed illusory. Halsbury found the solution in a detailed, copper-bottomed list of sexual acts, the description or depiction of which would fall within the ambit of the 1959 Act. He admitted he had spent a considerable time researching and preparing its contents. The list is worth reproducing, if only because it provides a wonderful dinner party game in which the person who manages to define the highest number of acts, without the use of a dictionary, wins.[13]

Activities relevant to the definition of obscenity
Anal fisting
Analingus
Anal sadism
Auto-erotism
Bestiality
Bisexuality
Bondage, or other acts of force or restraint associated with such activity
Buggery
Cunnilingus
Coitus
Coprolagnia
Coprophilia

Display of human genital organs

Ejaculation

Erection

Exhibitionism

Fellatio

Flagellation

Gynaecomastia

Hermaphroditism

Human urinary or excretory functions

Interlingual kissing

Masochism

Masturbation

Mutilation, torture or other acts of gross violence towards humans or animals,
    whether real or simulated

Necrophilia

Nymphomania

Paedophilia

Sadism

Sado-masochism

Scopophilia

Sodomy

Trans-sexualism

Troilism

Urolagnia

Urophilia

Vaginal fisting

Voyeurism

Grateful to the Leader of the House, Lord Williams of Mostyn, for pointing out that the list included nymphomania, but no equivalent male condition, Lord Halsbury returned at committee stage with an amendment to add 'satyriasis' which, as with the Bill as a whole, was accepted without a division. Lord Rowallan, whose father, the Chief Scout, had produced some of the choicest words to condemn homosexuality during debates in the 1960s, observed wryly, 'If it succeeded in passing through the other place and became law surely the first thing that would run foul of its terms would be the Bill itself, which could not even be printed or published' – as would also be the case with this book.[14]

The new willingness of the House of Lords to consider changes in the criminal law relating to morality at the head of, or beyond, public opinion during the 1960s did not last long. During the Thatcherite hegemony of the 1980s the House of Lords did not challenge some of the more conservative initiatives such as Section 28. Even with the exit of most of the hereditary peers in 1999, an alliance of Conservative, crossbench and Labour peers continued to exert a conservative brake on policies which the Commons overwhelmingly supported, notably the equalisation of the age of consent at sixteen, the repeal of Section 28, and adoption by non-married couples. However, this alliance has now begun to break down. The age of consent was equalised in 2000 using the Parliament Act. But following the death of Baroness (Janet) Young in 2002, who had galvanised much of the opposition to these reforms, the effective whip behind the alliance was absent, and by 2003 both these other measures passed the Lords with surprisingly solid majorities. However, the Lords has not stood still in tackling new moral issues. Its Science and Technology Committee, established in 1979, has in recent years been at the forefront of discussion of the moral implications of new technologies, conducting important inquiries on subjects including the medical use of cannabis, the development of a genetic database and the relationship between science and society.

The Home Office has been the department at the centre of most of the postwar battles over morality and the law. In the words of one wartime Home Secretary, Herbert Morrison, 'the corridors of the Home Office are paved with dynamite.'[15] Because the Home Office patrols the border between the state and the individual citizen, its role is fraught with political dangers, with almost every decision and almost every action taken in the name of the Home Secretary, of which he may only become aware afterwards, being the subject of the parliamentary or media spotlight. Whether or not a Home Secretary aims to go down in history as a liberal or a reactionary there is a warning, as Sir Brian Cubbon, former Permanent Secretary at the Home Office (and Northern Ireland) made clear to new incumbents:

The thing about the Home Office I used to tell Home Secretaries rather pompously when they arrived was, 'Look out of that window, and every person you see thinks he can be Home Secretary tomorrow, and they won't aspire to being Chancellor or even Foreign Secretary, but they'd all take on being Home Secretary.[15]

Perhaps not surprisingly, the Home Office sees itself rather differently from its critics. Though Jenkins is famed for his shepherding of liberal reforms on homosexuality, abortion and penal policy, according to one former Home Office official who served there from Attlee to Thatcher, his effect on the department was as much about the culture of its work as the promotion of liberal policies. According to Sir Brian Cubbon, after the war

officials knew best, they were liberal and sensible, clear thinking, short-term in their outlook totally, but Ministers just read the speeches in Parliament. The arrival of Jenkins, and particularly special advisers, was really an affront to those who thought they were in charge ... It was a cultural, machinery-of-government revolution, as well as an ideas revolution.

The idea that Home Office officials were a conservative obstacle to considering reform is not borne out either by the recollections of politicians and officials, or by the Home Office records, which show a willingness to try to implement the wishes of their political masters, whether Conservative or Labour. In Cubbon's words:

The Home Office has been used since time immemorial to react to irresistible public and parliamentary pressure when it turns out to be irresistible. Not certainly out of reactionary reasons, [but] for idleness, in the sense you've got to find people to do this work. But also from the bitter experience of the law of unintended consequences.

There was a strong tradition that I was brought up in that the Home Office was the final guardian of the liberty of the subject, and the other departments were always rushing ahead and stopping people doing things, creating criminal offences and that it was the Home Office that would stop these nonsenses in the interests of the liberty of the subject.[16]

Whereas former Home Office ministers seem forever to be reliving the political nightmares surrounding their law and order responsibilities, their officials can be keen to play down this 'negative' side of the department's responsibilities. Lord Allen of Abbeydale, who as Sir Philip Allen was Permanent Secretary from 1966 to 1973, was at pains during a conference to mark the Home Office's bicentenary in 1982 to emphasise reforms covering censorship, prostitution, abortion and homosexual behaviour with which he dealt in the department.[17] Echoing Cubbon and Allen, Lord Armstrong of Ilminster, Home Office boy before disappearing 'in clouds of glory' into the Cabinet Office, was quoted by Hugo Young as remembering 'concern for individual liberty' to be the most intrinsic quality of the Home Office and its officials.[18]

Such natural sympathy for individual liberty complemented the more liberal attitude heralded by Jenkins' arrival at the Home Office. Jenkins himself agreed with these views. Speaking in November 1999, and perhaps consciously echoing his words from his prospectus for the Home Office written in 1959, he dismissed suggestions that civil servants had resisted his ideas:

The Home Office was pretty good on this. There was no significant Home Office obstruction. The only sort of social measure of this sort that I had any sort of trouble on was second time around ... that was on the Sex Discrimination Bill [in] 1975. That was a dedicated Under-Secretary who was a woman, and she did try to sabotage it. I had to come down with firm Secretary of State authority on her. [Officials] broadly thought the Home Office was due for a bit of opening of windows and fresh air.[19]

Alan Travis, in his 'secret history' of obscenity, *Bound and Gagged*, identifies how civil servants reacted to attempts to prosecute such works as *Last Exit to Brooklyn*, by Hubert Selby Jr, and Henry Miller's *Sexus*.[20] Officials were also quick to tack to Jenkins' desire to push his Cabinet colleagues on homosexual law reform, abortion and theatre censorship. The Home Office of the postwar period has often been characterised as being run consecutively by a conservative authoritarian and then a relaxed liberal under Sir Charles Cunningham between 1957 and 1966, and Sir Philip Allen until 1972, the handover neatly coinciding with Jenkins' *annus mirabilis*. Like a vintage episode of *Yes Minister*, with Sir Humphrey successfully foiling Jim Hacker's attempts to change anything about the way things are done, Jenkins recalled in his memoirs a monumental battle to reform the centralised, authoritarian submission procedures under Cunningham. Only the purest, distilled essence of policy options were submitted to the Secretary of State, leaving little scope to challenge the prevailing view, a strategy which, he says, had contributed to failure for the two previous Home Secretaries.[21] But according to Cubbon, this did not mean that Cunningham was a 'do-nothing' permanent secretary, rather a 'do-everything' permanent secretary: 'Cunningham came up in a school that thought Parliament was the public, and that if you persuaded Parliament … you'd done it. And the thought of having to prepare opinions below that through the media was a new world to him.'[22] This tradition of centralisation did not, however, die a death with the arrival of Jenkins. According to Jim Callaghan it was still, frustratingly, alive and well when he was Home Secretary, though easing gradually, with a more open and discursive atmosphere among officials.[23]

Perhaps the most significant innovation on the official side of government in the postwar period was the creation, following an election manifesto commitment in 1964, of the Law Commissions (for Scotland and for England and Wales). The idea for a body which would advise the government on legal reform was worked out in opposition by Gerald Gardiner, subsequently one of the most successful Lord Chancellors of the twentieth century, who oversaw its birth and infancy throughout the first Wilson administration.[24] The Commission agreed an annual programme of work with the Lord Chancellor, but was independent, staffed and run by lawyers. Though some of its work has always been technical and uncontroversial, from the beginning it also risked controversy by looking at areas of law which it considered were ripe for overhaul – family law being one of the first. This meant that when pressure for divorce law reform reached its peak after 1966, the Law Commission was in a good position to attempt to take some of the heat out of the controversy by producing an options paper, *The Field of Choice,* on which legislation could draw.[25] The Law Commission was innovative in another way, because it set a pattern of institutional reform which was followed closely thereafter, whereby semi-independent public bodies or 'quangos', an increasingly pejorative acronym, were entrusted with the task of reviewing existing practices, regulating administration or the activities of outside interests, or representing and promoting the interests of different groups in society. In addition to the Law Commission, the Wilson Government also established in 1965 the Race Relations Board and, in its second incarnation, the Equal

Opportunities Commission. In the 1980s, the recommendation of the Warnock Commission that such a body be set up to regulate human fertilisation treatment and embryology research was enshrined in the Human Fertilisation and Embryology Authority, established in 1990. In 1998 the Disability Rights Commission was added to the two existing equalities bodies, and following the incorporation of the European Convention for the Protection of Human Rights (ECPHR) in the Human Rights Act 1998, there were increased calls for a Human Rights Commission to be established to oversee the Act's operation and promote a culture of human rights, something which existed in many other countries. To date, this is a move which the Blair Government has resisted, preferring to move towards combining the existing equalities bodies in a single 'Equalities and Human Rights Commission'. This mania for establishing quangos to oversee the development and administration of policy was partially an attempt to lend their decisions a degree of political impartiality which keeping the work 'in house' would lack. However, Cubbon, who as a senior Home Office official worked closely with these bodies, suggests:

> *I think it's true that in those days governments wanted to have control of changes. The thought of giving the courts principles to apply was not part of the normal course of things. There was legislation but it was mainly setting up the bodies and providing for the actual manning of anti-discrimination. The culture was to have bodies to do it.*[26]

The attitude of other central government departments at the forefront of regulation and reform of public morality and individual behaviour since the Second World War also reflects their different perspectives and organisational cultures, and has often resulted in sharp interdepartmental clashes. The Department of Health, which during its incarnation as a 'super-ministry' combined with Social Security, from the late 1960s to the 1990s, was known as the Department of Stealth and Total Obscurity, approached moral issues from a predominantly medical perspective. While this could often manifest itself in a practical concern for the health of groups within society and individual citizens, for example over the spread of contraception and combating disease, it also had a restricting influence on people's access to new services, treatments and technologies. As advances heralded greater liberation, particularly for women, from the 1960s, a shift from the prohibition of women's behaviour to its medicalisation occurred. Hence the strict provision within the Abortion Act that two doctors must certify legitimate grounds for an abortion. At least in theory, there was no abortion on demand in Britain, unlike much of the rest of Europe by the 1990s.

The traditional decentralisation of education provision in Britain has meant that postwar educational responses to changing social structures, behaviour and attitudes have been inconsistent and diffuse. Many on the right, and even some on the left, apportion much of the blame for a post-1960s collapse in moral standards and behaviour amongst the young to the spread of fashionable child-centred teaching methods, which minimise the importance of discipline and instruction for the sake of individual development. Whitehall was responsible mostly for the structure of educational provision, much of the funding and issuing guidance on different areas of policy. There was little central direction, particularly where sensitive issues like sex and religious education were concerned. From the early 1960s, when changes in sexual behaviour and attitudes began to influence what some teachers and educationalists thought should be included in sex education, this became a fierce battleground. By the 1980s it had assumed central importance, with the government bowing to pressure to outlaw anything which might 'promote' homosexuality, and allowing parents to opt out of sex education for their children. No government until 1997 made any concerted effort to use sex education to tackle increasing health problems, and even then there was a paralysis of fear at the idea that sex education should be standardised.

The Lord Chancellor's Department has consistently punched above its weight where the law impinges on fundamental matters of moral principle. Since the Second World War those who have graced the Woolsack in the Lords, from Kilmuir and Gardiner to Hailsham and Irvine, have played a significant role in relation to family law and sexual morality. In recent years the department has accrued new responsibilities for human rights and other areas of policy from a shrinking Home Office. Responsibility for the Law Commission greatly increased the department's capacity for innovation and influence across Whitehall.

The Treasury's fiscal responsibility has put it at the centre of the debate about the relative morality of high or low taxes, but it is only more recently that it has assumed a dominant position in shaping debate about the family. In 1964, when

Callaghan became Chancellor, the Treasury discussed possible plans to subsidise teenagers in order to influence their social behaviour, though nothing came of these proposals.[27] By the early 1990s, political concern about the spiralling cost to the Exchequer of social security led Tory ministers to question the morality of those on benefit, particularly single mothers. More recently, under the chancellorship of Gordon Brown, greater Treasury control over the benefits system has resulted in a more unified approach to support for families, with clear implications for state approval or disapproval for different family structures, notably the move from special treatment for married couples to extra help for any parents with children. Fiscal incentive has increasingly been seen by moral conservatives as the most potent tool to indicate the state's approval of the traditional nuclear family and marriage and maintain any social stigma attaching to single parenthood, divorce or other 'undesirable' domestic arrangements. But even during the Thatcher and Major administrations, these carrots and sticks were being withdrawn, and by the beginning of the twenty-first century, Tory policy was swinging dramatically behind the idea of helping all parents, regardless of their status.[28]

Though most politicians have tried to avoid issues of morality like the plague, a few dominant individuals have directed debate about public morality and the law in the postwar period. By the mid-1950s, with the urgent issues of postwar economic and social reconstruction largely settled by the establishment of the welfare state and a mixed economy, politicians began to look to wider social changes which had partly been encouraged by the war itself, but which had then been ossified as postwar priorities imposed themselves. In 1956 Tony Crosland published his seminal work, *The Future of Socialism*, in which he focused on greater equality in society on a much wider canvas than before: 'Socialists cannot go on indefinitely professing to be concerned with human happiness and the removal of injustice, and then, when the programmes are decided, permitting the National Executive, out of fear of certain vocal pressure-groups, to become more orthodox than the bench of bishops.'[29]

Crosland's thesis was reflected in detail in the personal manifesto of his friend and rival Roy Jenkins for the post of Home Secretary, which the latter coveted and attained in 1965. Writing in *The Labour Case* in 1959, Jenkins listed a number of reforms, from the abolition of capital punishment and relaxation of theatre censorship to decriminalising homosexuality. The Labour leader Hugh Gaitskell's liberal credentials were not quite as pure as those of some of his younger lieu-tenants. During the drafting of Labour's 1961 policy statement, *Signposts for the Sixties*, he supported Harold Wilson's assertion that endorsing the Wolfenden recommendations on homosexuality would cost the party six million votes, saying, 'Can't we be sure this time not to say things which are going to lose us votes?'[30] Although more instinctively liberal than Wilson,[31] Gaitskell also remained aloof from parliamentary efforts at reform during the early 1960s.[32] Gaitskell's deputy, the frequently lubricated George Brown, was repulsed by his colleagues' fondness for embracing and encouraging the trends underlying the 'Swinging Sixties', regaling them before a vote on homosexuality in 1966 with his view:

> *This is how Rome came down. And I care deeply about it – in opposition to most of my Church [he was Anglo-Catholic]. Don't think teenagers are able to evaluate your liberal ideas. You will have a totally disorganised, indecent and unpleasant society. You must have rules! We've gone too far on sex already. I don't regard any sex as pleasant. It's pretty undignified and I've always thought so.*[33]

Wilson had personally committed Labour to giving time for Parliament to come to a decision on capital punishment. However, his nonconformist background disinclined him to wider consideration of sexual morality. In a typically Wilsonian exposition of inoffensive agnosticism, and a wonderfully Pythonesque version of his famous comment that he preferred tinned salmon to fresh, Wilson compared his Yorkshire childhood atmosphere of chapel preachers with his Oxford years in a toe-curling interview for the *Daily Express* in 1960:

> *In later years I came to spend long hours grappling with the thoughts of the world's greatest philosophers, Plato, Aquinas, Descartes, Leibniz, Spinoza, Kant. I spent memorable hours listening to some of the greatest philosophers and theologians of our day. But I cannot say they added more to my conviction than those simple homely phrases which carried with them the burning sincerity of faith.*[34]

The first postwar government to accord questions of personal morality and the family a central place in its philosophy and rhetoric was Margaret Thatcher's. Just as its economic liberalism owed much to the failings of state planning under

Wilson in the 1960s, so Thatcher's traditional social outlook was reinforced by what she saw as the insidiousness of the permissive society which Labour had encouraged under Wilson. Yet, as Thatcher herself admits in *The Path to Power*, she had voted for decriminalisation of homosexuality and abortion law reform during the 1960s. She regretted this, arguing that these, together with other reforms, amounted to more than the sum of their parts, rather than simply removing legal anomalies as she and others had intended, and had led to further, unacceptable demands.[35] However, as will be seen in the chapters on the Thatcher and Major administrations, this rhetoric was only occasionally matched by the reality of government policy. While ministers demonised certain groups such as single mothers and homosexuals, the demands of moral campaigners like Mary Whitehouse, whom Conservative politicians including Thatcher professed to support, were rarely met.

The position of prime ministers on moral issues, as elsewhere, is particularly exposed. During the Heath Government, apart from the extension of family planning, it was questions about censorship and pornography which were the dominant moral controversies, with ministers being pursued vigorously by Whitehouse and her supporters. But in this area the first unmarried prime minister since Arthur Balfour had a potential weakness which even an uncharacteristically hard-nosed Mary Wilson noted to Barbara Castle:

> *Mary Wilson said to me, as we escorted her and Harold from the [International Women's Year] reception, that she was always telling Harold's office they ought to make more use of her. 'With the Leader of the Opposition a bachelor we have an advantage we ought to exploit, but they won't listen to me.'*[36]

At the opposite end of a scale of sexual activity, Labour would hardly have needed to take advantage of Heath's Conservative successor but one, John Major, had knowledge of his four-year affair with Edwina Currie emerged at any time during his premiership, but the effect would have been most keenly felt after Major's 'Back to Basics' speech in October 1993. Although Major maintains that he never meant it to apply to personal morality, given the number in the party for whom personal morality was a front line, this was almost wilful naïveté. Since his adultery became public knowledge in 2002 this now looks more like recklessness.

Tony Blair's '1960s' speech was not, of course, the first time the most religious Prime Minister since William Gladstone had stepped into this territory. In September 1999 he made a broad appeal to moral values in response to press coverage of two pregnant twelve-year-old girls, and against a background of failing attempts to 'crack down' on juvenile anti-social behaviour. Calling for 'a new moral purpose' in Britain, Blair said that:

The idea that we should live in a moral and social vacuum is an abrogation of responsibility as adults. It is entirely different to moralising and preaching, which is not what the government is getting at ... No-one is talking about back to basics or a return to Victorian hypocrisy.[37]

However, Blair's comments did earn a 'friendly' rebuke from George Carey, Archbishop of Canterbury, about the dangers of governments moralising to the public.[38] Despite such injections of moral language into his rhetoric, Blair forcefully supported equal rights for minorities more than any of his predecessors. Although his government fell into the habit of timidly refusing to push through measures like the repeal of Section 28 as part of government legislation, Blair roundly condemned the prejudice which he saw behind Conservative support for the clause, voting consistently for its repeal and an equal age of consent.

There is a common misconception that politicians have been either white or black in their approach to moral issues. Leo Abse, non-practising Jewish sponsor of homosexual and divorce law reform, remained fervently opposed to abortion on the grounds that it destroyed life. Similarly, Shirley Williams, devout Catholic and opponent of abortion, was a supporter of contraception as well as homosexual law reform. She consistently voted against the passage of David Steel's Abortion Bill but, as she makes clear in her book of reflections on politics and religion, she and other Catholic Labour MPs found their efforts to win broader support hampered by their church's refusal to relax doctrine on contraception and family planning.[39] John Smith, though impeccably liberal on most social and moral issues, was also passionately opposed to abortion, voting consistently to restrict the 1967 Act during the 1980s. Another strand within the Labour Party which resisted liberal reform was led in the 1960s by Dame Edith Summerskill, who, fearing that it would be a 'Casanova's Charter', opposed Abse's divorce law proposal to remove the concept of fault from divorce proceedings. Anti-pornography feminists within the Labour Party supported censorship through Clare Short's bill to ban topless models from tabloid newspapers in the 1980s. This division within the Labour Party on pornography continued through to the Blair Government. When Richard Desmond, the new proprietor of the *Express* newspaper titles, donated £300,000 to the Labour Party in 2001, a great deal of hand-wringing and preaching wrestled over whether it was appropriate to take money from the man whose other publications included *Asian Babes* and *Readers' Wives*. Some Labour MPs, like Glenda Jackson, retorted with evidence that pornography actually reduces violence against women. Just as the picture among Labour MPs, generally more supportive of liberal social reform, has actually been more mixed, Conservative politicians also buck the opposite trend – the liberal wing of the Conservative Party is larger than the conservative wing of the Labour Party. It is easy to forget that, had it not been for Harold Wilson calling the February 1966 general election, it would probably have been the Conservative MP Humphrey Berkeley's Sexual Offences Bill which decriminalised male homosexuality in private, and another Tory, Simon Wingfield Digby, responsible for abortion law reform. It is also likely, from discussions in Downing Street before the 1964 election, that the Commons would have been given another opportunity to abolish capital punishment. Norman St John Stevas, a prominent Catholic, actively supported homosexual and divorce law reform but, like Abse and Williams, opposed easier abortion. This fissure within the Conservative Party became more significant after 1997 as the party attempted to come to terms with social changes and the success of New Labour.

Circling the wagons of political debate about moral issues have been the Red Indians of the fourth estate, and particularly the tabloid press. The greater freedom to discuss sex from the early 1960s gave licence for prurient comment and investigation into the sexual lives of public figures and private individuals. After the watershed of Profumo, an insatiable appetite for political sexual scandal reached its apotheosis in the sleaze-obsessed years of the Major Government when no sexual peccadillo, however minor or legal, was allowed to escape the tabloid glare. Coincidentally, political sex scandals seem to have been working on a ten-year cycle since Profumo in 1963. In 1973, two ministers resigned over their use of call girls and it was more by luck than judgement that no others followed them. In 1983, Thatcher's finest hour in the wake of the Falklands victory was marred by the news that her golden boy, Party Chairman Cecil Parkinson, had fathered an illegitimate daughter. Major was brought close to his nemesis in 1993: after successfully squashing rumours that he himself was having an affair, he reaped a whirlwind following his infamous 'Back to Basics' speech at the Conservative party conference. Perhaps this cycle was finally broken by the relatively calm year of 2003. Certainly the revelation in the summer of 2004 that the divorcé Home Secretary, David Blunkett, had been conducting an adulterous relationship with the married publisher of the right-wing *Spectator* magazine, Kimberly Fortier, showed that, if such extra-curricular activities could no longer bring about their downfall, they could not pass entirely unnoticed. Chief amongst those to condemn Blunkett was William Hague's former spin doctor, Amanda Platell. She managed to milk the story not only in the *Daily Mail's* stablemate, the *Evening Standard*, but also in the *Independent on Sunday*, where she profited from a second swipe at this evidence of Britain's 'moral malaise':

> *what would have been considered sleaze under the Tories has become merely a love affair under Labour – and one talked about in the most chaste terms … I do feel for them. But it does make me wonder what you would have to do these days to be disapproved of.*

Clearly aghast that so few fellow journalists felt the same level of 'revulsion' as she did, she rammed the point home in despair:

> *What are we to teach our children about the importance of marriage, partnership, family and fidelity if we cannot point to the Blunkett affair and say, simply and without equivocation, it is wrong?*[40]

*

One of the least well-covered aspects of public morality in Britain is the divergence between different parts of the UK. Since 1999 the gap in public policy between London and Edinburgh, and to a lesser degree between London and Cardiff, has yawned. While Labour has dominated all three executives, differences have often been nuanced, rather than explicit. But long before the process of devolution was kicked off by the Blair Government in 1997, the handling of issues of morality within the UK varied widely. Scotland's separate legal system attempts to promote the public interest, rather than preserving public order and protecting the citizen from exploitation and corruption as in England and Wales.[41] Some examples. The Sex Offences Act 1967, which implemented the Wolfenden recommendations on homosexuality, decriminalised consenting male homosexual acts in private in England and Wales only. The continuing legal bar on such acts in Scotland was not enforced following the passage of the Act, but the fragility of this *entente* was highlighted in 1976 when the law covering other sexual offences was tidied up, and the criminality of homosexuality was restated. Ministers argued that the legal anomaly was irrelevant because the prosecuting policy was the same. Despite passing up this opportunity, they nevertheless insisted that it was up to backbenchers to address the question, and the government would accept the will of Parliament on the issue. Yet backbenchers in both Houses were thwarted in attempts to remove this provision until 1980, when an amendment to the first Criminal Justice Bill of the Thatcher administration became the unlikely vehicle for equalising the law within Britain.

Characteristically, the first Mayor of London, Ken Livingstone, presiding over the new Greater London Authority, instituted in 2001 a same-sex partnership registration scheme. Constricted in the formal powers which the Mayor exercises in the capital, this symbolic political move (which would confer neither legal status nor rights on those registering) was designed to put pressure on ministers in Whitehall on behalf of London's large gay population. Just two years later, in 2003, the Government published its own proposals for civil registration of same-sex partnerships which would entail some of the rights enjoyed by married couples. However, the restriction of the proposals to England and Wales threatened to throw up new anomalies within the United Kingdom, particularly as under the devolution settlement, social security (one of the areas most affected by partnership issues) is a matter dealt with at a UK level, but at that point the Scottish Executive had not put forward plans for a similar scheme north of the border. Even more sensitive, given the actual likelihood of Edinburgh following suit, was the possibility that couples registered under the proposed scheme could obtain their rights if living in Northern Ireland.

In 1966 a 'Save Ulster from Sodomy' campaign had little trouble in excluding the province from the provisions of the Sexual Offences Act which decriminalised homosexual acts between two consenting adults in private. Despite having resisted changing the law in Scotland, the Callaghan Government made an abortive attempt in 1978 to extend the Act to Ulster, where the prohibition was rigorously enforced, unlike in Scotland. Faced once again by a broad alliance of Unionists and Catholics opposed to the move, the proposal was dropped. However, the necessary order finally went through in 1982, against the concerted opposition of most Ulster politicians. In the words of one senior civil servant, this sort of social reform was perhaps 'the price they had to pay for avoiding [power-sharing under] Sunningdale'.[42] Major differences between Northern Ireland and the rest of the United Kingdom have been retained. The age of consent remains set at seventeen (for men and women since equalisation under the Sexual Offences Act 2000). The 1967 Abortion Act never extended to the province, and women wanting abortion on any but strict medical grounds still have to travel to the mainland to obtain a termination.

At a more local level, cultural differences can also weigh heavily, particularly with regard to abortion in areas of high concentration of Catholic Irish immigrants, most notably Harold Wilson's Huyton constituency. Although there is no indication that this caused him to take a definite stance against abortion during his first administration, when the subject became politically sensitive again in 1975, he became more irritated. Barbara Castle, then Social Services Secretary, was herself MP for a constituency with a large Catholic population, though a smaller one than in Wilson's, as Blackburn was further up the historic path of immigration for Irish settlers.[43] In Wales, Methodists, championed in Parliament by George Thomas, Welsh Secretary and later Speaker of the House of Commons, successfully resisted the relaxation of Sunday observance laws well into the 1970s, despite the concession of 'local option' referendums. Similar nonconformist abhorrence of the spread of drinking punched far above its weight in debates on licensing. Conversely, state support for alcohol consumption was, in some areas, extremely high. In 1970, the new Heath Government, attacking one of the less monumental areas of public ownership early on, made plans to sell off the state's interest in the brewing trade. Though it was considered that this would be popular in the areas concerned in Scotland, it was feared Carlisle would be a different matter. Apart from the threat of job losses and any socialist opposition to privatisation, the Home Secretary, Robert Carr, commented that the locals 'like the beer', to which Ted Heath replied constructively that perhaps it was time that people in Carlisle be given a choice of drinks.[44]

The responsibility of local authorities for licensing cinemas gave an opportunity for vociferous local campaigns against certain productions and films to have them banned. These licensing provisions had originally been intended to protect people from physical harm rather than moral corruption, and in 1952 the BBFC (British Board of Film Censorship, later Classification) became legally responsible for censorship and classification of films. However, the ultimate power of censorship still lay with the local authority, which could still ban a film given a certificate by the BBFC. Councils could also permit a film to be shown to which the BBFC had declined to give a certificate. Some councils, as late as the 1970s, insisted that the synopsis of all films rated X by the BBFC be submitted to the council for examination before approval. When the film version of James Joyce's *Ulysses* was cut by the BBFC in 1967, fifty-one councils, from Aberdeen to Woodstock, banned the film entirely. Twenty-seven councils granted a licence uncut. The pyrrhic nature of the victory of those councils appalled at the foul language of the film is clear from the fact that, in many areas, a short bus ride would have enabled those living in places where the film was banned to find a cinema where it had been licensed: in Staffordshire, for example, Newcastle-under-Lyme refused a licence, whereas Leek and Stoke-on-Trent did not[45] Local censorship powers also extend to advertising, and these have often been exercised. When the Greater London Council was under Conservative control during the 1960s, London Transport banned advertising of a political nature, for example for meetings held by Amnesty International about international political prisoners in 1962, and on the Underground by the Family Planning Association in 1967 because it was 'controversial on religious grounds'.[46] The support of some Labour councils in London for gay rights during the 1980s fuelled a battle over sex education which rumbled on until Parliament repealed Section 28 in July 2003.

More routinely the national application of laws allowing abortion up to a certain time limit, or governing child care, child protection or fostering and adoption, is belied by the kaleidoscopic variations in local rules which have operated within the National Health Service and local authority social services departments. The provision of legal abortion on the NHS since 1968 has depended on the local availability of sufficient numbers of doctors willing to perform terminations and the interpretation of the regulations by the local health authority and certifying doctors. Similarly, local control over social services has meant that historically those wanting to become parents, and particularly single mothers, have been judged and treated very differently according to where they live. The way in which spasms of local concern about moral issues have continued to affect debate at a national, as well as local, level is remarkable, and has perhaps increased with modern media communications and the 24-hour news day. Pictures of groups of residents protesting against the presence within their community of suspected or actual paedophiles, asylum claimants, users of drug clinics, mental-health patients or other despised groups, whether or not any fears are justified, imagined or externally provoked, have increasingly become the battleground for moral guardians in the media.

*

In 1945 the criminal law largely reflected traditional Judeo-Christian morality in the context of the rapidly industrialising society of late Victorian Britain, when laws concerning abortion, marriage and divorce, the protection of children, homosexuality, alcohol and licensing were all stiffened by the rising influence of religious, and particularly nonconformist, moral concern. The Second World War forced a rather more pragmatic approach to moral issues. But, as with the temporary *bouleversement* of the labour force during the war, retrenchment was the watchword after 1945. Perhaps the most important document in the postwar history of law and morality is the *Report of the Departmental Committee on Homosexuality and Prostitution*, published in 1957, and thereafter known as the Wolfenden Report after its chair, the Vice-Chancellor of Reading University, Sir John Wolfenden. Much recent comment about Wolfenden has focused on the self-destructive behaviour of his homosexual son, Jeremy, as an impetus for Wolfenden's liberal approach to homosexuality in the Committee's investigation, in a way similar to other reformers like Lord Arran. The principle underlying the report was that the concept of 'sin' should be separated from the criminal law and replaced with a utilitarian philosophy that the public should be protected from harm and offence in public from acts which would not be criminalised in private: 'To preserve public order and decency, and to protect the citizen from what is offensive and injurious and to provide sufficient safeguards against exploitation or corruption of others, particularly those who are specially vulnerable because they are young, weak in body or mind or inexperienced…'.[47]

Soon after the publication of the Wolfenden Report, public moralists struck back, with Lord Devlin's defence of the link between Christian morality and the law. Devlin argued that the basis of Western morality was essentially Christian and that in the modern world the 'right-thinking man' in society would agree with, the Christian ethic and the importance of the Church in maintaining the moral order.[48] Making vague reference to historical precedent, presumably Rome, Devlin also considered the strict control of public morality to be as essential to the survival of society as the suppression of sedition and treason.[49] Devlin answers for himself three questions which are determined by his, and many other people's, certainties about public morality:

i) Has society the right to pass judgement at all on matters of morals?

ii) If society has the right to pass judgement, has it also the right to use the weapon of the law to enforce it?

iii) If so, ought it to use that weapon in all cases or only in some; and if only in some, on what principle should it distinguish?

Wolfenden would have answered 'yes' to the first two questions. However, Devlin argued from an *a priori* assumption that the preservation of public morality is essential to the survival of society, and that this morality is a basically Christian one upon which all right-thinking people can agree. Devlin refuted the Wolfenden notion of privacy where no harm is done to others, insisting that the breach of the moral principles of the criminal law is an offence not merely against the person who is injured but against society as a whole.[50] Therefore there can be no withdrawal of the sanction of the criminal law from any area of traditional (Christian) public morality. In response, the jurist H. L. A. Hart said that Devlin leaped from

the acceptable proposition that some shared morality is essential to the existence of any society, to the unacceptable proposition that a society is identical with its morality as that is at any given moment of its history, so that a change in its morality is tantamount to the destruction of a society.[51]

However, from the Street Offences Act on prostitution and the Obscene Publications Act giving new protection to literary works from censorship in 1959, the principles behind Wolfenden began to permeate the criminal law. Its philosophy became so current to debates about changing British society at the beginning of the 1960s that it found its way into films as diverse as *Victim* and *From Russia with Love*.

By the late 1970s the Wolfenden strategy was being updated for new circumstances. The Obscene Publications Act was widely discredited, and a new way of protecting people from offensive material and pornography was needed. Merlyn Rees, Roy Jenkins' successor as Home Secretary in 1976, established a new inquiry under the philosopher Bernard Williams, which recommended a clearer separation between a small category of violent images which should be banned, other pornography, which should be restricted, and the written word, which should be left untouched. This was anathema to the incoming Thatcher Government, who shelved it. The development of new fertility techniques, which had led to the birth of the first 'test-tube baby' in 1977 through in-vitro fertilisation (IVF), and the prospect of embryo research called for a new set of ethical principles on which law could be based. In 1982 the Secretary of State for Social Services, Norman Fowler, announced the appointment of a committee. Its chair was to be another Oxbridge moral philosopher, Mary Warnock. The appointment of this 'wise woman' was vital to the inquiry, according to Fowler, and its work put Britain 'ahead of the international game' on fertilisation and embryology.[52] As with similar inquiries since Wolfenden, Warnock recognised that public and private morality were not the same thing, and that the committee could only weigh the evidence of the consequences of different policies against the balance of public opinion, and provide a coherent set of proposals for public policy, rather than individual conscience.[53] The unprecedented difficulty which this inquiry faced was that even for those who considered their moral compass to be fixed rigidly by traditional moral teaching, this was uncharted territory. In Warnock's words, 'If morality is indeed obedience to rules, then the rules were yet to be invented.'[54] Another novel aspect to the inquiry was the international implications of any recommendations, given the fast-moving nature of scientific research. Hereafter this was to be a major concern of policy-makers, particularly with innovations like the internet. The public and political debate that ensued lasted six years until the report's basic approach and recommendations were incorporated into the Human Fertilisation and Embryology Act 1990. Given the fast-moving nature of the science, it was perhaps remarkable that proposals put forward in 1984 held in legislation until the end of the twentieth century. By that time many, including Warnock herself, felt they were coming unstuck, or had not been proved correct. However, the basic principles of the committee's report, that a regulatory body, independent from government, should be set up to monitor developments and regulate treatments and research, has not been challenged. Neither has the basic assumption that IVF treatments and embryo research should be permissible within a moral framework generally acceptable to society. The questions have centred on what is acceptable and whether science has indeed stepped over any boundaries.

During discussion about implementing Wolfenden in the mid-1960s, officials had been reminded of the minefield of complicated and often anomalous provisions relating to other sexual offences on the statute book, and suggested that these could be reviewed at some point in the future after the Act had been in force.[55] However, there was little political pressure to iron out the problems involved, particularly when the Thatcher Government came to power. It was only in 1998 that the nettle was grasped by Jack Straw and an inquiry under Home Office civil servant Betty Moxon was charged with a wholesale review of sexual offences which resulted in a new report, *Setting the Boundaries*. This recommended a radical overhaul of the legislation based on the principle of equality of treatment for men and women, heterosexual and homosexual, and enhanced protection for children. In 2002 the Government introduced a bill to implement this new strategy on sexual offences. On the family law side, it also took the first step towards removing discrimination between heterosexual and homosexual couples by publishing a White Paper on the civil registration of same-sex partnerships. Opponents of such a move argued that this undermined heterosexual marriage, and any discrimination could be avoided by piecemeal reform and contractual arrangements, rather than this comprehensive approach to establishing a new legal form of partnership.

Since incorporation of the ECHR into UK law in the Human Rights Act 1998 domestic judges have been able to test laws and the actions of public bodies against the rights enshrined in the Convention without citizens having to have resort to Strasbourg. This has been perhaps the most important step taken by the Blair Government in the field of constitutional reform. It has also been the most controversial. Ever since, a continuous stream of jeremiads from the right has complained about political interference from the judiciary and the erosion of parliamentary and national sovereignty. In addition, it is claimed, such rights-based law is alien to British traditions and encourages a selfish individualism which will further undermine social cohesion and morality. The ECHR's influence on UK law is a sixty-year story stretching back to its genesis at the hands of UK lawyers including the Conservative David Maxwell-Fyfe (later the Earl of Kilmuir) after the Second World War. Although Britain had signed the Convention, there continued to be some disdain for what were seen as its woolly, and politically dangerous, provisions, particularly in relation to the colonies. James Griffiths opposed ratification because it was

> *likely to cause considerable misunderstanding and political unsettlement in many colonial territories [where] the bulk of the people were still politically immature … This confusion would undoubtedly be exploited by extremist politicians in order to undermine the authority of the colonial government concerned.*[56]

Setting a precedent for the next two decades of debate about the application of the Convention to overseas territories, Griffiths admitted, 'If it were possible for the United Kingdom to decline to accept it, so that the question of its application to the colonies would not arise, the Colonial Office would very glad.'[57]

Governments continued to resist acceding to the 'optional' clauses of the Convention which would allow individual petition of the Commission in Strasbourg and recognise the jurisdiction of the court in the UK, although ironically it had been Maxwell-Fyfe who had insisted on the right of petition of individuals being reinserted into the Convention after it had been removed from an earlier draft.[58] When the Wilson Government finally took the decision in the autumn of 1965 to accede to these clauses, the number and range of concerns about the application of the Convention became clear. A continuing caveat applied to many of Britain's dependent territories, particularly Hong Kong, where it was obvious that human rights did not meet the standards in the Convention. In the UK the Home Secretary listed a number of objections: immigration, prison discipline and, most importantly, Northern Ireland. The abuses of the O'Neill Government were increasingly becoming an embarrassment in London, as some of the provisions of the Special Powers Act were directly incompatible with the Convention's obligations, and necessitated a derogation which had been in place since 1957.

A similar story can be told of Britain's obligations under the Genocide Convention, which was signed in 1951. Labour ministers after the war were reluctant to ratify the convention because of objections to the legal principles it laid down. Frank Soskice, the Solicitor General, wrote to the Home Secretary, James Chuter Ede, in 1949:

> *I cannot, however, pretend that our existing law is at all points consistent with the obligations laid down by the Convention. What amounts to an offence 'of a political character' has, I think, never adequately been defined. It does seem to me a most monstrous thing that plain murder on the ground that a man is a Jew or a nigger should ever be regarded as a political offence, and I am most doubtful whether the courts would so regard it in this country.*[59]

Although the fear that Britain would be overwhelmed by complaints to the European Court proved unfounded, by the early 1970s the few cases which did reach Strasbourg were significant, particularly in relation to the further tightening of immigration laws and internment and torture in Northern Ireland. By the late 1970s anomalies in the laws governing a number of areas in different parts of the UK, including homosexuality since the Sexual Offences Act 1967, were the subject of claims to Strasbourg, and this was a primary motivation for Labour and then Conservative governments to standardise the position throughout the UK. By 1984 constitutional lawyers were concluding that 'in recent years, the [Strasbourg] Court's decisions have invariably been the impetus behind that small ration of liberalisation that has been forced upon Mrs Thatcher.'[60]

Despite this, there was little pressure from the left to incorporate the Convention into UK law until the early 1990s. Towards the end of his second period as Home Secretary, Jenkins had commissioned a paper on the arguments for and against incorporation, which was written by Anthony Lester and Brian Cubbon. At the suggestion of the permanent secretary, Sir Arthur Peterson, this was published as a Green Paper in 1976.[61] Despite a similar recommendation from a House of Lords Committee and support from Tories such as Norman St John Stevas, Lord Hailsham and Sir Keith Joseph, the proposal foundered, with Margaret Thatcher answering that 'we believe that it is for Parliament rather than the judiciary to determine how these principles are best secured.' Though an internal Labour Party document in 1976 had recommended incorporation, it was squashed by the ruling National Executive Committee,[62] which was dominated by the fear on the left that the Convention would be used by conservative judges as a weapon against industrial and political radicalism. The fact that the chair of the working group which produced that document, Shirley Williams, along with Jenkins, defected in 1981 to found the SDP, probably did not help the cause of incorporation within the Labour Party.

*

Going back to the 1950s, perhaps the most pertinent sentence in Lord Devlin's attack on the threat posed to public morality by a utilitarian criminal law is this: 'No society has yet solved the problem of how to teach morality without religion.'[63] He goes on: 'So the law must base itself on Christian morals and to the limit of its ability enforce them, not simply because they are the morals of most of us ... but for the compelling reason that without the help of Christian teaching the law will fail.'

More recently this view has been upheld, perhaps not surprisingly, by religious leaders including the then Archbishop of Canterbury, George Carey, when he said in 1996:

> *There is a widespread tendency to view what is good and right as a matter of private taste and individual opinion only. Under this tendency, God is banished to the realm of the private hobby and religion becomes a particular activity for those who happen to have a taste for it.*[64]

Even allowing for a degree of self-interest on the part of the Archbishop, is it true that a shared morality is synonymous with widespread religious belief? Support for public morality to be rooted in non-humanist, spiritual values is still a prevalent one, even among liberal, secular commentators. But the development of a human rights culture in the UK, according to its supporters, contains, potentially, the seeds of exactly this social development. As Francesca Klug has chronicled, until the mid-1990s a Bill of Rights or incorporation of the ECHR was largely seen in quite technical legal terms about parliamentary sovereignty and positive versus negative rights. The development of the 'Third Way' philosophy under Tony Blair saw the domestication of the language of human rights within new Labour rhetoric about community and the symbiotic relationship between rights and responsibilities.[65] Mary Warnock, whose pragmatic liberalism has been influential on public debates about morality since the early 1980s, rejects the idea that human rights can be the basis for ethical principles. To her this is putting the cart before the horse. Moral principles, motivated by an instinctual altruism are, for her, the fount of legal and social mores on which human rights themselves are based.[66]

In more popular discourse, one phrase has successfully encapsulated debate about the moral state of Britain since the 1960s – 'the permissive society'. Permissiveness, in the context of morality, long predates discussion of the emergence of a 'permissive' society in Britain. Geoffrey Gorer, in his ground-breaking *Exploring English Character*, considered the 'ideas about sex' of the respondents to his questionnaire largely in terms of their 'permissiveness' or 'rigidity'.[67] However, its emergence during the 1960s as a catch-all term for liberalisation of law and behaviour, or loosening of moral standards, was gradual. The first time the phrase was used in *The Times* was in 1962, but on that occasion it was employed by the violinist and conductor Yehudi Menuhin, describing the musical culture of India, which he considered the 'most permissive society' in the world. It was not until 1964 that the phrase was used in relation to the immorality of young people in Britain, when condemning bank holiday rioting in seaside towns. But by the late 1960s the phrase had become a neat shorthand for conservatives to condemn the tsunami of change which they saw around them, and for the government's opponents to pin the blame firmly on their shoulders. In 1970, Conservative MP John Selwyn Gummer penned the first political analysis of the permissive society, arguing that 'we are as restrictive materially as the Victorians were morally ... The twentieth century permits a great deal less than did the nineteenth and only in the sphere of private morality is it more permissive.' In relation to the Profumo affair, Gummer thought that 'the Victorians would have made no bones about it. They would have said quite clearly that public men should set an example in private morality. They would have seen such behaviour as harmful per se. This was certainly the reaction of the majority of the population even in 1963.'[68]

However, this is not a judgement with which even Margaret Thatcher agreed. Gummer argued that there was no public support for the liberal reforms which the Labour Government had allowed through in the late 1960s, and laid the wider blame for permissiveness at the feet of women and their demands for greater freedom. During the 1970s, as economic and social upheaval created an atmosphere of greater uncertainty, many Marxist sociologists, influenced by the feminist and gay liberation movements, began to criticise even the liberal changes of the 1960s, saying that they merely changed the way in which society controlled women, the young and minorities, particularly by 'medicalising' their problems and putting them in the hands of doctors. Such criticisms were clearly born of frustration that the terms on which Labour allowed discussion of moral issues was about removing unjustifiable restrictions rather than a pursuit of equality and complete freedom for the individual, regardless of the fact that such views were in a clear minority, even among liberal politicians, let alone the public.

The dominance throughout the 1980s of a Thatcherite view of public morality was only partially reflected in what the Iron Lady's Governments actually did. But it faced no coherent challenge until the mid-1990s, when discussion about human rights and their relationship to moral values in a secular society became the liberal left. As Klug argued, 'once you bring concepts like "a fair hearing" or "a private life" into the law, extra-legal moral theory is required to interpret them.'[69] However, contrary to the claims from the right that this entailed a throwing up of social and political control over the criminal law or social values, people like Klug insist that human rights principles challenge everyone to consider the competitive claims between all individuals and wider society.

Decisions have to be made as to where to draw the line between, for example, protecting the rights of even the most despised groups like rapists or paedophiles and adequately defending their victims or potential victims. Outside clearly defined boundaries, such as no death penalty and no torture, this line cannot be permanently fixed. It is inevitably going to have to be porous enough to absorb some prevailing norms without compromising on fundamental human rights principles.

This leaves space for some 'democratic' involvement in where boundaries between rights should lie. If human rights are to play the crucial role now allotted to them, then wider participation in such debates is both inevitable and to be welcomed. Even though the final decisions in actual cases must lie with the law courts, the same does not apply to the issues that underlie them. Without this 'democratisation', there is little hope … that the idea of human rights can help to fill the values void in Western societies.

Peter Hitchens, in his blistering attack on contemporary British society, *The Abolition of Britain*, published in 2000, contests that decriminalisation of homosexuality was inevitable once the Pill was accepted by a governing class whose morals were laxer than those of the masses, an assertion which is contradicted by research as early as Gorer's 1955 study, which found the highest proportion of those in favour of premarital sex among the lower working class.[70] 'The Pill removed all these practical punishments for promiscuity and made women much more willing to contemplate abortion if for any reason they found themselves expecting an unborn child.'[71] Clearly, 'practical punishments' for using the Pill continued, not least in the risk of sexually transmitted diseases, higher risks of certain cancers and possible cardiovascular disease, and attempts by men to use the Pill as an excuse for having sex. But the Pill was never the subject of legislation, and although single women increasingly found ways to obtain the Pill from the mid-1960s, officially it was aimed at married women at this time, and a woman's marital status was specifically ascertained before prescribing. Sometimes, indeed, doctors sought the permission of a woman's husband before agreeing to prescribe. In fact, as the most recent, detailed study of the history of the oral contraceptive pill, by Lara Marks, argues, 'it would be a mistake to associate the oral contraceptive with a revolution in sexual behaviour among single women. Indeed there is plenty of evidence to suggest that single women were engaging in premarital sex well before the introduction of the Pill.'[72]

Melanie Phillips' 1996 analysis of Britain's moral crisis, *All Must Have Prizes*, ploughs a similarly doom mongering furrow about the state of contemporary Britain, seeing many of its problems in the same domino effect of loosening moral standards and collapse of 'authority' and the spread of progressive education, quoting Lord Devlin's defence of traditional, Christian, public morality. Her experience as a social affairs journalist for the *Guardian*, however, contributes towards a more balanced critique which also heaps blame on the social and economic damage wrought by Thatcherism in the 1980s.[73] The idea that the reform of laws governing family relationships has a significant effect on family stability is a persistent one, which has been little resisted, even on the liberal left. To take the example of divorce reform, which Phillips herself highlights, although the 1969 Divorce Law Reform Act, which finally dented the concept of exclusively fault-based divorce, was followed by a steep rise in the number of divorces, this rate had been increasing even faster during the 1960s.

Looking abroad, almost all countries saw a rise in their divorce rate during the same decade, regardless of what changes were made to the ease with which marriages could legally be ended, suggesting a rather more complex mixture of reasons for the Western increase in divorce.[74]

Phillips focuses her withering gaze on the 'progressives' among educationalists, academics, lobbyists and politicians of various left-wing heresies. Curiously, although she broadly condemns the callous neo-liberalism of the Thatcher years, few individual conservatives come in for criticism. Particular opprobrium is heaped on the notorious comment which Sir Edmund Leach made in one of his 1967 Reith Lectures, when he said, 'Far from being the basis of the good society, the family with its narrow privacy and tawdry secrets, is the source of all our discontents.'[75] The conservative consternation which this comment caused at the time led Leach to explain it laboriously in a footnote to the published version of the lectures the following year, although on reading it the context is quite obvious. Only those looking for scapegoats could still, thirty years later, seize on this as part of a crazed liberal plot to destroy the family. Leach may or may not have been right, but he was arguing that, since the dispersal of extended kinship networks, the nuclear family, a relatively new sociological unit, was placed under new and particular emotional strains. This is a proposition that has, more recently, been supported by the British Social Attitudes Survey. In 2002 the survey found 'hints of a less desirable side to high levels of family contact – a possible inward looking tendency that precludes "joining in" with more formal networks outside the family'.[76] Phillips is scathing of the liberal argument that the distressing evidence of emotional problems experienced by children from broken families is caused by poverty more than the failure of the nuclear family. She focuses on research which claimes to show that single-parent families, families where the parents are unmarried, or step-families, are more unstable or result in worse outcomes for adults and children than those in which two parents bring up their own children together. However, in 2003 the Policy Studies Institute published research which showed that, allowing for the work status within the family, there was little difference in the situation of children between single- and two-parent families.[77] Phillips does attempt to chart a alternative culture of 'attachment'. But this is not the same form of reciprocal 'attachment' embodied in the ECHR, which, to Phillips, is individualistic anathema. It implies, essentially, restoring the moral framework which existed in the 1950s, privileging the married over other relationships.

However, among liberals, there are those who view with concern a range of contemporary social ills which greater individualism and commercialism have encouraged. For example, according to Jonathan Freedland:

> One Forbidden Zone, where progressive feet have long feared to tread, beckons especially. It is morality – not the sexual conduct kind, dished out by the Tories in the dying days of the Major administration. But the moral questions about the health of our society and the coarsening of our culture: the troubling phenomena ... of a new 'age of selfishness'. That covers a range of dysfunctions, from the rudeness of strangers in the street to the bombardment of near-pornographic images in mainstream advertising; from the loneliness of individuals adrift in places that were once communities to the struggle millions wage to keep work and life in balance.[78]

Globalisation, the internet and the ubiquitous power of multinational companies and commercial advertising makes it seem more difficult than ever before for governments to effect changes in social attitudes and individual behaviour. This is a very different world to that which faced the first majority Labour Government in 1945.

2. In the Ripeness of Time: 1945–1957

'In a few years, marriage licences will be sold like dog licences, good for a period of twelve months, with no law against changing dogs or keeping more than one animal at a time.'

Aldous Huxley, *Brave New World*[1]

'I believe – and so do a large number of religious and social organisations of all creeds and shades of thought … that it is wrong to withhold the protection of the law from any citizen on grounds of his or her moral character.'

Barbara Castle MP[2]

'What a confession of impotence it was that the Prime Minister and the Cabinet, who did not dare to stand for their declared convictions of what they thought was right and necessary in the present circumstances, should have cast their duty to the wind and left this grave decision on capital punishment to the casual vote of the most unrepresentative and irresponsible House of Commons that ever sat at Westminster.'

Winston Churchill[3]

'The trouble about Royal Commissions … is that they do eventually report, and the Report comes home to roost. It does not always come home to roost in the nest of the particular bird that hatched it …'

Lord Silkin[4]

The postwar construction of the welfare state focused, in Jeffrey Weeks's words, on the conditions of reproduction, and set the parameters of debate about the balance between individual freedom and state intervention in sex and the family for the postwar era, particularly over population policy, domestic life and sexual behaviour. This balance was reflected in a number of ways in the 1942 Beveridge Report and the legislative and administrative architecture which the Attlee

Government erected to span the cradle and the grave after 1945. Family allowances and other benefits were paid alongside the growth of social work in local authorities. Welfare benefits were to be paid to deserted, separated or divorced wives only if the woman could prove she was not the guilty party in marriage breakdown. However, the withdrawal of women from much of their wartime employment was tempered by an admission that confining women solely to the home and hearth would 'run against the democratic conception of individual freedom', and amount to a 'rebuking of the tide'. The dominant attitude towards women was reflected in an influential book by John Newsom, Chief Education Officer for Hertfordshire. In *The Education of Girls*, he warned that women who did not recognise the primacy of motherhood were 'normally deficient in the quality of womanliness and the particular physical and mental attributes of their sex'. Their value was primarily as housewives and 'it is not an exaggeration to say that woman as a purchaser holds the future standard of living in this country in her hands ... If she buys in ignorance then our national standards will degenerate.'[5]

The Government's refusal to relax divorce law (once some allowance had been made for mistakes among war marriages) was balanced by a greater appreciation of the need for marriage guidance to nurture relationships, including advice on improving sex for couples and an extension of legal aid to divorce to benefit working-class couples. The Marriage Guidance Council's postwar publication *How to Treat a Young Wife* had, by the late 1960s, sold half a million copies under the more progressive title *Sex in Marriage*.[6]

The Royal Commission on Population had begun work in 1944 when concern about a declining population was still high. The Beveridge Report itself had warned that 'with its present rate of reproduction the British race cannot continue'. Churchill had even declared in a public broadcast during the war that 'our people must be encouraged by every means to have larger families'. However, by the time the Commission reported, such fears had subsided, as the evidence they had taken indicated that family size had stabilised. It recommended removing economic and social obstacles in the way of large families, but it balanced this by supporting married couples' voluntary limitation of the number of children by encouraging and praising the work of the Family Planning Association in dispelling widespread ignorance about fertility and contraception and for providing safe and reliable services to married couples.

The report was also alive to the long-term effects of the war on women, despite the return to domesticity:

> *It should be assumed also that women will take an increasing part in the cultural and economic life of the community, and* [public policy] *should endeavour, by adjustments of social and economic arrangements, to make it easier for women to combine motherhood and the care of a home with outside interests.*[7]

The report was condemned by Catholics for advocating 'artificial birth control'. Only two years later Pope Pius XII re-emphasised the anathema of all forms of artificial contraception from appliances to *coitus interruptus*. Only the rhythm method fell outside this prohibition. There was no parliamentary discussion of the Royal Commission's report, although ministers were only too conscious of its recommendations. Herbert Morrison, Deputy Prime Minister, commented that the Chancellor of the Exchequer wouldn't like some of the report's more costly suggestions and that, personally, he didn't want 'to become the Population Minister!'[8]

Despite the encouragement given to the growth of contraceptive services by the Royal Commission on Population, provision for married couples was still extremely restricted in the decade after the war. In the early years of the National Health Service family planning was not considered a proper role for it, and such services continued to be left to the discretion of local authorities, although local health authorities could also make grants under the NHS Act to voluntary bodies providing services on strictly medical grounds. Only in one area, Aberdeen, was comprehensive, free family planning available at this time. Others, such as Bristol, also pioneered more extensive provision. In many places both councils and new health authorities were dissuaded from funding family planning because of opposition from Catholics, the threat of a prurient media and the prior demand on scarce resources of other, less controversial treatments.[9] Beyond this piecemeal growth of voluntary local services alongside the new NHS, the issue of contraception remained highly controversial for Labour ministers. A classic clash of morality and economics occurred in 1949 when public outrage was sparked by the growth of vending machines selling contraceptives in public places with easy access for children and young people. Such machines had been around since the 1920s, but they were now spreading. Individual government departments viewed this deveolopment very differently. Clement Attlee was inundated with complaints from members of the public, magistrates and MPs. These totalled over one hundred in the course of a few weeks – negligible in twenty-first-century terms, but then quite a postbag. According to two JP correspondents, the sin of juvenile greed was less of a worry than lust:

> *The temptation to children – and adults – to break them open in the hope of obtaining a quantity of half-crowns is nothing like so serious as the advertisement and easy sale of the contraceptives to any adolescent boy or girl. If these machines were in chemists' shops, at any rate the storekeeper would have them under supervision and youngsters would hesitate to be seen obtaining a packet in order to indulge in promiscuous intercourse. Placed in the streets, boys and girls are invited to buy them and no one will ever know that they have done so.*

Given that there was so little to spend a cache of half-crowns on in Austerity Britain, the temptation of promiscuous sex might admittedly have been higher. Attlee was 'unimpressed' by the response given by an official at the Ministry of Supply, responsible for licensing the manufacture of such vending machines, to one MP. This explained that the makers wanted to develop the machines for export markets which had expressed an interest, but which needed evidence from the domestic market that they were 'tamper-proof'. In the official's words, 'we cannot afford to lose a chance of increasing our exports to hard currency areas.' This 'horrified' one of the magistrates, who wrote to Attlee that the Archbishop of Canterbury was also anxious to take action against 'the grave moral danger' which the machines posed. George Strauss, Minister of Supply, was forced to explain his position to the Prime Minister. His defence was emollient and practical. Without attempting to justify the sale of contraceptives in vending machines directly, he did refer to the sale of sanitary towels, 'the social value of which is obvious'. Strauss was, however, more concerned about the wider morality of criminal behaviour: 'Elements of the public in all countries consider automatic machines "fair game"', hence the need for home trials to improve their security. Experimenting in this way with the morality of Britain's youth might not be thought to be a weighty argument, but the clincher for

Strauss was purely practical. He explained that this new-fangled technology, which probably baffled the famously technophobic Attlee, worked by the weight and size of the article for sale, and the size of coin used to operate the machine. Without banning the sale of all products of a similar weight and size as contraceptives and those purchased with a half-crown, vendors would have complete freedom to switch between different products on sale. Such a ban would 'seriously damage' the slot machine industry. According to Strauss the only other option would be a legislative prohibition on the sale of contraceptives in vending machines. At this point Strauss passed the buck to the Home Secretary for advice on introducing legislation. James Chuter Ede, who had also been lobbied by outraged citizens and worthies, supported action against a practice he considered 'detrimental to the public interest'. However, primary legislation was out of the question. Apart from lack of government time, he was worried that ministers would be drawn into a wider discussion about the advertising and sale of contraceptives and the provision of contraceptive advice by local authorities. Previous attempts by backbench MPs to restrict contraceptive sales through machines in the 1930s had failed, and there was little prospect of a more successful Private Member's Bill now. The solution arrived at, which was approved by the Attorney General, Sir Hartley Shawcross, was the introduction of a by-law giving local authorities the power to stop the practice in their area.[10] This was greeted in the House of Commons by widespread cheers, and welcomed in the Church Assembly by the Archbishop of Canterbury, although he warned that a proper legislative ban was also necessary, something which Anthony Eden also pressed on the Home Secretary.[11]

Resistance to the active spread of contraception or family planning services continued. It was augmented by religious support for larger families, and not just from Roman Catholics. In 1952 the Archbishop of Canterbury addressed the Mothers' Union, saying 'One child deliberately willed as the limit is no family at all but something of a misfortune, for child and parents. Two children accepted as the ideal limit do not make a real family – a family only truly begins with three children.'[12]

Such sweeping excommunication of so many families was, however, becoming more unusual. The political silence on contraception was eventually ended in 1955 with the appointment of Iain Macleod as Minister of Health. He was invited by a personal friend, Lady Monckton, wife of Churchill's Minister of

Labour, Sir Walter Monckton, to visit the Family Planning Association (FPA), of which she was a leading supporter, to help break the taboo surrounding the subject. Macleod eagerly agreed to a highly publicised occasion. The occasion even merited a lengthy *Times* editorial on the progress of modern parenthood, welcoming Macleod's support for family planning being 'accepted as part of the ordinary affairs of life'. The paper also approved the minister's care to give equal weight to different moral and religious views about contraception: 'It is this cleavage of opinion that justifies the constitution of family planning services as a voluntary movement, used by the public health services within defined limits, but remaining free of control or direction by the State.'[13] According to one historian of family planning, the media ban on discussion of contraception and the work of the FPA was broken almost immediately, with only minimal protest from Catholic quarters.[14]

*

The temporary surge in divorce after the Second World War, caused by the fragility of many wartime marriages, prompted the first critical examination of the basis of divorce law. Just before the war, after a long campaign waged by Sir Alan Herbert, MP for Oxford and Cambridge Universities, the grounds for divorce were extended to include desertion for more than three years, cruelty, incurable insanity, habitual drunkenness and imprisonment under a death sentence. However, it was only after the war that it was more apparent, except to the most immovable religious zealot, that in many of these wartime marriages the moral blame of one or other partner for their adultery or other sufficiently cruel behaviour was symptomatic of the harshness of circumstances beyond their control. The effects of the war on legitimacy, family breakdown and divorce were felt across many belligerent countries, perhaps most strongly in the USA. Support for allowing marriages which were clearly dead to be dissolved, even if no adultery or other offence had been committed, began to rise.[15] Such situations had in fact been well known to some, particularly Labour politicians and reformers working in deprived areas, for over a decade. As Leo Abse, one of the primary sponsors of divorce law reform during the 1960s, has pointed out, the operation of the means test during the 1930s, forcing young men to travel long distances to find work, had a similar effect to that of war on young marriages, without the widespread sympathy which military conflict generated.[16] In 1948 and 1949 the Labour Party's Research Department produced two papers on divorce, advocating divorce by consent after long separation or without consent after two years' desertion, which did not become party policy.[17]

The political sensitivity of tampering with divorce proceedings, let alone the fundamental principles underlying divorce law, was evident from the beginning of the Attlee Government in 1945. It is important to remember that at this point all divorce cases were still heard in the High Court, as they had been since the need to obtain an Act of Parliament had been removed in 1857. With the sudden increase in divorces resulting from wartime conditions, the system was now unable to cope. The Lord Chancellor, Lord Jowitt, petitioned the Cabinet for authority to handle the impending avalanche of cases by appointing, as a temporary measure, more county court judges as commissioners in the High Court. Even this was highly controversial, as many people, including the President of the Divorce Division, Lord Merriman, thought this was as bad as downgrading divorce case hearings to the county court itself, because of the impression it would create in the public's mind. This more radical suggestion was supported by Labour voices including Gerald Gardiner QC, president of the Haldane Society of Socialist Lawyers and the future Lord Chancellor under Harold Wilson, who would help shepherd a radical divorce law, as well as other legal reforms, onto the statute book. Jowitt had already had to reject this proposal because of the opposition which it would have faced in the House of Lords. However, Jowitt argued that the ballooning delays were already undermining the solemnity of divorce, because the pressures meant that in only a very small percentage of cases was there any real investigation of the facts for possible collusion between the parties. Some ministers were nervous of treading on such sensitive ground as the divorce law which did not form 'an essential part' of the Government's programme, something which the Cabinet Secretary, Sir Norman Brook, felt needed emphasising to the Prime Minister. However, the underlying concern of some ministers, including Jowitt and Attlee, was the cost of divorce proceedings for ordinary working people. This was increased by the necessity of cases being heard at the High Court as well as other procedural formalities. The cost of an ordinary undefended divorce case was about £75. A group of ministers recommended an inquiry, which, under the chairmanship of a youthful Lord

Denning, supported moves to reduce costs and delays.

The passing of the postwar peak in divorce by 1947 did not reduce demands for a fundamental reform of the law, particularly from Labour MPs, and in 1949 ministers had to face the possibility of a vote in favour of widening the grounds for divorce to include separation without consent after seven years. As Jowitt emphasised to Attlee, this would mean a profound break with the existing principle of divorce law, introducing the possibility of a guilty party divorcing the innocent without their consent. On the other hand, it was well recognised that the existing law enabled a long-separated spouse to refuse divorce, not because of religious scruple, but out of spite or bitterness towards the other spouse and a new partner. Jowitt peered over the edge of an abyss: 'If we accept this proposal, what guarantee have we that the seven years may not be whittled down to five, to three or even to one, so that the whole institution of marriage is placed in jeopardy?'

At the beginning of 1949, Attlee had, at Jowitt's instigation, rebuffed suggestions that a Royal Commission should be established to examine the whole basis of the divorce law. Jowitt also argued that the introduction of legal aid for divorce that year should be given time to demonstrate its effect before any further steps were taken. By the middle of the year, however, the position had changed. Labour MP Marcus Lipton had tabled an amendment on separation after seven years to a private members' bill dealing with less controversial aspects of divorce, and attracted massive support. Jowitt made a tactical retreat, arguing that a Royal Commission might now be established because there was no prospect of it reporting this side of a general election.[18] Ministers were torn, but agreed that 'the time was now ripe' to concede an inquiry, but only if necessary in order to defeat the amendment.[19] In the event the Speaker ruled the amendment out of order, so no mention of this decision was made. Attlee reverted to rejecting Lipton's plea for a Commission which would address the plight of 'thousands of men and women who are now condemned to life-long frustration and misery' by saying the time was not yet ripe. Having averted a potential crisis, the Cabinet agreed that 'there was no widespread public concern over this question, and that this was not an opportune moment at which to launch a further enquiry into it.'[20]

This line was held for another year, with ministers happily sticking their heads back in the sand, agreeing again in 1950 that 'there was no widespread public concern over this question.'[21] However, in early 1951 a new Commons bill introduced by Eirene White focused on extending the grounds of divorce to include separation after seven years. The Bill received a second reading by 131 to 60 votes. Divisions between ministers now began to appear over whether to remain completely neutral and let the Bill take its course, or to offer a Royal Commission again in return for withdrawing the Bill. The Attorney General, Sir Hartley Shawcross, and Solicitor General, Sir Frank Soskice, later to be Wilson's first Home Secretary, were both sympathetic to reform and wanted at least a Royal Commission to be set up. Herbert Morrison and the Secretary of State for Scotland, Hector McNeil, formed the main opposition to any concession in the way of an inquiry, Morrison because any government would be bound to act on its recommendations (how wrong that would prove), and McNeil from the more basic position that 'better opinion', particularly in Scotland, was against it and the government should not be indifferent.[22] Jowitt managed to overcome this opposition in Cabinet, and ministers then considered what tactics to employ. At this point, Attlee's normally efficient management of the Cabinet seems to have come rather unstuck. It was agreed that the Chief Whip and others should persuade the sponsors of the Bill to withdraw it in return for the appointment of the Royal Commission. However, it was not made clear what latitude should be given to ministers if there was still a vote on the Bill, or whether, as previously, the Royal Commission was conditional on the Bill's withdrawal. Attlee, Morrison and others said that ministers should not be allowed to vote as they liked, but were opposed by Aneurin Bevan, who was in the middle of fighting a rather larger battle with Hugh Gaitskell over imposing NHS charges to help cover the re-armament programme triggered by the Korean War.[23] According to Shawcross's recollection, 'after a confused discussion the matter rather went off on the assumption that there would be no vote anyway.' He and the Chief Whip managed to agree with the leading MPs for and against reform that a Royal Commission would be acceptable, but was unexpectedly asked point blank by Sydney Silverman whether it was a conditional offer, to which he said that the Government would have to reconsider its position if the Bill were approved. This was greeted with scorn by Labour supporters of the Bill in particular.

One can only feel sorry for Shawcross. His speech clearly indicated his sympathy for the Bill, posing the question whether the existing state of the law was satisfactory when *the vast mass of the people do consider that in practice divorce by consent is possible, provided that one party or the other will go through the distasteful process of spending a night in some hotel with some unknown woman and then submitting, at some additional expense, to proof of the fact in the High Court.*

He was, of course, experienced as a barrister who had practised in the divorce courts.[24] However, when the vote was taken, he invited more opprobrium from the supporters of the Bill by standing in front of the division lobbies and telling MPs that if they wanted a Royal Commission they should vote 'no', as this was what he thought had been the Cabinet's decision. He was rebuffed as the Bill was approved by 131 to 60 votes.[25] Shawcross complained bitterly to Attlee:

I was myself always in favour of a Royal Commission and was, in Cabinet and have been for six years, its main protagonist [sic]. It was for this reason that I had hoped to be allowed ... to announce on Monday that one would be established. As it is people will feel that the whole thing has been taken out of my hands and I have been impliedly rebuked.[26]

Ministers did make good the promise, with Attlee making the announcement in the very week that Gaitskell's rearmament Budget prompted Bevan and Wilson to resign. He almost gushed, for him, from the despatch box that 'in my experience people have had to wait a considerable time on these questions of the divorce laws.' Challenged by Conservative MP Cyril Black, the main defender of the status quo, whether the Commission would be able to look at ways of strengthening the sanctity of marriage, Attlee responded drily that 'I have always understood that that was one of the points taken into consideration by Royal Commissions on this subject.'[27]

That decision did not quite mean the issue was safely in the long grass. As successive governments were to do, ministers now got themselves into a tangle over the appointment of the Commission. What weight should be given to religious opinion among its membership, and should the different denominations themselves be represented? The previous Royal Commission on divorce in 1912 had included the Archbishop of York. Many ministers were also keen that there should be an adequate working-class voice. What exactly was a Commission being asked to produce about such a contentious moral issue?

Northern Ireland was excluded from its remit because of the conservative views of both the Roman Catholic and Protestant communities. McNeil and James Chuter Ede wanted the Churches to be directly represented, McNeil no doubt meaning Scottish denominations. Shawcross and Soskice thought this pointless as the Churches' views were well known and the Commission's report would be more likely to be disregarded. Jowitt, writing to the Prime Minister about these difficulties, quoted from a 1910 Departmental Committee on the Procedure of Royal Commissions, whose observations should still be noted by governments today, that

> *those selected as Commissioners should, as far as possible, be persons who have not committed themselves so deeply on any side of the questions involved in the reference as to render the probability of an impartial inquiry and an unanimous report practically impossible ...*
>
> *A Commission selected on the principle of representing various interests starts with a serious handicap against the probability of harmony in its work, and perhaps even of practical result from its labours ...*
>
> *The true object of the appointment of a Royal Commission is to obtain a carefully considered judgement on the matters within their terms of reference; and this object is imperilled when the preliminary considerations mentioned above are disregarded, because its members are apt to divide almost from the date of their appointment into two or more opposing parties.*

Jowitt thought the arguments evenly balanced. He recognised that those wanting denominational representation would be likely to view the omission as 'one further step towards the separation between the Christian and the secular conception of marriage', but was inclined to agree with the Law Officers. Reflecting on the 1910 report, he thought it would

> *no doubt ... be exceedingly difficult to discover anyone who is suitable for appointment to a Royal Commission on the divorce law who has not already reached some provisional conclusions ... but to invite anyone as deeply committed to a particular point of view as a representative of any of the Christian Churches must be, it is argued, to court [these] very difficulties.*

Perhaps most shockingly for the period, he also questioned how religious or secular an inquiry on divorce in the modern world should be:

> *It may be said by those who oppose the Churches' representation on the Commission that such representation would necessarily imply acceptance of the Christian view of marriage and that this is not a matter which should be regarded as beyond controversy in the appointment of the Commission. This argument is not, perhaps, a strong one, as it can readily be answered by saying that the Churchmen were appointed as representatives of an important element in the national life, but nevertheless it may well be an argument which it might be desirable to avoid if possible.*[28]

Norman Brook, against appointing unnecessary Royal Commissions just for political expediency, was clearly bored by this navel-gazing, and asked whether ministers understood what they meant by representation. An ordinary member of a Christian denomination would be in a sense 'a representative' of that denomination and hold, in greater or lesser degree, the views on marriage professed by the denomination to which he belonged. He presumed that the Lord Chancellor would not propose to ask a man whether he was a Christian before appointing him to the Commission, and refuse to appoint him if he said that he was.[29] Ministers tossed possible names around at Cabinet. The actuarial point was made that the 1912 Royal Commission had included only one representative of the Churches, and that the influence of the Churches in national life had decreased substantially since then. It would therefore be 'out of accord with contemporary opinion if the Churches took a dominant part in the work of the Commission'. They were content to ensure that the broad range of religious opinion was represented without asking different denominations to nominate actual 'representatives', so long as the working-class interest was beefed up.[30] With the Commission safely appointed on this basis, ministers could sit back in the sure knowledge that the other lot would have to deal with the problem. Lord Morton, chosen to chair the Commission, pleaded that duodenal ulcer trouble limited his workload, adding to the likely delay. Considering the poor reception which his report would receive, such a burden might have been viewed as particularly galling.

*

At the same time that Eirene White's battle to relieve some of the hardship of marital breakdown was being frustrated, one small step was taken to remove the greater stigma conferred on immorality among women compared to men. The instrument of this progress was another female Labour MP, the youthful member for Blackburn East, Barbara Castle, Parliamentary Private Secretary to an equally youthful President of the Board of Trade, Harold Wilson. She had been on the official British delegation to the UN General Assembly in 1949, where she made her first media splash back home with a vitriolic speech attacking the Soviet 'genocidal habit of mind'. To her dismay, she had been put on the Assembly's Social Committee,[31] which was discussing the white slave trade and prostitution at the optimistically named (at least for the venue for a UN meeting) Lake Success. At these talks, Britain had been rather embarrassed by the fact that in England and Wales, the protection of the law from the parasitic corruption of men procuring women for sex or to work in brothels did not extend to women or girls already in the sex trade, or, as they were then known, 'common prostitutes'.

When the Criminal Law Amendment Act 1885 had been passed, a distinction was made between ordinary women and girls, and those of 'known immoral character'. As Castle and the women's organisations pointed out, these were exactly the individuals most likely to need the protection of the law. One cannot imagine that the fiery young Barbara enjoyed being embarrassed in this way, especially considering, as she relayed to James Chuter Ede, 'we did indeed take a very lofty line in the matter [of brothels] particularly vis-à-vis the French.' Her dismay soon turned to enthusiasm, and it did not take much persuading from women's organisations for her to pursue the injustice back in Britain. In the summer of 1950 a helpful, but rather patronising, Sir Oswald Allen at the Home Office interpreted her feelings about the legal anomaly for the Permanent Secretary, Sir Frank Newsam, saying that she found the position 'intolerable' and was 'emotionally disturbed' by it. It seems that Castle may have deliberately given the impression that she was the helpless victim of outside pressure by merciless women's organisations, from which the gallant officials should rescue her. It was clear that the Government would not find time for such a measure, but an imaginative Allen suggested to Castle that it might be possible to 'ventilate' the problem through private members' legislation, if the procedure was restored, as was hoped, in the following session. When Castle and a deputation from the

Association for Moral and Social Hygiene met Chuter Ede in September he rebuffed Castle's plea that the Government should take the issue on itself, saying that it would be better dealt with as a private members' bill because 'the moral issues would command the sympathy of members of all parties.' However, his officials had already drafted a bill for her, keeping closely to the restricted issue of removing the disabilities conferred on 'common prostitutes' in the 1885 Act. The difficulty of preparing a bill, he said, was to avoid controversial issues and to make it impossible for others to introduce them by moving amendments.[32] Unfortunately, Castle failed to win a place in the ballot for private members' legislation in November. Undaunted, she tabled a motion under the new Ten Minute Rule. Introducing the Bill, Castle explained: 'It does not seek either to condone or persecute prostitution as such. It is concerned with the procurer, with the man or woman who exploits the vice of others, and therefore has an interest in its encouragement.' The law helped to trap women in prostitution and gave them no assistance in escaping from it, she said, as men could have no fear of prosecution for their parasitic control over women who were already prostitutes.[33] Crucially, her political patron, Herbert Morrison, was the other key minister on the Home Affairs Committee which now agreed to allow her Bill a fair wind.[34] In the Lords it was sponsored by Lord Chorley, who said that Castle's action demonstrated the virtue of having women MPs, and he looked forward to the time when the Lords would also benefit from the wisdom of the fairer sex in its deliberations. Perhaps the two most distinguished former Home Secretaries, Viscounts Simon and Samuel, were also roused to support the Bill.[35]

Quite how much the women which the Bill intended to help were able to avail themselves of this new protection and equality with other women might be questioned, especially given the later reinforcement of the difference in penalties between women prostitutes and their clients. However, Castle had struck the first significant legislative blow for women of her long career, leading to the award of Backbencher of the Year.[36] It was also the first ten minute rule bill to reach the statute book. Amazingly it was on an issue of sexual morality.

*

James Chuter Ede, who had been 'Rab' Butler's Labour deputy at the Board of Education during the war, and whose name might as easily have been pinned to the 1944 Education Act as his boss's, was a moderate social liberal as Home Secretary under Clement Attlee, but in the most controversial issue with which he had to deal in his long tenure, which lasted until he was transferred to be Leader of the House of Commons shortly before the 1951 general election, he supported retention of the death penalty. This was to cause Chuter Ede considerable pain in later years. In 1938 he had voted for a Commons motion for a five-year suspension of the death penalty, four years after the Labour Party conference had voted unanimously for abolition. Within a few years of leaving ministerial office he had reconverted to abolition. Why were his abolitionist instincts suppressed after 1945, and why did they resurface so quickly? Chuter Ede's public case made during the parliamentary debates in 1948 rested on his appraisal since becoming Home Secretary of civil service evidence of the deterrent effect of capital punishment, and the risk of 'experimenting' in the context of sharply rising crime during and since the war. The Home Office, despite its reactionary image, was divided on the question. Crucial in the context of the new move for abolition in 1948 was the retentionist influence on penal matters of Sir Frank Newsam, who eclipsed the more abolitionist Permanent Secretary, Sir Alexander Maxwell, eventually replacing him in late 1948. Perhaps equally important were feelings within the Home Office services, principally the desperately undermanned Police and Prison Board, where officials and ministers were unwilling to risk damaging morale.

Like several home secretaries after him, the issue which swung the case for abolition in Chuter Ede's mind after 1951 was the risk of miscarriage of justice. This was learned in the hardest way possible. In 1949 Chuter Ede allowed the law to take its course in the Rillington Place murders. John Evans had been convicted of killing his wife and child. Despite retracting his confession and accusing John Christie, Evans was hanged. Four years later Christie was himself hanged for the murder of several other women in the same house. Despite an investigation into the Evans case, it was not until 1966 that he was granted a posthumous pardon. Chuter Ede campaigned for abolition of capital punishment until his death in 1965. Poignantly, he died just one day after Evans's remains were transferred from prison to his family, as Chuter Ede himself had urged, and only months after Parliament had passed the five-year experimental suspension of capital punishment.[37] However, as Home Secretary, he defended the status quo, though perhaps without the vigour shown by his predecessor, Herbert Morrison.

Morrison once expressed a morbid desire to see a woman hanged, and confessed an inclination to pardon a man for killing a nagging wife, though according to his biographers he had always approached each case that had come before him as Home Secretary with dispassionate care, and was influenced by the more liberal instincts of Maxwell.[38] Morrison performed a similar volte-face to Chuter Ede just before the next Commons debate on the death penalty in 1955, under the influence of younger colleagues and Sir Ernest Gowers, chair of the Royal Commission on Capital Punishment, though with a rather merciless attitude towards those whom he had hanged as Home Secretary, considering society well rid of them.[39]

Following the Labour landslide, supporters of abolition had galvanised with the Howard League organising a Parliamentary Penal Reform Group. This garnered 187 signatories for a letter to Chuter Ede calling for a five-year suspension of capital punishment as part of the Government's programme of reform of the criminal law, which was about to be enshrined in a Criminal Justice Bill. This was rejected, but the Government cleared the way for a debate on an abolitionist amendment to the Bill at the report stage, when all MPs could participate. At this point, however, ministers began to get themselves into difficulties. Should they, as well as backbenchers, be allowed a free vote?

The question of free votes on issues of conscience had recently been aired within the Parliamentary Labour Party (PLP). A 'conscience clause' in the standing orders of the PLP dated back as far as 1906, when the Liberal Government's Education Bill caused personal difficulties for the sole Catholic Labour MP, who could not accept the party's policy of secular education (a far cry from the Blair Government's support for religious education). Until 1945 the clause was most often employed in relation to defence, where genuine pacifists were given a dispensation for political or religious objections to party policy. In 1945, the clause was defined more narrowly in relation to 'religion and temperance'. However, this still only allowed abstention, but in 1946 the standing orders were suspended, reflecting a more relaxed attitude in the context of a Commons majority of nearly three figures. With collective responsibility, however, ministers were not to be allowed this degree of latitude, but the Cabinet was split on how to handle the question. Morrison, as Leader of the House responsible for the legislative programme, was all for imposing a three-line whip against the abolitionist amendment. Chuter Ede was more pragmatic. He recognised the strength of feeling within the party, including among ministers. A compromise was reached whereby ministers were not permitted a free vote, but a blind eye would be turned to abstention.

The atmosphere surrounding the vote was extremely charged. Both camps had several months from the time the Government announced it would allow a vote to the point when the Bill returned from its committee stage to the floor of the House. Press and public debate raged. Predictably, and consistently, public opinion supported retention by a margin of over two to one, with little differentiation, as would later become the case, between the sexes, or between different generations or social classes. The press was divided between national newspapers, which tended more towards abolition, and regional and local press, which reflected more closely public support for the death penalty. Their influence was enhanced in 1948 when a freak series of particularly bizarre and shocking murders were reported in lurid detail, all grist to the mill of retentionists in Parliament. One case involved a ship's steward, who assaulted and murdered a young actress and pushed her body through a porthole into shark-infested waters (though if already dead when she entered the water, the added ingredient of sharks might be thought only to have added a further sinister indignity to her demise). The murder of a policeman by a youth in London sparked a particularly intense wave of publicity, with the *Daily Express* splashing the headline 'Kill the killer'.[40]

On the morning of 15 April 1948, when debate on the abolitionist amendment was due to begin, Morrison announced to a meeting of the PLP that the free vote would be restricted to backbenchers. Abstention would be tolerated if ministers opposed the death penalty. The meeting exploded, with abolitionists saying they had been misled, and retentionists arguing that collective responsibility must be maintained. The strongest support for the death penalty during the debate came from Sir John Anderson, that quirk of Whitehall who achieved the unique distinction of serving ten years as Permanent Secretary at the Home Office and then becoming Home Secretary himself. In response to Labour protests at his contention that the risk of miscarriage of justice was 'so small, indeed, so infinitesimal that consideration can be dismissed', he asserted that no innocent man had been hanged in the twentieth century. Rather more convincing was the argument repeatedly used, including by Chuter Ede, that the alternative to hanging, life imprisonment, was felt to be more inhumane by many people, notably the former Prison Commissioner, Sir Alexander Paterson.[41] Forty-four ministers failed to vote, including the Chancellor of the Exchequer, Stafford Cripps, Aneurin Bevan, Harold Wilson and all four Law Officers. Chuter Ede gave his own junior minister (who was responsible for the Government's Criminal Justice Bill) Kenneth Younger, permission not to vote. Several ministers stayed conspicuously on the front bench during the division. The amendment to suspend the death penalty was carried, amidst jubilant cheers, by 245 to 222 votes. Winston Churchill's reaction to the government's defeat was typical of his less temperate opposition style. Rousing the massed ranks of the Conservative Women's Association in the Royal Albert Hall to the theme of creating a new national Conservative Government, 'devoid of party prejudices', he proceeded to employ party prejudice to the nth degree:

> As I listened the other night to the crazy cheers with which the Socialist back-benchers … swept away the death penalty … I could not but wonder that these were the same men who regarded the slaughter by their mistakes of at least half a million Indians in the Punjab alone as a mere incident in the progress of Oriental self-government.[42]

The stage was now set for the Lords to position themselves as the champions of the people, a role that would not fall to them over another issue of morality until peers resisted the Commons' decision on gay rights and adoption by unmarried couples under the Blair Government. A double parallel with the position half a century later was provided by the concurrent row over House of Lords reform. Negotiations over reform had just broken down in 1948, and Parliament was then recalled from its summer recess for a special session to consider a Parliament bill reducing the Lords' delaying power from two years to one. Peers' support for retention of the death penalty was hardly dimmed by the way in which Lord Chancellor Jowitt intervened in the two-day debate on the question, damning with faint praise the abolitionist arguments put forward by the Commons. He conceded only that 'since it has been decided, however, that it is the right thing to do, let us now go forward.' Only twenty-eight peers 'went forward' with the Government's hollow support for this clause of its own Bill, with 181 against.[43]

In a move now reminiscent of the Blair Government's tortuous search for consensus over fox-hunting where none existed, Chuter Ede, Morrison and

Cripps now effected a compromise which they persuaded Labour abolitionists to accept on tactical grounds. This would involve differentiating between classes of murder, retaining the death penalty only for aggravated crimes, including those compounded by robbery, burglary or housebreaking, the use of explosives, sexual assault, administration of poison, resisting arrest or killing a policeman or prison officer. Press and public reaction was derisive. Churchill returned to the fray, quoting Elizabeth I's comparison between poetry and blank verse:

'*Marry, this is something. This is rhyme! But this* [the blank verse] *is neither rhyme nor reason.*'

He preferred to rely on the Home Secretary's existing power of reprieve as 'by far the most elastic, sympathetic and comprehending process that can possibly be used'.

Conservative opposition to this plan was, in retrospect, highly ironic given the involvement within the next decade of many of the Tory front bench in steering just such a compromise on to the statute book under Anthony Eden. Unafraid even of Churchill, Sydney Silverman attacked the opposition leader's ignorance of the evidence and his party politicking, but bowed to the will of his Government.[44] However, there was no certainty that the Lords would be any more inclined to accept this proposal, which arguably brought the criminal law into greater disrepute than abolition did by flouting public opinion. In the words of an early historian of the episode, 'two more widely separated stools would be difficult to imagine.'[45] Back in the Lords Jowitt again equivocated. The best he could say for the proposals was that they were a compromise, and that any jury could be expected to be as divided on the question as Parliament and the public as a whole. The Lords threw it out by almost the same margin as before.[46] With the Parliament approaching its fourth session and more important matters crowding in (not least the question of the delaying power of the Lords) it was clear the Government was not going to test peers again over a compromise in which hardly anyone, including themselves, believed. Nor could they use the Parliament Act because the compromise had not been part of the original Bill when it left the Commons. Despite bitterness among core abolitionists like Silverman, the Commons accepted the recommendation of the Home Secretary to drop reference to capital punishment from the important Criminal Justice

Bill. Churchill was scathing about the circumlocution which Chuter Ede had performed over the course of the Bill, and downright rude about Sir Hartley Shawcross's legal expertise.[47]

Norman Brook now gave the knife a good twist in a memo to Clement Attlee which reeked of 'I told you so'. Brook pushed strongly the arguments in favour of the status quo, and ridiculed the compromise proposal. The only point which he used to soften his argument was the suggestion that the number of individual cases in which the death penalty would be exacted might continue to decrease:

> *Home Office practice, in advising on the prerogative of mercy in capital cases, takes account, not only of the code of rules ... but also of the prevailing attitudes of public opinion towards the general question of capital punishment ... It is after all, the change in public opinion which has caused the progressive 'humanisation' of those principles over the last fifty years or so; and that development can continue, and can be accelerated.*

This rather ignored the mercurial, emotional nature of public opinion on capital punishment. While a consistent majority supported its retention, whenever an individual murderer faced the rope, public sympathy tended to swing behind him or her, fuelling calls for mercy. Brook also dismissed the suggestion that a Royal Commission should be appointed as a 'waste of time and effort', arguing:

> *What is required is a judgement – not on the moral issue, but on the question whether a majority of people in this country wish to see a change in the law. Is it not arguable that that is the responsibility of Government and Parliament?... so far as the general public are concerned, I should have thought that after last summer's debates most people would be content that the subject should now be dropped.*[48]

Brook was undoubtedly correct in his assessment of the state of public opinion, but also ignored three political factors: the majority support among MPs for abolition; the fact that, had ministers been given a free vote, this majority would have been three times larger; and Labour MPs' resentment at being twice thwarted by unelected peers, whom they were concurrently engaged in shackling further by restricting the Lords' power of delay. The political considerations won out on this occasion, and Attlee conceded a Royal Commission, over whose appointment he took a particular interest. Characteristically, he showed his unyielding respect for British institutions when suggesting John Foot, elder brother of future Labour leader Michael, to serve on the Commission, commenting that 'I know of no other family where the four boys in succession have been President of the Oxford Union ... the most balanced is John.' However, he also showed particular sensitivity to how such a controversial inquiry would be viewed by the public, criticising the obscure list of names which the Home Office submitted, demanding better-known, less academic, figures.[49]

*

The establishment of the Arts Council in 1946 marked a watershed in the funding of the arts in general, and theatre in particular, which began to encourage innovation, and represented the cultural side of Labour's postwar nationalisation programme. However, the theatre was still tightly controlled by a system of precensorship ruled by the Lord Chamberlain. He was unaccountable to government or Parliament, and was under no obligation to give reasons for refusal to grant a licence to a play, and there was no form of appeal against his decisions.[50] The 1843 Theatres Act laid down no criteria for refusal of a licence. Moreover, appointees to the post of Lord Chamberlain (a Crown appointment on the advice of the Prime Minister) were always peers, and usually former soldiers who had little, if any, experience or sympathy for the theatre or the arts in general. Theatre censorship was only one function of his office, which was otherwise responsible for royal ceremonial occasions (arguably just another form of theatre).[51] Although the background of the play-examiners, who wrote reports on submitted scripts on which the Lord Chamberlain partly based his decisions, broadened considerably after the war to include actors, producers and university lecturers, their social milieu remained distinctly military and aristo-cratic.[52]

However, the creative atmosphere of postwar British theatre did little to challenge this archaic system of regulation. Theatre was still divided into two very different genres separated by social class. Plays featuring drawing rooms looking out through french windows over gardens hosting tennis parties attended by the leisured upper-middle class were watched by largely middle-class audiences. Against this was the music hall tradition (in decline since the development of cinema between the wars) and touring nude revues, watched largely by the working class.[53] In the words of one historian, 'theatre was continually trying to set standards. Writers on all levels were ready to chip in with sturdy defences of traditional values.'[54] In the face of this stultified and undynamic scene, there was little to challenge the moral and artistic prescriptions which the Lord Chamberlain's pre-censorship applied. However, in 1951 the Lord Chamberlain considered for the second time since the war relaxing the *de facto* ban on the discussion of homosexuality on the stage. He had recently been visited by a deputation appealing for a licence to be given to *The Children's Hour*, a play dealing with lesbianism. His visitors argued that, as lesbianism was not a criminal offence, and the play in no way encouraged it, an exception should be made.[55] In 1946 Lord Clarendon had consulted a 'cross-section of the play-going public', albeit a rather exalted cross-section of clerical, medical, scholastic and legal luminaries, who affirmed the need to retain the ban. In the last months of the Attlee administration he ventured to test the water again. The Lord Chancellor, Lord Jowitt, was part of Clarendon's cross-section. The Lord Chamberlain outlined to him the arguments for and against, that the public was now more broad-minded and that theatre, being the 'mirror of the age', should not be fettered by censorship. On the other hand, he argued that 'the subject will be very distasteful and embarrassing in mixed company of all ages and also that the introduction in plays of these new vices might start an unfortunate train of thought in the previously innocent'. He continued:

Another view is that the British public is apt to be intolerant of attempts at moral reform and there may be an inclination to ridicule, which would be unfortunate. I can ensure that the subject is not treated with levity in stage plays but I do not control music-hall artistes, who might tend to give the subject distasteful notoriety.

Jowitt replied in uncensorious tones that the question of whether or not to allow a play on homosexuality would depend on the seriousness with which the subject was treated. He and, he suspected, modern responsibly-minded young girls would be revolted by any indecent discussion of homosexuality:

You and I are probably rather old-fashioned in our outlook and personally I would very much rather not see plays which are based upon the theme either of homosexuality or lesbianism … I suspect, however, that I am Victorian in my outlook … I think we Victorians are always apt to confuse innocence with ignorance.

Potentially devaluing his own advice, Jowitt admitted that

I hardly ever go to the play and I certainly should not go to plays if I knew that they dealt with these topics … I think, however, the censorship frequently defeats its own object, and that under modern conditions there is much to be said for free and open discussion.[56]

However, the weight of contrary advice carried the day, and the ban remained until after the publication of the Wolfenden Report in 1957. Leslie Stokes's *Oscar Wilde* had been refused a licence in 1946. In 1948 a private production was seen by members of the Lord Chamberlain's staff, who wrote to Clarendon that 'it is undoubtedly a good play, but I do not recommend you to pass it. It is entirely about perverts, and as Game [another play-examiner] says in his 1946 report this subject is taboo as a dramatic theme.'

The officials who viewed and read plays for the Lord Chamberlain were clearly softening in their approach towards discussion of homosexuality. In the early 1950s Donald Duncan's *The Catalyst*, which included lesbian leanings between a man's wife and mistress, was considered very good by one examiner, who suggested to Clarendon that 'this is the exceptional play for which to loosen up.' Clarendon replied:

I have read this play with great interest and I should think it could be a real success, but I am not prepared to pick and choose between the good and the bad plays which deal with the subject of homosexuality and lesbianism, and so long as that policy prevails I regret I cannot license the play.[57]

In 1953 Philip King's *Serious Charge* was submitted for licence, featuring a vicar wrongly accused of sexually assaulting a young boy. Examiner Heriot wrote: 'The play is strong and sensible. We are in no doubt at any time that the vicar is innocent of the "serious charge". Clarendon relented on this occasion, though rejected the suggestion that the false nature of the sexual allegation meant that 'no question of propriety can arise.' *Tea and Sympathy*, which again had a lesbian theme, was refused a licence in 1954 despite a successful Chicago production starring Deborah Kerr. In 1949 the playwright MPs Ben Levy and E. P. Smith introduced a bill to abolish precensorship which was carried by seventy-six to thirty-seven votes, but then ran out of time. The doctrine of 'unripe time' was once again invoked by James Chuter Ede as well as the hoary official line that there were many anachronistic and illogical things about the British constitution which should not be swept away without a firm idea of how their replacement would work.[58] In a real demonstration of how such constitutional anomalies could work, the play *Pick-up Girl* was seen by an unperturbed Queen Mary on her seventy-ninth birthday in 1949, but changes were insisted upon by the Lord Chamberlain for a public version.

*

If theatre censorship remained strictly under the Lord Chamberlain's control in the decade after the war, equally immovable was the opposition to any relaxation of the mediaeval prohibition of entertainment on Sundays. The obstruction by the Lord's Day Observance Society (LDOS) of Sunday entertainments ranging from the South of England Table Tennis Championships to a concert by Tommy Handley in 1949[59] jarred with the growing unease at continuing postwar austerity, and a yearning for fewer controls on consumption and greater gaiety in life.[60] It certainly sparked the first organised campaign for law reform, the Sunday Freedom Association, which attracted the support of screen stars such as Jack Warner and the parliamentary sponsorship of John Parker, Labour MP for Dagenham, who unsuccessfully championed the issue until the fall of the Wilson Government in 1970.[61] The LDOS successfully harried the Attlee Government's plans for the 1951 Festival of Britain so as to prevent the amusement part of the Festival Gardens operating in Battersea Park from opening on Sundays. In the event, because of the illogicality of the existing laws, merry-go-rounds were still allowed. Not for the last time, a government with a slim majority and MPs from marginal seats allowed a liberalising measure to be castrated by a small but vocal minority.[62] Parker's first attempt to introduce a bill in 1953 was defeated by 281 to 57 votes, and a subsequent proposition that a Royal Commission be appointed fell by 172 to 164, after the LDOS organised a campaign which produced a petition with over half a million signatures. The Tory Home Secretary, David Maxwell-Fyfe, was advised by Downing Street effectively not to touch the subject with a barge-pole.[63] He breezily reported to the Cabinet's Legislation Committee, in the sure knowledge that the Bill would not make progress, that 'he did not believe that there was much public support for the Bill or that performers themselves generally would be in sympathy with its objects.'[64]

There were two particularly interesting features of this bill. First was the inclusion of a compulsory contribution to charity of a proportion of the profits from Sunday opening of cinemas and theatres.[65] This was a sop to the Christian injunction that works of charity should be the only occupation other than divine worship on the Sabbath. Secondly, a local option, aimed to appease Welsh nonconformist opposition, would allow councils to exempt themselves from the Bill's provisions after a referendum for a period of three years. However, it was realised that the potential ease of evading the law and the local variations which would be created was hardly an improvement on laws which had already come into disrepute.

If the late 1940s had witnessed some popular frustration with controls and shortages, then the rise in family incomes from the economic upturn from 1952 and the increasing employment of married women gave families more scope for leisure activities on Sundays. Public debate after the 1953 Bill led to a growth in Sunday entertainments, some within the law, others not, and organisations such as the National Trust discovered the popularity of visiting their properties on Sundays.[66] The cause of those opposed to relaxation of the Sunday observance laws might not have been assisted, however, by the participation of the young Duke of Edinburgh in Sunday polo matches.[67] The Archbishop of Canterbury, Geoffrey Fisher, was sufficiently worried about the impression this was having to write the duke a highly critical letter:

> *Many people speak or write to me about your Royal Highness's occasional taking part in Sunday polo or cricket. I have always said little except to call their attention to the glorious example which you set Sunday by Sunday of regular and faithful Church attendance. And I have tried to restrain some people who wanted to write to the papers or send petitions to you. But I have*

had an uneasy feeling that though I said no more to them, honesty required that I should say what I thought to you. Once or twice this holidays I have begun an attempt, but torn it up. Now I am very sorry to see that the Free Church of Scotland has criticised you publicly and their words have been given further publicity in the Observer and other Sunday papers...

Your Royal Highness will I am sure read what I have written on this matter with patience ... but the question raised is one which depends more on a judgement of social values than one of religious values, so far as they can be separated: and judgement of social values is always complex and difficult ... I do feel the strength of the argument that when you take part in Sunday polo or cricket, inevitably you are the cause of a great concourse of ten or twenty thousand people or more and that thereby the general defences of Sunday as a day when as few people as possible should make demands upon other people for their services are weakened, and great encouragement is given to all who now are constantly seeking to invade the domesticity of Sunday rest and recreations, and who when the time comes will press very hard for legislation to remove all restrictions upon the full secularisation and commercialisation of Sunday.[68]

This was given fairly short shrift by Prince Philip, although he was prepared to make one rather impractical concession:

I don't think there is any need to be apprehensive about Sunday observance. I believe it is only necessary to have clearly in mind the limits and extent of your defensive position and confidence in its strength so that instead of waiting for it to be gradually eaten away you could go over to the offensive and attack the most glaring cases of the misuse of Sunday ...

As far as I am concerned I would not mind playing behind a screen without anyone looking on but unfortunately the club which organises the game cannot afford to do this. It encourages people to pay to come and watch in order to reduce to some extent the expense of the game.'[69]

*

If the Festival of Britain had prompted some delicate questions about Sunday entertainment, the international focus which the festival and, indeed, the coronation in 1953 threw on London raised even more profound moral questions for the Churchill Government over the visibility of prostitutes in Mayfair and the West End. When David Maxwell-Fyfe decided that something needed to be done about this problem, discussion expanded to include the even more controversial topic of homosexuality, despite what he amusedly called his 'Old Testament attitude' (a label given him by *Punch* magazine).[70] Maxwell-Fyfe has always been viewed as a reactionary force in the story of the Wolfenden Committee and homosexual law reform. The spread of a moral panic about homosexuality during the early 1950s among the political class and in the press was a reaction to numerous celebrated trials and scandals; the flight to the Soviet Union of Guy Burgess and Donald Maclean in 1951, and the prosecutions of Lord Montagu and Peter Wildeblood, and Robert Croft-Cooke and Michael Pitt-Rivers in 1954.[71] It was also in response to the rapid increase in indictable offences at the time – five-fold between 1945 and 1960. But this itself was a reflection of the political drive, particularly by Maxwell-Fyfe, to impose greater uniformity across the country in the prosecution of homosexual offences.[72] What seemed to be an increase in incidence was, more likely, an increase in police activity. Entrapment was frequently used and, in court, the charge of conspiracy was revived, the more easily to obtain convictions than could a simple charge of indecency or sodomy.[73] The fear of an increase in homosexuality was succinctly captured by Wolfenden in his memoirs: 'Nobody had any idea how much of it there was ... but there was an impression that it was increasing; and there was a feeling that if it was then it ought to be curbed.'[74]

What liberalising pressure there was came initially from the Church of England Moral Welfare Council (CEMWC), which, in 1952, published its report *The Problem of Homosexuality*. This recommended an inquiry into the law relating to homosexuality and the separation of 'sin' from the criminal law.[75] For itself, the Labour Party Research Department as early as 1948 produced a paper on 'Reform of Substantive Criminal Law', which included a section on homosexuality advocating decriminalisation of acts committed by those over eighteen, pointing out that lesbianism was not even recognised in law, and criticising the judiciary's cruel and outdated attitudes.[76] Further support came from the Howard League for Penal Reform and the *New Statesman* after the Montagu–Wildeblood trial.

As Maxwell-Fyfe would have been very satisfied with the custodial sentences handed down at that time, it is curious that the establishment of the Wolfenden Committee has often been attributed to a head of pressure which built up in 1954 after those trials. In fact it was prostitution, not homosexuality, which was the original remit of the Committee. The latter area was only added to balance out the inquiry with a 'related' problem. Lord Allen of Abbeydale, Deputy Secretary at the Home Office in 1954 and later Permanent Secretary under Roy Jenkins, when interviewed in 1994 recalled that the visibility of prostitution on the streets of the West End and elsewhere was the prime motive behind the establishment of the Committee; 'and as we were having an inquiry into prostitution, almost as a make-weight as I recall, we threw in the other half … It [homosexuality] wasn't a live issue … to that extent … although I know the contrary has been said since.'[77]

Another reason is provided by Bill Deedes, a Home Office minister at the time of the establishment of the inquiry, who cited the concentration on reconstruction after the disruption of the Second World War as the reason why social reform had not been addressed before: 'It was fairly natural that around the middle 1950s a change of view began to take place; we hadn't reviewed the social scene for twenty years … people hadn't got the mind, at least in government, to deal with these matters until roughly the middle 1950s.'[78]

It has even been said that Maxwell-Fyfe could not bear the subject to be discussed in Cabinet, although this is not quite the picture revealed by the Cabinet minutes. It is true that, in his own words, he 'doubted the expediency of amending the existing law', and would not countenance any suggestion that homosexuals should not be prevented from being a danger to others, especially the young.[79] However, even before an inquiry had begun, he recognised the weight of 'responsible' opinion calling for decriminalisation of homosexuality. Maxwell-Fyfe brought the questions of prostitution and homosexuality to the Cabinet in February 1954, seeking permission to appoint a Royal Commission. The scourge of public soliciting by prostitutes, particularly in London, was now, in his opinion, only ameliorable by legislation to strengthen the penalties available. This, he argued, would prove highly controversial and be opposed by women's groups. At the same time, there had been an even larger increase in the number of homosexual offences, for which he had no clear explanation. Public opinion was being increasingly excited by this phenomenon, and would reject action on the former without the latter. A commission should therefore look at both.

Some of his colleagues were palpably aghast at the discussion. No government could emerge from a change in the law 'with any credit', it was suggested. However, there was keen support for a clamp down on prostitution by increasing penalties to Scottish levels, where it was thought that greater severity had had an effect on the number of offences. 'Special doubt was expressed' about moving on homosexuality. Ministers echoed calls made a few days previously in the Commons for a new law restricting the reporting of 'gross and unnecessary details' of criminal cases involving homosexuality.[80] This ostrich-like approach was based on similar reporting restrictions in divorce cases, where delicate moral sensibilities, and the young and vulnerable, were protected from corruption by any salacious publication of the sordid details of immorality.[81]

The following month Maxwell-Fyfe again sought approval for an 'independent and authoritative' inquiry into prostitution and homosexual offences on which government could base legislation or other action. This time reluctant ministers were openly led by the Prime Minister. Winston Churchill rejected any action, except supporting a private members' bill to introduce reporting restrictions on criminal cases involving homosexuality. Maxwell-Fyfe agreed to bring back an analysis of the arguments for and against such legislation, but warned that 'even if it had the effect of allaying public anxiety about homosexuality, [it] would make no contribution whatever towards a solution of the problem of homosexuality', which he considered the greater evil. Churchill's intransigence also overruled the majority of ministers, who recognised that an inquiry into prostitution was the necessary prelude to an increase in penalties for soliciting.[82] Maxwell-Fyfe returned once again to Cabinet in April, this time armed with an exposition of the arguments against imposing reporting restrictions, that the practical obstacles of definition were too great, and that 'if the Government supported this legislation and at the same time declined to hold an enquiry, they would be open to the criticism that they were trying to suppress the publication of evidence showing the need for an enquiry'. He was prepared, however, to downgrade the proposal to a less high-profile Home Office departmental inquiry, rather than a Royal Commission. Visibly washing his hands of the matter, Churchill gave way, provided that Maxwell-Fyfe 'take responsibility' for a departmental inquiry, clearly indicating his and his colleagues' distaste.[83]

*

Some of the Attleean chickens were also now coming home to roost. First, the Gowers Commission on Capital Punishment reported after nearly five years' leisurely deliberation. Given that it had been restricted to looking at whether the operation of the death penalty should be reformed, not abolished, the report's main conclusion could perhaps be described as the right answer to the wrong question. They concluded that 'the outstanding defect of the law of murder is that it provides a single punishment for a crime widely varying in culpability.' However, they rejected the creation of different classes of murder. Clearly leaning towards an abolitionist conclusion which they were precluded from reaching, they grasped for a compromise reform of the present ministerial power of reprieve. The option they plumped for, jury discretion over the sentence, was widely criticised. At least this gave Norman Brook a sense of satisfaction. When the Conservative Cabinet finally got round to considering, and rejecting, the report, nearly a year after its publication, Brook fired off a sharp note to Winston Churchill which one might think had been gestating since the Commission was appointed against his advice:

> The Cabinet had no hesitation yesterday in rejecting the main recommendations of the Royal Commission on Capital Punishment – and deciding that there was no urgent need to introduce legislation to give effect to its minor recommendations.
>
> The work of this Royal Commission occupied 4½ years and cost £23,000. I thought you might be interested in these figures, especially as you have been active lately in preventing the appointment of further Royal Commissions. This one, at least, seems to have been a lamentable waste of public time and money.

Churchill willingly reinforced the point to his Cabinet colleagues.[84] The Commission's report was not even debated by Parliament while Churchill remained Prime Minister. When MPs were given a chance to chew over its recommendations in February 1955, Sydney Silverman tabled an amendment for a five-year suspension, and the Cabinet was faced with the same dilemma which had confronted Labour in 1948 – what whip to impose on an issue on which they were divided? Ministers lined up behind the deterrent effect of hanging with David Maxwell-Fyfe, now Lord Kilmuir and Lord Chancellor, declaring that 'its removal would prejudice the maintenance of the Queen's peace and tend to undermine the morale of the police.' In a further ironic twist, Gwylim Lloyd George, the new Home Secretary, had expressed abolitionist sentiments in 1948, only to renounce them at the Home Office as James Chuter Ede had done. He now said the choice could only be between straight retention and abolition, not an experimental period. He also pointed to a four-fold rise in violent crime among youngsters in the past two decades as a reason for rejecting another of the Commission's recommendations, namely to raise the minimum age at which a murderer could be liable to be hanged from seventeen to twenty-one. However, without Churchill's obstinacy, ministers were able to agree the more pragmatic line in the Commons that as many of their government colleagues as possible should be informally be encouraged to vote against Silverman's amendment, without imposing a formal whip.[85] In these efforts they were assisted by wide-spread hatred of Silverman among Conservative MPs, many of whom could not distinguish between his position on capital punishment and his far-left sympathies on other matters, suspecting him of being activated more by party than moral motives.[86] The majority, 245 to 214 against suspension, was slimmer than the change in the strength of the parties since 1949 would have implied.[87] This was due to the influx of a large number of younger Conservative MPs, some of whom were to have considerable influence for abolition of capital punishment during the following decade. Added to this was growing public disquiet over a number of recent cases including those of Derek Bentley, Ruth Ellis and the Evans/Christie case which so disturbed Chuter Ede.

By the end of 1955, however, the Government was under pressure to give its considered response to the Gowers Commission's report. Their firm rejection of its main recommendation was balanced by the realisation that the parliamentary arithmetic was moving against them. Robert Carr, Anthony Eden's Parliamentary Private Secretary, warned the Prime Minister that he calculated that the newly inflated ranks of Conservative abolitionists probably tipped the balance in the Commons against capital punishment. Cabinet accepted that the boil would have to be lanced in the near future, but were divided on the tactic most likely to ensure the retention of the status quo. Lloyd George proposed that he should announce an extension of the use of the prerogative of mercy, though even he conceded that this would make little material difference to the present annual tally of thirteen hangings, as he already took account of every possible circumstance in trying to find enough evidence to recommend a reprieve.

Kilmuir and the Law Officers were outraged at this suggestion. They had two constitutional objections. The first was that to analyse publicly the factors involved in recommending the exercise of the Royal Prerogative was unsound. Secondly, to extend ministerial interference with the judiciary would bring the law further into disrepute by increasing the number of cases where the death penalty was not carried out, and only encourage calls for the law to be changed.[88]

Lloyd George and other ministers fronted the Conservative backbench Home Affairs Group with a defence of the status quo, receiving broad support, although moderate reform was supported by Godfrey Nicholson, who caused considerable hilarity with the suggestion that the death penalty should be exacted only for the most horrible crimes but should not be applied to 'the ordinary man who murders his wife'.[89] The dam was now breached on the initiative of the Government. It agreed to look at the minor recommendations of the commission on provocation and diminished responsibility, though with no firm commitment to a timetable for legislation, and tabled a motion supporting the death penalty but amending the law of murder. This provided the opportunity for abolitionists to press their case again. Led this time by a repentant Chuter Ede, their amendment was carried by 293 to 262 votes.[90] Forty-eight Conservatives had supported abolition of the death penalty. A number of rising ministerial stars abstained, including Selwyn Lloyd, Iain Macleod, Derek Heathcoat-Amory, Edward Boyle and Carr himself.[91] The Commons had, of course, come to such a decision on more than one occasion previously. However, 'Rab' Butler, winding up the debate for the Government as Leader of the Commons, made one of his less heroic speeches, employing, not for the last time, the formulation that 'the time was not yet ripe' for reform. Even less commendably, in view of his interest in penal reform which would soon blossom at the Home Office, he trotted out the familiar official arguments that no innocent person had been hanged in living memory and that life imprisonment was crueller than hanging. He was pilloried in the press, and suspected of being put up to convince more liberal Tories to vote for retention.[92] To make matters worse, he had rather rashly promised that the Government would take action on whatever MPs decided.

The Cabinet was now faced with a more difficult choice than its predecessor in 1948. Having had its advice to the Commons rejected it was impossible that they should introduce a government bill giving effect to a decision which had been opposed by the majority of its own supporters. The stakes were raised in the press with the anger among Conservative activists reverberating through the leader pages of the *Daily Telegraph* in particular. The *Daily Mail* erroneously claimed that Lloyd George had threatened to resign rather than introduce a government bill to abolish capital punishment as implied by Butler's statement, leading Eden to complain bitterly that government public-relations officers had not done enough to rebut such rumours.[93] Some ministers supported the idea of forcing the Labour opposition to promote its own abolition bill. Instead, Lloyd George proposed that they provide time for debate on a private members' bill. Despite the fact that this would inevitably be Silverman's Bill, he felt that Silverman had been

swallowed up in victory, and the Bill will be not so much his as that of his more eminent and respected supporters ... as you know, his Bill is backed by, among others, Chuter Ede and Clement Davies [the Liberal Party leader], and I see nothing undignified or inappropriate in finding time for a measure which has wide and respected support.

Norman Brook, on the other hand, tried to forestall such a move by arguing that MPs should wait for the Lords to pronounce on the question, on the basis that with public opinion in favour of retaining the death penalty, the voice of the upper house should be allowed to balance that of the Commons. Using an argument which he knew would play well with Conservative ministers, he cited 1948 when the Lords 'appeared to be a better judge of public opinion than the Commons – at a time when the Government, in proceedings on the Parliament Bill, were anxious to claim that the Lords could not represent the popular will'. Alternatively, Brook warned, protracted scrutiny of the Bill would eat into an unforeseeably large amount of the Government's own legislative programme with the remaining (welcome) possibility that it would not even pass during the session. Cabinet backed Lloyd George, and Silverman swiftly introduced a bill to give effect to abolition.

One other alternative not considered previously was the possibility of a referendum on the question, something which several Conservative MPs lobbied Eden for. Despite the easy way out this would have presented the supporters of the death penalty, Eden firmly rejected such a derogation of parliamentary sovereignty.[94] The opposing camps, particularly within the Conservative Party, now began unofficial whipping in earnest. However, this had little effect on the result. MPs confirmed their earlier vote by the remarkably consistent margin of 286 to 262, a majority against capital punishment which was to rise steadily over the years beyond suspension in 1965, abolition in 1969 and successive attempts by recidivists to reintroduce hanging up to the 1990s.[95] The rejection of abolition by a large number of Conservative backwoodsmen in the House of Lords was derided in *The Spectator*: 'The retentionist army was largely composed of hitherto unknown rustics who thought, perhaps, that abolition was in some way a threat to blood sports.'[96]

Indeed, it took peers two whole days for the, rustic and not the so rustic, to plough through the familiar arguments, only to reject abolition once again, if by the slightly less shattering margin of 238 to 95.[97] Labour veterans of 1948 could now be forgiven expressions of *schadenfreude* at the similar position in which Eden's Government found itself. Unwilling to attempt to overturn the decision of peers, and encouraged to find a compromise by figures including Archbishop Fisher, ministers plumped for the option which had been rejected by the House of Lords in 1948, the Royal Commission, the Cabinet Secretary and themselves only two years before, by the Home Secretary only months earlier, and in total on ten occasions in ninety years – that of creating classes of murder for which the death penalty would be retained. If Labour in 1948 could be accused of foolishness or weakness, the Eden Government was more open to the charge of cynicism. The Cabinet had continually supported the retention of the status quo and rejected differentiation between different types of murder. Now the Home Secretary admitted that, unless they implemented a scheme with which they profoundly disagreed, the Commons would again vote for abolition and the Parliament Act might be invoked.

The Home Secretary insisted, just as his Labour predecessors had done, that the question of maintaining the Queen's Peace meant that the Government was justified in taking a stance against abolition, whatever the moral implications. However, he argued that the compromise would result in a reduction of seventy-five per cent in the number of hangings. Just as Churchill and Lord Hailsham had done in 1948, so Labour members mocked the potential anomalies which the Government's Homicide Bill threw up. Using the recent highly emotive case of Ruth Ellis, hanged for shooting her lover, it was pointed out that if she had used a hatchet, she would not have faced the rope. In contrast, the Conservative abolitionists, who had suddenly strengthened the case for reform in the Commons, melted away just as quickly. They had faced huge pressure since the previous session from their constituency associations and the party machine, with the Chief Whip, Ted Heath, personally interviewing them to convince them to accept a compromise. It was made clear that their attitude towards the Bill would materially affect their parliamentary career. Those sitting on larger majorities in their constituencies were warned that they were expendable and would be left to the mercies of their constituency associations.[98] When one of their leading number, Nigel Nicolson, flaked off, it was clear the Government was going to get its way. To be certain, Lloyd George moved quickly. His speech was remarkably similar to Chuter Ede's in 1948, amounting to 'Look, my advisers and I think the threat of hanging deters potential murderers, but the vote by MPs obliges us to support a woolly compromise.'[99] The Bill was introduced at the beginning of the session, and was on the statute book inside three months. No Conservative did more than abstain on the Bill, and most whole-heartedly supported it. Neither House was filled to capacity for debates on the Homicide Bill as they had been on previous occasions. This was due as much to the wider political context as to ennui. The second reading debate was held just as the double crisis of Suez and the Soviet invasion of Hungary was breaking. With the Government thrown increasingly on to the ropes during the passage of the Homicide Bill, its minor amendment of the law seemed even more marginal, and left potential Conservative rebels with little appetite to add to their Government's woes.

*

Despite his ulcer trouble, Lord Morton delivered his Commission's report on marriage and divorce in 1956, just shy of five years after its appointment. The evidence which they had collected fell into three broad spheres, according to Owen McGregor: 'institutionalists', who argued for the retention of the matrimonial offence; 'abolitionists', who argued either that the existing system encouraged collusion and perjury and brought the law into disrepute, or that keeping people in 'holy deadlock', as A. P. Herbert had described it, harmed the institution of marriage and the individuals trapped by it; and finally those who supported the extension of the grounds outlined in Eirene White's 1951 Bill to include long separation – weakening, but not replacing, the matrimonial offence.[100] Despite its wide terms of reference, the Commission failed to employ or recommend any social scientific research of the kinds that had informed most other such inquires for over half a century, being content merely to collect opinions.[101]

One indication of Morton's unsuitability to chair the Commission should have been the plan which he supported in 1953 to separate Christian from civil marriage, under which access to the divorce courts would be denied to those who had married in church. Not surprisingly senior churchmen swiftly rejected this idea.[102] His timidity did not even justify a Commons debate on the subject, although Lawrence Stone sees the report as yet another lurch down the slippery slope towards 'the unknown waters of no-fault divorce on demand'.[103] In fact, the Government was only forced into taking a position on the report by the imminent prospect of a debate in the House of Lords, tabled by Lord Silkin. Silkin commented drily that

> *the trouble about Royal Commissions … is that they do eventually report, and the Report comes home to roost. It does not always come home to roost in the nest of the particular bird that hatched it …*

Silkin, who supported extending the grounds for divorce in the way which the Commission had rejected, nonetheless heaped praise on its work, concluding, in a phrase that must have made Norman Brook choke, that its budget of £35,463 4s. 6d. was well spent.[104]

At the Cabinet's Home Affairs Committee before the debate, Lord Kilmuir displayed a certain anxiety that the Government would be exposed to the criticism that such reports were left to gather dust. However, he and his colleagues were confident that because the Commission had been divided, they would be justified in not acting in such an 'explosive' area. Even on the subsidiary recommendations, which were less controversial, the Government did not feel able to move during the current session. Ministers agreed to look again at the report in the light of the report from an official committee which would look at the Royal Commission's report.[105] That is, if they could still see it through the long grass. However, just as they were dismissing the Morton Report on divorce, another inquiry was preparing to deliver its findings which would completely alter the philosophical and political debate about the relationship between the criminal law and sexual morality in Britain.

3. Buggery and Bingo: 1957–1964

'The criminal law ... is to preserve public order and decency, to protect the citizen from what is offensive or injurious, and to provide sufficient safeguards against exploitation and corruption of others, particularly those who are specially vulnerable ...

'It is not, in our view, the function of the law to intervene in the private lives of citizens ... further than is necessary to carry out the purposes we have outlined. It follows that we do not believe it to be a function of the law to attempt to cover all the fields of sexual behaviour.'

Report of the Committee on Homosexual Offences and Prostitution[1]

The lower classes are such fools
They waste their money on the pools.
I bet, of course, but that's misleading.
One must encourage bloodstock breeding.

'The Higher Motive' – Bernard Fergusson[2]

Alison: Helena – even I gave up believing in the diving rights of marriage long ago. Even before I met Jimmy. They've got something different now – constitutional monarchy. You are where you are by consent. And if you start trying any strong arm stuff, you're out. And I'm out.

Look Back in Anger, John Osborne[3]

'You can – you owe it, if you step into the front line, and if you can use a very reactionary, an old-fashioned sentence, which hasn't done much harm to our country through many centuries, you should behave like an officer and a gentleman.'

Harold Macmillan[4]

'He has been one of our national heroes. His has been a marvellous life. It's time to forget the Keeler business.'

Margaret Thatcher[5]

The Eden Government had found itself forced by its own backbenchers into a messy compromise over capital punishment but had resisted other changes such as divorce reform. Under Harold Macmillan there slowly began a fresh approach to social questions. 'Rab' Butler, passed over for the premiership after his star had waned under Anthony Eden, found a new lease of life as Home Secretary. Initially there was little indication of change. Unlike Roy Jenkins' rapid opening of the windows in 1965, Butler's support for social reform involved a more cautious inspection of the Home Office cupboards. In some areas his liberal instincts led him to begin a clear-out of lurking Victoriana. In others awareness of the limits of Tory liberalism forced the drawers shut, despite mounting pressure from Parliament and beyond. What was this tentative spring cleaning in response to?

Rising affluence since the early 1950s had transformed the opportunities available to ordinary working-class people, but especially women and young people. One of the most enduring images of the 1959 election is the Trog cartoon of Macmillan sitting surrounded by a television, a car, a fridge and a washing machine, concluding: 'Well, gentlemen, I think we all fought a good fight.' The cosy confidence of the second Elizabethan age had soon proved superficial. The spirit of the coronation in 1953, a religious revival of the Anglican Church, the popularity of evangelical missions such as Billy Graham's, and a fall in divorce all ground to a halt by the mid-1950s. In 1956, secularisation began to take hold. From then on, fewer and fewer people were basing their personal morality on the direct influence of the pulpit or the Bible. A number of long-term trends were behind this, including the postwar dispersal of inner-city communities, growing economic affluence, and the development of alternative forms of entertainment which were increasingly affordable to working-class people. The advent of widespread television ownership from the late 1950s meant that the home became more and more the focus of wider family gatherings, rather than other traditional places like the church.

Restrictions on consumption via the ration book were finally lifted in 1954. Between 1951 and 1961 average male earnings rose from £8 6s. per week to £15 7s. and by 1966 they were £20 6s. Significantly for consumption, prices of consumer goods were steadily falling over the same period. This fall in prices increased spending power among the working class, fuelled by a period of continuous full employment, and led to a reduction in inequalities between the working and middle classes, between women and men, and perhaps most importantly between the young and the old. As parents became far less economically dependent on the incomes of their children with the rise in their own wages, so youth became proportionately better off than their parents, and achieved a spending power from the late 1950s which they had never previously enjoyed. It was estimated that compared with their parents, the income of the young had risen twice as quickly, and disposable income four times as fast.[6] Coupled with this was the unprecedented variety of things to spend your money on, particularly for the young. New styles of popular music influenced by America, a burgeoning fashion industry, the cinema, television, and the concomitant advertising, all began to be focused more on the appetites of a younger generation. The advent of commercial television with the launch of ITV in September 1955 encouraged the explosion in television ownership (which reached seventy-five per cent of households by 1961) and viewing,[7] although in 1960 only two thirds of the viewing public were regularly watching ITV.[8] Importantly, leisure time also increased with a reduction in working hours during the 1950s. For young men conscription was reduced from two years to one in 1955 and finally abolished in 1960. According to the most recent analysis of secularisation in Britain, after the brief postwar revival, from 1956 all indices of religiosity started to decline, and from 1963 most entered free fall.[9]

New technology and communications prompted the development of mass culture, transcending for the first time class, geography and gender, which allowed youth to be seen as a separate and problematic group in society. The coming of independent television and advertising during the late 1950s was an important agent in synthesising the cultural and consumer habits of the young.[10] Social conservatives were so concerned by the explosion in teenage consumerism that American-style capitalist consumption became a *bête noire* of the right as well as the left. John Selwyn Gummer wrote at the end of the 1960s that 'society has become more free largely because the young have become the prime target of the advertising man and the marketeer.'[11] Working-class commentators such as Richard Hoggart bemoaned the influx of American 'candy-floss' mass art and 'sex in shiny packets' at the expense of morally and culturally more profound British working-class traditions and activities.[12] At the same time there was an explosion in music and fashion styles. The teddy boy cult of the mid-1950s spread throughout the country and was demonised by the media and older commentators, soon followed by the explosive arrival of rock 'n' roll with Bill Haley and the Comets' 'Rock around the Clock'. Older Britain was shocked by the rise of the pugnacious mods and rockers.

At the same time as these mainly working-class cultural phenomena were emerging, middle-class youth was also asserting its identity in relation to its elders. One outlet was to adopt working-class modes of fashion and music unappealing to parents. However, political expression was also an important factor for middle-class youth from the late 1950s onwards. Support for radical political movements like the Campaign for Nuclear Disarmament (CND) (and later the anti-Vietnam movement) could be one avenue for anti-establishment rebelliousness against one's parents. Alternatively many young people were drawn to CND by family socialisation within the movement.[13]

The increasing generation gap of which parents and grandparents were so apprehensive was also represented in literature, drama and film, the walls of which, for the first time in the late 1950s, were breached by writers who were often working class. They were not always exactly young, as the soubriquet 'Angry Young Men' suggested. Neither, as John Osborne, Alan Sillitoe and others have since insisted, were they particularly angry. However, they were at least fifteen years younger than the middle-class writers and intellectuals who dominated the early 1950s. For the first time they addressed issues relevant to working-class men and, also for the first time, women, in a naturalistic environment. Shelagh Delaney's *A Taste of Honey*, written as a play in 1958 when she was just nineteen and translated to the cinema in 1960, was the first such work to place women at the centre of the action around whom the male characters revolve.[14] The insecurities, disaffection and aspirations of youth were major themes, as were the ubiquity of sex and violence in society. Such innovations gradually punched holes in the dam of the Lord Chamberlain's stage censorship. The portrayal in film of Osborne's *Look Back in Anger* and John Braine's *Room at the Top* in 1959 was also a litmus test for the new Secretary of the British Board of Film Censors (BBFC), John Trevelyan. His pragmatic, liberal approach towards 'New Wave' film-makers became an important part of the blossoming of realist films during the 1960s.[15]

With this explosion of a visibly different youth culture and the artistic portrayal of previously taboo subjects came the threat, as far as conservatives were concerned, of a decline in moral standards amongst the young. The depiction of non-marital sex, abortion, homosexuality and violence in film, drama and print confirmed for older generations the abandonment of Christian morality, which had to be resisted and reversed. Undoubtedly there occurred a greater degree of openness in the discussion of sex and sexuality. Indeed the changing attitude of the press towards the discussion of sex was an important barometer of how social and political attitudes were already changing. As Arthur Marwick suggests, newspapers were increasingly a part of mass consumer society rather than a mould for public opinion.[16] Another crucial development was the gradual separation of sexual behaviour from sexual reproduction as a result of technological leaps in contraception, most famously in the release of the oral contraceptive pill in 1961. Also the development of antibiotics with which to fight sexually transmitted diseases took off during the 1950s. It should be emphasised, though, that contraception was still predominantly used by married couples, and birth control advice was available only to married couples until the mid-1960s. The spread of contraception, including the Pill, was, however, barely mentioned in Whitehall and Westminster at this time, despite the profound social and medical implications for the future.

The 1950s pattern of idealised female domesticity was gradually challenged by pioneers such as Betty Friedan, whose study of American women's attitudes towards themselves, *The Feminine Mystique*, dissected the social and economic pressures exerted on women (including by each other) to focus on the home and family.[17] Paid employment during the 1950s and 1960s was already a double-edged sword for women in respect of their position within the family. Despite the extra spending power, often from work in the commodity-producing industries, the social pressures on women to remain at home remained considerable, and were a positive bar to many for whom there was no financial imperative. For those mothers who did work, the newly 'discovered' phenomenon of 'latch-key' children was a reminder of where their real duties were supposed to lie. 'Maternal deprivation' was thought to be contributing towards the problems which were leading Britain's youth into moral decline. An important difference between the social and cultural temptations for newly affluent youth and the pressures exerted on women was that of class. Whereas there was an increasing uniformity of appeal for middle- and working-class youth in the cultural attractions available, for women, the message of the media still depended very much on their class. As Carol Smart points out, the more down-market weekly women's magazines approved of women taking two jobs (and presumably few working-class women had the choice), whereas the monthly magazines like *Good Housekeeping*, read by middle-class women, exhorted the virtues of child-rearing and husband-tending.[18]

*

Among Conservative politicians, 'Rab' Butler was certainly more sensitive to the implications of these social and economic trends for the Government's own policies. According to Bill Deedes his 'influence was not always on the record', but he had a great effect on young Conservative MPs; 'he made the Tories feel it was respectable to indulge in social reform.'[19] However, there were limits. Hugo Young gave a rather harsher verdict:

> *He was among those Conservative politicians who were usually more sensitive to what the party might not like than to what it ought to be persuaded, against its better instincts, to accept. Although a reformer, he seldom went about the business of social change by means of explicit challenge to the past. He did not, in that sense, have a brave political imagination.*[20]

During his 'Pooh-Bah' years, when he combined being Home Secretary and Leader of the House of Commons and, amazingly from a twenty-first-century perspective, party chairman from 1959, Butler bestrode the three key offices for a Conservative politician interested in achieving radical legislative reform. In control of policy at the Home Office and management of legislation in the Commons, he was also subject to the relentless barrage of the Tory faithful. Travelling the country he grew increasingly exasperated by 'the very strong feelings of a huge section of the party in favour of birching and flogging', not to mention hanging. Butler was proud that he managed to have inserted into the 1959 Conservative manifesto a commitment to social reform, starting with penal reform and then betting, gambling and licensing, where the law was anomalous or led to abuse and corruption. Interestingly it acknowledged that an expansion of educational and social services was needed to 'strengthen' national character and 'uphold' moral standards.[21] Harold Macmillan's reaction to this passage in the draft manifesto, when it was discussed at a party meeting in his room at the

House of Commons, was to hold it out two feet from his face, hood his eyes and say very slowly: 'I don't know about that. We already have the Toby Belch vote. We must not antagonise the Malvolio vote.'

Ted Heath, the Chief Whip, supported Butler, saying that they had already publicly committed themselves to such measures.[22] Butler wanted to bring the same spirit of reforming zeal for progress as had imbued the 1944 Education Act. His White Paper on penal reform, *Penal Practice in a Changing Society*, struck out in a newly enlightened direction for prison policy, and held out against the 'Colonel Blimps of both sexes' demanding the reintroduction of corporal punishment.[23] Macmillan himself was not without a socially radical bent. Looking back to the interwar period Clement Attlee described him as 'by far the most radical man I've known in politics ... He was a real left wing radical in his social, human and economic thinking'.[24] However, according to Alistair Horne, Macmillan had a favourite tease for his unusually liberal Home Secretary: 'I understand what it is you want to do. You want to popularise abortion, legalise homosexuality and start a betting shop in every street. All I can say is if you can't win the Liberal nonconformist vote on these cries you never will!'

According to Horne, while Butler agonised over capital punishment, Macmillan supported its retention and didn't 'remember Dorothy ever expressing views ... it was not her kind of interest'.[25] Butler boasted that not once in his stewardship of the Home Affairs Committee did he ever need to call on the authority of the Prime Minister. Macmillan was confessedly happy to leave the business of the Home Office to Butler, and later Henry Brooke.[26] This was in stark contrast to his greater interest, and interference, in economic and foreign policy.[27] However, Butler did use the ultimate threat of resignation to ensure that penal reform was included in the 1959 manifesto. Tory modernisation was also stimulated by the new generation of politicians, many of whom founded or joined the Bow Group, including Iain Macleod, Geoffrey Howe and Christopher Chataway. Howe described their purpose as 'seeking to make the Tory Party fit for *Observer* and *Guardian* readers to live in'.[28]

*

The Wolfenden Committee on homosexual offences and prostitution had worked from the premise that the function of criminal law was to protect, in particular, the weak in society and maintain public order and decency. It was not, however, the function of the law to set or reinforce a particular moral code, save that necessary for the maintenance of public order and decency. In the same way that prostitution was not in itself a criminal offence, the Committee quickly concluded that homosexual acts in private should be no longer be so. Conversely, they concluded that the penalties for soliciting and for importuning should be strengthened in order to preserve public decency and curb the visibility of the offences which had given rise to the Committee's inquiry.[29] The limited extent of the reform proposed reflected the utilitarianism of the Wolfenden strategy, removing private sin from the ambit of the criminal law where no harm was committed, or where the harm was less than the effect of the present law (a distinction Sir John Wolfenden described as being 'incredibly unnoticed by so many of our fellow countrymen'), whilst retaining strong sanctions against public offences and the corruption of the young.[30] In fact the Committee argued that its proposals would increase protection for the young because 'with the law as it is there may be some men who would prefer an adult partner, but who at present turn their attention to boys because they consider that this course is less likely to lay them open to prosecution or blackmail.'

What is most interesting about the Committee's deliberations is the uncertainty among its members about how far their recommendations might offend, or be misunderstood by public opinion, and how much they should lead or be guided by the national mood. This was a problem that was to trouble politicians ever after. How much should the Committee, and politicians, be educators? The direction of the Committee appeared to be heading towards setting the age of consent at eighteen for homosexuals and abolishing buggery as a separate offence. However, several members were concerned about the public and political reaction to this. During a general discussion in 1955 William Wells, Labour MP for Walsall, and a Roman Catholic, said that 'public opinion had perhaps produced the Committee; politicians were timid folk and there would be nothing politically attractive in its recommendations. In consequence it must be very careful about its relations with the public.' Other members of the Committee, like Wolfenden himself, took a longer view, that 'the primary objective was not immediate legislation, but an educational process which might perhaps have the effect that one day public opinion would accept these changes.'[31] As Philip Allen later assessed it,

I suppose ... to some extent the Rab Butlers of this world did set ... going policies which in the end had influence on ... the public. But no politician can afford to get too far ahead of public opinion ... he can't really get away with policies which fly flat in the face of public opinion.[32]

Despite the Anglican support for Wolfenden (who was appointed Chair of the new Church of England Moral Welfare Council), Geoffrey Fisher, Archbishop of Canterbury, agreed with Butler that immediate implementation might cause 'the vulgar' to 'suppose that it was legalising vice'.[33]

Wolfenden thought the response to the report positive.[34] Most politicians, regardless of public opinion, just wished such an unpleasant topic would go away. There was no mood in Parliament to act on the report's conclusions on homosexuality. However, in March 1958 a letter to *The Times* calling for implementation of the Wolfenden Report was signed by such respected figures as Lord Attlee, Bertrand Russell, Isaiah Berlin and the Bishops of Birmingham and Exeter.[35] This was followed in April by another from fifteen eminent married women.[36] The Government demonstrated that it was in no way inclined to promote a course of action which it considered to be way ahead of public opinion, although it remained officially neutral on the issues themselves. Butler initially favoured implementing the whole Wolfenden Report, but his junior minister, David Renton, said his own conscience would not allow him to pilot a homosexual bill, awakening Butler to the feeling within the Conservative Party. So he suggested that public opinion might not actually disagree with the Wolfenden principle of removing sins such as homosexual behaviour from the ambit of the law, but would be likely to misinterpret the recommendations as a general approval of homosexuality per se, which would outrage public morality. At a meeting of the Cabinet's Home Affairs Committee in November 1957, Butler emphatically stated that there was no prospect of introducing legislation to implement Wolfenden's recommendations on homosexuality. This was reinforced a year later, shortly before the Commons debate on the report at the end of 1958.[37]

However, impressed by the level of support shown for the Wolfenden recommendations in the press and a debate in the House of Lords, there was considerable discussion among ministers and officials about the possibility of some kind of compromise solution. Sir Charles Cunningham, Permanent Secretary at the Home Office, and W. S. Murrie at the Scottish Home

Department both suggested to Butler that decriminalisation of gross indecency, but not buggery, might be a workable compromise. This would restore the law to the position before the Labouchère amendment to the Criminal Law (Amendment) Act of 1885. Conservative public moralists would be comforted by the retention of sanctions against the age-old offence of buggery, which so excited many of them in debates on the subject, whilst the difficulty of proving the commission of buggery would mean the same practical effect as acceptance of the whole of Wolfenden and might satisfy the reformers. Cunningham suggested that this would have the support of the Lord Chief Justice, Lord Goddard, and other members of the judiciary.[38] This strategy ignored the new legal anomaly which it would create, when one of the main arguments for reform was that the law was illogical. However, even Lord Kilmuir had some sympathy with the desire to prevent blackmail and stale offences being brought up, and a number of MPs and peers pressed for all offences over a year old to be referred to the Director of Public Prosecutions (DPP).[39] However, the DPP, Toby Matthew, would not countenance this. Writing to the Home Office to oppose any of the subsidiary proposals in the Wolfenden Report, he insisted: 'I am sorry to be so unhelpful, but my experience of compromise legislation in the criminal field is that it inevitably leads to anomalies that disturb public confidence, and it makes the task of judges, juries and prosecutors extremely difficult.'[40]

Butler seems to have taken the point and admitted that it was 'impractical, in the present state of public opinion.'[41] One minor recommendation of the Wolfenden Report which Butler was prepared to sanction which did not require legislation was the reintroduction of oestrogen treatment for prisoners convicted of homosexual offences. This had been discontinued during the Attlee administration by the Director of Medical Services in the Prison Commission in October 1950 because of the risk of sterility inherent in the treatment. David Maxwell-Fyfe, later Lord Kilmuir, had wanted to reintroduce the procedure, but had instead referred it to the Wolfenden Committee in order to deflect any political controversy. Now, following Wolfenden's approval of oestrogen treatment for homosexuals where a prisoner requested it, and where the prison medical officer considered it might be beneficial, Cunningham recommended Butler approve the treatment.[42] The extra safeguard that prisoners should sign a written acknowledgement that they understood the risks involved was added. The Prison Commission had already agreed with the reintroduction in discussions with the Wolfenden Committee and the

Home Office.[43] Butler concurred with the recommendation.[44] The terrible, futile effects of this treatment did not halt its use for some years.

The Labour front bench did not demur from the Government line of inaction on the Wolfenden Report.[45] Neither party wanted to be seen to endorse a proposal with dubious public support and considerable opposition based on religious feeling, defence of traditional public morality and the perceived danger to the family and the young. Furthermore, a considerable amount of indignant protest had been stirred by the circulation to MPs before the debate by the Homosexual Law Reform Society (HLRS) of a number of publications advocating reform. Sympathetic parliamentarians who worked with the society warned that this was alienating support and urged it to concentrate on the attitude of the public at large.[46] It was clear that no immediate prospect of parliamentary action lay ahead. The HLRS, which was founded in the spring of 1958, saw itself as the main instrument of the process of public education which the report and the Government advocated. Having enlisted the support of some 100 public figures, its small active staff (the secretary, Rev. A. Hallidie Smith, the chairman, Kenneth Walker, and a small executive committee, including the university lecturer A. E. Dyson) embarked on a campaign of public meetings and speeches to educate progressive public opinion, and thus indirectly politicians. Crucial to the later influence of the HLRS with the Labour Government was the involvement of Kenneth Robinson, Minister of Health from 1964–7 and C. H. Rolph, the barrister and journalist.

The society was in a delicate position. Although it was not a group promoting homosexuality, its membership ranged from those who advocated a change in the law for purely humane or judicial reasons but were still opposed to homosexual acts, to others of a more liberal mind or who were themselves homosexual. Its middle-class, moderate membership clung to the cautious, liberal utilitarianism embodied by Wolfenden. Its politics were opportunistically sympathetic to Labour, and necessarily ignored the merits of homosexuality.[47] Their work involved mainly Hallidie Smith touring the country and providing speakers for meetings of university student unions, church organisations, constituency parties and humanist groups. Walker has written that at no meeting was there a 'predominantly hostile audience'.[48] However, most, it is fair to presume, were held in broadly sympathetic surroundings. Its first public meeting in 1960 was counted an unqualified success. More than a thousand people filled the Caxton Hall, Westminster on 12 May 1960, including notable supporters of reform as well as unknown members of the public. The audience again displayed a wide range of attitudes loosely collected under the banner of reforming the 'monstrous injustice' of the present situation, as the Bishop of Exeter put it.[49]

However, the reaction of the press to the publication of the Wolfenden Report, even amongst the popular papers, was far more balanced. The *Daily Mirror* declared: 'Don't be shocked by this Report. It's the Truth. It's the Answer. It's Life.'[50] *The Times*, the *Daily Telegraph* and the *Manchester Guardian* gave less dramatic approval to the modest, utilitarian proposals of the Committee. The *Daily Express*, the *Daily Mail* and the *Sunday Times,* conversely, were more concerned with the threat in the report's proposals to public morality.[51] When the Commons came to debate Wolfenden in 1958, *The Times* neatly outlined the disjuncture between the reformers and progressive opinion on the one hand, and what Parliament thought that public opinion would tolerate on the other:

> *It is a foregone conclusion that the homosexual laws will not be reformed yet. It is equally a foregone conclusion that reform must eventually come. For the majority of well-informed people are now clearly convinced that these laws are unjust and obsolete in a society which refuses to punish lesbian practices, adultery, fornication or private drunkenness.*[52]

A Gallup poll conducted shortly after the Commons debate showed forty-seven per cent against the main Wolfenden recommendation and thirty-eight per cent supporting it. The margin of disapproval was slightly higher among women.[53] According to officials the Lord Chancellor's postbag was fairly evenly divided on the report.[54]

*

Even without immediate action, a number of events gradually shifted the political debate, supporting Oscar Wilde's observation sixty years earlier that it was public officials rather than public opinion which needed educating.[55] In 1958 the Lord Chamberlain, responsible for licensing stage plays, relaxed the rules on the treatment of homosexual subjects. This led to two, largely factual, plays about the trial of Oscar Wilde, and the 1961 film *Victim,* which starred Dirk Bogarde as the dashing and successful married barrister whose homosexual liaisons with young men become embroiled in a web of blackmail, facing him with the moral dilemma of whether to crush the allegations against himself, or confess the truth and destroy his marriage and reputation. Bogarde had to fight strongly with the censor to prevent the removal of key scenes in which homosexuality and homosexual desire were referred to directly. *Victim* discussed law reform, and endorsed the Wolfenden proposals and the liberal view of homosexuality as an unfortunate and abnormal condition to be pitied but not condemned.

Because of the imminent publication and parliamentary debate of the Wolfenden Report, the Lord Chamberlain, Lord Scarbrough, was forced to reconsider his position on licensing plays dealing with homosexuality. He went to see Butler in June 1957 to discuss the problem, prompted by the production of a number of plays dealing with homosexuality, including *Tea and Sympathy,* by the New Watergate Theatre Club at the Comedy Theatre.[56] The regular abuse of this loophole of the 'private theatre club' to present unlicensed plays had created a position in which the law and the censorship was, in Scarbrough's own words, 'becoming rather farcical'. Scarbrough, asserting that the censorship had always adjusted gradually to changing social attitudes, for example towards the discussion of prostitution, thought that 'the same position was arising with regard to perversion'.[57] Some plays dealing with homosexuality the Lord Chamberlain 'recognised to be of substantial literary and artistic merit'.[58] Both Butler and Scarbrough agreed that it was undesirable to launch prosecutions against theatre clubs for presenting such plays, for fear of inciting press and public outcry against the censorship. The New Watergate's productions had indeed aroused considerable press comment, which generally remarked on the mildness of the plays presented, the sensible function of the theatre club and the archaism of the Lord Chamberlain's powers of censorship over the stage. The *Daily Mail,* in advocating that the censorship be either abolished or reformed along the lines of a classification system like that applied to films, commented that 'neither of the two plays so far presented under the New Watergate's cloak of legalised hypocrisy could be called a shocker. They were not "plays about homosexuality" as the gossips loosely called them; they only lightly touched on the theme'.[59] The *Daily Express* followed the same line, arguing that theatre should be left to the laws of obscenity, as were books. It also compared contemporary work to relatively much bawdier classical plays like Shakespeare's *Titus Andronicus* or Sophocles' *Lysistrata*, although the latter, as an adaptation, continued to be banned by the Lord Chamberlain.[60]

Scarbrough and Butler's instinct was to relax the censorship 'and permit for limited audiences plays dealing seriously with what could be regarded as a social question'.[61] The proposal, as worked out between the Home Office and the Lord Chamberlain's Office, was to confer on the Lord Chamberlain the power to declare a play unsuitable for children under eighteen, and create a new offence of admitting a child to a performance of such a play.[62] By the time it reached the Home Affairs Committee of the Cabinet in June 1958 other ministers were alarmed at the prospect of the pre-censorship system being submitted to parliamentary and press scrutiny, although they were keen to liberalise the censorship of controversial issues. This resulted in the idea of a voluntary classification scheme which the Lord Chamberlain would agree with theatre managers.[63] However, at the next meeting of the committee, Butler had clearly had second thoughts about the Lord Chamberlain seeking 'informal agreements' on censorship.[64] The failure of the Conservative Government to legislate for a more sophisticated system of censorship along these lines left the Lord Chamberlain in a difficult position. By the end of 1958 he was forced to deal with the reality of plays continuing to push the limits of the censorship when dealing with homosexuality, swearing and other controversial topics. Scarbrough therefore outlined strict terms on which homosexuality might now be dramatised:

I ... propose to allow plays which make a serious and sincere attempt to deal with the subject ... Licences will continue to be refused for plays which are exploitations of the subject rather than contributions to the problem [sic]...

a. Every play will continue to be judged on its merits. The difference will be that plays will be passed which deal seriously with the subject.

b. We would not pass a play that was violently pro-homosexual.

c. We would not allow a homosexual character to be included if there were no need for such inclusion.

d. We would not allow any 'funny' innuendos or jokes on the subject.

e. We will allow the word 'pansy', but not the word 'bugger'.

f. We will not allow embraces between males or practical demonstrations of love.

g. We will allow criticism of the present Homosexual Laws, though plays obviously written for propaganda purposes will fall to be judged on their merits.

h. We will not allow embarrassing display by male prostitutes.[65]

The only merit of these prescriptions could be said to be that it was the first time that rules operated by the Lord Chamberlain were set out in such detail. However, this did not leave much scope for a profound discussion even of the limited legal and penal content of the Wolfenden Report, let alone the moral issues involved or the real-life experiences of homosexuals. However, opinions within the Lord Chamberlain's Office on the operation of these rules were contradictory, as with other subjects. Shelagh Delaney's seminal play *A Taste of Honey* received differing assessments by play examiner Charles Heriot and Comptroller General Sir Norman Gwatkin. Heriot, while sympathising with the merits of the play and recommending a licence, was keen to see the 'queerness' of the Geof character toned down, and referred to homosexuality as 'the forbidden subject', despite the relaxation of the ban the previous year.[66] Gwatkin was repelled by it and was strongly against allowing it through. Scarbrough sided with Heriot, and noted that 'for one thing this subject had now become one which was much talked about, and it was bound to appear rather ostrich-like that it should never be mentioned on the stage.'[67] This highlighted the impossible dilemma in which the Lord Chamberlain stood. The arbitrary system of bartering over controversial subjects to be presented on stage in realistic vernacular language could not be squared satisfactorily with his other declared role of protecting the public from distasteful or shocking material, especially once ground had been conceded in a liberal direction.

It is true that both Scarbrough and Lord Cobbold, former Governor of the Bank of England and the last Lord Chamberlain to exercise powers of theatre censorship, refused a licence to only a tiny percentage of plays. However, there was an increasing number during the decade before abolition where the Lord Chamberlain's Office required significant alterations or cuts before granting a licence. There was also an increasing number of so-called 'waiting box' plays, where the producer would not assent to the required alterations and was in dispute with the Lord Chamberlain's Office.[68] This masked the number of 'banned' plays because they were often performed without a licence under the illegal but permitted loophole of the private theatre club. What added to the pressures on the Lord Chamberlain to relax the censorship, and swelled the calls for its reform or abolition, was the increasing permiability between the theatre and other media. The regulatory regimes for BBC and commercial television, cinema, literature and the press were all more relaxed than that operated by the Lord Chamberlain for the theatre. Scarbrough had some right to feel the ground was constantly shifting underneath him. No sooner did one public episode result in a modification of his rules, for example that over Wolfenden and homosexuality, then another medium relaxed its rules further, for example the degree of liberation afforded to writers of literature by the new era of the Obscene Publications Act 1959. Whilst this Act meant that 'literature of merit' such as D. H. Lawrence's *Lady Chatterley's Lover* could be published for the first time, containing descriptions of adulterous sex embellished with 'four-letter' words, such genuine expressions of real life and use of the vernacular could not be tolerated in any realistic measure on the stage.

By the mid-1950s the activities of Her Majesty's Customs and Excise against the works of well-known authors, whether or not they contained anything sexually explicit, was bringing the operation of the Victorian obscene publications legislation into disrepute. The puritanical Maxwell-Fyfe had, as Home Secretary, stoked the fires among magistrates to pursue any hint of indecency, leading in one case in Doncaster to an attempt to ban the Kinsey Report. The Swindon destruction of the Renaissance classic, Boccaccio's *Decameron*, was the final straw for many, including senior Home Office officials. A cack-handed attempt to separate out a 'white list' now ensued, reflecting, as Alan Travis points out, the Oxbridge, classicist sensibilities of Whitehall. Aristophanes, Aristotle, Boccaccio, Daniel Defoe and *The Arabian Nights* would now be safe. Marie Stopes, Havelock Ellis and such contemporary social scientists, dabbling in a more murky world of birth control and sexology from which the public should be protected, could be left to fend for themselves. Resistance from the police to the proposal thwarted this plan. Enoch Powell, Treasury minister responsible for Customs, ducked the question of whether there was actually an index of proscribed books, claiming that individual books were judged on their merits, although in evidence to a Commons select committee, Customs officials blurted out the existence of the list the following year. The Society of Authors and its powerful parliamentary lobby launched their campaign to reform the obscenity laws, with a first abortive Private Members' Bill by Roy Jenkins in 1955. However, following intervention from Butler to prevent it being blocked, the Bill was considered in the next session by a select committee, taking evidence from witnesses.[69] This continued until 1958, when it was expected that the Government would introduce its own bill after showing itself prepared to compromise. However, nothing was forthcoming until Sir Alan Herbert threatened to stand against a Conservative candidate in a pending by-election in Harrow East. Miraculously, the Government now found time for Jenkins' Bill.[70] Jenkins later wrote fulsomely to Butler that without his help, the Bill would not have become law.[71] The Obscene Publications Act introduced for the first time a defence against obscenity of 'public good' if the work contributed towards science, literature, art or learning. The test of obscenity became whether an article, if taken as a whole, tended to deprave and/or corrupt persons who were likely, having regard to all the relevant circumstances, to read, see or hear the matter contained or embodied in it.

What Travis's account of the shenanigans over the *Lady Chatterley* trial reveals is that having allowed the Obscene Publications Act to introduce into the law a defence of literary merit and public good, ministers, including Butler, and his officials, were immediately seized with horror at the first serious implication of allowing a notorious book to be produced in a paperback edition which would be cheap enough to attain a mass circulation among wives and servants, in Mervyn Griffith-Jones' nightmare scenario.[72] Claims after the trial by the DPP, Sir Toby Matthew, that he had received no instruction from the Home Office or ministers are belied by the correspondence from senior Home Office officials, including Sir Austin Strutt, making clear that they had agreed the importance of prosecuting the book. In contrast, Jenkins mocked the judge's concentration in his summing up on the adultery in the book rather than the question of its alleged obscenity. He wondered whether a decree nisi for Sir Clifford Chatterley might have been more appropriate than an acquittal.[73]

However, at least there was a new legal test against which books and films could be judged. An unfair decision by the Lord Chamberlain could not be challenged. The failure of the Government to establish an adult certificate play licence threw the system's archaism into greater relief as other media enjoyed more subtle and sophisticated regulation. Some supporters of the censorship failed to recognise the logic of stage plays being on the same footing as literature, with living persons and others afforded the same protection through the courts.

The BBC enjoyed considerably more freedom than either cinema under the BBFC or theatre to broadcast material which challenged the stuffy, conventional middle-class perspectives of the 1950s. BBC Radio soon had a close relationship with new authors. Despite some adverse comment, audiences reacted well to new radio plays such as Bill Naughton's *Alfie Elkins and His Little Life* (1962), broadcast on the Third Programme, which later became the film *Alfie*.[74] The large audiences which radio, and increasingly television, could garner for new playwrights made these media very attractive to writers – Harold Pinter's *A Night Out*, which featured on ITV's *Armchair Theatre* programme in 1960, attracted 6,380,000 viewers.[75] In addition, BBC executives had a specific remit to find as many new writers as possible and explore 'contemporary British themes', especially with the advent of *Play for Today* in 1962.[76] However, when a book or radio play was translated into a stage play or film, writers and producers found that the liberalising rhetoric of censors like John Trevelyan at the BBFC about 'moving with the times' did not prevent them from trying to impose much severer restrictions than had heads of department at the BBC. Because of the nature of external pre-censorship of cinema and theatre, and the grey area in which controversial scripts found themselves, both sides were dragged into a process of often lengthy discussion about the level of swearing or the explicitness with which abortion, homosexuality, violence or sex could be depicted. The Lord Chamberlain and the BBFC kept in close contact, and followed a policy of keeping in line with each other over what they would permit.[77] Cobbold met Lord Harlech, President of the BBFC, frequently, and Johnston had a similarly close relationship with Trevelyan.[78] Yet, despite the younger, mass audience to which the cinema was catering, Trevelyan's regime at the BBFC always inclined towards greater liberality than the Lord Chamberlain's Office. Whereas plays licensed for the theatre rarely had trouble being passed as X-certificate films, scripts which had made it to the big screen could have their content questioned by the examiners of plays. When the play of the film of the book of Alan Sillitoe's *Saturday Night and Sunday Morning* reached their office they took the same attitude towards the use of the word 'bogger' as had the BBFC, but also cut other far more innocuous swear words.[79]

The Lord Chamberlain's Office had, of course, contributed considerably towards creating this untenable position by trying to balance liberal and conservative demands with increasingly bizarre restrictions on, and alterations to, controversial plays. The Lord Chamberlain even refused a production of Samuel Beckett's *Endgame* on grounds of blasphemy the year after a French version was allowed, giving rise to speculation that either 'the Lord Chamberlain did not understand French, that he thought that God did not understand French or that he thought that Englishmen who understood French were already so corrupted as to be beyond salvation'.[80]

However, the acrimonious and litigious atmosphere between the Lord Chamberlain's Office and producers and writers was partly due to connivance with successive attorneys general in an illegal loophole. This permitted plays which had been refused a licence for fear of the outrage or offence they would cause to be produced in a 'private theatre club', where the audience was restricted to paying members. This was a ruse dating back to the nineteenth century designed to evade the Sunday observance laws. Some theatres had developed into proprietary clubs catering for a special audience, rather than staging individual private performances of unlicensed plays.[81] However, as an increasing number of plays fell foul of the blue pencil during the second half of the 1950s, normal theatres recreated themselves specially for the purpose of selling membership to view an unlicensed play 'in private'. The Lord Chamberlain allowed such performances in the following circumstances:

a. Tickets must be sold only to its members, on production of a membership card, who may bring up to four guests.

b. No tickets to be sold at the door or money taken there.

c. Any advertisement must clearly state that performances are for members only.

d. No alcoholic drinks (to comply with the Theatres Act 1843).[82]

Despite the clear lack of provision under the Theatres Act for such arrangements, the Lord Chamberlain's Office, Conservative and Labour governments, theatre managers and production companies all connived in this fictitious loophole in order to allow, in the words of Lord Scarbrough, 'experimental laboratories for the theatre',[83] and avoid having to relax or abolish restrictions generally. Many newspapers agreed. *The Times*, in tones more suited to Pall Mall than the West End, thundered:

> *If the tolerance of the Lord Chamberlain is not to be tested, then clubs may be trumps … Elected members can witness scenes and hear lines that would perhaps be kept from the ordinary public … Still, doubts persist – aesthetic rather than moral. When no holds are barred, you may get a rough house, a free fight, instead of a display of hard skilful boxing.*[84]

In 1957 the Home Secretary was asked by Labour MP Marcus Lipton whether, in the light of the performance of unlicensed plays, the censorship would be abolished. A flat denial was given.[85] But the upsurge in unlicensed performances continued, with Actors' Equity expressing concern at the conditions in such clubs and suggesting a legal challenge to them should be made. The Theatres National Committee, representing theatre managements, also complained to the Home Office.[86] While the Home Office and Lord Chamberlain waited for Parliament to debate the Wolfenden Report, the New Watergate staged *Cat on a Hot Tin Roof*, refused a licence by the Lord Chamberlain. The press response to the play was generally favourable, the *Manchester Guardian* reporting that 'its extraordinary, gripping speech rhythm … and the fearsome soul-baring nor the psychological surgery … lifts the play above a mere sexual *grand guignol* … and stamps it as a very impressive if distressing study in neurosis and marital misery.'[87] However, one Home Office official noted:

> *This type of club uses the fact that a play has been 'banned' for publicity purposes; in fact I understand that they sometimes deliberately arrange for a play to be submitted to the LC so that it can subsequently be billed as 'banned'. The 'X' certificate given to films is similarly abused and it is likely that the 'adult' classification of plays will be too.*[88]

Officials were clearly not convinced of the efficacy of moving to a BBFC-style regime as considered by Butler and Scarbrough. Another official commented that 'the Act of 1843 is obscure and unsatisfactory in many respects but the local authorities and theatre managements have evolved a workable system which we should not wish to disturb or call in question at this stage.'[89] They were supported by other ministers on the Home Affairs Committee, who did not wish the boat to be rocked by increased public interest in the Lord Chamberlain's control of theatre censorship.[90] In any case, there were a number of technical difficulties encountered during attempts to draft a bill covering the whole of Britain which would satisfactorily amend the 1843 Act as well as the numerous regulations governing different types of performance and location.[91] Private theatre clubs were left undisturbed for the time being.

*

Butler's liberal instincts were finally allowed to blossom in 1959 as the Conservative Party put together its election manifesto. At the beginning of the year the youthful Bow Group published an edition of its magazine *Crossbow* on 'politics, morals and society'. This advocated a wide-ranging series of social reforms to give the party a modern image more in tune with contemporary attitudes and aspirations, alongside its support for individual prosperity in the fields of gambling, licensing, Sunday observance and censorship. Butler immediately gave the magazine to Sir Charles Cunningham to see how its ideas could be translated into policy. 'There is no doubt that much of our legislation in the fields mentioned – and some others – dates from an age which is now past, and we should prepare our pigeon-holes for some, at any rate, of the pigeons to fly out!'[92] Cunningham agreed that it was 'quite wrong that the existing law should be so totally inconsistent with practice' and that there was 'much dead wood' that would have to be 'lopped off and some of the trees ought probably to be knocked down'. Such Gladstonian imagery masked a determination that this should really only amount to a bit of 'tidying up' or pruning, rather than root-and-branch reform. Philosophically, Cunningham thought that 'the law is powerless to set standards and can only reflect standards that are already generally accepted.'[93] Although history has tended to lay most of the credit and blame for the subsequent relaxation of betting and licensing laws at Butler's feet, as Mark Jarvis has demonstrated, these moves were very much a collective attempt by senior ministers to adapt Tory social policy to the modern world – Lord Hailsham, Iain Macleod, party chairman Oliver Poole, Chief Whip Ted Heath and Harold Macmillan included. After the election Macmillan noted that the 'great thing is to keep the Tory Party on *modern* and *progressive* lines'.[94]

The aim of Butler's betting reforms was, in Jarvis's words, 'to give the small punter without a telephone the same opportunity to back a horse as a rich punter' who could already take advantage of credit betting.[95] The elitist nature of the existing betting laws had actually been under scrutiny since the 1940s. In 1951 a Royal Commission had recommended legalising off-course betting, but religious opposition to reform was sealed when the Archbishop of Canterbury condemned gambling as a social evil. Despite a Commons committee arguing in 1956 that the law was now untenable, the Conservative administration continued to stall on the question. On taking over the Home Office in 1957, Butler pushed for the party to accept reform because the betting laws could 'no longer operate in favour of the rich against the poor'. Politically, Michael Fraser advised that Labour was reluctant to oppose it because this would alienate their natural working-class supporters, who would benefit from the introduction of cash betting. However, the Tory Party would not bite, and Macmillan ruled that it was too contentious.

According to Bill Deedes, Macmillan became convinced at this time that his Government was out of step with the Church of England, still very much the 'Tory Party at prayer' in the late 1950s. He and Charles Hill, the original 'Radio Doctor', who was Chancellor of the Duchy of Lancaster and responsible for government information services, came up with the idea of breaking bread with some of the bishops whenever the Church Assembly was meeting in London to try to improve understanding between the two. Deedes acted as chairman and host for what might be termed their 'wine and wafers' diplomacy, in contrast to Harold Wilson's 'beer and sandwiches' with the trade unions: 'I appointed the best food and wine the House of Commons could offer, reckoning that for the most part our bishops no longer lived in the style of Anthony Trollope's Barchester. Good wine eased the faint tension and loosened tongues.'[96] Despite such pleasantries, Macmillan noted another angle in the social inequalities which marked legitimate financial speculation from sinful gambling: 'Buying equities to the ecclesiastical mind has all the fascination of gambling without its moral guilt.'[97] Certainly religious opposition in the parliamentary party was ready for them. Stout defender of traditional morality, the Baptist Cyril Black warned the Prime Minister that there was 'legitimate cause for real concern regarding the decline in the moral standards of large sections of our people ... the fever of gambling is taking an ever stronger hold upon masses of the people'.[98]

The Betting and Gaming Act introduced the licensing of off-course betting shops and legalised gaming and gambling amusements including non-commercial entertainments. The Home Secretary billed the reform as one plank of the party's effort to banish the '"Victoriana" attitude in legislation relating to our social habits'.[99] Unfortunate consequences of the legislation quickly became apparent. Much of the focus of attention had been on betting shops, and nothing prepared politicians or the public for the explosion in gaming which now occurred. According to Bernard Levin the Act was supposed to enable 'innocent housewives to play whist ... and no less innocent vicars to hold raffles ... [but] although the blameless housewife and the deserving vicar had indeed benefited ... so had many people far less innocent'.[100] Not only did it unleash a mania for bingo – sixteen million people were playing it by 1963 in nearly eighteen thousand clubs – but slot machines or 'one-armed bandits' evaded restrictions on prizes and became ubiquitous in high streets. Butler had wanted to 'permit innocuous forms of gambling in innocuous places', but the amount of cash to be made from gambling soon attracted organised criminals to this new racket.[101]

Wilson was quick to take advantage. In his 1962 party conference speech, in which he famously said that the Labour Party was a 'moral crusade' or nothing, he mocked the Government: 'Mr Macmillan has said that British industry would have to concentrate on the more complicated, sophisticated, specialised groups. He was referring, no doubt, to those sophisticated products of the Tory affluent society – the one-armed bandit or Blue Streak [the cancelled missile project].'[102]

The Government tried to get some of the toothpaste back in the tube by tidying up the legislation in 1963, although once the beast of commercial gambling and casinos had been unleashed it proved difficult to control. Butler and his colleagues were forced to admit that they had 'failed to see the development of commercial gaming'.[103] It is tempting to think that the rapidly deteriorating position after the 1960 Act came into force had some effect on the Government's willingness to tackle other areas of social reform which had become a quagmire. By 1961 Butler, Brooke and Macmillan had to admit that the 1957 Homicide Act, the compromise by which Conservatives had managed to retain capital punishment, was a mistake: it had been 'inherently unsound' to distinguish between capital and non-capital murder. However, reluctant to concede that capital punishment had no deterrent effect, they proposed to do nothing about it until after the next general election, despite increasing public clamour about the Evans/Christie case. By 1964, with the election imminent, Macmillan's successor, Sir Alec Douglas-Home, confessed that the law was now 'unworkable' and that the next Home Secretary, of whatever party, would have to tackle it.[104]

*

One of the other anachronistic controls which Butler was keen to sweep away was the raft of laws, some dating back to mediaeval times, prohibiting Sunday entertainment. A vote in favour of an inquiry in 1958 was not sufficient to stimulate immediate action.[105] However, the Government was also prompted to consider reform by other difficulties over its proposal to relax pub hours. One provision in its Licensing Bill would have extended the Sunday opening hours, but against considerable protest from housewives that Sunday lunch would be affected this proposal was dropped.[106] One can only have sympathy for Sir Charles Cunningham, who seemed torn between a desire to see archaic social legislation gradually tidied up, and his palpable horror at the difficulty the Government would have in legislating on any proposals which would be broadly acceptable. He recommended that 'if something is to be done, there may be something to be said for putting off the evil day and setting an enquiry on foot.'[107]

Despite Butler's personal support it was not mentioned in the 1959 Conservative election manifesto because of political sensitivity.[108] After the election, discussions at the Home Office resumed on the possible lines and form of an inquiry. It was agreed that an inquiry should be set up quickly, to avoid demands for controversial legislation in the last session of the next Parliament, close to a general election.[109] There was not unanimity, however. A junior Home Office minister, Dennis Vosper, claimed he had never, in ten years, received any constituency correspondence on Sunday observance and could detect no parliamentary pressure for reform. However, he advocated legislation in the first session of the next Parliament, following a manifesto commitment. In the intervening period an inquiry could gauge public opinion. There was vociferous opposition within the backbench Conservative Home Affairs Committee to the principle of reform and the dangerous timing of any legislation close to the next general election.[110] In Cunningham's words the Government should plan 'the timing of any enquiry in such a way that its results would not be available before the next general election, so that the way for legislation would have been prepared and legislation could follow at the beginning of the new Parliament'.[111]

Vosper, more nobly, and despite party concerns about the timing still preferred a report before the next general election on the basis that he 'would rather electioneer with the facts ascertained rather than otherwise'.[112] The Crathorne Committee, chaired by Lord Crathorne, formerly Sir Thomas Dugdale, Conservative minister from the 1930s to the 1950s, was eventually established by Butler in July 1961.[113] The most notable aspect of the appointment of its members was, once again, the consideration given to religious affiliation. When the Catholic Sir Peter Rawlinson resigned from the Committee on his appointment as Solicitor General in July 1962, ministers were anxious that no impression should be given by appointing another Catholic that they were conceding denominational representation. This would hand a weapon to the nonconformist Churches, who were not represented on the Committee, and who might feel that the Government was 'being craftily seduced into Romish practices' in any liberalising report. Because of the less reactionary position of Catholics on this issue, it felt that it was not necessary to replace Rawlinson with another Catholic.[114] The Committee took some two and a half years to produce its report, though this was because of its leisurely approach to its schedule from the beginning, which was designed to fit in with its chairman's other commitments.[115] The report was not published until December 1964. It had been completed in June but its presentation was delayed to avoid becoming, as ministers had feared, an issue in the coming election.[116] As Mark Jarvis concludes, Sunday observance was another example of the limitations of the Conservatives' modernisation agenda.[117]

*

Only months after a general election, in June 1960, the Labour MP Kenneth Robinson, later Minister of Health in the Wilson Government, decided to test the water again on the Wolfenden recommendations on homosexuality. His motion was heavily defeated, by 99 votes to 213.[118] However, signs of change were there. The 1959 New Year edition of *Crossbow* had included homosexual law reform among its list of important social reforms which the Conservative Government should adopt.[119] Bill Deedes indicated that he had moved from outright opposition to acceptance of the inevitability of reform.[120] He denies that he had significantly changed his mind, but was influenced by Butler on the issue, as he was on many others: 'Butler, in this instance – what he did was to shift me from downright hostility to reluctant neutrality. That's about as far as he changed my mind.'[121]

Twenty-two Conservatives voted for the motion, including one Margaret Thatcher, who had become MP for Finchley at the 1959 general election.[122] Many of those supporting Robinson's motion on the Labour side were also to become ministers under Harold Wilson after 1964. Most significant of these was the future Home Secretary Roy Jenkins. Informed debate was hampered by the undetailed nature of the criminal statistics, which gave no geographical breakdown nor identified which offences were consensual, in private, or committed by adults. Nor was it possible to ascertain how many cases involved an element of blackmail. Butler refused to sanction the work on grounds of cost, blocking the evidence for two of the main arguments for reform: that the law as it stood was unevenly applied and that it encouraged other criminal offences.[123]

In stark contrast, the Government moved quickly in 1958 over the prostitution recommendations of the Wolfenden Report. Butler found himself in some personal discomfort over the Street Offences Bill. Though he strongly supported the utilitarian principle of removing the offensive nuisance of prostitution from the streets of central London, he was under pressure from women's organisations to give equal weight to measures against pimps and clients of prostitutes. This position was given added piquancy by the fact that Rab was related to Josephine Butler, who had been instrumental in the campaign to protect women and girls from sexual exploitation which had led to the 1885 Criminal Law Amendment Act, warts and all. He was regretfully obliged to resign from the Association for Moral and Social Hygiene.[124]

However, at Butler's request another look was taken at decriminalisation of gross indecency between men, despite Sir Toby Matthews' earlier objections. This had been suggested during the 1960 debate by William Shepherd, Conservative MP for Cheadle, and was supported by Archbishop Fisher.[125] One of the advantages of this course of action was thought to be the retention of buggery as a *symbol of society's moral disapprobation of homosexual conduct ... which has been part of the criminal law for 400 years, and before that was part of the ecclesiastical law.*

Later the paper added the quixotic hope that

with the absence of discriminatory legislation and the virtual absence of proceedings for homosexual conduct in private public interest in and sympathy for homosexuals would decrease.[126]

However, no further work was done on this proposal. Recognising that the current parliament would not countenance the main Wolfenden recommendation, Leo Abse, Labour MP for Pontypool, sought to introduce a ten minute rule bill to enact some of the minor Wolfenden proposals which had been dismissed in 1957 and 1958. These would require the DPP to authorise all action against offences in private between consenting adults; require that prosecutions must commence within twelve months of their commission; and order the courts to ask for psychiatric reports before sentencing.[127] At a meeting with Abse, Charles Fletcher-Cooke, Parliamentary Under-Secretary at the Home Office, was unforthcoming. For the Conservative opponents of reform even Abse's minor reform represented the thin end of the wedge, Charles Doughty complaining that such 'abominable offences' should be distinguished from ordinary sexual crimes in the title 'Sexual Offences Bill'.[128] At Cabinet's Legislation Committee it was agreed that the Bill should not be allowed to receive a Second Reading.[129]

Shortly after Abse's Bill was blocked Butler received a deputation from the HLRS including Robinson and the Conservative MP Christopher Chataway. As well as pressing for Wolfenden, the deputation strongly urged Butler to step up resources for treatment of homosexual offenders.[130] However, Home Office officials dealing with research projects already undertaken were beginning to realise that, despite such work providing interesting information about homosexuality, it had little bearing on the political feasibility of achieving reform.[131] Neither Sir Charles Cunningham nor Butler felt that there was any imminent prospect of successful legislation. They both felt that repeal of the Labouchère amendment was the best way forward, but that the legal anomalies created ruled this out. As Cunningham wrote, 'this distinction between one form of indecent conduct and others would have no apparent basis in logic or in morals.'[132] Butler made it clear that it was too near to the next general election to act, and that there was no point until a fresh House of Commons had been elected. This was reinforced by the Prime Minister, Sir Alec Douglas-Home, in a letter to Lord Arran, as well as by Butler's successor, Henry Brooke.[133]

Brooke has gained a reputation as one of the most illiberal home secretaries of the twentieth century. Yet in relation to ongoing pressure on Wolfenden this is not entirely deserved. Brooke made no effort to push reform. After all, as Butler had pointed out, the parliamentary arithmetic remained the same as it had been in 1960. However, he did begin discussions about the alleviation of blackmail of homosexuals, prompted partly by a parliamentary question from Shepherd on behalf of the HLRS.[134] He felt that, whilst the police rarely prosecuted in cases where a bona fide complaint of blackmail had been made, the threat of prosecution deterred complaints.[135]

Cunningham, Fletcher-Cooke and Lord Jellicoe, Minister of State at the Home Office, whose own sexual meanderings were to prompt his resignation from the next Conservative Government in 1973, all voiced their support for the implementation of the main Wolfenden recommendation on homosexuality. In fact Jellicoe attended a lunch with Edgar Wright from the HLRS to discuss reform that was arranged by David Astor, editor of the *Observer*, in May 1963.[136] In the previous year's reshuffle Sir John Hobson, who was to be a main participant in debates on abortion and homosexuality throughout the 1960s, had been made Attorney General. He favoured some public encouragement of complaints of blackmail.[137] However, as Fletcher-Cooke pointed out, to make the practice of non-prosecution in blackmail cases more widely known would be impracticable unless an absolute rule were introduced.[138]

*

The last three years of the Conservative administration under Harold Macmillan and Sir Alec Douglas-Home were a period of intense political controversy in which any general change in attitudes towards Wolfenden was strongly affected by rumour and scandal in which homosexuality was a recurring theme. The Vassall spy scandal in 1962 gave grist to the mill of those who thought such behaviour should be more strongly rooted out, not accommodated, in public service and politics.[139] Lords Arran and Longford were careful to emphasise the disconnectedness between the homosexual and security aspects of the scandal, except that a bad law made homosexuals easy targets.[140] Sir John Hobson warned that any announcement of new procedures on the prosecution of homosexuals must wait until July 1963, well after the tribunal report and parliamentary debate on Vassall.[141] When accusations surfaced against John Profumo, Secretary of State for War, that he had had a sexual relationship with Christine Keeler, a call girl who was alleged also to be having a relationship with a Russian diplomat, Macmillan's failure to investigate properly Profumo's denials was greeted with scorn and incredulity. As the events have become increasingly distant, Profumo's reputation, particularly given his devotion to work for East End charities since his resignation, has soared. The opportunism of those who pursued him on the basis of quite flimsy evidence of a security risk, and those who persecuted Stephen Ward, Keeler and Mandy Rice-Davies, is thought increasingly cynical. The rapid erosion at the beginning of the 1960s of the social deference previously accorded to the political class coincided with these events. Macmillan's later bitter judgment was that.

> *Profumo had behaved foolishly and indiscreetly, but not wickedly. His wife ...*
> *is very nice and sensible. Of course, all these people move in a selfish, theatrical,*
> *bohemian society, where no one really knows anyone and everyone is 'darling'.*
> *But Profumo does not seem to have realised that we have – in public life – to*
> *observe different standards from those prevalent today in many circles.*[142]

The insidious George Wigg, who was soon to become Harold Wilson's security adviser, had been passed details of the rumours about Profumo. Wilson briefly reined him in, but on 19 March 1963, during the debate on the Vassall report, Wigg used parliamentary privilege to raise them, supported by Dick Crossman. Barbara Castle also raised the disappearance of Keeler. Only the eccentric, fox-hunting Labour MP Reginald Paget queried their interest: 'What do these rumours amount to? They amount to the fact that a minister is said to be acquainted with an extremely pretty girl. As far as I am concerned, I should have thought that was a matter for congratulation rather than an inquiry.'[143]

When Profumo was forced to confess to the Chief Whip, Martin Redmayne, that he had lied, prompting his resignation, many of his colleagues were merciless, none less than Lord Hailsham. On the BBC's *Gallery* programme, he railed:

> *It is intolerable for Mr Profumo in his position to have behaved in this way, and a tragedy that he should not have been found out – that he should have lied and lied and lied. Lied to his friends, lied to his solicitor and lied to the House of Commons.*

Almost a lone voice, Paget called that a 'virtuoso performance in the art of kicking a friend in the guts'. He added: 'When self-indulgence has reduced a man to the shape of Lord Hailsham, sexual continence involves no more than a sense of the ridiculous.' On 11 June under the headline 'It *is* a moral issue', *The Times*, 'whose high moral tone had always been uncomfortable with Macmillan's encouragement of materialism', thundered:[144]

> *Everyone has been so busy assuring the public that the affair is not one of morals, that it is time to assert that it is. Morals have been discounted too long. A judge may be justified in reminding a jury: 'This is not a court of morals'. The same exemption cannot be allowed in public opinion, without rot setting in and all standards suffering in the long run. The British are not by and large an immoral nation but through their pathetic fear of being called smug they make themselves out to be one ...*
>
> *Eleven years of Conservative rule have brought the nation psychologically and spiritually to a low ebb ... It is time they [the Conservative Party] put first things first, stopped weighing electoral chances, and returned to the starker truths of an earlier day.*
>
> *Popularity by affluence is about played out, especially when it rests on so insecure a basis. Even if the call had metaphorically to be for 'blood, sweat and tears', instead of to the fleshpots, they might be surprised by the result. The British are always at their best when they are braced.*[145]

Ministers were pole-axed by the scandal, with fears that further resignations would follow. Henry Brooke wrote to John Boyd-Carpenter to say that he calculated from the Denning papers that they were the only two ministers 'not at the moment the subject of scandalous rumours'.[146] *The Times* had asked to what extent Wilson would dare elide the question of morals with the question of security. In the debate on the report which Lord Denning was asked to write after inquiring into the affair, the leader of the opposition skilfully did just that:

> *This is a debate without precedent in the annals of this House. It arises from disclosures which have shocked the moral conscience of the nation. There is clear evidence of a sordid underworld network, the extent of which cannot yet be measured.*

The degradation of Keeler continued, with Nigel Birch summing up the general attitude towards her: 'Miss Keeler is a professional prostitute. There seems to me to be a basic improbability about the proposition that their relationship was purely platonic. What are whores about?'[147]

The Government's reputation, and more particularly the Prime Minister's, never recovered, although there was some electoral resuscitation under Douglas-Home during 1964.[148] With the Conservative Government already battered, the summer of 1964 saw rumours of homosexual links between the Conservative peer Lord Boothby, the Labour MP Tom Driberg and the East End gangster Ronnie Kray. Papers in the Prime Minister's file at the Public Record Office record the paranoid tension which seems to have overcome senior government figures at the prospect of yet another scandal, making any idea of homosexual law reform even less likely. After Macmillan's resignation in October 1963 nervous attempts to remove politics from investigations into such rumours were made. In a note to Douglas-Home on 19 July 1964, his Principal Private Secretary wrote, regarding the Boothby/Driberg/Kray allegations, that 'the key-note of the handling of the whole situation would be that it was being removed as rapidly and as far as possible from members of the Government as politicians.'[149]

Senior ministers, including Lord Blakenham, Chancellor of the Duchy of Lancaster, Brooke, Deedes and Hobson, met on 21 July to decide what action to take. Hobson voiced fears of a homosexual version of the Profumo affair: 'He said that his information was that a number of Labour backbenchers were plotting something with the *Mirror* which they intended should be detonated on August 1 ... the right day to start off a new series of rumours similar to 1963.'[150]

These exchanges indicate that Boothby's protestations of innocence were not entirely believed by all his colleagues. Shadowy minor players from the Profumo affair were named in connection with Boothby. In a note to Brooke on 30 July, Redmayne made clear the extent of the paranoia now gripping the Government. He pointed to the two MPs who started the rumours and their East German connections:

> *Without being unnecessarily suspicious[!], one does not forget that the Profumo affair was seriously thought to have been based on Soviet subversion and I do not think that this should be lost sight of in this case*[151]

At the 21 July meeting the discussion of the rumours was preceded by one about the directive from the new DPP, Sir Norman Skelhorn, to chief constables that all proceedings where homosexual acts had been committed in private or more than twelve months ago should be referred to him.[152] This makes clear that Skelhorn did not consult either the Attorney General, the minister to whom the DPP is responsible, or the Home Secretary. Hobson said that 'in his opinion the DPP should have consulted him in his capacity as chief adviser to the Government on prosecutions.' Interestingly he also made the fine distinction that in carrying out his 'statutory duty to advise Chief Constables on any cases that might give rise to points of difficulty … he [the DPP] was not acting on behalf of the Executive'. Both Hobson and Brooke agreed to say that they knew nothing of the directive. In Brooke's answer to parliamentary questions from Robinson and Leo Abse the same day he insisted that 'there is no question of any general change in prosecuting policy or law enforcement or of any reflection on the exercise by Chief Constables of their discretion to prosecute where they see fit.'[153] However, Deedes insists that the two issues were coincidental, and that the Boothby affair was 'fatuous'. He also denies any link between the series of scandals and the issues surrounding homosexual reform.[154]

*

Despite the will among some reform-minded Tories to adapt to the new social and cultural currents which affluence had unleashed, others had trouble relating to ordinary working-class sensibilities. Sir David Eccles, President of the Board of Trade, had been Butler's rival to become the leading Tory liberal immediately after the Second World War. Now eclipsed, with 'preening elegance and apocalyptic smugness' according to *The Spectator*, he smiled condescension on the public, declaring, 'We're all working class now.'[155] In July 1959 he minuted Harold Macmillan on the exciting explosion in youthful cultural activity, though from a rather rarefied perspective:

> *The case ... rests on the obvious desire of a growing number ... (especially the young) to bring something into their lives which is not money or the cruder diversions of sport and sex. Politicians could give different answers to this compound of guilt and boredom; one is to go witch-hunting after sinners; that we can leave to Mr Harold Wilson. Another is to extend the field of the Arts. The second suits our party. Public interest in the arts is gathering force without, as yet, the Government being very plainly identified with it. E.g. we see growing rapidly gramophone record clubs; paper-back editions of the classics; ballet and drama societies; visits to historic houses; amateur classes in drawing and painting etc.*

We may wonder whether by 'paper-back editions of the classics' he meant *Lady Chatterley's Lover*, and whether many young Albert Finney characters were joining ballet classes. Eccles, claiming the support of the Chancellor, Derek Heathcoat-Amory, recommended that the arts should all be brought under the Ministry of Works. Tourism should also be included because it would be 'easier to justify the spending of money to promote the earning of foreign exchange than for the purpose of subsidising the arts. But if the latter were done well the results must attract the tourist.'[156]

He pursued this strategy more vigorously on becoming Minister of Education after the October general election, arguing for a scheme of emergency aid for the arts, supported by a *Crossbow* pamphlet entitled 'Patronage and the Arts'.[157] However, strong Treasury resistance neutered the plan. Describing Eccles' paper as 'wordy and diffuse',[158] officials, including an ascendant Burke Trend, then Second Permanent Secretary at the Treasury, argued merely for an interdepartmental committee to coordinate arts and leisure policy more closely.[159] Heathcoat-Amory disabused Macmillan of any idea that he wanted to shed responsibility for the arts on the grounds that he did not want to 'disturb the excellent relationship which has developed over many years between the Treasury and [funded institutions]'.[160]

Despite his more comical aspects, Eccles did demonstrate an understanding of and concern for the problems which affluence was bringing to the first teenage generation. One source of concern was a lack of training in moral instruction at teacher-training colleges. Eccles entered into discussions with the colleges about how this could be remedied. Responding to a report based on responses from college principals, Eccles began with a characteristically crashing but unintended insult. He wanted to spread knowledge about work in teacher-training across Whitehall, but worried that 'to gentlemen who have been educated at Oxbridge the training colleges are as unknown as Chinatown.' Officials were understandably nervous about stepping into discussion about religion and morality, but Eccles remained firm:

> *I would be against an exercise to tone down passages which link morals with religion, and more often with the Established Church than any other denomination.*
>
> *I smiled a small smile to see the [Chief Inspector of Schools] anxious not to offend the Non-Conformists ... concerned for ... the humanists with someone no doubt ready to champion the Romans. Such delicacy of feeling breeds the very neutrality which is so debilitating in contemporary England.*
>
> *By all means make it clear that moral standards may be firmly held on other grounds than religion. My wife grows fine plants in a thermostatically-controlled greenhouse. Electricity, one may say, is a manufactured substitute for sunshine, but the plants would be much easier to grow if the winter sun were as strong here as it is in mid-summer.*

Officials deployed typical Sir Humphrey tricks to try to delay any action on the issue. The problems were extremely delicate and would require a number of working parties to be established to examine them thoroughly. More alarmingly it was thought that the colleges' task would be made much more difficult if their problems were seized upon by the press and given the kind of publicity which suggested a scandalous state of affairs. They were also anxious that those colleges which had disapproved of Eccles' strictures should not be further antagonised. Very soon Eccles fell in Macmillan's 'Night of the Long Knives', and could only send plaintive missives to his successor, Edward Boyle, about progress on his pet project.[161]

Boyle, less determined to channel youthful exuberance into the performing arts, was also more relaxed about the moral integrity of the new generation. Far too relaxed for some. In July 1963 a storm broke over comments by the Ministry of Education's Principal Medical Officer, Dr Peter Henderson, that he could not condemn couples who had sex before marriage as immoral if they were planning to wed, but were delaying marriage perhaps for economic reasons. Newspapers vented all their fury on Henderson. Conservative-minded teachers 'marched' into the Commons, demanding of ministers how they could be expected to teach morality when a senior medical civil servant made such statements.[162] The *Daily Express*, raking up Profumo, trumpeted:

> *Sir Edward must know the damage that has been done to Britain's good name abroad by recent incidents which have suggested that crime and vice are rampant in this country. The impression is false. But it is necessary all the same that strict moral standards should be championed.*[163]

The Marriage Guidance Council tried to pour oil on the water by reasoning that 'many couples who had sexual intercourse before their wedding day now have happy marriages. But we do not recommend it as a way of starting married life.'[164] Boyle fought back by giving a lengthy interview to Susan Barnes of the *Daily Express*, who, coincidentally, was married to Tony Crosland, Boyle's Labour successor but one at Education in 1965. It revealed an extremely thoughtful and humane man, without the black and white opinions that some in the press were looking for. Speaking just after Profumo's resignation, he said he deplored the tendency to use this rather 'tragic' affair as an occasion for general denunciations about moral decadence in Britain. He thought there were grave dangers in simply equating morality with sexual morality, and that he doubted if an 'effete or morally decadent civilisation' would show such concern about education and the state of other public services as did people in Britain. Deploying a very sixties turn of phrase he said:

> *When you're estimating the morality of teenagers you've got to consider other things besides their sexual morals. You've got to consider their group loyalties they show to each other, the belief they oughtn't to let their friends down. They may have different values from an earlier generation, but you*

can't write them off as nihilists – as people with no moral sense.

I happen to be something of a Puritan myself ... in the sense that I think all of us are totally responsible for finding the values we believe in. The people who depress me most are not those whose values are different from mine but those who never seem to have asked themselves seriously what they think life is about.

Reminding his audience of the hypocrisy of former generations, like the Duke of Devonshire's attack on Parnell for associating with Mrs O'Shea, despite his own multiple affairs, he mused that

we traditionally have liked bear-baiting and public executions. Even now they'd get an audience and while we devote a lot of our energies to avoiding violence and aggressiveness, once our defences break down, we're capable of becoming rather disagreeable. Notting Hill [the 1958 race riots] and all that sort of thing. I am always impressed with the depths of the recesses of the human psyche.[165]

More pertinently he defended Henderson's position, though without concurring with his conclusions:

Whether or not one agrees with Dr Henderson's views it would be wrong for me to appear to lay down the law on a difficult moral issue with regard to which equally good and honest men, both inside and outside the Christian churches genuinely differ[166]

Members of the medical profession, as well as a large section of the public, were outraged. The Assistant Secretary of the BMA declared that, 'speaking as a doctor ... I say that the idea of premarital intercourse is medically dangerous, morally degrading and nationally destructive.' A Gallup poll for the *Sunday Telegraph* found that in no age group was there a majority who supported Henderson's views on premarital sex. The *Telegraph* concluded that the poll provided

an index more of opinion than of practice, and it would be optimistic to assume that all those who favour chastity also practise it. In some respects, however, what people believe in is as valuable evidence of the moral health of a community as what they do, and the impression ... that contemporary England is a generally promiscuous society, has been strikingly refuted.[167]

Though the *Daily Herald* weighed in to support Henderson against the 'hysterical' response, he was condemned by Archbishop Fisher as one of the 'amateur moralists' getting out of hand. With equal sagacity and grace Barbara Cartland, billed in the *News of the World* as a 'novelist and writer on youth', launched a withering attack on Boyle, asserting that he had disclaimed to a visiting group of female American educationists any aim in Britain of trying to produce better citizens through education, because this would verge on the field of morals and principles. To this she added some anecdotal evidence of the pernicious effect of the Profumo affair on Britain's youth:

I have been told of three schoolgirls whose first experiments in sex occurred after they had seen a TV programme which elaborately described the immorality revealed in the Dr Ward case. Taxed with their misbehaviour, the girls pointed out that Christine Keeler and Mandy Rice-Davies seemed to be admired by men of all ages. Why not them?[168]

The Bishop of Exeter, Robert Mortimer, one of the Anglican voices trying to negotiate a theologically sound and socially realistic path through the changes in contemporary society for the Anglican Communion during the 1960s, spelled out the importance of maintaining fornication as a sinful act, though within a hierarchy of sin:

Rape is very bad, and so is the seduction of a young virgin, generally speaking. Less reprehensible is sexual intercourse between two persons in love with each other. No one really doubts this. The modern insistence on almost complete freedom of association between the sexes gravely increases the strain on young people, and it is this, I think, rather than the contents of books, plays, television and advertisements which accounts for the increase of promiscuity among the young. Open social approval of pre-marital sexual intercourse, even within limits, would surely create a position of intolerable strain at least for the girls. Their interest at least is better served by a total social disapproval of any premarital intercourse.[169]

Clearly, any feminist idea of an autonomous female sexuality had not yet pene-trated Mortimer's consciousness. His boss, Fisher, now appealed to Macmillan and Boyle for the government to show some moral leadership, particularly given Boyle's position '*in loco parentis*'. He argued that, as the Government was increas-ingly making interventions of a moral nature in private behaviour, for example the new advice to young people about the dangers from smoking of lung cancer, they could not argue that they should remain aloof from warning of the dangers of premarital sex, for example from venereal disease. Macmillan parried the blow in typical style:

> As I think is fairly generally known, I am a communicant member of the Church of England and fully accept the morality which has always been held by the Church. That is my own position [although not that of his wife of course]. But if I am asked, as Head of the Government, to make a statement of policy on behalf of my administration as a whole I think it only prudent to hesitate.
>
> On this point our views coincide. But what if on some equally important question they did not?
>
> I think he [Henderson] is absolutely wrong and I am prepared to state that as my own view as a Christian, and I have so stated it. But, I am not his 'superior' – nor for that matter is Edward Boyle.

Boyle made what would become the standard disclaimer for education ministers over the next four decades when faced with denunciations of teaching in schools. The ministry only set the legislative framework and policy guidelines. The detail of what was being taught in schools was the responsibility of schools themselves and local education authorities. He also corrected Fisher on the question of smoking, responding that ministers had not instructed teachers to teach children not to smoke because of the dangers of lung cancer; what had happened was that the minister had given information and advice to local education authorities and teachers.[170] However, the episode did contribute towards a greater concern among ministers about teenage pregnancy, sex education and VD, which continued after the change of government in 1964.

*

Despite little progress over the ageing recommendations of the Wolfenden Committee, Leo Abse also tried to nudge forward on the chaotic result of the Morton Commission on Marriage and Divorce towards the end of the Conservative Administration. He introduced a Private Members' Bill in 1963 to make separation after seven years a ground for divorce, over which the commission had been divided. In addition he sought to bolster the support for reconciliation between estranged couples. According to Abse, attempts by his Labour colleague Eric Fletcher, the party's home affairs spokesman and a member of the Church Assembly, to wreck the Bill at second reading and in committee met with resistance at a meeting of the Parliamentary Labour Party from Charles Pannell and Bert Bowden, Labour's Chief Whip. Fletcher had sought to stack the Labour membership of the Committee to examine the Bill with like-minded conservatives. His ineptitude, however, allowed Abse to employ, not for the last time, the tactic of rallying his Welsh colleagues.[171] As he later recalled:

> With the aid of my Welsh colleagues I managed to get a Committee that was packed with Welsh MPs, some of whom were fiercely anti-clerical, and they would smell incense about a thousand miles away, so all the conspiracies of the Church lobbies were defeated, and by 1 vote [it was in fact 2 votes] we got it through Committee.[172]

However, ministers on the Cabinet's Home Affairs Committee were chary of such radical reform whilst admitting the strong case behind it. They felt that 'it would scarcely be possible publicly to support major innovations so soon after a Royal Commission had reported [seven years earlier].' As with the main Wolfenden recommendation on homosexuality, the Conservative Government could not countenance the thought that public opinion had shifted enough. The committee did approve, with some amendment, the Bill's provisions aimed at improving the chances of reconciliation, though 'the impression should not be given that support for this ... implied an official government view on the wider issues of divorce law'. The Lord Advocate, Ian Hamilton Shearer, stated that Scottish ministers took a firm stance against any part of the Bill applying to Scotland, and, in a jibe at the Welsh, that the long separation clause 'would meet with objection in Scotland, looking to the source of the Bill'. The Committee agreed to his suggestion that, tactically, Scottish members should therefore be included on the Committee.[173] With the Bill scraping through the Committee stage by two votes, this nearly worked.[174]

Startled at the prospect of easier divorce, and in stark contrast to the divisions among denominations only four years later, the Churches now combined to condemn Abse's Bill publicly,[175] and their representatives of all parties in the Commons succeeded in 'castrating' it on report. Abse was left with the crumb of comfort of the reconciliation clauses to pass as the Matrimonial Causes Act 1963.[176] The impressive ecumenical consensus which had successfully defeated Abse's 1963 Bill masked Anglican doubts. At this stage, Archbishop Fisher made clear to ministers his opposition even to moving divorce hearings from the High Court to the county court, despite the fact that county court judges already heard divorce petitions as commissioners in the High Court, for the same reason that had been given in 1945 – that it would indicate to the public that the importance of marriage had been downgraded. One official wrote to Sir Alec Douglas-Home in exasperation: 'It is farcical that the taxpayer should pay £300,000 a year because a county court judge trying divorce cases as he does at present, wears a different robe and is addressed as 'My Lord' instead of 'Your Honour.'[177]

However, following lengthy discussions during 1963 with the Lord Chancellor, Lord Dilhorne, and Henry Brooke, a group was established in April 1964 by Michael Ramsey, Fisher's replacement as Archbishop of Canterbury, to 'review the law of England concerning divorce', virtually at the request of these ministers.[178] According to Lawrence Stone, 'the national mood had changed drastically from what it had been even a decade before.'[179] By 1963 the movement within the Churches to adapt to the new social realities and rescue Christianity from the tide of secularisation had acquired a philosophical edge with the publication of two seminal books, Bishop John Robinson's *Honest to God* and the Friends Home Service Committee's *Towards a Quaker View of Sex*.[180] *Honest to God* in particular sent shockwaves through the Anglican hierarchy and the Establishment. It advocated a reassessment of traditional Christian teaching in the modern world, and the adoption of a system of 'situational ethics', in which a measurement of harm involved in personal behaviour should be considered.[181] 'Our moral decisions must be guided by the actual relationships between the persons concerned at a particular time in a particular situation, and compassion for persons overrides all law. The only intrinsic evil is lack of love.'[182] This was very close to the new Quaker position: 'Surely it is the nature and quality of a relationship that matters: one must not judge it by its outward appearance but by its inner worth. Homosexual affection can be as selfless as heterosexual affection and therefore we cannot see that it is in some way morally worse.'[183]

Christopher Booker, looking back from 1970, condemned *Honest to God* in particular: 'In no way was the disintegration of authority more subtly and profoundly reflected, however, than in a book [which] brought to a head all the doubts and insecurities which had recently been afflicting many leading members of the Church of England.'[184]

However, the other key ingredient which would hasten reform of the divorce law and so many other areas of public morality was, of course, the election of a Labour Government in 1964 under Harold Wilson.

4. Letting the Wolf Through the Door: 1964–1970

'*The Labour Party is a moral crusade or it is nothing. Let that be his epitaph*'
Tony Blair[1]

'*The public opinion behind the [abortion] Bill is millions of women up and down the country who are saying 'we will no longer tolerate this system whereby men lay down, as if by right, the moral laws, particularly those relating to sexual behaviour about how women should behave.*'
Christopher Price, Labour MP for Birmingham Perry Barr[2]

'*The fewer the people who go out to a public entertainment on Sunday the more who will stay at home, wilfully mentally inhaling the claims for some detergent or breakfast cereal.*'
Lord Moynihan[3]

Hacker: That bloody place [the National Theatre] is always putting on plays attacking me. They set The Comedy of Errors *in No.10 … I knew who they were getting at … There was a whole play attacking my nuclear policy, a farce.*

Sir Humphrey: What, the policy?

Hacker: No, Humphrey, the play. Why do they do it?

Sir Humphrey: It's very healthy, Prime Minister … Practically no one goes to political plays, and half those that do don't understand them, and half of those that do don't agree with them and the seven who are left would have voted against the government anyway. It helps people let off steam, and you're seen as a democratic statesman for subsidising your critics … Plays criticising the government make the second most boring evening.

Hacker: What are the most boring?

Sir Humphrey: Plays praising the government.

Yes Prime Minister [4]

Despite a decade of gradual rehabilitation, the record of the first Wilson administration remains low in the taxonomy of postwar governments. From the National Plan to *In Place of Strife* and the school-leaving age to House of Lords reform, much of its key attempted reforms remained unfulfilled. Although less high-profile achievements including the creation of the Open University and legislation on race relations and equal pay are counted successes, its enduring legacy is still considered a range of reforms which it did not even explicitly support: abolition of capital punishment, homosexual law reform, abortion, ending theatre censorship and relaxing the divorce law. The Government effectively allowed the Commons its head on a range of issues which previous postwar administrations had opposed or delayed. For conservatives these changes have not led to the 'civilised society' heralded by proponents such as Roy Jenkins, but have fulfilled the expectations of those who warned that they would lead to the collapse of the family and the spread of immorality and crime. Even for some of the proponents of these limited reforms, what has come since has not been welcome. A. P. Herbert was soon decrying the spread of pornography in the 1970s and Leo Abse looked aghast at the demands of gay rights campaigners.

If Harold Wilson's background inclined him to consider such issues at best a distraction and at worst unpalatable he was, as ever, attuned to the political weather. He famously understood, and exploited, the symbols of cultural change in 1960s 'Swinging London', most famously by awarding OBEs to the Beatles. Similarly, his antennae enabled him to overcome personal reservations about his Government being associated with a relaxation of laws governing public morality to give way to the overwhelming pressure within the Labour Party. However, this accommodation was tempered with concern about how far such moves were ahead of public opinion, and the electoral harvest that might be reaped, particularly in areas like his own constituency of Huyton with a large Catholic vote. His close friendship with Cardinal Heenan fuelled this anxiety. When Labour was drafting its 1961 policy statement, *Signposts for the Sixties*, Wilson, supported by Hugh Gaitskell, warned in exaggerated terms of the potential electoral cost of endorsing the Wolfenden recommendations on homosexuality, saying it would cost the party six million votes. Nonetheless, even before October 1964 Wilson was putting in place the mechanism which would allow reformers within the party to drive through reform once in government.

In a pre-election address to the Society of Labour Lawyers, he promised a free vote on capital punishment, and suggested there could be more free votes on areas of Home Office policy, if only non-controversial ones (quite what the point of allowing free votes on non-controversial issues would be is not clear, as the whole point is to remove controversial matters from party responsibility).

Wilson had been one of the most prominent Cabinet ministers who had failed to vote with the Government to retain hanging in 1949. He also foreshadowed action in the fields of race relations and women's rights. Though there was no direct reference to wider issues of morality, he did attack the Tory Home Secretary, Henry Brooke, for his lack of humanity and liberality. In the words of one young Labour MP at the time, Gwyneth Dunwoody, Wilson was 'quite happy if people did controversial things, to try and balance the interests of all the different groupings'.[5] If he never explicitly mentioned such matters either at the time or in retrospect, perhaps the most compelling evidence of Wilson's willing acceptance of what was to come is his appointment of Jenkins as Home Secretary in December 1965. No potential candidate for the job before or since has striven so openly, and with such an explicit and radical agenda, to be Home Secretary. Wilson could hardly complain he had not been forewarned of Jenkins' plans. Indeed it is clear from the records that Wilson had fixed firmly on Jenkins' move to the Home Office three months before the reshuffle came, after briefly flirting with the option of the rather grey Colonial Secretary, Arthur Bottomley.[6] Jenkins himself certainly felt Wilson was knowingly giving him the opportunity to implement some of the vision he had set out in *The Labour Case* in 1959. According to Jenkins, questions such as abortion and homosexuality 'did not make his blood run cold'.[7] When Jenkins was called to No. 10 during the December 1965 reshuffle, Wilson spoke to him:

> *'You surely wouldn't like to be Home Secretary, would you?' he said. I said that I would very much indeed: it was no moment to beat about the bush ... I then told him some of my ideas about letting fresh air into the Home Office, about which he became enthusiastic. He had apparently been upset by an article by Jo Grimond in that morning's* Guardian *which had said the Government was competent but not radical. He thought my appointment might redress the balance. I hoped he meant by increasing the radicalism not reducing the competence.*[8]

In contrast, the response of Wilson's deputy, George Brown, to some of Jenkins' ideas was visceral. Barbara Castle recorded in her diary for 11 February 1966 that, when she and other ministers proposed to leave a meeting in order to go and vote for Abse's Bill implementing this part of the Wolfenden Report;

> *George set off on a remarkable diatribe against homosexuality ... 'This is how Rome came down. And I care deeply about it – in opposition to most of my Church [he was an Anglo-Catholic]. Don't think teenagers are able to evaluate your liberal ideas. You will have a totally disorganised, indecent and unpleasant society. You must have rules! We've gone too far on sex already. I don't regard any sex as pleasant. It's pretty undignified and I've always thought so.'* [9]

Brown's biographer, Peter Paterson, has chronicled the sad demise of Brown's own marriage, including his bullying treatment of his wife Sophie. Wilson's own marriage was the model of an enduring political partnership. But it endured, and survived, despite repeated allegations of Harold's infidelity with Marcia Williams, who had been his Political Secretary since 1956 and remained so throughout the roller-coaster ride of Wilson's leadership of the party, ending in the debasement of the honours system that was the infamous Lavender List in 1976. During the 1964 election campaign, the Conservative Secretary of State for Education and Science, Quintin Hogg, parrying a heckler who raised the Profumo scandal, declared, 'If you can tell me there are no adulterers on the front bench of the Labour Party, you can talk to me about Profumo.' Hogg's remarks caused a brief panic in Labour's campaign headquarters, where it was feared that Wilson's relationship with Williams might be misrepresented by the press. Lord Attlee rebutted Hogg's remark and accused him of acting like 'a schoolboy', though Hogg repeated the allegation in August 1965 on the television programme *Late Night Live*. The question of Wilson's alleged affair with Williams was recently re-aired by two members of Wilson's 'Kitchen Cabinets', Joe Haines and Bernard Donoughue.[10] However, Wilson was not above using allegations, or evidence, of other people's sexual infidelities to his advantage. His reputation as one of the most successful leaders of the opposition rests partly on his skilful use of the Profumo affair to his, and Labour's, benefit. In 1967 he also used rumours of sexual 'irregularity' against Colonel Sammy Lohan, the Secretary of the Defence Notice Committee, whom Wilson suspected of leaking

stories to journalists in order to damage the Government.[11] One curious observation is that, among Matthew Parris's exhaustive and wonderfully humane
catalogue *Great Parliamentary Scandals*, there are none from the 1964–70 Labour
administration. Not, surely, for lack of sexual adventure on the part of Labour
politicians in the 1960s?

Sir Frank Soskice's reputation has always suffered in comparison with his
successor at the Home Office, Roy Jenkins, not least at the hands of Jenkins
himself, who dismissed him as indecisive and uninterested in the Home Office
questions of reform which formed Jenkins' own manifesto for the job. This is
somewhat unfair. Although not fired with the same youthful passion for such
issues as Jenkins, Soskice had been a supporter of divorce law reform since his
time as Solicitor General under Attlee, as we have seen, when his liberal opinions
on the subject prevented him from opposing Eirene White's Reform Bill from the
despatch box. Much like 'Rab' Butler, Soskice weighed the influence of public
opinion more heavily than those who were more strongly committed. However,
this could lead to him making distorting claims about public opinion. When an
abortion law reform deputation came to see him in February 1965, he suggested
that their task was to crystallise public opinion in support of legislation, and that
'a rapid change of opinion could come about, as in the case of the abolition of
capital punishment.'[12] This was a curious reading of public opinion, which never
moved significantly or rapidly in favour of abolition of the death penalty,
whereas support for a more liberal abortion law remained consistently high and
ahead of the political will to address the issue. In an uncanny echo of Butler's
attitude after the publication of the Wolfenden Report, Soskice argued that the
Government could not 'force this on an unwilling public opinion, which is not
yet ready for it. There is nothing we can do at the present.'[13] However, Soskice did
support decriminalisation of homosexuality. It was he who initiated the first
review of the position after Labour took office by asking Sir Charles
Cunningham for a note on possible options. To his reform-minded junior
minister in the Lords, Lord Stonham, he said: 'It is, I think, best to have the
debate. I very much dislike, in effect, sweeping social questions of this sort under
the carpet; (and personally would like to give effect to Wolfenden).'[14] When the
issue was forced by the introduction of a Private Members' Bill in May 1965,
Soskice was considerably ahead of the agreed Cabinet line of neutrality,
explaining that 'I am reluctant … to adopt a wholly neutral attitude, without

offering some guidance to the growing body of opinion in favour of a change in the law on how in the Government's view a change might be brought about.'[15]

The difference between the Wilson Government and its predecessors, both Tory and Labour, is neatly demonstrated by the instructions to ministers on how they might vote on capital punishment abolition in 1965. In 1948 and 1956 members of the Government had been told if they supported abolition they should abstain. Now Cabinet agreed that ministers should preferably abstain rather than vote against Sydney Silverman's Bill, although consciences would not be pressed.[16] The Murder (Abolition of the Death Penalty) Bill received its second reading on 21 December 1964 by 355 to 170 votes. However, the ability of the Government merely to withdraw and allow the Commons to reach a decision was immediately challenged. Retentionists wanted the Bill taken on the floor of the House, rather than in a standing committee, so that it would eat into the Government's own time. When a vote was taken on this, it was only narrowly defeated, and the Government was accused of 'putting the Whips on' to protect it. Progress in the standing committee was extremely slow, but the attempts by retentionists to amend the Bill were frustrated until one Conservative sprang a surprise on a quiet Friday by tabling a motion for the Bill to be returned to the floor of the House. This passed by eight votes.[17] The Government was now in a quandary. It could hardly attempt to reverse the decision, but equally was reluctant to use its own parliamentary time for protracted scrutiny of the Murder Bill. The solution was to propose special Wednesday morning sittings for the Bill. Not only would this save time, but it would severely inconvenience Conservative MPs with other professional engagements, give the Bill a fairer wind and serve as a warning against future attempts to restrict scrutiny of bills to the main chamber.[18] Amendments were all defeated except, significantly, the proposal that the Bill last for an experimental period of five years, at which point both Houses would need to vote again to make it permanent. The Government gave more time to complete the final stage of the Bill, and the Lords, energised by the growing ranks of life peers, also passed it with large majorities.

*

When in May 1965 the Cabinet considered what to do about the forthcoming debate of a motion on homosexuality tabled by Leo Abse, several ministers pointed to 'the present political situation' – the small parliamentary majority and impending second general election – as a reason for not giving him any assistance. Sir Frank Soskice hoped, however, that they would be able to find time for a debate in the future. Harold Wilson demanded that a strictly neutral attitude be adopted by ministers, though this 'need not preclude reconsideration of the matter in the light of any later developments in public opinion'.[19] This question was rendered temporarily irrelevant at the end of the month, when Abse's first attempt to introduce a bill was defeated by 178 votes to 159 – so much for the newly liberal House of Commons. According to Abse himself, this was due in part to the influence of the veteran Emanuel Shinwell, Minister of Fuel and Power under Clement Attlee and now chairman of the Parliamentary Labour Party, over his fellow trade union members, warning of the intellectual follies of middle-class liberals such as Abse.[20]

However, two days before this set-back for Abse and other reformers, peers struck their first significant liberal pose, approving a similar bill introduced by Lord Arran by ninety-four votes to forty-nine, in the face of fierce opposition including Lord Denning and the two previous Lord Chancellors, Dilhorne and Kilmuir. Kilmuir warned darkly about known 'sodomitic societies' and 'buggery clubs', demanding, 'Are you Lordships going to pass a bill that will make it lawful for two senior officers of police to go to bed together'?[21]

Both Archbishops spoke in favour of reform, leading a majority of the Lords Spiritual who supported the Bill. However, Michael Ramsey, a vice-president, though not an uncritical one, of the Homosexual Law Reform Society (HLRS), insisted to Arran that 'reforming the law should be presented in the best way for edifying the public.'[22] The majority among hereditary peers, twenty-six to thirteen, was similar to that among life peers. Most startlingly, Lord Queensberry, the descendant of Oscar Wilde's nemesis, wrote supportively to Antony Grey, secretary of the HLRS, that 'the House of Lords must represent, on the whole, a conventional and reactionary approach to most subjects and if they are so very much in favour of reform, then it seems unlikely that public opinion in the country holds the opposite view.'[23] This educated guess was now backed up by opinion poll research which indicated the public might well now support Wolfenden. One NOP poll for the *Daily Mail* (of all papers) in October 1965 found that only thirty-six per cent of people thought that homosexual acts between adults in private should be criminal, and sixty-three per cent thought that they should not. Even broken down by gender, age, region and social class, a majority supported reform in each case.[24]

'Boofy' Arran's own motivation for taking the lead role in the House of Lords was extremely personal. In 1972 he wrote in an article in *Encounter* of the effect of a newspaper colleague who 'went to prison over a case so contrived as to stink for ever in the annals of the police and the judiciary'. However, he also alluded to the need through stress for a 'new anxiety' to distract him from other troubles.[25] It is now clear that was an oblique reference to his older brother, the previous earl, who, it seems, had a homosexual past and died after a long psychiatric illness. Abse writes in his memoirs that he had met a man who claimed to have been the lover of the older brother.[26] With the Bill now in committee, some ministers and officials began to work around Wilson's injunction on neutrality in the face of the practical need to pronounce on the form which amendments to the Bill might take. In the words of Sir Charles Cunningham, that supposedly reactionary Permanent Secretary, if the Government sat back while amendments were passed to which it would have to object for legal or administrative reasons, 'it is hardly dignified for the House to be frustrated in this way when its wishes were made known at the Committee stage.'[27] The Bill passed its final stage in the House of Lords at the end of October by 116 votes to 46. Lord Stonham reassured Arran that, following the private members' ballot in the Commons at the beginning of the new session, he would give 'any assistance as a persuader' and that 'whatever the discouragement or ignorant abuse there can be no question of giving up.'[28]

The initiative now passed to an unlikely quarter. Humphrey Berkeley, Conservative MP for Lancaster, came near the top of the ballot and risked the opprobrium of his colleagues by adopting a homosexual law reform bill. The promotion to the Cabinet a few weeks later of the soi-disant 'Young Home Secretary', Roy Jenkins, changed entirely the terms of play. He immediately pushed the Cabinet's Home Affairs Committee to adopt a more positive line towards Berkeley's Bill as well as abortion law reform and the abolition of theatre censorship, arguing that a 'benevolent neutrality' should include giving more drafting assistance and the possibility later of parliamentary time. Though this was not agreed by the Committee, Jenkins was adamant that he should be allowed to indicate his personal support – not to do so would have made him look ridiculous, given his previous pronouncements. When approval of this was omitted from the record of the meeting, Jenkins wrote to the Committee's chairman, Bert Bowden, demanding they be rewritten. In private he discussed with Berkeley the best tactics for success with his Bill, and he and Bowden indicated that they hoped to be able to give the Bill more time if it reached its report stage. When the second-reading debate came on 11 February opposition collapsed and the Bill received its second reading by 164 to 107 votes.[29] If Wilson had decided to hold out longer until calling another election in 1966, the sponsor of the decriminalisation of homosexuality might well have been a Conservative MP just as, nearly thirty years later, another Tory MP, Edwina Currie, tabled the amendment to reduce the homosexual age of consent from twenty-one to eighteen. However, a general election did intervene, and when Parliament returned, Labour's majority had soared to ninety-seven, including Berkeley's Lancaster seat, where the swing to Labour of 5.25 per cent was much higher than the national average of 2.7 per cent. Berkeley certainly felt that he had suffered as a result of his prominent support for homosexual law reform, writing to the Archbishop of Canterbury that he had encountered much hostility from 'church-going people' in his constituency, who had been unaware that their spiritual leaders generally backed reform as well.[30] Berkeley had certainly made no secret during the election campaign of his homosexual law reform bill, even including it in his eve-of-poll address. In contrast, his Labour opponent, Stanley Henig, concentrated on the need for a new bridge across the river Lune in the constituency, something that would undoubtedly benefit heterosexuals as well as homosexuals. He did, though, go on to support the successful reform bill in the next parliament. When he was then defeated in 1970 by the Conservative Elaine Kellet-Bowman, the swing against him was less than the national average. If on balance Berkeley lost more votes than he won through his position, Henig would still have won on a lower swing than actually occurred.[31]

If a key supporter of reform had been sacrificed along the way, the inflated Labour majority, and the political latitude which this gave the Government, meant that Jenkins could press his case once again with less concern about the electoral implications. Ironically, Wilson's early move at the end of February to seek an enhanced mandate provided the best opportunity for reform from the back benches, because it ensured that the first session of the new Parliament would run for about eighteen months until the autumn of 1967, rather than the usual twelve months. Time, the best weapon in the armoury of opponents of reform, was now on the side of the reformers. The ballot for private members' bills on 12 May produced the hope among reformers that David Steel, the youthful Liberal MP for Roxburgh, Selkirk and Peebles, would choose to introduce a homosexual law reform measure. Arran lobbied Steel, using fair means and foul to persuade him. He pointed to the majorities in both Houses in favour of Wolfenden and a similar endorsement by the Liberal Council, arguing that this meant the issue should have precedence over abortion law reform, which Steel was also considering. He claimed, more dubiously, that homosexuality concerned the happiness of more people than abortion and was concerned more with personal liberty. Willie Ross, the Scottish Secretary who achieved something of a political record by serving in the same post not just for the length of the 1964–70 administration, but also for Wilson's second stint as premier from 1974 to 1976, flatly refused the cooperation of his department with Steel's idea for a border development bill,[32] a decision which, given his staunchly anti-abortion and anti-homosexual views, he might have come to regret. Steel carefully gauged the opinion in his new constituency (he had won it from the Conservatives in a by-election only in March 1965), and announced in the *Sun* that he would welcome all suggestions about which reform he should champion.[33] This produced the usual enormous postbag of advice and supplication from the rational to the insane, which probably tipped the balance still further from homosexuality towards abortion. The most interesting aspect of these letters is the widespread view amongst Liberal supporters that Steel should not be pressurised into sponsoring a controversial measure that might cost him a valuable Liberal seat simply to satisfy Labour's reforming impulses, and that Labour MPs should be performing the task.[34] This was also a strongly held view among reform-minded Labour MPs. Lena Jeger, MP for Holborn and St Pancras South, writing in the *Guardian* in 1966, stated:

What worries me much more than the rightness or wrongness of … [a] partic-ular piece of legislation is the possibility that members of Parliament should accept sanctions in which they do not themselves believe for the sake of electoral considerations. A government cannot govern by the counting of correspon-dence'[35]

Despite urging from Jenkins that a homosexual reform bill would be easier to pilot through the Commons, Steel plumped for abortion. This was not surprising, since Arran's Bill did not even cover Scotland.[36] Arran, for one, was becoming increasingly frustrated with resistance to allowing the Commons to reach a decision on the issue. He complained to Archbishop Ramsey's assistant, Robert Beloe, that he was 'honestly beginning to wonder whether there is any purpose in the House of Lords at all, and whether we are not just being used as a platform for the airing of progressive views on which no action will be taken'.[37]

His resolve was stiffened by, amongst others, a sympathetic Peter Henderson, Clerk of the Parliaments, later well known as a campaigner in the House of Lords on gay rights, abortion and cruelty to children. Arguably exceeding the limits of his official capacity, he had earlier written to Arran that 'I should be strongly in favour of your introducing the Bill next Session in exactly the same form as it was passed last Thursday in this Session. If you do not do so you may well be open to the charge that you have broken faith with ... your supporters.'[38]

Arran's Bill was indeed again approved by peers in June 1966. It was now that Leo Abse stepped into the limelight. When he sought approval to introduce a bill under the Ten-Minute Rule in July, the change in the arithmetic was clear, as MPs voted 244 to 100 in favour. Asked whether other MPs objected to Abse's obsession with Freud, including psychoanalysing his parliamentary colleagues, Jenkins commented wryly, 'Yes, I think they did, rather. He wasn't exactly the person I would have chosen to be the sponsor of the Bill, but given that he didn't do it badly at all.'[39]

With a thumping Commons majority Jenkins now tried once again to push his ministerial colleagues on the Cabinet's Legislation Committee to adopt a more positive attitude.[40] Despite an agreement that giving a bill extra parliamentary time in the future would not be ruled out, there was no commitment at this stage. However, over the summer the pressure increased. Wilson personally fielded appeals from impatient Labour backbenchers including the future Cabinet minister Edmund Dell. A critical mass behind facilitating the passage of a bill came with the replacement of Bert Bowden as Leader of the House with the more radical Dick Crossman in August 1966. Crossman's diaries reflect his strong support, even his proud claims to leadership, of the emerging government strategy to enable the Commons to come to a decision on the range of controversial moral issues which were decided between 1965 and 1970. Yet his attitude towards homosexual law reform was ambivalent. According to his biographer, Anthony Howard, he 'never sought to conceal the fact that in his early years at

Oxford he had operated predominantly as a homosexual', as a peripheral member of the social circle dominated by W. H. Auden.[41] But Crossman also voiced doubts about the desirability of the issue of reform, worrying to Tam Dalyell that the only benefit of the 'Buggers' Bill' was that it was creating a 'boomerang effect' of support for abortion law reform which he saw as being a pretty popular measure, especially among working-class women, in stark contrast to the public response to homosexual law reform:

> *Frankly it's an extremely unpleasant Bill and I myself didn't like it. It may well be twenty years ahead of public opinion; certainly working-class people in the north jeer at their Members at the weekend and ask them why they're looking after the buggers at Westminster instead of looking after the unemployed at home.*[42]

In any case, he and Jenkins agreed that an extra half day of time might be made available and suggested that Jenkins raise the matter again at Cabinet. Having promised Abse that he would secure extra time for a homosexual law reform bill if it was approved by MPs, Jenkins cued in the arguments for shifting the government's stance: both Houses had now approved reform, the Lords twice; until the issue was decided the criminal law would be increasingly difficult to administer; and finally, the precedent of Sydney Silverman's capital punishment abolition bill.[43] According to Crossman's diary it was Wilson, Jim Callaghan and George Brown, supported by others, who resisted Jenkins' appeal. Crossman himself pointed out the risk of letting the subject drag on until nearer the general election. He recorded that 'with this highly tactical argument we persuaded the PM to drag the rest of his colleagues with him.'[44] This did not mean that the issue was settled among Government supporters in the Commons. Many conservative-minded Labour MPs were staunchly opposed to their Government providing extra time for such measures, and this became clear during Abse's Bill's second-reading debate in December 1966. Among them were several government whips. According to Crossman: 'Like a lot of our northern Members [George] Lawson [MP for Motherwell] is passionately opposed ... much more so than those of us who come from the Midlands and the South. He and several other Whips objected fiercely that it was turning our own working-class support against us.'[45]

An influx of younger, more liberal, Labour MPs in 1964 and 1966 had fuelled demand for reform. According to David Butler's analysis, the proportion of university-educated Labour MPs rose from thirty-nine per cent in 1959 to forty-six per cent in 1964 and fifty-one per cent in 1966. However, even after 1966 the PLP had a higher average age than Conservative MPs.[46] According to Crossman, the PLP after 1966 contained '120–150 Labour people who are progressives', by which he meant those committed to the Crosland/Jenkins vision of a 'civilised' society. This represented less than half the parliamentary party.[47]

Abse and his ministerial supporters were prepared to make repeated compromises in order to get any bill through the Commons. His Sexual Offences Bill was already a watered-down version of the Wolfenden recommendations, with a tighter definition of concepts such as 'in private' and a blanket exemption for the armed forces. Now Abse side-stepped difficulties in the committee examining the Bill by immediately accepting amendments to exclude the Merchant Navy as well. This followed intense lobbying of ministers by both the National Union of Seamen (NUS) and the National Maritime Board. Their case was championed by the Board of Trade, led by Douglas Jay and Roy Mason. The NUS were clearly bullish only months after their successful strike, which had threatened to cripple the British economy and led Wilson to make his infamous accusation about a 'tightly knit group of politically motivated men' leading the strike, which included a youthful John Prescott, future Deputy Prime Minister. Abse was determined to avoid antagonising the union at such a delicate time, and bowed to their demands for an exemption.

Though the Bill had avoided death by a thousand cuts in committee, there was still no certainty that it would survive its final stages when it returned to the full House in the spring. Crossman returned to Cabinet to plead for extra time for Abse's Bill as well as David Steel's Bill on abortion. The atmosphere between conservatives and liberals in the PLP exploded in ferocious clashes about the possibility of further special treatment, but Wilson approved the move provided that it did not jeopardise either the Government's own legislative programme or the date fixed for the beginning of the summer recess. This shifted the focus of attention back to the reformers in the Commons, still not out of the woods, because of the need to have 100 supporters present to vote on each division on the Bill during the all-night session fixed for 3 July. According to Crossman, he and the Chief Whip, John Silkin, 'spent the night going round the lobbies and encouraging the troops', despite the Government's own neutrality on the Bill. At 5:50 a.m. the Bill passed its third reading by ninety-nine votes to fourteen after a session lasting over twenty hours. Conservative MP Gerald Nabarro launched a fierce attack on the 'depravity' among Labour MPs, saying that the 'long hair of Mr Wilson's intellectuals on the back benches would strangle him' at the next election.[48]

Peers now cantered round the familiar arguments once more, with even less opposition than had been seen previously. Lord Kilmuir, who had set the whole process in train by establishing the Wolfenden Committee in 1954, had died in January 1967, and Lord Dilhorne became less obstructive once the age of consent was set at twenty-one. Arran himself, who had doggedly pursued reform, was still recovering from two mild strokes which he had suffered only weeks before, but set the seal on the Bill with a speech of studied moderation. The Bill was in no way a condoning of homosexuality. It was merely an acknowledgement that homosexuals found themselves in an unfortunate and abnormal condition through no fault of their own, that they deserved to be pitied not persecuted, and that criminal sanction was not the way to discourage such practices. However, he warned those from whom the shadow of the criminal law was being partly lifted:

> Homosexuals must continue to remember that while there may be nothing bad in being a homosexual, there is certainly nothing good. Lest the opponents of the new Bill think that a new freedom, a new privileged class has been created, let me remind them that no amount of legislation will prevent homosexuals from being the subject of dislike and derision, or at best of pity.[49]

*

If Sir Frank Soskice had been only mildly encouraging towards reformers who approached the Home Office about homosexuality in 1964–5, he was even less positive about the chances of relaxing the law on abortion. Although he indicated his support for limited reform on grounds of maternal health, and in cases of rape and severe deformity such as the recent Thalidomide tragedy, he opposed 'complete legalisation', abortion on social grounds or on demand. The deputation was stonewalled about lack of parliamentary time. Undeterred, Labour's Renée Short tried to introduce a bill under the Ten-Minute Rule in May allowing for abortion by a medical practitioner until the thirteenth week of pregnancy. The radical Scottish Labour MP Willie Hamilton also kept up the pressure by judicial questioning of ministers, which eventually elicited from Alice Bacon, a junior Home Office minister, in July 1965 the agreement that the Government might look more favourably on a private members' bill in the coming session.

The sudden quickening of the pace of parliamentary activity on abortion in 1965 meant an explosion of activity on the part of the Abortion Law Reform Association (ALRA).[50] Much of its growing income now financed surveys from NOP covering, apart from the views of the general public, the division of opinion among doctors and Catholic, Protestant and nonconformist clergy.[51] The results of these opinion polls gave the lie to claims that the public was not ready for reform, that the medical profession was lukewarm, that general opposition was not mainly Roman Catholic or even that Roman Catholics were solidly opposed to legal abortion.[52] In July 1966 an NOP survey revealed that seventy-five per cent of women favoured easier legal abortion and only twenty per cent were opposed.[53] In 1965 NOP found that sixty-six per cent of doctors agreed with the provisions contained in the Silkin Bill or thought them too restrictive, whilst only ten per cent were totally opposed to abortion.[54] NOP also demonstrated that Catholic women were no less likely to have had an abortion than other women,[55] and that forty-four per cent of Catholic women surveyed in March 1967 supported abortion 'if the woman is unable to cope with any more children'.[56]

Unlike homosexuality, abortion was a subject which serious political debates, documentaries and dramas were eager to tackle, and ALRA took full advantage of the opportunities this development gave for promoting the cause of reform, particularly from 1965. Catholic opponents, and the Society for the Protection of the Unborn Child (SPUC) from 1967, also vigorously pursued these avenues for publicity, if sometimes demanding exposure on different terms. Mary Whitehouse complained that Diane Munday of ALRA had been allowed to appear on the BBC *24 Hours* programme on abortion on the grounds that she might influence public opinion, against the terms of the BBC Charter. This despite the appearance in the same programme by members of SPUC.[57] Whilst most of the press and broadcast media were favourable to reform, two prominent exceptions were *The Times* and the *Daily Telegraph*. According to reformers, the Catholic William Rees-Mogg's editorial policy at *The Times* sought to exclude pro-reform arguments from the paper, despite his attention to other changing social attitudes among the young.[58] However, *The Times*'s editorial line was not all in one direction. A number of leaders pointed to the need for some reform and a clearer government position.[59]

As with homosexual law reform, the running was soon being made in the House of Lords where Lord Silkin, former Minister of Town and Country Planning in the Attlee Government and father of Harold Wilson's Chief Whip, introduced an abortion bill in November. Silkin was undogmatic about the issue, ready to take compromise amendments or consider another departmental inquiry, and this made opposition more difficult. The bill won a second reading by seventy-seven votes to eight. Simultaneously, Simon Wingfield Digby, Conservative MP for Dorset West, introduced a Commons Bill. Roy Jenkins now intervened, and he argued with colleagues on the Cabinet's Home Affairs Committee on 12 January 1966, just days after his appointment, that to continue with the present policy of strict neutrality after the positive Lords vote would amount to hostility towards reform. The Committee was chaired by Douglas Houghton, Chancellor of the Duchy of Lancaster and supervisory Cabinet minister for health and social services, whose wife Vera was a leading lobbyist for ALRA. Houghton was as committed as she to reform. Despite this high-profile advocacy, there was still considerable opposition from other members of the Committee to any diversion from strict neutrality as a result of a vote in the House of Lords. Others emphasised the appalling statistics for maternal mortality and injury which illegal abortion resulted in, and the fact that the Conservatives had been prepared to consider limited reform by putting the existing case law on a statutory footing. The most that they could agree was that spokesmen should advise on the practicability of amendments and assist in putting any which were approved in a proper form. A special group of ministers was convened to consider the Government's position on abortion further. It was to be chaired by Houghton and included Lord Gardiner, who had been an adviser to ALRA during the 1950s and felt he had only prevented from taking a more prominent role because of his candidature in the marginal seat of Croydon West.[60] He had publicly stated his personal support for abortion on social grounds in an interview with *The Economist* before the 1964 election when discussing Labour's plans for law reform, as well as co-editing a volume on legal reform which supported abortion law reform in 1963. Kenneth Robinson, Attorney General Sir Elwyn Jones, Judith Hart, a left-wing junior Scottish Office minister, and Jenkins made up the reforming numbers. This left only poor Lord Longford, Leader of the House of Lords, as the only avowedly anti-abortionist represented. He was in particularly unyielding (and ungenerous) mood, reportedly describing Silkin as 'an old man, a Jew, who had given up practising his religion and, like such men, radical in his views and not caring any longer about the family'. Longford realised that the Government would not risk supporting Silkin's Bill with such a slim Commons majority, and made threatening noises about resigning if the policy of neutrality on the issue were breached.[61]

On the substantive questions raised by the Silkin Bill, ministers rejected a rape clause because it might encourage false allegations of rape to obtain an abortion. According to one voice, it 'might be thought anomalous that a promiscuous girl of fifteen who had consented to intercourse should thereafter be able to have pregnancy terminated lawfully, while the 16-year-old victim of rape would not'. If the present case law were on a statutory footing, however, doctors 'would probably be readier to hold that to bear a child resulting from rape would be detrimental to the mother's health'. They considered the wording in Silkin's Bill allowing for the doctor to consider the 'total environment, actual or foreseeable' too vague, but agreed that social concerns should be tied to the question of maternal health, and that doctors should be entitled to take into account 'all circumstances, present or prospective, relevant to her physical or mental health'. When Cabinet considered the results of the discussion on 3 February, neutrality on the substance of the Bill continued subject to advice on practicality of amendments and the use of parliamentary draftsmen, although ministers would now be allowed to express their personal sympathies either way.[62] The dissolution of Parliament at the end of February intervened, Wingfield Digby's Bill having already been felled by the intervention of two Catholic Labour members from the north-west, the Mahon brothers Peter and Simon.[63]

In the private members' ballot at the beginning of the extended first session of the new Parliament David Steel had come third and, as we have seen, spent some time considering his options. In his memoir, Steel refutes the idea that the abortion issue made much difference at the 1970 general election, saying that the local brouhaha caused by the South African Springboks' rugby tour was far more damaging.[64] The second-reading debate for Steel's abortion Bill was held on 22

July 1966, and was the first full-scale debate on a bill on abortion in the Commons, reflected in the large number of MPs wanting to speak. The majority was overwhelming, 194, but presaged a far more tortuous path than Leo Abse's homosexual reform Bill running parallel with it.

Rather late in the day, the opponents of abortion now mobilised against the Steel Bill. SPUC gained widespread exposure from its inaugural press conference in January 1967. Their explicitly non-Catholic council included the Anglican Bishops of Exeter and Bath and Wells, and prominent gynaecologists including Professor Hugh McLaren of Birmingham University, a Presbyterian father of seven who was particularly active in the programme of meetings and debates which SPUC organised across the country.[65] However, the vociferous and personal nature of many of the attacks made by members of SPUC, particularly some of their Catholic members, had a counterproductive effect on some sections of the public and of Parliament. Iain Macleod, Conservative Shadow Chancellor, writing in his column in the *Daily Mail*, commented, 'I would have thought that it would infuriate any doubter into voting for and not against the Bill.'[66] The activities of SPUC were, however, not as broad-based or sophisticated as those of its opponents. According to Paul Tulley, general secretary at SPUC in 2000, there was little lobbying by them of ministers, MPs and professional groups. Instead they concentrated in their early years on grassroots canvassing of support, organising petitions and encouraging people to write to their MPs individually against the abortion bill.[67] What their tactics lacked in sophistication they made up in fervour. As Gwyneth Dunwoody recalls, 'People don't understand now, I don't think, just exactly how much pressure there was. I was told in my constituency that I was a murderess. You got an absolutely vicious type of letter. A lot of people found it very difficult to deal with that kind of pressure.'[68]

The acceptance of a conscience clause which would allow doctors to decline to perform abortions blunted the absolutist opposition. A greater restraining influence on the progress of the Bill was the non-religious opposition of abortion in Parliament, from Abse in the Commons and Baroness Wootton in the Lords. They were held in extremely high regard in Parliament, especially by reformers and the uncommitted. They did not argue from a condemnatory, absolutist position like Roman Catholics, but saw the danger of abortion in terms of the pernicious eugenic effects that social abortion would have on the deprived groups whom they saw as the targets of abortionists.[69] As Wootton phrased it, 'women in this position who are pregnant may often be subject to very considerable pressure from within the family and sometimes, I think, from doctors who have their own ideas about who ought to have children and who ought not.'[70] They also heartened the more moderate religious opponents of abortion because of their rationalism. Norman St John Stevas, Conservative MP for Chelmsford, later wrote: 'One of the things that has convinced me that the present struggle is more than sectarian has been the support given to me by people of no religion. Lady Wootton is one, Mr Leo Abse is another. I am indeed grateful for their dedication and enthusiasm.'[71]

Others opposed to abortion were less publicly vocal, but no less determined. Shirley Williams' first ministerial post in 1964 was as Kenneth Robinson's Parliamentary Private Secretary, which gave her ample opportunity to argue with him about abortion law reform. As junior minister at the Ministry of Labour after that, she was still active behind the scenes, though she felt the Catholic position was undermined by Pope Paul VI's refusal to countenance artificial birth control.[72] Abse, however, was less generous about some of his opponents. In his memoirs he shows considerable respect for the pro-choice doctor, Glanville Williams, saying of one television debate, 'we ended the occasion with the same quality of mutual regard and esteem for each other as we began.' However, his description of the female pioneers of ALRA and their successors is a less flattering picture of twisted and barren female sexuality: 'The Association was originally dominated by a cluster of intelligent, shrill viragos, Janet Chance, Stella Browne and Alice Jenkins. The three women all resented their feminine identity, and their writing and speeches reveal their keen sense of deprivation.'[73]

There had been little organised interest within the medical profession on abortion before 1965. However, soon after ALRA's publication of the surprising findings of its North West London Group Survey of NHS doctors,[74] there were studies conducted by the Royal Medico-Psychological Association, the BMA, the Royal College of Obstetricians and Gynaecologists (RCOG) and the Medical Women's Federation on Abortion.[75] The resulting reports produced a picture of a partially divided profession, generally supporting some element of reform but more conservative than the general public and MPs. What was becoming apparent was that the medical leadership were also more conservative than their grassroots members. The only medical organisation which staunchly supported radical reform was the Socialist Medical Association, which declared at its annual conference that 'the law on abortion is outdated, unclear, cruel and should be reformed ... We call on the Government to draw up new legislation to enable abortions to be carried out under the NHS before the twelfth week of pregnancy.'[76] Such collective voices were represented by individual Labour MPs with real experience of the horrors of illegal abortion. According to Dunwoody, 'when I was a young doctor's wife large numbers of working-class women did the most horrendous things to themselves ... [Abortion] existed in different ways for those who were able to go into a private clinic and those who had to do terrible things to themselves on a Friday night.'[77]

The cautious concerns of the medical profession were of the utmost importance to the Government, and the doctors' prime concern, their professional autonomy from both the provisions of the law and the demands of the female patient, became a central plank of the Steel Bill as the government sought to remove as many specific provisions for legal abortion from the Bill as possible in order to allow doctors the maximum discretion.[78] The publication of Steel's Bill in November 1966 prompted the BMA and the RCOG to publish a joint report on abortion. Their main target was the social clause, which would require doctors to consider non-medical factors which would be outside their expert knowledge.[79] This was not unwise, considering some doctors' understanding of some non-medical issues. When two doctors from the BMA met Lord Silkin in December 1965 to press him to remove social conditions as grounds for abortion Silkin was 'surprised' when one of them 'referred to the fact that there were adoption societies and other means to look after a child if it were necessary to take it out of the charge of the mother and that this was, therefore, not particularly a ground for an abortion'.[80] Instead the BMA/RCOG report argued that 'account may be taken of the patient's total environment actual or reasonably foreseeable.' This phrase was lifted directly from *Abortion: An Ethical Discussion* – the views of the two most influential interest groups, the medical profession and the Church, had coalesced.[81]

The 'social clause' became the main focus during debates on the Bill between January and April 1967 with many MPs and officials wanting to confine the grounds for legal abortion to those based strictly on health, leaving doctors to take into account the patient's 'total environment'. For critics of easier abortion this satisfied the BMA argument that a social clause contravened medical ethics, and for reformers it allowed liberal doctors sufficient leeway to approve abortion on social grounds. There was no question of allowing the woman to make the decision, only authorised professionals.[82] Division among doctors about whether abortion should be restricted to consultants, something the BMA and the RCOG demanded in a letter to *The Times*, allowed the Home Office to support the sponsors of the Bill in opposing this amendment.[83] The pay-off was that all mention of the 'well-being' of the mother, which Steel had inserted during the committee stage to widen the grounds for abortion in Clause 1(a), was removed. On this point the Ministry of Health agreed with the medical organisations, saying that 'well-being' was unworkable.[84]

David Owen, who in 1974 became health minister under Barbara Castle at the DHSS, and helped her lead a successful rearguard action to protect the Abortion Act from those seeking to reverse it, was a prominent supporter of the Bill, seeking to explain, as he later put it, 'some of the complex medical aspects that underlie the legislation'.[85] Steel's own comment about Owen's contribution to the passage of the Bill is that he 'did not join the [pro-reform] team but supported it in the way he thought best'.[86] Owen also courted controversy by recalling movingly his experiences as a junior doctor in south London:

Only a short distance away I have coached patients to say to the doctor, when asking for a termination, that they are desperate and are thinking of suicide, because I know that doctors will not terminate pregnancy on social grounds. I have seen doctors themselves encourage patients to widen their case – because they do not feel that social grounds are of themselves sufficient.

As the time available in the committee designated for private members' legislation was rapidly eaten away by other bills, Silkin and Dick Crossman agreed to switch the abortion bill to a committee usually reserved for government measures. There the composition of the committee was the first focus of controversy. Members of ALRA felt that Catholics and other opponents were overrepresented, considering the large majority the bill had received, as some of those who had voted for the Bill on second reading turned out to be sceptics who would vote consistently against the Bill's provisions in committee. The Bill emerged from committee in April amended but intact. However, as with Leo Abse's Sexual Offences Bill, there was little chance that it would survive obstruction without extra time being provided by the Government. When Cabinet discussed the Bill on 11 May, along with the various other controversial Private Members' Bills on the go, a decision on Steel's Bill was held back until Roy Jenkins and the Home Affairs Committee had decided how to handle those parts of the Bill that had been amended by MPs.[87] Lord Longford, Willie Ross and other ministers vigorously opposed giving it any further assistance because of the electoral implications. It would give Labour a 'permissive, not to say, beatnik, image which would not go down well in the provinces'. Alternatively, abortion was not important enough to be worth valuable time.[88] The opposition was certainly strong enough to cause Harold Wilson to suspend the rule, which he had himself introduced in 1964, that only the chairman of a Cabinet committee could decide whether an issue on which there was some dissent from the majority should be brought to full Cabinet for further discussion.[89] Longford was being further accommodated. However, despite concern about Catholic opinion both within the Government and in areas like his own constituency of Huyton, Wilson realised that the abortion issue would be raised every session until it had been settled, and that extra parliamentary time would be necessary to allow MPs to come to a conclusion.[90]

Despite Longford's continued complaints, particularly in the light of a new statement by the most senior Anglican bishops in *The Times*, ministers agreed that extra time should be given to the Bill, provided its sponsors were prepared to compromise on the wording of the social clause. They were clearly tiring of the Lord Privy Seal's persistence. As Crossman recorded in his diary: 'He [Longford] made the most menacing speech and when I pointed out that Cabinet was neutral he shouted, "Neutral be blowed. You have all the hierarchy against you. I warn you of it."'[91]

In a rather transparent attempt to prove the Government's neutrality, Crossman and Silkin left the House as soon as debate began on Thursday 29 June in order to keep 'my management above suspicion'.[92] Longford unsurprisingly exercised the latitude given him by Wilson to refer the matter back to Cabinet, despite the majority on the committee for giving time to Steel's Bill.[93] The familiar arguments were deployed once again on 1 July, with Longford adding the weight of opinion demonstrated by the recent petition of over five hundred thousand signatures organised by SPUC. Ross said that he opposed the Bill on the grounds that the law in Scotland, where there were fewer prosecutions for illegal abortion, was satisfactory.[94] It was suggested, not unreasonably, and with a simplicity that was too disarming for abortion's opponents, that the mere fact that there was a free vote on which ministers, and not just backbenchers, would vote in different lobbies, demonstrated the Government's neutrality. Cabinet agreed to give the Bill a night to complete its final Commons stages.[95] In the Chamber before this all-night session, Crossman was asked by Willie Hamilton whether, if this time proved insufficient, the Government would provide further facilities to complete the last stages of the Bill.[96] As he admitted, this caught him unawares, because Steel's supporters had been told, allegedly by Jenkins' Parliamentary Private Secretary, Tom Bradley, that the following Monday would be given if necessary. Crossman accused Jenkins of 'throwing his weight around'.[97] Not something Crossman himself would ever have done, of course. When this did indeed prove insufficient, Cabinet had, once again, to decide the Bill's fate. This time there seems to have been greater agreement that the Bill should be given as much time as necessary in order to forestall any further filibuster. The Government had clearly been persuaded of the PLP's support for the measure by the consistently large votes from Labour MPs during the inconclusive all-night sitting of 29 June. There were also repeated appeals made by sympathetic MPs to the business managers at PLP meetings during June and July.[98] Crossman and Silkin had already discussed the possibility of postponing the parliamentary recess for a week to complete the Bill, exactly what Wilson had said should not happen.[99] The Prime Minister wobbled again, but was stiffened by Jim Callaghan, who reminded him that abortion would haunt the Government until it was settled, and Longford's last 'comical intervention' was thwarted.[100] Unlimited time was provided for the abortion Bill after normal business on Thursday 13 July.

Crossman admitted that the extra time had 'pulled us off our neutrality fence. The Government will be pushing the Bill through and will get the credit or discredit for it'. At Business Questions he clung to 'the fig-leaf of neutrality', as John Boyd-Carpenter, Conservative MP for Kingston-upon-Thames, described it. This was made all the more embarrassing by the 'resounding cheer from our own side organised by Douglas Houghton as a response to the announcement of the all-night sitting'.[101] In the end Anthony Greenwood, Minister of Housing and Local Government, was the only Cabinet minister in the Commons to vote against the Bill on third reading. He was joined in the 'No' lobby by six other ministers including Shirley Williams, now Junior Education Minister, and Bob Mellish, Minister for Public Works, both Roman Catholics.[102]

This was not quite the end of the story. When the Bill returned to the Lords after the summer recess, Lord Dilhorne and his supporters reintroduced a 'consultant clause' and an amendment removing reference to the woman's 'existing children', which were passed by the House before being reversed in the dying days of the session. This threatened a constitutional crisis. In a letter to the *Daily Telegraph*, Lord Salisbury argued that there was a distinction between government legislation which had received an electoral mandate and private members' bills.[103] In a furious reply Lord Silkin refuted these claims, saying:

> *No such distinction is made in the Parliament Act … There can be no doubt that it was the will of the Commons that the Bill should go forward without the amendments passed by the Lords … to insist upon these amendments against the will of the Commons surely involves a constitutional issue which may have far-reaching effects on the House of Lords.*[104]

Silkin was alluding to ongoing discussion about House of Lords reform, which was, once again, running parallel with the discussion of controversial backbench legislation, as it had in 1949–51, and would again after 1997. Whilst the Government was appalled at the prospect of a clash between the two chambers occurring over an issue such as abortion, Crossman had to admit that the Parliament Act could be invoked in such a case.[105] In order not to entangle the Lords reform proposals with the abortion bill, the Government decided to prepare the ground on the former measure with opposition leaders to prevent them using the impasse as ammunition in the abortion debate in the Lords.[106] According to Crossman, however, embittered by defeat in Cabinet and Parliament on abortion, Longford had already leaked the government plans to the Conservatives.[107] Had poor attendance by many peers not reversed the anti-abortion majorities then a crisis might have resulted, which Crossman was personally starting to relish.[108] Significantly for the future implementation of the Bill, Dilhorne and his allies, who had been grappling with the concept of relative risk to the health of the mother, introduced the wording allowing abortion if: 'the continuance of the pregnancy would involve risk … greater than if the pregnancy were terminated.'[109] Their motivation was to allow doctors a clearer basis on which to reach their medical judgement about the need for an abortion. However, the implications of this, considering the increasing safety of the abortion operation, were not immediately realised by the Bill's opponents. Despite Edith Summerskill pointing out the effects of the amendment, Dilhorne ignored it and Lord Waverley used misleading statistics based on those women who were currently seen in hospitals for abortion, who were more likely to be suffering abnormal pregnancy, to dismiss her claim.[110]

Even at this stage, there was considerable disquiet about the legislative result. As one Home Office official commented, Steel's 'inexperience had led to a rather botched-up bill ... because he had not stuck to one line all through'.[111] Leo Abse blamed the 'ham-handed' spinsters from ALRA.[112] Alistair Service admits that more experience of piloting a bill would have given Steel and ALRA a marginally better act.[113] The complexity of the abortion issue, like divorce law reform, and the wide-ranging implications for the NHS and wider government health policy support the argument that this was unsuitable for a private members' bill. It was certainly the Government, and principally Crossman, one of the Bill's most prominent political advocates, who had to shoulder the burden when the Act came into operation in 1968. Very soon there were concerns about commercial exploitation by a rash of new private nursing homes in London, and sensational press stories about forty thousand Danish women being imported to take advantage of the newly relaxed law. Despite the mounting political pressure, DHSS officials were reluctant to intervene in these commercial operations, saying that if they did anything to interfere with the doctors they would be transgressing the Abortion Act itself. Wilson, tipped off by Mellish, now Chief Whip, ordered Crossman not to go on *The World at One* to make a statement about the scare stories because he didn't want him to get too close to the abortion row. However, it was clear, although it took some time for ministers to be informed, that such clinics were essentially fiddling the figures in the notification process, and that the figures which they were giving to Parliament showing the tiny proportion of total abortions involved were not reliable. Crossman hit the roof and, even on his own assessment, was 'rude and violent and unpleasant' to his staff.

> Bea [Baroness Serota, his junior minister] and I are uneasy because we hate this private sector. I think it's outrageous that our Abortion Act should be sullied and smirched by the activities of these money-making commercial doctors, and I ferociously believe that if they refuse to let me discipline them, they should discipline themselves through the GMC.[114]

Not that Crossman had much faith in the General Medical Council bringing doctors into line. He thought the professional body 'disgusting', observing that 'they say there are only two crimes for doctors, advertising and sleeping with other people's wives.' Only by getting the police to crack down on any illegal activities, his other line of approach, would they catch out doctors breaking the terms of the Act. However, he was exasperated, as often, by what he found to be the 'pertinacious' attitude of his own civil servants and those in the Home Office 'who refuse to spy on' the private nursing homes.

The Act's opponents did not waste much time waiting to see how its implementation worked out. In July 1969 Norman St John Stevas tabled a motion under the Ten-Minute Rule to introduce a Bill to restrict approval for abortions to two consultant gynaecologists. This would have the effect of severely restricting the number of abortions which could be performed in the NHS, whilst probably stoking further the private abortion trade. The motion was defeated by only eleven votes on an unusually high turnout because MPs were waiting to vote on a three-line whip on the Finance Bill to implement the Budget.[115] Unbowed by this result, another Tory MP went a stage further than St John Stevas by introducing a bill stipulating that a consultant gynaecologist be present at each abortion operation. Crossman insisted to colleagues that he wanted the Bill talked out because the Act was so new and he didn't want it changed yet. According to Crossman, Wilson, Mellish and Barbara Castle said that there would have to be a free vote, to which he responded that ministers should vote against it, but Wilson objected that ministers couldn't be made to vote for abortion. Jim Callaghan piled in with a characteristic 'I told you so' moan that he had been against giving time to these controversial private members' bills in the first place. Crossman was forced to admit to himself that, although he felt justified in asking that an act which he had to administer should not be tampered with in this way, politically Wilson was right that it had to be a free vote: 'It will be extremely difficult to run the Health Service when part of it can be chopped this way and that by a free vote, and that's something I certainly didn't think of when I was Leader of the House.'[116]

Castle would, in a few years, find herself in a position identical to Crossman's – 'Secretary of State for Abortion', as he felt he was seen by the general public. The only advantage to this soubriquet was that abortion was such a controversial topic that when Crossman made a strong speech supporting the Act in March

1970, saying that it had prevented the birth of twenty thousand illegitimate babies and all the consequent social problems, it overshadowed a row about him reserving for himself a whole first-class carriage on the train from Paddington to Banbury, his home station.[117] In the meantime, the Bill was talked out in the Commons.

*

Dick Crossman was understandably rather more keen to be seen as a Secretary of State for Family Planning. The extension of family planning services is one of the less well-known reforms of the first Wilson administration, and there is little explanation why politicians did not make more of its potential to ameliorate the controversy surrounding the Abortion Bill. Until 1967 local authorities were allowed to provide family planning services only where the mother's health was at risk from pregnancy, rather than on social grounds. In 1966 the Minister of Health, Kenneth Robinson, made clear that he supported such an extension, but that legislation would be needed, and the moral issues involved suggested that it would be more suitable coming from a backbencher than the government. The Labour MP Edwin Brooks duly obliged, introducing a Bill in February 1967 which was largely drafted by the Ministry of Health.[118] The Government was quite happy to approve the financial implications of his Bill but not to assume responsibility for piloting it through Parliament, although Robinson admitted during debate on the Bill that they would have stepped in if Brooks had not, conveniently, beaten them to it. In the words of *The Times*, never can a social reform have received such a loving reception.[119] Only one MP complained that the supply of housing should meet the rate of procreation, rather than the other way round, and no fuss was made about the supply of contraceptive advice and services to the unmarried or to teenagers. Much of the support for the Bill seemed to be motivated by the current scares about the British population rising by one third by the end of the century, and comparison was drawn between the annual cost of an NHS prescription for the contraceptive pill at £3 5s. and of keeping an unwanted child in an adoption home at £600.[120]

However, two years after this Act was passed and over a year after becoming Secretary of State for Health, Crossman made the startling admission that he didn't know the Pill was not on the NHS and that unless people get it through the FPA [Family Planning Association] or through the local authority we make them pay for it. Apparently people usually have to pay a considerable sum themselves. He overturned departmental advice to reject an offer from chemists to begin providing the Pill on prescription, and began to consider how the scheme might work. Officials objected on the grounds of the cost, £5 million, which Crossman thought a bargain for such a social good, although he wondered whether moral qualms lay behind their reluctance.[121] The Chief Medical Officer, George Godber, wrung his hands over family planning, 'saying it was terribly difficult and that there would be major trouble'. He regarded family planning and the Pill as not 'pukkah doctoring of the sort the Ministry deals with'. There was even resistance within the department to publicising the fact that vasectomies were available on the NHS in certain circumstances with medical approval.[122] Promotion of the Pill was, however, increasingly fraught, as some of the health risks associated with some of the high-dose oestrogen pills became known. The former Labour minister Baroness Summerskill and her MP daughter Shirley led a campaign warning of the health risks of the Pill, against the tide of its growing popularity among women, the medical profession and government. *The Times* supported the continued use of the Pill as the most efficient and safe contraceptive available, although it warned, rather unrealistically, that 'it must never be used as a social convenience but when family planning is carefully carried out by a married couple then [its] use is justified from a medical point of view.'[123]

Unsurprisingly, other parts of the media handled such health stories in a more sensationalist way. When the Committee for Safety on Drugs was preparing to release a report on high-dose oestrogen pills, the *Daily Express*'s Chapman Pincher broke the story, leading to thousands of women suddenly coming off the Pill and a massive increase in the number of abortions. At the same time, Professor Victor Wynn, an endocrinologist and expert on the metabolic effects of the Pill, now did the rounds of the TV studios, including not one but three David Frost programmes, talking about the risks to women of thrombosis, depression and cancer. Crossman complained that his officials were overly concerned with the niceties of publishing the information through the medical press and not enough with giving the information in a responsible fashion to women taking the Pill, and he went as far as to write to Charles Hill at the BBC and Bert Bowden at ITV to ask for responsible coverage of the news.[124] Under this political and media pressure, Dr William Inman was rushed into publishing his preliminary findings for the committee, which effectively recommended banning seventeen of the twenty-one pills then on the market in Britain.[125]

If the Ministry of Health tried to resist the pressure for extensive family planning services, the Government had a similar problem dealing with concerns about rising levels of VD and promiscuity among the young. In 1964 a junior Home Office minister, Lord Stonham, had shown unprecedented interest in the problem of the increase of VD among young people by opening a BMA conference on the subject. However, he stated that 'the problem of VD in young people is the concern of everyone, and it does not follow that the best way to tackle it would be by a direct initiative of the Government.' If more instruction in schools were needed, that was the job of the Department of Education, not the Home Office. However, when concerned MP Julian Snow wrote to Crosland as Education Secretary about it, the reply came that the possibility of extending medical advice in schools had not even been discussed at ministry level but that, unsurprisingly, it was the responsibility of local education authorities (LEAs) and schools to decide what sex education and nursing advice was provided. By the late 1960s, however, some LEAs, for example Birmingham, were taking the initiative to promote sex education more rigorously in their schools. At the same time that they were promoting reforms of the abortion and divorce laws, ministers were concerned about the growing numbers of unmarried mothers of school age and the rising rate of divorce among young couples – prior, of course, to the relaxation of the law which was implemented in 1971.[126]

*

Most contemporary commentators and historians see Jennie Lee's tenure as de facto 'Minister for the Arts' as a highly fruitful period when the Government enabled an enormous expansion of the arts, and the theatre in particular, encouraging quality and stylistic innovation as well as quantity.[127] Harold Wilson's support for Lee was, of course, more than matched by that of Lord Goodman, Chairman of the Arts Council, who worked very closely with and, indeed, was in love with her.[128] However, the expansion of national and local state subsidy of the theatre involved, in Lee's terms, a good deal of discrimination.[129] At a time when the continued pre-censorship of plays was seen as increasingly absurd, the control of policy and subsidy could be used by various interested parties to stifle writing which was considered unsuitable. Local councils could, and did, withhold or withdraw grants to productions. For example in August 1968 Waltham Forest Borough Council, which had been captured from Labour by the Conservatives in the previous year's local elections, refused the necessary grant for the local youth theatre company to stage Edward Bond's *Saved*. That play's violent and foul-mouthed West End reputation no doubt failed to endear it to the borough's councillors (though whether they had actually read the script or seen the production is doubtful).[130]

The heavily subsidised national companies and others quickly presumed that their grants were sacrosanct and bound to expand as their ambitions did.[131] As these were the companies which were producing the most experimental and, for the censor, risqué plays, there was inevitable conflict between the role of the Lord Chamberlain's Office and the more liberal, artistic priorities of the Arts Council as a grant-making body. These came to a head over the legal challenge made by the authorities to the use of private theatre clubs to stage unlicensed plays in 1966–7, when Goodman took the decision to stop funding such productions because of a court ruling against their legality.[132] Even the subsidised companies exercised their own forms of censorship. John Osborne's creative dynamism, it has been argued, was impeded by the commercial priorities of the Royal Court Theatre.[133] Furthermore, the National Theatre, without the coercion of the Lord Chamberlain, refused to produce Rolf Hochhuth's *Soldiers* because of the implication that General Sikorski's death during the Second World War was the responsibility of Winston Churchill. The National Theatre's chairman, Lord Chandos, had been a member of the wartime Coalition Government with Churchill and Lord Cherwell, both portrayed in the play.[134] When the Royal Shakespeare Company and the Royal Court expanded their 'club' performances and their unrestricted membership, the new Lord Chamberlain, Lord Cobbold, felt compelled to act against any unlicensed production where paid acting and charging was involved, which technically breached the 1843 Theatres Act. The Royal Court staged Osborne's *A Patriot for Me* in 1965 under the thin disguise of a private theatre club production after a licence had been refused because of two significant scenes in which physical homosexuality was displayed and which 'exploited the subject',[135] contrary to the terms under which Scarbrough had relaxed the censorship in 1958.[136] Both the Lord Chamberlain and the Director of

Public Prosecutions, Sir Norman Skelhorn, were of the opinion that a successful prosecution was likely against the theatre.[137] However, the Attorney General, Sir Elwyn Jones, and the Solicitor General, Sir Dingle Foot (who had introduced the last private members' bill for abolition in 1962), decided for political reasons not to proceed: 'We were strongly of the opinion that it would be inexpedient to institute such a prosecution in connection with a play which had attracted a great deal of public interest and a good deal of support and had, in any case been running for some time.'[138]

The production of *Saved* as an eight-week run 'club performance' at the Royal Court, which followed soon after *A Patriot for Me*, was a step too far for the Lord Chamberlain and Ministers. Cobbold pointedly said that if no action were taken against such productions then the 1843 Act would be difficult to administer (as if it had been easy before),[139] and suggested that an intervention might 'serve to mark a point of principle and hold the line'. Jones still moved carefully, worried about stirring controversy against the current regime, and argued for a fresh inquiry along the lines of the 1909 select committee.[140] The Home Office's view of the position seems to have changed little since reform was last discussed in 1958. Commenting on the Attorney General's letter, an official note remarked:

> *Our view has always been that it would be best to let sleeping dogs lie; we continue to receive very few complaints ... This does not mean that there is not some rumbling dissatisfaction in literary or dramatic circles which finds occasional expression, but certainly there is no evidence yet of what could be described as a campaign.*[141]

This display of Civil Service *sangfroid* against all the evidence of which way the wind was blowing at least chimed in with the thoughts of Sir Frank Soskice, Home Secretary at the time. When Soskice, Foot and Lord Gardiner, the Lord Chancellor, met to discuss the matter, Soskice cheerfully argued that 'it continued to work by and large remarkably well.' He concluded that 'as regards an inquiry, his greatest fear was that the wrong sort of public interest would be aroused by it and pressures thus engendered which would result in the institution of a fresh system which, though more logical than the present one, would be effectively more onerous.'

Foot and Gardiner, who later married the film-director and Oscar-winning co-writer of *The Seventh Veil*, Muriel Box, were much more positive about reform. Foot attempted to mollify Soskice by saying that what he proposed would retain a voluntary use of the Lord Chamberlain's licensing system to protect producers against libel. The Lord Chancellor, however, made a special plea for improvisation and spontaneity in the theatre. At a meeting with the Home Secretary in November 1965, Cobbold threatened to go public about his concerns. He continued to support an inquiry, in conjunction with proceedings against the Royal Court, but, in a remark that sums up neatly the blindness of successive Lord Chamberlains, ministers and officials to the anachronistic position of the Lord Chamberlain being responsible for censoring stage plays, he said that

> *any inquiry should be handled in such a way that The Crown should not in any way whatsoever be thought to be implicated: he and his predecessors, though Court Officers, had always sought to disassociate their public function as theatre censors from their other functions as Officers of the Household.*[142]

It simply did not register that the public, press, actors and playwrights did not make such a distinction between public and royal duties, and for the changing social and political mores of the 1960s it was the Lord Chamberlain's complete identification with 'the Establishment' which the censorship protected that barred him from performing such a function, were that function necessary at all.

From the end of 1965 supporters and opponents of reform or abolition were beginning to press the Government for some resolution of the absurd anomalies and contradictions of the powers exercised by the Lord Chamberlain. As William Gaskill observed in his memoirs, 'the *Saved* affair had brought to a head the case against the Lord Chamberlain's power of pre-censorship. The following three years were dominated by the fight to break his power.'[143]

The decision to ban *Saved* had been a swift one. Eric Penn, Comptroller General, and Lord Nugent, his predecessor, found the language and plot revolting, particularly the scene where a baby is stoned to death in its pram. But even in this case there was some uncertainty about refusing the play a licence. Nugent worried that because the themes of 'hopelessness, fecklessness and the complete amorality which springs from them' had been broached before they should grant a licence with the script 'cut to ribbons', even though this would allow the 'tasteless' George Devine managing director of the Royal Court to put it on as a club performance.[144] Cobbold was 'not disposed to compromise very much' with *Saved*. Following the prosecution of the Royal Court in April 1966, the Lord Chamberlain's Office was inundated with requests for clarification about the legal status of the play and the exact conditions under which club performances would be tolerated by the Lord Chamberlain, principally by university theatrical companies. His responses to these letters were often opaque, and failed to correct the common misapprehension that the Lord Chamberlain, rather than the DPP on the advice of the Attorney General, instituted criminal proceedings.[145] This confusion, resulting from the lack of detailed rules by which the censorship operated, was compounded, in Lord Goodman's words, by the fact that 'the authorities have exercised a considerable element of caprice in the past.'[146]

Despite some prevarication Harold Wilson had not been hostile to reform when challenged by several MPs over the position of the Lord Chamberlain in July 1965,[147] and continued to be supportive of Jennie Lee's arts policy, despite the Arts Council's increasing largesse towards companies producing avant-garde and controversial works. In response to William Hamling, Labour MP for Woolwich West, in November, he virtually committed the Government to an inquiry.[148] The Attorney General outlined in his memo to the Home Secretary in October 1965 the criticism levelled against the censorship in terms which showed the anachronistic position in which theatre stood when compared to other media in the modern world:

1. Censorship applies only to the theatre. Nowadays a play vetoed by the Lord Chamberlain may not be performed on the stage before a few hundred spectators. But it can appear before millions of viewers of the television screen.

2. No other country censors stage plays. The result is that a play which can appear in Washington, or in any other capital, may be prohibited in London.

3. The rules laid down from time to time by the Lord Chamberlain appear to many people to be quite absurd. For example, no representation of the Deity or of the head of a foreign State can appear on the British stage.

His suggested approach, given the messy position in which the law, the Lord Chamberlain and the Government found themselves, was a fresh inquiry into the subject, either a Royal Commission or, he commented rather wearily, 'a Committee of Inquiry of a type with which we are all very familiar'. However, there had been some concern within the Government to avoid an investigation into theatre censorship until the current furore caused by Mary Whitehouse's 'Clean up TV' campaign had subsided.[149] Cobbold had already expressed his view that this was an opportune moment for a broader inquiry to include all the arts, including film and broadcasting. A more partisan view came from the Scottish Secretary, Willie Ross. In response to Soskice's draft paper to the Home Affairs Committee, Ross said that Scottish opinion favoured greater restriction for television than for the stage. He was strongly suspicious that Soskice's motives were to relax the censorship:

> I do not dissent form your main thesis that public attitudes and social custom have changed so much since 1843 that a review of the Theatres Act is overdue … [But] if we touch this subject at all, what we need, I think, is an examination of the whole question of what control over entertainments modern society requires, or is prepared to accept, in the interests of public morality and decency.[150]

The Home Affairs Committee of the Cabinet was anxious to prevent the widening of any inquiry, despite the fact that this would delay reform of theatre censorship, which it supported.[151]

However, two events precipitated swifter action. The first was the replacement of Soskice by Jenkins in December 1965. The fact that the new Home Secretary had been instrumental in reform of the obscenity laws in 1959 heralded a new attitude across Whitehall to action against suspect literary targets, as Alan Travis has revealed in *Bound and Gagged*.[152] Jenkins saw an inquiry in theatre censorship as essential once proceedings were launched against the Royal Court Theatre in January in respect of *Saved*. He took his cue from Wilson's positive responses to parliamentary questions, and suggested the inquiry be limited to London theatre, which would cut out the necessity of hostile Scottish representation on the inquiry committee.[153] Having pressed forward with the progress of private members' Bills on abortion and homosexuality,[154] Jenkins turned to theatre

censorship at his second Home Affairs Committee meeting. Using the proceedings against the Royal Court as a reinforcement of the case for launching an
inquiry, he argued that 'it should be possible to confine the inquiry to theatre
censorship on the ground that the arrangements in this field, unlike those for
films and broadcasting, were plainly outmoded.'

The second spur to action was the pressure being exerted by Cobbold to
delegate his powers of pre-censorship to some form of 'board of theatre censors'
like the BBFC whilst the future of the censorship was decided. His own view was
that such a board might be a longer-term solution. This idea was backed by both
archbishops and senior Methodists.[155] However, Jenkins argued that the
Government must take the initiative. The Lord Chancellor was more direct. His
Private Secretary reported to the Home Office his minister's view that to anyone
'interested in the free expression of ideas in the theatre, a Board of Theatre
Censors would be as objectionable as the present censorship. What he actually
said was "Over my dead body".'[156]

The main opposition to reform was coming from Whitehouse and those who
found the contemporary theatre's profanity, sex, violence and attacks on religion
and the Royal Family outrageous, and from a number of theatre managers, who
feared the removal of protection from libel and obscenity laws and the growth of
local watch committees.[157]

In the debate in the House of Lords which was used to air the proposal of an
inquiry, many crossbenchers and Conservatives, including Lord Scarbrough, Lord
Harlech, chairman of the National Theatre and the BBFC, and Lord Dilhorne, a
former Conservative Lord Chancellor, favoured some system of censorship. Other
crossbench, Labour and Liberal peers were generally more abolitionist, but with
some reservations about the actual effects on artists' freedom and the protection
afforded to ordinary people. Lord Kennet, the writer Wayland Young pointed to
the fact that the only other non-Communist Western country which operated a
system of pre-censorship of the theatre was Franco's Spain.[158] The composition of
the joint committee, when it was finally announced in July 1966, pointed immediately to abolition. Only Lords Scarbrough, Kilmuir (who was replaced by Lord
Brooke on his death in 1967) and Tweedsmuir, plus Sir David Renton,
Conservative MP for Huntingdonshire and Home Office minister from 1958 to
1962, were obviously pro-censorship out of a total membership of sixteen. The
only evidence, oral or written, submitted to the committee which supported the

existing system was from the Society of West End Theatre Managers, who saw the censorship as protection against prosecution and local watch committees, and the Association of Municipal Corporations.[159] Even the apprehensive Church of England had come to the conclusion that 'it would be morally healthy for the nation both if responsibility for maintaining standards were transferred to the theatrical profession itself and also if the adult population were faced with the choice of condemning by withholding patronage.'[160]

Cobbold was a lone voice for the continuation of pre-censorship by another body than the Lord Chamberlain's office. But his suggestion that this might be the Arts Council because of its independence and good relationship with the theatre drew a swift rejection by Lord Goodman, precisely because the Arts Council was independent and had a good relationship with the theatre.[161]

The Committee's report was finally published officially in the autumn of 1967, but its findings were made public in June 1967, very soon after its final deliberations. The report was sanguine and rational about the future position of the theatre without pre-censorship:

> *Censorship in the widest sense of the word will inevitably continue and by various means control will be exercised over what appears on the stage. Managements will continue to refuse to put on plays whenever they think fit. Theatre critics will continue to describe plays as they wish. The public will be free to refuse to attend plays or to walk out if they do not like them. Finally the courts will have the task of ensuring that those responsible for presenting plays which transgress the law of the land will receive appropriate punishment.*[162]

There was no swift end, however, to pre-censorship of the theatre. Summonses were eventually issued against the Royal Court Theatre in respect of *Saved* in January 1966. The position of 'private club' performances was not entirely clarified by the judgment which followed in April 1966 – that any unlicensed public productions were illegal, and the fig-leaf of a 'private theatre club' gave no protection against prosecution. What actually constituted a public rather than a private performance was not clear. In the event, both the Lord Chamberlain and many producers backed off. Cobbold desisted from further prosecutions, but warned the Vaudeville Theatre not to accept a transfer from the Royal Court of a 'private' production of the satire *America Hurrah*.[163] The ruling alarmed the

Arts Councils, which in England, Wales and Scotland were financing such productions. The Scottish Arts Council decided to continue its grant to the Edinburgh Traverse Theatre Club.[164] Goodman consulted Cobbold, who indicated his willingness to seek a prosecution again if he thought necessary. This persuaded Goodman that the Arts Councils should end all grants to theatre clubs.[165]

However, during the spring and summer of 1967, around the time the report's findings were made public, there was increasing concern raised among ministers about the protection of living persons after abolition of pre-censorship. This had been one of Cobbold's main concerns in the evidence he gave to the Committee.[166] But he received little encouragement to press the issue until the controversy stirred up by Richard Ingrams and John Wells's play *Mrs Wilson's Diary*. This was a rather gentle satire, nevertheless described by the Lord Chamberlain's office as 'so cheap and gratuitously nasty, and so completely worthless that it is not recommended for licence',[167] in which the *dramatis personae* included the Prime Minister and his wife, the Foreign Secretary, George Brown, Jim and Audrey Callaghan, and the Governor of the Bank of England, Lord Cromer (coincidentally the son of the previous Lord Chamberlain but two).[168] Cobbold sent the script to the Prime Minister for those portrayed to comment on, as was the practice with plays depicting living persons.[169]

By the time it had been vetted by the Wilsons, the Callaghans, Brown and even George Wigg, Wilson's insidious security adviser, eight scenes had been excised from the script.[170] The 'Balmoral Game' scene, in which the Wilsons were entertaining the Callaghans and Brown, went:

Harold: Ah, Audrey, do come in. We were just playing a little game we picked up during our brief stay at Balmoral Castle. It's called Crawling Round Under The Table Pretending You're Drunk.

George: Yes. I've been playing it for years.

Audrey: I think a little drink is called for.

The Lord Chamberlain agreed the scene should go, saying it was one thing to make fun of Brown's addiction – 'which I suppose every one knows' – but he was not going to have the Royal Family portrayed in that light. Nor would he allow a spoof poem by Mary Wilson on similar grounds:

And who should it be
Just in time for tea,
Harold makes a deep low bow
Her face turns green,
It was Her Majesty the Queen
Cos we're in the Big Time now

A song about Brown's drinking and womanising which was also deleted by the Foreign Secretary, who reportedly commented defensively to Harold Wilson that he had 'had just about enough of this sort of thing',[171] went:

So off I do my business
With the nation's good at heart
I'm tanked up to the brim,
Bloody, resolute and grim
A bastard, a master of art.
I'm the toast of every lady
When I am out on the town
So brothers you may laugh
But I'm a member and a half.
I'm the redoubtable,
The colourful,
The flamboyant,
The excitable,
Drunken Mr Brown.

This was replaced with the arguably funnier:

So brothers you may laugh
But I'll just have a half.
I'm the sober,
The statesmanlike,

The responsible,
The reliable,
Sagacious Mr Brown.[172]

Cobbold, having discussed the play with Michael Palliser, one of Wilson's private secretaries, concluded that refusing a licence would be unwise and futile, since it would only be produced as a club performance. Wilson, in any case, was content to leave the decision to Cobbold's discretion.[173] As Examiner Fletcher remarked over Rolf Hochhuth's *Soldiers*, 'where there is a political context to a play the Lord Chamberlain is at his weakest, since the last thing he can afford to be accused of is political bias.'[174] The Prime Minister, however, did lead a rearguard action to see a clause protecting living persons inserted into any bill. In July he requested information on the division of opinion within the Home Affairs Committee on the issue. The reply came that only Wigg favoured some restrictions, and both the Home Secretary and Patrick Gordon-Walker, former Foreign Secretary and now Minister without Portfolio, pointed out the anomalies that would arise with other media. Wilson's Private Secretary, Peter Le Cheminant, had to point out to Wilson that it had been Labour backbenchers who had insisted on a living-persons clause being removed from the Television Act in 1963, which recast the law relating to commercial television, which had previously been unable to broadcast satirical programmes like *That Was The Week That Was*.[175] The report was discussed by Cabinet on 27 July, where Wilson followed the usual line about heads of foreign states and the sovereign, adding, 'While no exception could be taken to political satire as such, plays portraying public men for purposes of political advantage or private malice might well do harm to the public interest.'[176]

This meeting coincided with the submission to the Lord Chamberlain's office of Ronald Millar's adaptation of William Clark's novel *Number 10*. The scrupulousness with which the Lord Chamberlain prohibited reference to foreign states was reiterated by the requested alteration of the name of the capital city of the fictional country in *Number 10* from Lusaka to the inoffensive Lusimba. This despite Clark's assurance that he had 'sent my friend Kenneth Kaunda [President of Zambia] an inscribed copy of the novel and got a grateful reply.'[177] Examiner Heriot, consistently the Lord Chamberlain's official with the most liberal outlook and driest sense of humour, failed to see what could be objected to in *Number 10*, commenting in his report that *this seems to me to be an amusing, exciting play without any personal axes to grind. I do not know why the Commonwealth Office should be 'interested' in it – but admit that, politically speaking, I am a moron, and that the interplay behind the scenes may be either too close to life or too flagrantly false to it.*[178]

Wilson was assisted by the gentle urgings of Cobbold, and the convenient legal assistance of Lord Goodman, who produced a draft amendment on living persons.[179] Against this Jenkins explained that, as a matter of principle, different media should be treated equally. In practical terms the protection of living persons was objectionable because of the popularity of political satire and the intransigence of many MPs, especially George Strauss, Labour MP for Lambeth and the sponsor of the Theatres Bill, not to mention the difficulty of casting a workable solution.[180]

The wielding of the prime ministerial axe, or, more to Wilson's style, the shuffling of the ministerial cards, intervened at the end of November 1967, Jim Callaghan resigning as Chancellor of the Exchequer after the humiliating devaluation of the pound, and swapping places with Jenkins.[181] This might have been expected to strengthen the hand of the Prime Minister and a living persons clause, given Callaghan's own outlook compared to Jenkins'. However, this does not seem to have been the case. Callaghan gave assurances to Cobbold at a meeting shortly before Christmas that he would raise the matter in Cabinet. This he did on 21 December, but, although still keeping the door open to such a clause, Callaghan clearly sided with Jenkins, the minutes recording that 'he agreed with his predecessor's conclusion that the best course of action was to make defamation in a play ... a ground for libel.'[182]

Strauss's Bill did not receive its second reading until 23 February 1968. It became clear to Wilson and Cobbold individually that the main pressure was now that of parliamentary time. The Lord Chamberlain pressed the Prime Minister on this, emphasising that if the Bill were not passed that session he 'would have to continue with his responsibilities as Lord Chamberlain for censorship in circumstances when everyone knew that a bill was about to be passed and would in consequence cause not only embarrassment to himself but would bring the existing law – about to be amended – into disrepute'.[183] Wilson realised that, having started on the road to abolition, the Bill had to be passed, and assisted in having the Bill moved from the normal committee for private members' legislation to another standing committee. Despite amendments put down by Cobbold in the Lords and Norman St John Stevas, Conservative MP for Chelmsford, in the Commons on living persons, the Bill emerged untarnished and received royal assent on 26 July.[184]

*

If Roy Jenkins, as Home Secretary, was the Labour minister most closely identified with homosexual and abortion law reform, then Lord Gardiner, as Lord Chancellor from 1964 to 1970, was the minister who made the running on divorce. As with Jenkins' *The Labour Case* in 1959, Gardiner had set out a comprehensive plan of law reform for a new Labour administration in *Law Reform Now*.[185] Gardiner's four immediate objectives as Lord Chancellor were to abolish capital punishment, to establish the Law Commission, to reform the system of assizes and quarter sessions and to alter the divorce law. By the time of Labour's 1970 defeat, all these, and many other reform proposals, had been implemented.[186] Compared to most of his colleagues, Gardiner had a strike rate in another league of an administration of notable disappointments and failures. The main instrument for executing this plan was the Law Commission, consciously modelled on such bodies in other countries. The first President of the Law Commission was Sir Leslie Scarman, a similarly liberal lawyer with immense practical experience on which to draw in the enormous task of modernising English law. Scarman himself was bullish about the impetus which the Commission could give to legislative reform, saying that its work would improve communication between courts and legislature, as well as advising 'an amateur and indolent' Parliament on law reform and spurring it into action.[187] As Sir Brian Cubbon says, the Commission was just the first of a series of arm's length bodies which governments increasingly trusted with overseeing reform.[188] Its detachment from government made it better placed than the short-termist and politically febrile House of Commons or government ministers to initiate and develop reform touching on controversial issues of the family and morality. The radicalism of the Law Commission's work on its inception reflected the Government's own instincts and policy in this area and the general demand for the law to catch up with the huge social changes the country had undergone since the war after a period of Conservative timidity and complacency. It stands as one of the most durable results of the 1964–70 administration.

One of the main planks of the Commission's work, as Gardiner and Andrew Martin had proposed, was family law. The aim was to reflect the modern recognition (in theory) of equality of men and women in marriage, and the elevation of the status of children above that of mere property. However, in the field of divorce the Commission felt it wise to wait until a group appointed by the Archbishop of Canterbury, Michael Ramsey, had published a report before presenting its own proposals.[189]

Putting Asunder was a seminal document in that it recognised for the first time the fact that secular divorce law could no longer be dictated by a religious ideal: 'In a modern plural society the concept of human law is very different from that which is obtained when the traditional theology of law was being formulated.' The group recommended that 'breakdown of marriage' be substituted for matrimonial offence.[190] This confluence of the thinking of the established Church with reformist opinion paved the way for the introduction of a bill with some chance of becoming law. However, the system of administration recommended in *Putting Asunder*, that the courts should hold an inquest to determine whether a marriage had reached the point of irretrievable breakdown, was both impractical and inquisitorial in a paternalistic way, which divorce reform was supposed to move away from.[191]

The speedy publication of the Law Commission's own report, *The Field of Choice*, pointed up these shortcomings, and while it presented three options for consideration by Government and Parliament – divorce by consent, divorce based on separation, and irretrievable breakdown of marriage without an inquest – it hesitated to favour one option until the various proposals had been debated.[192] At this point Gardiner began to get restive about the increasing range of options on offer and the lack of progress. Shortly before the House of Lords debated these two reports in November 1966, the Cabinet's Home Affairs Committee discussed what the Government line should be. Gardiner, strongly supported by colleagues, argued that divorce should not be left to the vagaries of a private members' bill. The importance of divorce, the implications for wider family law and social policy and the exhaustive nature of deliberations so far meant that the time had come for the Government to take charge of legislation on divorce itself. He proposed that after the Lords debate the Government should bring forward its own bill and, incidentally, take a more positive line on other areas involving issues of conscience.[193]

A gradual consensus built up during the first half of 1967, based on the expressions of optimism of key figures in the House of Lords debate in November 1966.[194] The Law Commission and the Archbishop of Canterbury's Group thrashed out a joint set of proposals, published in June 1967, in which the Church's proposed inquests were dropped and the old matrimonial offences retained as evidence of breakdown of marriage.[195] Gardiner presented these proposals to the annual conference of the National Marriage Guidance Council (NMGC), with a passionate personal statement of support. However, even his radicalism was somewhat tempered. He strongly supported the proposal that the traditional matrimonial offences should be treated as evidence of breakdown, saying that they 'are often very reliable indications that the marriage has, in fact, broken down … such offences could be used by the law as guide posts – pointing in the absence of evidence to the contrary, or forgiveness, to breakdown.'[196] Similarly the Law Commission had recoiled from the idea that divorce by consent should be the sole ground for divorce, arguing that this 'might lead to the dissolution of marriages that had not broken down irretrievably'.[197] The courts still held the power of discretion over petitions if errant behaviour did not prove to be satisfactory evidence of 'irretrievable breakdown'. It was a fudge, but at least for reformers a radical fudge.

A solution was frustrated for two years because of the complexity of the issues involved. Ramsey was particularly concerned that the issues should be thoroughly discussed before a bill was introduced, partly because this would prevent the mobilisation of Church opinion against reform.[198] In addition, opposition from women's groups to divorce reform, a 'Casanova's Charter' as Baroness Summerskill called it, without prior reform of the financial provisions for divorced spouses, combined with outright opponents of reform.[199] Cabinet approved the drafting of a bill to be given to a private member, William Wilson, partly due to the absence of notable opponents of reform, especially Scottish Secretary, Willie Ross.[200] Wilson's constituency neighbour, Dick Crossman, chivvying the reformers, argued that a 'substantial' second-reading majority would justify the provision of sufficient government time to enable the House to come to a decision on it.[201] However, Wilson's Bill was thwarted at its report stage. Opposition from women's groups had been mollified by the provision that a divorce would only be granted when the court was satisfied that an adequate settlement had been made.[202] The main problem was the wider political weather, which was deteriorating rapidly for the Government.

Jim Callaghan, although no 'saboteur' according to Roy Jenkins, was, as we have seen, no enthusiast for 'permissive' reforms.[203] Except for the final abolition of capital punishment in 1969, no mention is made of them in his memoirs.[204] His official biographer, Kenneth O. Morgan, depicts a tolerant man who was alarmed at the idea of liberal reform meaning any more than tolerance for involuntary moral deviance.[205] Callaghan's standing, which fell as a result of devaluation, was revived in 1968 following his calm handling of the Grosvenor Square Vietnam demonstration in March. The student protest threat was never on the same scale in Britain as those which faced the French or US Governments during the late 1960s. British officials at the Foreign and Commonwealth Office were sanguine about danger to universities and the wider social order, saying that 'the reaction of the broad mass of British students to the disturbances at Grosvenor Square suggests that at present at least an explosion on the scale of the Sorbonne is unlikely to happen here.'[206] Ministers resisted plans by other European administrations to meet the student leaders, thinking this would strengthen the protestors' hand.[207] Whilst officials conceded that there was resentment at 'the survival of Victorian ideas of student discipline, and in dissatisfaction with the level of student grants', there were key differences in between British and continental student populations. These included a more socially mixed profile of students in Britain, leading Shirley Williams to conclude that 'student effervescence [on the continent] seemed therefore curiously to be a function of the proportion of students of "bourgeois" origins.'[208] The main official means of channelling the rising power of students and teenagers which the Government endorsed was the Latey Committee on the Age of Majority. This recommended the lowering of the age of majority from twenty-one to eighteen, concluding that

> by eighteen most young people are ready for these responsibilities and rights
> and would greatly profit by them as would the teaching authorities, the
> business community, the administration of justice, and the community as a
> whole.[209]

As Bea Serota, one of the members of the Latey Committee emphasised, this inquiry comprised one of the most important reforming episodes of the 1960s.[210] In July 1968 the Government announced that it planned to make a similar reduction in the age at which people could vote although, as was generally unappreciated, because of the length of the period between elections, the effect of this was in reality the reduction in the average age of first voting from 23½ to between 20½ and 21. Hardly the revolution. Harold Wilson is commonly accused of making the cynical calculation that these new voters were more likely to vote Labour. Willie Ross, for one, disowned any interest in the suggestion that young people in Scotland might 'go nationalist'.[211]

Callaghan famously drew a line in the sand when Baroness Wootton's report on drugs recommended reducing the penalties for cannabis offences and making a clearer distinction between soft and hard drugs. Unusually, when the report was published in January 1969, Callaghan made a statement within days to make clear his opposition to this part of her proposals, saying that it was time to halt the 'advancing tide of permissiveness' and that Wootton had been over-influenced by a 'pro-pot lobby'.[212] No politician would touch the cannabis issue again for over three decades until David Blunkett began to take on board the argument first made by Wootton that a distinction should be drawn between cannabis and harder, more pernicious drugs, in 2002. However, any public disquiet at the legislative encouragement of permissiveness, or the excesses of student protests and the counter-culture were, according to David Butler, less detrimental to the Labour Government's performance at the 1970 poll than the anti-establishment feelings of the early 1960s against the Conservatives.[213]

Another significant change in 1968, in April, was the replacement of Crossman as Leader of the House with Fred Peart, no enthusiast for these reforms either,[214] although he was eventually helpful towards the divorce bill introduced in the autumn of 1968.[215] Then in April 1969 Harold Wilson demoted the congenial Chief Whip, John Silkin, to the Ministry of Public Buildings and Works, and replaced him with Bob Mellish, a Catholic opponent of abortion and divorce.[216] Dingle Foot had been replaced by Sir Arthur Irvine as Solicitor General earlier in 1967. This meant the substitution of a declared opponent of the 1967 divorce bill for an ardent reformer in an important legal post. Irvine had briefly been a member of the Archbishop of Canterbury's Group, which produced *Putting Asunder*. However, he resigned from it after only a few months, having realised that the direction of its deliberations was leading towards the principle of matrimonial breakdown, with which he would be 'out of sympathy'.[217] Whilst speaking for the Government during the second reading debate of William Wilson's Bill in February 1968 he expressed his personal ambivalence towards reform.[218] With Lord Gardiner so publicly in the vanguard of reform, such confusion caused a complete rethink of the position of ministers during debate on private members' bills.

The 1967–8 session was the period of devaluation, violence in Northern Ireland and continued crises in Vietnam and Rhodesia. It was also subject to a heavy load of government legislation at a time when Labour supporters were becoming increasingly disillusioned with Harold Wilson's leadership. Reform in the field of personal behaviour and relationships, marginal at the best of times to most politicians, came to be seen by some Labour MPs and ministers as an irrelevant distraction.[219] Callaghan was also under intense pressure on yet another front in 1968 – immigration. Many of his Labour colleagues were appalled at the restrictive measures which he took in the Commonwealth Immigration Bill that year, which would have particular effect on the Indian Ugandans under pressure from Idi Amin. Shirley Williams said privately that she would resign, along with a number of other ministers, mostly other women, if there was a threat to their livelihoods. This exacted a concession from Callaghan on the record that if such developments occurred, Britain would accept these people, a commitment which was honoured by Ted Heath, much to the horror of some of his own party.[220]

Once abortion law reform seemed secure, the parliamentary officer for ALRA, Alistair Service, offered his skills to the Divorce Law Reform Union (DLRU) in a similar capacity, when David Steel's abortion Bill became law.[221] He reinvigorated the union, just as a new, younger generation of women had done to the ALRA in the early 1960s after their lengthy campaign became stale and dispirited. There was considerable interest in the press about Service, with laudatory comments by Madeleine Simms and others about his 'value and dedication'.[222] Leo Abse described Service as 'a charming political voyeur with considerable lobbying skill'.[223] During the passage of William Wilson's Bill, Service and his colleagues were deeply involved in press correspondence and motivating, persuading and cajoling wavering supporters. They also filled in some alarming gaps in the understanding by the sponsors of the Bill of the grounds for divorce contained in it.[224] Service was particularly subtle at 'smoke and mirrors' tactics, convincing MPs that their qualms had been addressed, even if no ground had been given. Service was active in 'educating' an important group of supporters in the House of Lords, including Baronesses Stocks, Serota, Birk and Gaitskell, in the details particularly of the financial safeguards in the proposed Bill, which would be important to winning round sceptical women's organisations, who feared that divorce without consent even after five years would encourage middle-aged men to abandon their wives for younger women.[225] Where supporters of the Bill described this provision as divorce after 'long separation', Baroness Summerskill described it as divorce by 'compulsion'. Representing the Married Women's Association (MWA) she had doughtily campaigned against Abse's 1963 Bill, including the 'kiss and make up' reconciliation clause which women's groups felt acted as an extra boon to adulterous husbands.[226] She was ably matched in the Commons by her daughter, Dr Shirley Summerskill, MP for Halifax. Abse and Service were concerned before the second reading of Wilson's Bill that Baroness Summerskill was deciding the major issue, whereas they wished to keep the debate focused on the substantive grounds for divorce.[227]

However, it is difficult not to gain the impression from her speeches in the Lords and from her memoirs that the concentration on campaigning for financial safeguards, which was supported by almost all, was less important than the moral concerns about the damage to the institutions of marriage and the family, which more conservative women's groups such as the MWA avowed.[228] Abse characterised their position: 'Just as a death certificate records the death of the individual, so does a divorce only record the death of a marriage … [they] would believe death certificates caused death.'[229]

Despite the vocal and well-organised lobby of Summerskill and the conservative MWA, who justifiably pointed to the long-term dependency of many married women, other women's groups supported the reformers' argument that married women stood to benefit from a new divorce act as much as men, and that statistics from Scandinavian countries which had already liberalised their divorce laws proved this. In February 1968 the National Council of Women approved irretrievable breakdown of marriage as the only ground for divorce.[230] The National Joint Committee of Working Women's Organisations, affiliated to the National Labour Women's Advisory Committee, actively supported divorce reform once they were satisfied that adequate financial safeguards were in place.

The pressure brought to bear by women's groups on the divorce bills was intensified by the assistance they received from the Church of England. Other denominations, notably the Methodist Church, rallied to the proposals in *Putting Asunder*, and official Roman Catholic doctrine on divorce could not prevent prominent Catholics such as Lord Iddesleigh agreeing that, despite personal convictions, reform was inevitable.[231] More ardent (convert) Catholics remained orthodox, Lord Longford blindly arguing that his position might be a Roman Catholic one, but of course that was the general opinion of millions across the country. The more mainstream Catholic view was that, despite the abandonment of full inquests into the breakdown of a marriage, reform would achieve the eradication of deceit by couples.[232] This accommodation between the religious and the secular was further smoothed by the successful negotiations between the Law Commission and the Archbishop's Group, which was chaired by the Bishop of Exeter, Robert Mortimer. However, Archbishop Ramsey found the emerging proposals hard to stomach and he shied away from consultation with the other Churches, damaging his reputation for ecumenical cooperation.[233] Ramsey's was not the only important source of dissent from the tide which seemed to be sweeping the Church towards divorce by consent. Canon Bryan Bentley, who had served on the Archbishop's Group, was particularly worried, writing melodramatically to Ramsey that 'divorce by consent ... would be evidence of regression to the morality and law that prevailed in the Roman Empire before Christianity came on the scene.'[234]

Despite an agreement by Cabinet to give the Bill extra time, by the summer of 1968 it was clear this would involve extending the parliamentary session, so Harold Wilson's inner Cabinet agreed that it would have to be reintroduced in the next session.[235] This caused considerable consternation among MPs supporting reform, especially on the Labour benches. Abse and others raised protests in the PLP.[236] There was also harshly expressed disapproval, notably in the *Sunday Telegraph*, about the waste of seventy hours of parliamentary time.[237] With an agreement already in place to provide sufficient time for the Bill to pass in the 1968–9 session,[238] the Lord Chancellor authorised a new bill to be drafted on the assumption that the Government position remained, as one official put it, 'quasi-benevolent neutrality'.[239] The Government's involvement in the divorce law reform bill continued to be a complicated one because of the introduction of a bill covering financial aspects of divorce by Labour MP Edward Bishop, who had won third place in the ballot for private members' bills. This bill would have introduced whole new principles into divorce proceedings and property law in general which the Government could not ignore. Most advocates of divorce reform supported Bishop's Bill, as did some opponents including the women's organisations seeking greater financial protection for divorced spouses and children. However, the Law Officers advised that the Bill was seriously defective.[240] Cabinet's Legislation Committee decided that the Government would oppose the Matrimonial Property Bill when it came up for second reading, with a three-line whip for ministers and a two-line whip for back-benchers. Ministers felt that this could be justified on the grounds that the Law Commission was already looking at the subject, and related matters would soon be announced in a White Paper.[241] This was reinforced at Cabinet the day before the second-reading debate.[242] However, at the PLP meeting later that day there was such a furore, including a defiant speech by Shirley Williams, that Wilson was forced to make a speech announcing that a free vote would now be given and a negotiated solution would be found.[243] Despite this climb-down the Bill passed at second reading by eighty-six votes to thirty-two, due in part to a less than inspirational performance on the part of Arthur Irvine. Jennie Lee was the only government frontbencher to vote for the Bill.[244] Williams, who had abstained, angrily protested that she had, as a matter of conscience, already promised to support the Bill.[245] Shortly afterwards, Bishop agreed to withdraw his Bill in exchange for a promise on government legislation based on the Law Commission's findings.[246] The general enthusiasm among MPs for the principles embodied in Bishop's Bill meant that the issue of matrimonial property assumed a new importance. The previous arrangement, under which a divorce would not be granted unless the court was satisfied that an adequate financial settlement had been agreed, was now not enough for the opponents of the new divorce reform bill sponsored by Alec Jones. Those who wished financial provisions to be strengthened secured a promise from Irvine that the Divorce Bill would come into operation at the same time as a government matrimonial property bill to be introduced in the next session, although for the most vociferous opponents of divorce reform this was merely an admission that the Divorce Bill had always been inadequate.[247]

The report stage of the Divorce Bill became extremely protracted, both because of the success of opponents of the Bill in spinning out debate, and because its sponsors were finding it increasingly difficult to motivate sufficient numbers of supporters to attend and speak. George Brown's complaint to the DLRU that he wanted some sleep rather than a divorce all-nighter reflected more than his own frustration.[248] Lord Gardiner once again went to Cabinet to secure extra time for the Bill's completion.[249] Despite the familiar complaint that this would antagonise public opinion and compromise the Government's line of neutrality, it was agreed that the Bill would be given as much time as necessary, on the same lines as the 1967 Abortion Bill. In order to galvanise party approval of this, Wilson instructed Bob Mellish to bring this decision to a meeting of the PLP.[250] At this point in the protracted saga it became clear why Mellish's appointment as Chief Whip in April had been disadvantageous for the sponsors of divorce reform. As Abse records, Mellish had been party to the 'cabal' that had 'done for' his 1963 Divorce Bill, although he is cautious about accusing him of malice in 1969.[251] However, as discussions within the Government about how best to facilitate passage of the Bill continued, Mellish's opposition to was well known. His mistake, whether deliberate or naïve, was to accede to the demands for a debate on a Conservative motion which condemned the Government's assistance for the Divorce Bill.[252] Mellish informed his colleagues of his decision at a meeting of the inner Cabinet on the morning of 12 June. Because of the serious implications it was immediately referred to that day's Cabinet meeting.[253] There was considerable impatience with Mellish for agreeing to the debate, which, it was said, was obviously a filibuster, and one which could set a dangerous precedent. To compound matters, Mellish admitted that 'he had subsequently realised that the motion amounted to a motion of censure and that they might have difficulty in securing its rejection, since the day's business was subject only to a one-line Whip.' Cabinet had to arrange for a three-line whip and a closure of the debate at midnight, before the Divorce Bill's report stage could, hopefully, continue into the night.[254] The hostile motion actually went to the heart of the whole debate about the Government's position. They were, it was alleged, pretending to be neutral whilst taking no responsibility for a measure they were assisting. However, the Government won the vote by 166 to 62.[255] In the Lords, although Baroness Summerskill kept up her attacks against the 'Casanova's Charter', the concessions made on financial provisions lessened the support she attracted. Perhaps her invocation of the timid Morton Commission, by then thirteen years old, rallied the supporters of radical change. In addition the Bill was suavely piloted through by Frank Soskice, now Lord Stow Hill, who belied his earlier reputation as an indecisive Home Secretary and half-hearted reformer.[256]

*

An even greater feeling of wading through treacle beset supporters of reform of the mediaeval Sunday observance laws. The Report of the Crathorne Committee, which 'Rab' Butler had set up when Home Secretary, began from the secular premise that

> there was no objection to these forms of entertainment in themselves, and that there was no theological or ethical reason why they should be prohibited. The modern view appears to be that if an entertainment is improper on Sunday it is just as undesirable on weekdays.

Its main proposal was that all activities permitted on weekdays should also be allowed on Sundays after 12.30 p.m., with safeguards to prevent unnecessary employment and noisy disturbances. However, in attempting to reconcile the divisions between those sports which wanted to operate on Sundays and those which did not, the Committee ignored its earlier premise and produced the illogical fudge that only amateur competition would be permitted, to the derision of some newspapers.[257] This despite their assertion that 'in framing our recommendations we have endeavoured to make proposals which, if adopted, would produce a law that would be respected and could be enforced. To achieve this, the law must be clear, certain, and acceptable to a majority of the public.'[258]

When the *Coronation Street* writer Ted Willis introduced a bill to implement the report in the House of Lords in 1965, he argued that the advent of television on a nationwide scale was the most significant change about Sunday in the previous ten years: 'Sir Laurence Olivier or Dame Peggy Ashcroft may appear in a Sunday night play on television, but they may not appear in their own theatres. If the law was absurd before, television has made it ridiculous.'[259] However, when a bill was introduced in the Commons in 1967, Dick Crossman recorded in his diary that he had received the night before a 'round-robin' from ten Welsh MPs objecting to this use of government time. At the meeting of the Home Affairs Committee this manifested itself as a concerted attack by the Welsh Secretary, Cledwyn Hughes, and the deputy Chief Whip, Charlie Grey, who, according to Crossman, was 'nearly as religious as some of the Welsh ... the Bill will be stopped all right.'[260] Crossman and Roy Jenkins duly met a contingent of Welsh

MPs to discuss the issue, at which the idea of local option was welcomed, but some members vowed to fight a bill tooth and nail, the division being between north Welsh Sabbatarians and south Welsh sports fans. By this time, however, Crossman seems to have gone off the idea of assisting a Bill even by providing time for a second-reading debate to demonstrate support for its provisions, preferring to use the time on legislation that could pass that session, and introducing a Bill in the next session.[261] Alice Bacon, Home Office Minister of State, and Dennis Howell, Minister of Sport at the Department of Education and Science, both vented their anger at the tiny minority of Welsh MPs preventing reform even for England.[262]

A lowly ninth place drawn by William Hamling, Labour MP for Woolwich West, who adopted the Willis Bill in the Commons, meant that the time for debate on second reading would be limited. As in other debates on Sunday observance bills there was considerable criticism that the subject was being left to the initiative of private members.[263] Speaking for the Government, David Ennals, Parliamentary Under-Secretary at the Home Office, ingeniously defended the Government's detachment on the grounds that the long history of statutory government intervention in Sunday observance law was the reason that reformers were so anxious for a liberalising measure.[264] As Peter Richards observed, 'a superb piece of parliamentary gamesmanship' on the part of John Parker secured a division just when the few opponents who had bothered to stay thought that Parker himself was going to talk the Bill out because of its poor chance.[265]

What became apparent during the committee and report stages of Willis' Bill in the Lords was the strength of opposition to the growth of noisy disturbances caused by large sporting events.[266] Opponents of the Bill tried to link this to the division between amateur and professional sports, although it was made clear by Hamling that this distinction did not work.[267] This concern about the prevention of disturbance was a demonstration of the utilitarianism of the Crathorne Report. As with the Wolfenden recommendations on homosexuality, vulnerable groups, that is those who wished to preserve a quiet Sunday, should be protected from the results of the liberties of others. In this case their own freedom (to have a quiet or religious Sunday) was also at issue.

Only at the report stage did the Sabbatarian opposition to the Bill rally its supporters, many of whom had no direct interest in the Bill as they were Scottish and Northern Irish members whose constituencies were not covered by it.

Objections on the grounds of noise disturbance were now combined with the fear of labour exploitation. The venerable Jim Griffiths, Clement Attlee's Minister for National Insurance and Wilson's first Welsh Secretary, rose as a trade union MP to defend the principle of double pay on Sundays, which his younger colleagues were prepared to throw away. He concluded:

> *In this modern, permissive, materialistic society, if we had not inherited*
> *Sunday as a day of rest, we should have had to invent it. With all the speed and*
> *noise of modern life, it has become even more absolutely essential to have one*
> *day on which people can get quiet and rest.*[268]

Parker's incredible luck in drawing third place in the 1968–9 session ballot was squandered through his unlikely ignorance of the parliamentary rule that a private member cannot pick up a Lords Bill in order to reduce debate in the Upper House.[269] The second reading of Parker's Bill did not take place until 28 February 1969.[270] Despite this difficulty and the previous mammoth efforts made, particularly at the Home Office, to help Hamling's previous bill, the Legislation Committee refused to give any indication of help before the second-reading debate.[271] Parker argued that the recent increase in Sunday working had been predominantly in industry, not entertainment. Public opinion, he said, was moving in the direction of liberalisation.[272] Cyril Osborne rose to make the moral case for resisting reform:

> *The general moral background is that, since the war, we have had many small*
> *Bills like this which have helped to produce the permissive state, one thing after*
> *another. If this Bill were by itself then, from my point of view, it would not be*
> *so objectionable. But it is only one more step, though a small one, towards a*
> *permissive society.*[273]

This standard conservative case, which might well have appealed to many MPs on both sides of the House, was rather spoilt by Osborne's comparison of the importance of Sunday observance with the law of perjury. The opposition's attack was somewhat rescued by that star performer Bill Deedes, journalist and former Cabinet minister. He was typically sanguine about the Bill, saying it would not be 'the end of the world' if it were passed. However, his ironic musings had a sting in the tail: 'It is one of the consequences of social reform by private members' bills that one tends never to reach a finite point. It is reform by instalments.' He criticised equally religious dogmatism and overzealous modernisation, but on balance, considering the possibility of disruption of working-class family Sundays, he was 'reluctantly opposed'.[274]

A small majority on second reading meant that in standing committee the Bill's supporters had a majority of only one. Despite having two sittings a week, this lasted until the very last day for private members' business on 15 July,[275] by which time there was no prospect of finding sufficient time for its passage. By the 1969–70 session the Government seems to have given up all interest in Sunday observance legislation. A Ten-Minute Rule motion introduced in December 1969 was given cursory examination at the Legislation Committee, with Shirley Williams concluding that 'the opposition of the Sunday observance lobby would probably ensure that the Bill did not make progress.' The Government would maintain its stance of neutrality, and no mention was made of its previous efforts on behalf of Willis, Hamling and Parker.[276]

This anti-climactic end to the Sunday entertainments debate during the Wilson Governments is puzzling. It is true that in 1969 the Statute Law (Repeals) Act repealed the relevant seventeenth-century legislation. However, as Parker points out in his memoirs, the 1780 Act remained on the statute book, 'a testimonial to British hypocrisy which refuses to bring the law into line with current practice.'[277] As has been seen, opponents of reform could not resist exploiting conservative fears about the 'permissive society', which after 1968 became more of a political *bête noire* than it had been even in the previous year. This spectre haunted politicians of every party, not least the new Home Secretary, Jim Callaghan, who, as his biographer points out, 'took pride in his public stance against permissiveness and spoke with contempt in later years of the cynical, unrepresentative, and destructive view of the bourgeois chattering classes.'[278]

*

If Callaghan and his colleagues could not muster sufficient enthusiasm to settle the issue of Sunday observance, they were prepared to lance a far angrier-looking boil – the abolition of capital punishment, which had been suspended in 1965. During 1969 it became increasingly clear that the Government would at least have to make a decision about whether there should be a decision on capital punishment before the next general election. The Murder Act was due to expire in July 1970, when the discredited 1957 Homicide Act would automatically revive if nothing was done. If left until then it would have to be dealt with uncomfortably close either side of a general election. Now the flaws of the 1965 experiment became clear. The Home Office prepared the ground carefully, including finessing the Scottish position. North of the border there had been a dramatic rise in violent crime, and officials were anxious that Scotland shouldn't be seen to be 'dragged along' by England in something with which Scottish people didn't agree, as had happened with the controversy over British Summer Time. Tom McCaffery, the Home Office chief publicity officer, on Callaghan's instruction initiated a publicity campaign in papers including the *Observer* and the *Daily Express* on the merits of abolition and the experience in countries which had already done so.[279] Callaghan and Willie Ross presented their colleagues with the options open to them in May 1969, and Cabinet approved their plan to take the initiative and go for outright abolition at the end of the session in the autumn. Their case rested on the analysis that the murder statistics, on which many people were waiting to judge the effect of the suspension of capital punishment, were useless. Even in 1970 there would only be four years of figures, and even then they would not be sufficient to make any scientific conclusions. The Home Office must have known this in 1965 but up till now the Government had been peddling the line that the experiment must be allowed to run its course. Now it turned the argument on its head, and said they could not wait because the experiment was meaningless, and the real judgement was a subjective one. More crucially, ministers were terrified that capital punishment would become an election issue.[280] However, by September, Callaghan was still edgy about the timing of the votes. The 1968 figures were now available, but would not be published until November. The number of capital murders had risen sharply but overall the murder figures were not much higher than the previous year. He felt that they were, on the whole, helpful to the Government's case. Perhaps equally weighty in the minds of his Cabinet colleagues were three impending by-elections in October. The decision was pushed back to the new session in November.[281]

Duncan Sandys, former Conservative minister and Winston Churchill's son-in-law, was the most vociferous supporter of reintroducing hanging and had kept up a campaign during the experimental period, backed by continuing public support for capital punishment. In fact, he hadn't been prepared to wait for the five-year experiment to run its course either. He tried to bring back hanging in 1966, but was given short shrift by fellow MPs. In October 1969 the Conservative party conference passed a motion to restore the death penalty, although by the surprisingly narrow margin of 1,117 to 958. During the conference, Ted Heath suggested that 'three wise men' be appointed to give an impartial ruling on the new murder figures. Heath and his colleagues at least wanted the Government to wait until 1970, and tabled a Commons motion to this effect.[282] At a private meeting between Callaghan and Quintin Hogg, the Shadow Home Secretary threatened that the Conservatives might apply the whip against abolition if the Government refused to consider extending the experimental period. This might bring out the backwoodsmen in the Lords who could defeat the Government. Callaghan argued that another temporary fix was likely to cause more confusion and give candidates more trouble, not less, at the next general election. He was anxious to prevent capital punishment becoming a matter of party controversy, but ministers could be fairly relaxed about Hogg's threats, as the advice of the Law Officers was that, even if they were defeated, they could still bring in legislation to extend the experimental period during the 1969–70 session. Hogg described himself as a 'mild hanger' for reasons including his inability to imagine any time when the Moors Murderers, for example, could be released and the bad influence such prisoners had on prisons as places of reform. Not one to be bullied, Callaghan shot back that that Hogg was 'attempting to walk in the middle of the road and was therefore liable to be knocked over. He replied that if we did not allow him to walk in the middle of the road he would walk on the right.'[283]

When the Government announced that it would ask Parliament to come to a decision before Christmas, the Tories tabled a censure motion. This was defeated on a whipped vote. The following day, permanent abolition was approved by 336 to 185. Among the abolitionists were fifty-four Conservatives, including Heath and Enoch Powell. Only three Labour MPs supported restoration.[284] The Lords agreed by 220 to 174, although this was somewhat confusing, as peers were voting on an amendment by Lord Dilhorne to extend the trial period to 1973. The motion to end capital punishment was then passed without a vote.[285]

5. Pornography and Population: 1970–1979

'I have never believed that it is a legitimate function of politicians to lecture citizens on the morality of how they conduct themselves in their private lives.'

Edward Heath[1]

'We cannot have our moral cake and eat our tax-reliefs.'

Barbara Castle[2]

'Looking back, one can see how deep ran the links between sexual and political anarchy.'

Mary Whitehouse[3]

'Lord Longford, Malcolm Muggeridge and Mrs Whitehouse can pack up and go home. We swing not, neither are we lechers. The majority of English people lead sexual lives of extreme respectability, in spite of Soho, television, and the erotic bletherings of the press.'

Anthony Storr[4]

Sir Humphrey: He [the Dean of Bailey College, Oxford] tends to raise issues which often governments would rather not be raised. He's a trenchant critic of abortion, contraception for the under-sixteens, sex education, pornography, Sunday trading, easy divorce and bad language on television. He would be likely to challenge the government policy on all these subjects.

Hacker: But these are subjects on which the government is hoping to have no policy. Our policy is to have no policy.

Sir Humphrey: He's against your no-policy policy.

Yes Prime Minister[5]

The Conservative and Labour Governments which spanned the 1970s were assailed by crises of economic turmoil which questioned the assumptions of the

Keynesian postwar world. Though the proverbial postwar consensus in British politics has often been exaggerated, the failure of either the Conservatives or Labour to deal with fundamental economic problems led to a greater polarisation of British politics during the decade, ending in the triumph of Margaret Thatcher in the 1979 general election with a philosophy, if not yet all the policies, of the 'New Right' – economically liberal and socially conservative. This polarisation was fuelled by conservatives' demonisation of the 1960s and by the morally permissive legislation which had been enacted between the Obscene Publications Act under Harold Macmillan in 1959 and the Divorce Law Reform Act ten years later – between allowing Lady Chatterley's adultery to be read by the masses and allowing the masses to divorce more easily without having to feign adultery themselves. If some Conservatives were more consistent in their libertarianism, they were in a small minority, with the Thatcherite wing of the party increasingly invoking the moral revivalist language of campaigners such as Mary Whitehouse. Thatcher herself declared that 'we are the party of the family now,' and at the same Tory conference in 1977 Patrick Jenkin argued that 'the pressure on young wives to go out to work devalues motherhood itself.'[6] Despite the socially authoritarian and religious traditions within the Labour Party, which were still strong, and the role of rampant commercialism driving the trade in sex, pornography and gambling, moral permissiveness was painted by the right as the alter ego of left-wing political radicalism. Rising crime, juvenile delinquency and family breakdown were the result of looser moral standards, the decline in the influence of religion and a collapse in respect for parental authority – the consumerism and commercialisation encouraged by rising affluence were rarely the culprits. Specific trends, such as the hike in the divorce figures when the 1969 Act was implemented in 1971, could easily be pinned on specific pieces of legislation.

Concern about the state of the family intensified with a growing number of houses headed by single, unmarried, divorced or remarried people. Though traditionalists within both the Labour and Conservative Parties could often unite to condemn permissiveness for its effect on the family, the force exerted by the party political divide was greater. Conservatives argued that moral responsibility was independent of social conditions, Labour that increasing public spending to alleviate poverty would cure endemic problems within families. Sir Keith Joseph's discovery of a 'cycle of deprivation' which bequeathed both social and moral disadvantage to successive generations of the poor represented a more sophisticated and sympathetic Tory view of the causes of endemic poverty, as well as a convenient shorthand which was still being used casually by politicians of every hue three decades later. His lack of political skill allowed his critics to suspect him of darker motives, but his championing of wider family planning targeted at the most disadvantaged shocked as many on the right as the left. Joseph's drift away from such interventionist policies later in the decade also allowed his successor, Barbara Castle, to take advantage of the clear ground, making the marginal removal of prescription charges for contraceptives in 1974 seem more radical than it really was. Indeed, for all the association of the left with the morally permissive 1960s, Labour in the 1970s made few concessions to a more libertarian society. With Roy Jenkins a 'recidivist' Home Secretary and Castle the 'overlord' of health and social services, the sphere of social policy might have made more strides in the direction of Jenkins' 'civilised society'. Instead, political debate was trapped in largely the same parameters as in the previous decade. One important example was the failure of the Labour Government to act on the ground-breaking Finer Report into one-parent families, published in 1974, despite pressure from its own supporters and an increasingly vocal lobby led by the Child Poverty Action Group (CPAG) and its director, the future Labour MP and social security minister Frank Field.

The moderate utilitarian approach of liberal reformers in the 1960s was increasingly under attack on two fronts. From the end of the decade, movements for women's and gay liberation and, less prominently at this stage, disabled groups rejected the language of toleration, harm and medicalisation of their 'problems' which was explicit in the legislation of the late 1960s, in favour of equality, eschewing the moderate tactics of parliamentary reformers for the publicly confrontational politics of protest. This radicalism had far more social influence than political impact, although by 1974 both main parties were careful to include in their manifestos sections on their policies for women, both at home and in work. Recent reforms on homosexuality and divorce still did not cover the whole of Britain, let alone Northern Ireland, and the legislation of the 1960s was under attack from moral conservatives, particularly on abortion. However, Jim Callaghan's successor at the Home Office, Reginald Maudling, was in many ways less hostile to the contemporary focus on individual freedom, and he firmly resisted suggestions that the Conservative Government should take a stand against permissiveness, rejecting the notion that governments in general could effect a change in individual attitudes. Speaking in the wake of a fierce row about a sex education film in 1971, he suggested there would be a natural reaction against the commercial exploitation of sex:

> *There is a rhythm in human affairs, and the impulse is bound to come from the public as a whole. It is not a matter of compulsion, it is a matter of leadership, by academics, the churches, journalists, and the mass media … These are matters of one's fundamental attitude to life which seem rather to transcend one's attitude on party politics.*[7]

The wisdom of such caution from Ted Heath and Maudling was graphically displayed in 1973 when the most serious political sex scandal since the Profumo affair briefly gripped the nation. Maudling had already had to resign over his links to the corrupt development deals surrounding the architect John Poulson in 1972. The following spring allegations of a vice ring involving a large number of high-profile public figures broke when a call girl, Norma Levy, shopped her husband for drug-trafficking after her flat was monitored by the police. She also revealed that one of the visitors to her flat was Lord Lambton, a junior defence minister. Levy's husband on his arrest began spilling the beans about the vice ring with a list of fifteen prominent men involved and photographs, one of which proved to be of Lambton in bed with two prostitutes, smoking a joint. Levy, who later told the press that she voted Tory because they had always been her best clients, made ambiguous claims that other ministers were involved.

When the police informed MI5 because of the security angle, ministers agonised over what to do. The shadow of the Profumo affair immediately hung over their deliberations. Peter Earle, one of the *News of the World* journalists involved, had been active in the events of 1963. Worse, rumours reached Francis Pym, the Chief Whip, from a lawyer who worked for Rupert Murdoch that his stable had 'on the stocks' a story about a minister involved in sex orgies with backbenchers. Robert Carr, the Home Secretary, remarked that it was not a crime to have a mistress, but the question of how to deal with Lambton resolved itself when police searched his home and discovered an amount of cannabis and amphetamines. Lambton immediately went to see Pym and offered his resignation.

Rumours of other ministers implicated were now swirling around Fleet Street and Westminster. Lord Jellicoe, the Leader of the House of Lords, was unfortunately at the top of the list. Robert Armstrong, Heath's Principal Private Secretary, was dispatched to bring him to No. 10 to see the Prime Minister from a performance of *Lucia di Lammermoor* at Covent Garden. When confronted with the allegations against him, though bewildered, he denied any knowledge of Levy. However, he returned to Downing Street the following morning to confess that he had indeed been using prostitutes on a regular basis for some years. The link with the Levy ring was purely coincidental. Jellicoe was amazed that his name had become known. The assignations were all at his own flat but remained strictly business like and he naïvely seemed to think that the women who visited him would remain unaware of his identity, despite his status as a Cabinet Minister. Presumably call girls were unlikely to have an interest in politics. Heath reluctantly accepted his resignation and drafted in Lord Goodman to help smooth things over. Lady Jellicoe, demonstrating more *sangfroid* than Donizetti's Lucia had the previous evening when confronted with allegations of infidelity, supported her husband throughout. The subsequent Security Commission Report concluded that 'Jellicoe's "casual affairs" were conducted with discretion. There was no abnormal sexual behaviour.'

The shades of Profumo did not go unnoticed in the Commons either, where the splendidly named Sir Henry d'Avigdor Goldsmid referred to 'the events of ten years ago' rather in the same way that actors avoid mentioning the name of 'the Scottish play'.[8] Labour MPs were understandably anxious to probe as far as possible, although Harold Wilson was considerably more restrained than he had been over Profumo, without the malign influence of George Wigg, largely supporting Heath over the setting up of the Security Commission inquiry. In the words of *The Times*, the 'excessive penalties' which Profumo had suffered still gave the Commons 'feelings of guilt'.[9] The question of whether further ministers were involved remained unclear. Police were now interviewing large numbers of prostitutes and others, persistence which would undoubtedly unearth such names eventually. According to one report, five political names had been given by the *News of the World* to *The Times*, which may have been communicated to the Government when William Rees-Mogg saw Heath about the allegations. A named third minister denied any involvement but one Labour MP, Charles Loughlin, said that there was 'no one in the House who did not know the name of the alleged third minister'. Although *The Times* and other newspapers declined to report the name, young Liberal firebrand Peter Hain, anti-Apartheid campaigner and future Labour Cabinet minister, had no such scruples, publishing the name of Geoffrey Rippon, the Environment Secretary. Shocked and enraged, Armstrong consulted the Attorney General's office about the possibility of reviving criminal libel in order to prosecute Hain.[10] Heath managed to diffuse the situation by fudging the issue. There was insufficient hard evidence to flush out further resignations and the Security Commission Report rejected the allegations. Its main target was Lambton's drug habit, which had laid him 'wide open' to blackmail or to revealing secrets while under the influence.[11] Lambton, rejecting suggestions that the secret photographs which had been taken of him were an invasion of privacy, remained consistently unruffled by the affair. In a television interview with Robin Day, he was asked, 'Why should a man of your social position and charm and personality have to go to whores for sex?' He replied, 'I think that people sometimes like variety. I think it's as simple as that and I think that impulse is probably understood by almost everybody. Don't you?'[12]

*

Sensing the very different temperature within the House of Commons after 1970, anti-abortionists wasted little time in attempting to reverse or mitigate as much of the 1967 Abortion Act as possible. They were aided in this by the well-publicised abuses in the private sector, which had also prompted supporters of the Act to want to tighten it up, as Dick Crossman had tried to do without much success. Publicity outlining the benefits of the Act, including the disappearance of back-street abortions, the disappearance of the illness and death which women had previously suffered, and the softening of the social stigma which had been borne by hundreds of thousands of women, was conspicuous by its absence, either from the press or in parliamentary debate. A constant rearguard action during the 1970s by supporters of the Act was necessary to thwart the increasingly well-organised anti-abortion lobby. In fact, the 1970s saw a massive increase in the availability of contraceptive and family planning advice and services, supported by governments of both parties – partly as a rather belated response to the high level of abortion.

Moralist campaigning groups began to coalesce around the questions of providing contraception to under-sixteens, particularly without parental consent, which they thought undermined the autonomy of the family and the authority of parents, and preventing more liberal sex education in schools. The fact that provision of sex education continued to be patchy in the hands of local education authorities and schools did not restrain them from demanding central government intervention to protect the prerogative of parents in this area of teaching, particularly from the philosophy of sexual permissiveness and experimentation, which they said was increasingly prevalent in the early 1970s. The threat from radical permissive ideas to Britain's youth was most evident in the celebrated trials of the underground press – *Oz* and the *Little Red School Book*. But the importance of obscenity to debates about public morality during the decade ranged wider than such juvenilia, as moralists such as Lord Longford attacked the greater availability of hardcore pornography on Britain's streets, made possible, as it turned out, by a corrupt Metropolitan Police Obscene Publications Squad. As Mary Whitehouse sought ever more ingenious ways to enforce some kind of obscenity law, the Labour Government was forced to concede an inquiry into the subject.

The question of allowing individuals and couples greater control over their own fertility and family size acquired a new potency from the mid-1960s as concern about a population explosion coloured many questions of domestic public policy, as well as overseas development and aid to the Third World. This reached a peak in the early 1970s. In Britain, the projections of postwar planners such as the 1949 Royal Commission on Population, which had warned of a crisis of a falling birth rate, proved wildly inaccurate. After the immediate postwar baby boom, the birth rate had fallen back to prewar levels, only to rise significantly from 1956 to 1964, falling thereafter, but still, at the proverbial 2.4 children, well above the wartime low in 1941 of 2.04 children. Less childlessness and fewer lone-child families were accompanied by a far more controversial rise in illegitimacy rates. Taken together with unplanned pregnancies to married couples, by the end of the 1960s researchers were talking of as many as two hundred thousand unwanted pregnancies each year. What seemed appropriate to prevent a population explosion in the Third World causing a world crisis now appeared to apply to an already crowded island. Extending birth control, voluntary for local authorities and the NHS under the 1967 Family Planning Act, became a rallying cry for population-planners, and lobbying groups sprang up to campaign on the issue. Parliamentarians led by former Tory minister Lord Renton, but including two veteran Labour figures in particular, Lord Houghton and Baroness Gaitskell, harried the Government in the Lords for a coordinated response to the question. Government and Parliament were stung into action, and there was soon considerable competition in Whitehall and Westminster among different bodies pronouncing on the question. However, as in 1949, no politician seemed terribly keen to become the 'Minister for Population'.

Widespread public concern about racketeering in private clinics had already led Crossman to attempt to clean up the commercial abortion sector, but with little success. Not surprisingly, a large number of foreign women were soon coming to take advantage of Britain's abortion laws, which were considerably more liberal than those of most European countries at the time, something that would continue with particular regard to women and girls from both the Republic of Ireland and Northern Ireland, which remains outside the scope of the Abortion Act to the present day. As the low-cost voluntary sector squeezed out some of the domestic market for private abortions, foreign women made up a greater part of the private sector. A Commons motion calling for an inquiry into the working of the Act attracted 260 signatures. Sir Keith Joseph, who straddled the monolithic DHSS for the whole period of the Heath Government, decided he must take some of the parliamentary heat out of the debate by setting up a departmental inquiry into the workings of the Abortion Act in 1971, at the same time that he announced an extension of family planning services. DHSS papers reveal that the Abortion Act was under real threat from the proposed scope of Joseph's review, and that it was saved, in the short term at least, by the intervention of the Prime Minister, Ted Heath, and the Home Secretary, Reginald Maudling, who both reined Joseph in. Writing to Maudling before putting his proposal to Cabinet colleagues, Joseph said that action on the related fields of family planning and abortion was essential:

> It seems clear that the lack of the first leads inevitably to the second. It is tempting to take action on the first and to mark time on the second, but the public pressures to which we are subject make me believe that this course is not open to us.

He proposed an inquiry into the Abortion Act which would include the grounds on which abortion was currently permitted, only restricting it from 'making recommendations which would restore the law to what it was believed to be before the liberalising influence of *R v. Bourne* in 1938'. (This case had established that abortions carried out in good faith to save the health of the mother, in this case a fourteen-year-old girl raped by four guardsmen, were legal.) Maudling clearly questioned the breadth of this remit, because Joseph answered his response by conceding:

> *I take your point about the difficulty of reviewing the criteria for lawful abortion. My trouble has been the difficulty of looking at the working of the Abortion Act without looking at these criteria, because imprecise criteria can facilitate misuse of the Act. I have however thought about this again in the light of what you say and I doubt whether we can improve the precision without being too restrictive.*

Joseph was also persuaded to 'mark time' on the question of restricting the number of foreign women obtaining abortions in Britain by Heath. He originally proposed to the Prime Minister that he should impose a three-month residence qualification on foreign women wanting an abortion, but Heath squashed the notion that this could be done in advance of the inquiry. However, when new figures in March 1972 indicated that the numbers of 'foreign' abortions had not fallen, despite attempts to stamp out the worst abuses through administrative means, Joseph attempted once again to get Heath's agreement to the ongoing inquiry, producing an interim report on the problem, which stated that 'action which might be criticised by some as being unduly xenophobic would be best based on the results of an independent study of the ill consequences of the foreign traffic.'

Cannily, Joseph was determined to find a woman to chair the committee.[13] However, this led to a considerable delay in establishing it, as ministers and officials demonstrated how restricted was the number of women in senior public positions at the time, as well as their own ignorance of suitable woman to sit on the committee. The problem was so severe that officials took up Joseph's suggestion of consulting the popular agony aunt Marjorie Proops about young unmarried women of 'child-bearing age' who might fit the bill as members of the committee. A trawl of the list of Foyle's 'Women of the Year' failed to bring forth any candidates. This female famine was compounded by the other stiff criterion which ministers laid down, that inquiry members should not have any previous known position on abortion – which might have been assumed immediately to exclude most women in public life, and indeed most women, though this never seems to have occurred to the men in Whitehall. Joseph's initial favourite for the chairmanship of the inquiry, Baroness Brooke of Ystradfellte, the wife of former Conservative Home Secretary Henry Brooke, fell foul of this rule, as a careful examination of her voting record on David Steel's Abortion Bill showed that she had voted for three restrictive amendments in the Lords. Again it seems it was Maudling who convinced Joseph that this record would disqualify her. The second choice, Alison Munro, headmistress of St. Paul's Girls' School in Hammersmith, was also compromised when she revealed that her brother was a gynaecologist chairing the BMA's own inquiry into the abortion law 'with pronounced views vis-à-vis the present Act'. The eventual choice of the other woman high-court judge, Dame Elizabeth Lane, must have been quite a relief, though Lord Chancellor Hailsham's caveat that she would have to fit the inquiry round her circuit commitments as a judge might have been thought to contradict the Prime Minister's stated determination to Joseph that the inquiry should be 'conducted with all possible speed'.[14] This was sufficiently wide of the mark that the problem eventually landed back in the lap of the next Labour Health Secretary, Barbara Castle, when the committee finally reported in 1974. Joseph's own prejudices also hampered the choice of an 'objective' committee. As well as a predictable aversion to sociologists for lack of objectivity, Joseph was sensitive to the fact that the city of Aberdeen had for several years been at the forefront of providing abortion and contraceptive services. He therefore blackballed one man, commenting, 'I am not especially happy to have an Aberdonian, even one with six children. Surely he will be attacked as biased?' Another candidate was erased because 'a Catholic who is liberal on this subject is surely not a good idea. He will be constrained to be liberal when what we need is objectivity.'[15]

After announcing the inquiry to Parliament in February 1971, Joseph emphasised at a press conference that it would seek to examine concerns that in some areas there was effectively abortion on demand, contrary to the intentions of Parliament and 'the declared intention of the sponsors of the Act', and that in other areas access to terminations was so restricted as to prevent women who genuinely qualified under the Act from obtaining one. However, he stated that the anecdotal evidence available suggested that the former problem was greater than the latter. At the same time Joseph announced an extension of domiciliary family planning advice by increasing the local government grant from the Exchequer by £800,000, rising to £2.25m in the following year. Advice would be free, as would equipment provided on medical grounds. However, Joseph rejected the idea of a free comprehensive service, saying that 'free contraception for all would be a gratuitous waste of taxpayers' money, as the vast majority of people in the country were capable of seeking and paying for contraception.' His attraction to domiciliary services, however, flew in the face of existing trends in professional opinion towards providing clinic services, as domiciliary services had proved expensive and unpopular. Nevertheless, Joseph continued to resist a extension of clinics for another eighteen months. Despite its limitations, birth control campaigners welcomed the move as a 'milestone' for central government money to be used for local family planning services.[16]

Following this announcement, campaigners for a comprehensive family planning system decided to reorganise themselves to focus on achieving this goal. Though the Family Planning Association was obviously committed to extending access to birth control, its charitable status precluded explicit lobbying activities, and it was already under attack from conservatives unhappy about some of its publications relating to sex education, and its new links to the British Pregnancy Advisory Service – concerns which were to continue for years to come. However, the new organisation, the Birth Control Campaign (BCC), was staffed largely by former activists in the abortion law reform movement and the wider movement for women's rights. Alistair Service, the BCC chairman, had been the energetic young parliamentary officer for the Abortion Law Reform Association (ALRA) and then the Divorce Law Reform Union, instrumental in persuading parliamentarians to support these two measures of reform between 1965 and 1969. Vera Houghton and Dilys Cossey, also from the ALRA, were the other key figures, and the campaign was supported in Parliament by pro-abortionists including Douglas Houghton and the former Lord Chancellor Lord Gardiner. However, the new campaign sought to draw support from as wide a spectrum as possible, including the Churches. The Bishop of Durham joined the campaign's Advisory Council.

Some anti-abortionists were caught in a bind over the new lobby group. Many Catholics of course opposed it on the grounds that artificial contraception breached doctrine recently confirmed after a more liberal policy was withdrawn by the Vatican just before publication. However, others were extremely supportive of better family planning and birth control, often seeing this as a way to reduce what they considered the horror of abortion, and that earlier steps towards comprehensive birth control might have obviated the need for abortion law reform in the first place.[17] Some resented the high profile which abortion campaigners played in the new organisation, including the Jewish Labour MP Leo Abse and the Conservative Anglican John Selwyn Gummer. Gummer was so outraged at the support being given by the Bishop of Durham that he wrote to the Archbishop of Canterbury, Michael Ramsey, to complain. Claiming to be a moderate 'who would strongly oppose the South African Government and whose record on race relations and discrimination is entirely liberal', Gummer accused the campaign of seeking 'to legitimise abortion as an acceptable method of birth control'. Becoming melodramatic he warned that the BCC would 'set back the family planning movement by a decade' and that 'some of our leaders seem to support so many causes promulgated by people who, in the last resort, are totally opposed to the faith of Christ and whose organisations are active in its destruction.' Finally, in a letter sent to and published in the press on the same day it was written, before the private covering letter could have reached Ramsey (in fact it was lost in the post), he urged him 'to give a further lead so that Christians will know that the Church is not prepared to be swept along by fashionable morality'. Ramsey responded that he trusted the Bishop of Durham's judgement on the matter, but the controversy was enough for him to decline Gardiner's request for him to support the campaign publicly. As Ramsey's Private Secretary, Hugh Whitworth, observed, political campaigns active in such a delicate area, drawing support from people with very different moral perspectives, inevitably encountered such problems:

> It is wrong to assume that members of the Advisory Council of this organisa-
> tion are committed in advance to any and every detail ... In fact, many of
> the Campaign's supporters are eminently respectable and even right-wing;
> but basically this is the same old problem as the C of E has with the World
> Council of Churches. What is remarkable is that an MP, who presumably

loyally accepts the Conservative Whip, should take this impossibly purist line.[18]

The conjunction of much of the personnel of the BCC with pro-abortionists remained controversial. In any case, public opinion seemed to be with the campaign. NOP polls commissioned by the BCC in 1972 showed about two thirds of people supported a free birth control service.[19]

While the Government reviewed family planning services during 1972, campaigners refused to wait, pressing the issue of access to vasectomy operations through a Private Members' Bill sponsored by Labour MP Philip Whitehead. The popularity of vasectomies had been rising rapidly as prejudice against such an invasive, surgical procedure receded with more enlightened attitudes towards family planning, and particularly with scare stories about the safety of the Pill for women. Waiting lists were frequently long, and access to the operation under the NHS was limited. The Bill sought to extend the same availability as for other forms of contraception under the 1967 Family Planning Act. The Bill had received cross-party support, by a margin of eighty to one on second reading in the Commons, and without a division in the Lords. The Government pledged not to oppose the Bill, and Labour indicated its neutrality. With the maximum time available for a private members' bill before it, there should have been a good chance of it becoming law by the summer. Some of those sympathetic to the principle of vasectomy had reservations about the Bill. In the Lords the surgeon Lord Brock worried that doctors were being encouraged to perform more operations, as with abortion, on social rather than medical grounds, contrary to the Hippocratic Oath. Abse, who in his memoirs admits an 'arrogant' determination to 'steal' the Bill during the second-reading debate, was in particularly self-regarding mood as he criticised the Bill's sponsors for distracting attention from what he considered a more important issue, the scandal of profiteering by the London Rubber Company (LRC) in its monopolistic pricing of the most popular form of contraception, the sheath. Using parliamentary privilege he named Sir Edward Howard, at the time Lord Mayor of London and chairman of the LRC, of being personally responsible for 'the high cost of loving'. He repeatedly raised the need for psychological counselling for patients by a psychiatrist before operations were authorised. Abse's obsession with interpreting all political motive and policy according to principles of Freudian psychoanalysis was at least consistently, if bluntly deployed. More divisively, Abse criticised the BCC, lobbying for the Bill, for being the 'discredited Abortion Law Reform Association in another guise'.[20] Privately, he also suspected Whitehead, who had himself been adopted as a child, of subconsciously attempting 'to work through his deep grievance [towards his own natural father] by precipitating the symbolic castration of thousands of natural fathers throughout the realm'.[21] Abse was eventually mollified, but more serious was the intransigence of a small number of Conservative MPs opposed to an extension on family planning, particularly when focused on men. After the Bill successfully negotiated almost its whole parliamentary passage through both Houses, they nearly talked the Bill out by discussing a technical amendment for almost the whole two hours available. With two amendments to be voted on when time was called on debate, the Bill fell because the Deputy Speaker ruled that they had to be voted on separately rather than together, exceeding the time limit.[22] The Bill's supporters were outraged, but the Speaker, John Selwyn Lloyd, later overruled his deputy, stating that the remaining vote could have been taken after the time limit. Given the predicament, Robert Carr, Leader of the House, agreed to breach the Government's policy of refusing to give government time to private members' bills, to allow this one to complete its remaining stages.[23]

There were other indications during 1971 and 1972 that Joseph's resistance to a radical extension of NHS contraceptive services was crumbling. These came not least from Joseph himself. In June 1972 he made a speech intended further to establish his credentials for intellectual analysis of the problems of social welfare. Speaking to the Pre-School Playgroups Association, he coined the phrase the 'cycle of deprivation' to describe the pattern of deprivation handed down from generation to generation. Rejecting the idea that eradicating poverty was the whole answer, Joseph also indicated that extending family planning in such areas was important, and that a departmental review of services would report later in the year.[24] Although no details of the review were given, correspondence with Downing Street reveals that Joseph had already accepted that a radical extension of family planning services was likely. A year earlier, in May 1971, he had written to Ted Heath giving him notice that the DHSS would be conducting the review, and giving a strong indication that even the extension of services which had just been announced would probably have to be revised and that radical new provision was under consideration:

Given the 150,000 or so unintended pregnancies that occur each year, half of which end in the traumatic experience of abortion, and the growing numbers of young girls involved, we have to ask ourselves whether present policies and services are adequate ... I propose to consider what further expansion of services would be appropriate, what form this should take and whether the benefits (in terms of reduced demand on the maternity and other services as well as of prevention or relief of distress) would justify any departure from the general principle that those who can afford to pay should do so.

An important question would be whether the Pill should be prescribable by general practitioners under the NHS not only, as now, when pregnancy would be medically harmful, but whenever a doctor thought fit to prescribe it.

Heath commended the approach but voiced anxiety that there should be no 'speculation or thinking aloud' until the review was complete.[25] However, external pressures were also mounting, notably from the medical profession, the Women's Institute, and the Church of England Board for Social Responsibility, all influential with the Conservative Party. The Duke of Edinburgh also gave his imprimatur to an extension of family planning services, including abortion. In 1969 he had shown his approval of the FPA by opening a new centre at the organisation's headquarters, and in 1971 he made a speech on the population explosion suggesting, in his inimitable way, that abortion and contraception be extended, although this was rather unfortunately linked to the idea that people might be taxed for having children. This understandably provoked an outcry, not least from anti-abortionists, one of whom accused the Duke of sounding like 'an early Victorian knocking the poor'.[26]

In August 1972 the Conservative-dominated Commons Committee on Science and Technology published another report on population policy, which recommended a raft of measures to control and plan population growth. Its central aim was the establishment of a comprehensive family planning and birth control service as a normal part of the NHS.[27] The Government was also under pressure because of widely diverging levels of provision across the country. Some local authorities, such as Birmingham, announced pioneering provision of comprehensive, free contraceptive services in conjunction with the FPA and Brook Advisory Centres. In some cases this was explicitly motivated by ongoing concern about a population explosion in densely populated urban areas.

However, spending on family planning services ranged from 175p per woman in Islington to only 1p in Burnley. According to the FPA, their worker in Dunoon, near Glasgow, was told by the local authority to 'go to India where her efforts were needed'. Despite the fact that an increasing number of women qualified for free advice and sometimes supplies through local authorities, it was clear that in such areas women were either not accessing, or not using such services. In one village in County Durham, where ninety per cent of women visiting the clinic qualified for free supplies, the average mother under twenty-five had six children.[28] In October 1972, at the Labour Party conference, Barbara Castle played to the gallery with a speech committing Labour to eradicating medical charges across the NHS, starting with prescription charges, and including providing free, comprehensive family planning services, saying, 'We cannot have our moral cake and eat our tax-reliefs.'[29]

In December Joseph announced the results of the department's review of family planning services, proposing their integration within the NHS from April 1974 and free advice to all, with exemptions from charges for contraceptive supplies for those in 'special social need' and those in 'financial need'. Women within twelve months of a birth or an abortion would also qualify. Those with a medical need would pay only a prescription charge, with the rest paying the full cost of the supplies as was already the case in 1972. Joseph stated that 'a substantial extension is needed if the numbers of unwanted pregnancies are to be reduced. With modern contraceptive methods available there should be fewer abortions, and much less of the unhappiness and ill-health which results from unplanned pregnancy.'[30] The announcement was greeted with a limited welcome from both sides of the House, but advocates of a free service, including David Steel, Renée Short and Shirley Summerskill, Labour's spokeswoman, criticised its limitation. Controversially, Catholics opposed to an extension of birth control failed to attract the Speaker's eye before he stopped questions on the statement, leaving Labour Merseysider Simon Mahon fuming that 'as one who comes from a large family ... very little chance was given to hon. members who opposed the new proposals.'[31]

However, the wind was now definitely behind family planning campaigners. The Bill to implement the proposals, the NHS Reorganisation Bill, involved a much wider structural reorganisation of the health service. Despite this, parliamentary debate on the Bill became 'swamped' by the argument about the extent of free contraceptive supplies.[32] Introduced in the Lords, the family planning proposals were ambushed by a concerted cross-party coalition, supported by lobbying from the BCC. In committee peers supported a backbench Labour amendment to make all contraceptive supplies free, with many pointing out that the Bill might actually involve a restriction of services in those areas where local authorities were already providing a totally free service. Only five of the eighteen women peers who voted resisted the amendment, one of whom was a junior minister, the mildly youthful Baroness Young, just embarking on a thirty-year career at the head of the praetorian guard protecting traditional family values in the House of Lords.[33]

When the Bill reached the House of Commons, it was clear that the Government would have to give some ground. Fifty four-Conservative MPs, including the Chairman of the 1922 Committee, Edward du Cann, and former Home Office minister Sir David Renton, had signed a motion calling for a totally free service, enough to make a government defeat likely (though with some churn from Catholic Labour MPs this was difficult to predict).[34] Joseph graciously bowed to the pressure, though was only prepared to go as far as reducing the cost of supplies to the level of a prescription charge for everyone – arguably in line with other NHS medicines and appliances. Die-hard rebels inevitably repeated concerns that existing free services would be curtailed, and that means-tested prescription charges would still deter.[35] However, Joseph had done enough to ensure victory, with a surprisingly large government majority of 117 over the 'free' family planners.[36]

However, when the Bill returned to the Lords, peers were in no mood to climb down, inflicting a heavier defeat than in December, insisting on a totally free service by 107 to 58.[37] This enraged Government supporters in the Commons, with Norman Tebbit accusing the life peers of being a group of trendy 'back-street' as opposed to 'backwoods' peers.[38] This was only partly justified. In this second vote, life peers divided sixty-three to eight in favour of a free service. The hereditary 'backwoodsmen' did indeed favour the Government's prescription charge, but only by fifty to forty-three, indicating the broad range of opposition which the Government faced. The Commons again reversed this decision by twenty-seven, a margin rather closer to its nominal majority than before. With a full-blown constitutional crisis now in train, both sides were under pressure to compromise. Peers were reluctant to back down, particularly as the measure had not been part of the Government's manifesto. The former Labour health minister Baroness Serota tabled an amendment to allow a free service to continue in the thirty-four areas where it already existed. However, as Lord Waldegrave pointed out, peers were on unsafe constitutional ground here, as they were challenging the financial privilege of the House of Commons to raise taxation. With the Lords anxious not to pull the pillars down around them, and ministers in emollient mood promising an ongoing review of the service with the possibility for extending it later, they capitulated.[39]

With the new system due to come into force on 1 April 1974, this looked to be the basis on which the NHS family planning service would begin, rather than the free one which birth control campaigners had hoped for. However, this failed to reckon with the consequences of the industrial turmoil gripping the country. As the miners' strike and the three-day week swept the Government from office unexpectedly early in February 1974, when Ted Heath called an election on the theme 'Who Governs Britain?', Castle, the new Social Services Secretary, was able swiftly to implement Labour's manifesto commitment to a free family planning service by not implementing the prescription charge in the March Budget. Geoffrey Howe, now shadowing social services, criticised Castle's doctrinaire insistence of abolishing all prescription charges across the NHS.[40] When the electorate was asked to boost the Labour Government's mandate at a second election in October, the Conservatives claimed the credit for introducing a comprehensive service in the first place, but rather opaquely said that 'we must leave it to every family to decide what use to make of the … service.'[41] However, the Tories' leading social reformer was soon accused of contradicting this 'permissive' attitude towards contraception.

Although Labour's tenuous grip on power was only marginally strengthened in the October election, the voters' narrow rejection of Heath was at least confirmed by a further loss of Conservative seats and votes, correcting the perverse result in February in which Labour won more seats but fewer votes than the Conservatives. The vultures were now circling the corpse of the Heath leadership, as rival candidates for the succession sought to lay out their credentials. Those who blamed Heath and his supporters for the betrayal of a philosophy and policies on which they had been elected in 1970 sought to reaffirm Conservative principles and move the party to the right. The first and most controversial such sally came hard on the heels of polling day. Joseph, moved from social services to shadow the Home Office, delivered a speech in Birmingham which, in the words of *The Times,* 'sparked a tinderbox of reaction, most of it hostile', on the subject of 'The Family and Civilised Values'. This was the second controversial oratorical foray which Joseph had recently made, displaying his characteristic intellectual grasp alongside a woeful lack of political judgement. The previous month, in the run up to the general election, he had made a speech on economic policy which had allowed Labour to claim that he was advocating higher unemployment. Now, at the end of a speech exhorting the country to 'remoralisation', Joseph added a coda on birth control in which he said that the 'stock' of Britain was being threatened with 'degeneration' by a higher birth rate among the bottom socio-economic groups in society. The lack of judgement was all the more telling because this phrase was Joseph's own, reinserted into the text after Sir Alfred Sherman, who wrote most of the rest of the speech, had removed it.[42] Recapitulating his 'cycle of deprivation' thesis, Joseph argued:

Many of these girls are unmarried. Many of them are deserted or divorced, or soon will be. Some are of low intelligence, most of them are of low educational attainment. They are unlikely to be able to give children the stable emotional background, the consistent combination of love and firmness which are more important than riches. They are producing problem children, the future unmarried mothers, delinquents, denizens of our borstals, sub-normal educational establishments, prisons, hostels for drifters. Yet these mothers ... are now producing a third of all births. A high proportion of these births are a tragedy for the mother, the child and for us.

Joseph advocated extending birth control more widely among such young women, despite inevitable disapprobation from moral conservatives: 'Is it not condoning immorality? I suppose it is. But which is the lesser evil, until we are able to remoralise whole groups and classes of people, undoing the harm done, when already weak restraints on strong instincts are further weakened by permissiveness in television, in films, on bookstalls?'[43]

Though there was some support for Joseph's views in the letters pages and in his own postbag, political reaction was severe. Enoch Powell, a politician whose experience should have told Joseph that a swollen and supportive postbag was no sign of winning an argument, criticised Joseph for moralising, but also indulged in a little *schadenfreude* by saying:

> *It's fun to see someone else getting into hot water over a speech. I almost wondered if the river Tiber was beginning to roll again. I think the morality of politics might be reconsidered by some of those who are talking about it. I do not like politicians preaching. We have a very slight effect on the progress of public morals.*

More predictably Labour opponents were outraged. Some were repelled by the eugenic implications of his remarks, though as some correspondents pointed out these were in almost complete alignment with the principles of George Bernard Shaw and other socialists before the Second World War. The real differences were two-fold. First, whether these problems were most acute among lower socio-economic groups. Labour MP Renée Short argued that they were not: 'Unwanted babies are born in every group. And when he relates this to a decline in national morality, it is not those in the fourth and fifth [socio-economic] groups who patronise call girls.'[44] The second, and perhaps more important, difference was whether poverty or immorality should be the prime concern of politicians with a social conscience. In his speech, Joseph had pointed to research published by the CPAG, which revealed that an increasing number of babies were being born to young mothers, many of whom were poor. However, Frank Field, the director of CPAG, was angered by what he considered Joseph's misrepresentation of the research, and retorted that the answer was not to 'scapegoat' such women, but to 'share more equitably the cost of raising our next workforce'.[45] He accused Joseph of 'deliberately attempting to unleash a national backlash against the poor'.[46] From the other extreme, the de rigueur response from Ronald Butt in *The Times* criticised Joseph for the clumsiness of this passage in his speech, suggesting it was the result of his realisation that he himself had actually assisted this process as a minister by providing the basis of a free birth control service for all, which is now to operate without regard to age or marital status.[47] It was indeed on this point that Joseph had laid himself open to attack, not just from moral conservatives like Butt, but also from the advocates, or 'missionaries' in Butt's words, of comprehensive family planning. Castle, typically, was unable to resist such an open political goal, and duly obliged the waiting media by launching a stinging attack on Joseph. Her speech, well researched by civil servants distressed at their former minister's comments,[48] undermined the evidential base for the conclusions he had drawn from the CPAG research. She pointed out that the statistics did not support Joseph's assertion that a third of births were to young, unmarried mothers from socio-economic groups 4 and 5, and that the statistics were unhelpful, even preju-diced, as the classification for illegitimacy was based on the mother's occupation, whereas for legitimate births it was based on the father's occupation. Even allowing for this, she claimed the rate of illegitimate births to teenage mothers was only three or four per cent in England and Wales.

> *On this flimsy basis, Sir Keith raises a cry of alarm about a threat to our 'human stock'. To do so on such inaccurate evidence is frighteningly irrespon-sible. And to talk about the need to remoralise our society by special reference to girls in socio-economic classes four and five is wickedly unjust.*

Castle also cited Michael Schofield's ground-breaking study, *The Sexual Behaviour of Young People*, to claim that children from broken homes were not more likely to have sex than other children, 'so it is wrong to claim that the cycle of deprivation is synonymous with a cycle of permissiveness'.[49] Castle was supported by a critical article by the *Sunday Times* Insight team, whose own research countered the claim made by Joseph and other moral conservatives, that the first Wilson Government, and the liberal left, was responsible for rapidly declining standards of morality and personal responsibility, and, as a result, a collapse in social stability and rising crime:

> *There has been a marked drop in the number of sexual offences and armed robbery. The murder rate is static and burglary fell last year. Drunkenness is certainly increasing, particularly among the young, though we are nowhere near the Victorian rate of some 100,000 cases a year in London alone. Even ille-gitimacy, which increased rapidly in the sixties, is now on the decline.*[50]

Joseph was also undermined by figures published by the Registrar General a month after his speech which showed that births to married couples in groups 4 and 5 had declined dramatically between 1970 and 1972.[51] He retorted that Castle had missed the main point of his argument: that, whatever the statistics, 'a high proportion of [poor teenage mothers] are likely to be unmarried, deserted or divorced. It is the "unmarried, deserted or divorced" that is the essence.'[52] Mary Whitehouse no doubt agreed with this emphasis on morality rather than poverty. She praised him as the coming prophet, even the Christ to her John the Baptist, clearly flattered by the supportive reference to her own work in Joseph's speech. However, as Joseph's biographers point out, 'the man who as a government minister could reply to a question about the growing incidence of venereal disease by coolly distinguishing "between Gonorrhoea, the incidence of which had greatly increased and Syphilis, which had not increased", was an unlikely ally for Whitehouse.'[53]

Joseph's humiliation continued for several weeks, essentially until he ruled himself out of an impending leadership election. He had been particularly stung by the reaction to the Birmingham speech because during the previous three years he had made similar, and even cruder, comments about the morality and degradation of the poor, with little or no controversy. *Private Eye* dubbed him 'Sir Sheath' in honour of his services to contraception. An interview with Polly Toynbee for the *Observer*, conducted in a state of extreme tiredness, was spiked, allegedly on the instructions of David Astor, who was possibly anxious to protect Joseph, but not before some fumbling, confused, apocalyptic comments were leaked across Fleet Street and Westminster.[54] Castle, never afraid to kick a political opponent when he was down, returned to the fray during the debate on the Queen's Speech at the beginning of November, saying:

> *In his speech ... he has weakened the national will to attack the evils of depri-*
> *vation and poverty. Most unforgivable of all, he has deliberately propagated the*
> *lie that socialism is synonymous with permissiveness. If this is to be the level of*
> *argument with which the Conservatives hope to restore their shattered*
> *fortunes, I hope they will at least have the decency to drop all their soggy*
> *sermons about 'national unity'.*[55]

The implementation of a free, comprehensive family planning service within the NHS was neither as free nor as comprehensive as campaigners and the public had been led to believe. Firstly, GPs were still levying doctors' prescription charges. Second, the service became embroiled in the wider deadlock between the DHSS and doctors over their contracts and fees. Long waiting lists built up at clinics during the period in which they were transferred from the voluntary FPA service to the new area health authorities, leading Castle to commit a further £1m to family planning. A fundamental flaw in the system was that GPs refused to give out free condoms to men under the scheme on the basis that they were not 'medical devices', despite the fact that this was, and remained, the most popular and effective form of contraception for married and non-married couples (as well as the best protection against sexually transmitted diseases). Conversely, there was much hostile reaction to the suggestion that contraception might be provided to single teenage girls, particularly those under sixteen, though the Health Minister, David Owen, rejected the argument that this would encourage greater promiscuity – an argument that would intensify over the following decades.[56] Though Leo Abse had been eclipsed over vasectomy and abortion, his persistent harrying of the LRC eventually paid off. With the medical profession and ministers increasingly concerned about the rising cost of contraceptive medicines and devices, the Monopolies Commission investigated the LRC's pricing of rubber sheaths, and their profits were slashed to a quarter of their 1972 level. Abse was able to crow wittily that, with government assistance, he had now 'brought down the cost of loving'.[57]

If Joseph had been 'naïve', as he admitted, over family planning policy, he could have been forgiven a degree of satisfaction at a less comfortable political legacy that he bequeathed to Castle in the shape of the report of the Lane Committee on the Abortion Act. In one respect the report made life easier for the Government in that it supported the status quo, saying that gains far outweighed any disadvantages for which it had been criticised. It resisted the suggestions of those campaigning for abortion on demand, at one end of the spectrum, as well as those wanting to restrict to differing extents the grounds on which women could obtain a legal abortion. However, it did provide enough meat for the Government to implement its recommendations immediately and with little controversy. Its recommendations focused on shifting the provision of abortion more towards the NHS and voluntary services, and trying to reduce the incentives for unscrupulous private practice, where the Committee had uncovered extensive evidence of abuse. This included pressure on women to abort as well as insufficient inquiry into their medical and social circumstances to justify granting an abortion. Such practices were motivated by the high commercial return for private abortion operations, particularly from foreign women taking advantage of Britain's more liberal law. However, the Committee thought that actively trying to suppress private practice through legislation might rekindle even more unsavoury underground activities.[58] This thinking chimed with the Government's own caution, but the problem was that many of the MPs who had signed the motion which led to the establishment of the Lane Committee in 1971 were not actually interested in making the Abortion Act work more centrally within the NHS, as the Committee recommended, or in removing the most glaring abuses of the Act in the private sector. They wanted to legislate to restrict the grounds on which abortion could be performed, and they wasted no time after the Lane Report in seeking to persuade Parliament to do just this. A minor bill, sponsored by Conservative Michael Grylls, seeking just to regulate pregnancy advice centres which made abortion referrals, encountered the wrath of anti-abortionists including the redoubtable Dame Jill Knight, propagator of the 'Babies for Burning' allegations about aborted foetuses being rendered down to make soap. These allegations, also gleefully supported in *The Times* by Butt, were revealed as fraudulent. This did not, of course, deter Knight from using other shocking evidence of abuse of the Abortion Act such as 'a relatively poor medical student who in six years had achieved a town flat, a country house and three cars through abortion'. She and three other MPs walked out of the standing committee on the Grylls Bill, complaining that it did not go far enough.[59]

Many anti-abortionists were, however, savvy enough to continue to cloak their recidivist aims in more moderate tones, as they realised that to be successful, legislation would have to win the support of those in favour of abortion as well as those opposed. The best opportunity was a Private Members' Bill sponsored by Glasgow Labour MP James White in 1975. This shrewdly ignored the 'social clause' in the Act, which allowed doctors to take into account a woman's 'actual or reasonably foreseeable environment', and sought to correct the mistake which anti-abortionists had made in 1967 when they themselves inserted into the Abortion Bill the qualification that a termination could only be performed if 'the continuation of the pregnancy involved *greater risk* [to the mental or physical health or the life of the woman or her existing child(ren)] than if the pregnancy were terminated'. It was soon realised that medical advances meant that an early abortion would almost always be safer than a full-term pregnancy, so certifying an abortion under this rule was easier than enquiring into a woman's physical and mental health or her social environment. White, Abse and their supporters said this provided abortion virtually on demand, which was not what Parliament had intended. They also wanted to tighten the provision for abortions on the ground of the risk to the physical or mental health of the woman, and lower the time limit to twenty weeks, except in an emergency. The Bill also wanted to make enforcing the law easier by reversing the burden of proof so that doctors and nurses would have to justify their actions, rather than the prosecution prove that they had not acted in good faith.

The Government was in a difficult position. Even if babies were not being turned into soap (and, as medical experts soon pointed out, aborted foetuses do not possess the layer of subcutaneous fat necessary to make them valuable ingredients for soap), the private abuses of the Act had been laid bare by the Lane Committee. Ministers were anxious to stamp these out without conceding the restrictions on the terms of the Abortion Act for which pro-life MPs were clamouring. Owen indicated that legislation was a possible option. However, in his memoirs Owen explains the tactics behind his words rather differently:

> *I was anxious about introducing any new legislation for the mood of the House of Commons in the middle of 1974 was very different from the reformist mood in 1966 when Labour had a large majority. I judged that any new legislation risked the imposition of restrictive amendments to the actual grounds on which an abortion could be authorised. I decided therefore to try to use existing legislation, though I might be taken to court for going beyond the powers those laws gave me … Even legislation to fix the number of weeks beyond which no abortion could take place could have had a restrictive amendment attached to it. So I deliberately delayed this legislation as well.*[60]

Owen and Castle were 'forced' into conceding a select committee inquiry into the provisions of the White Bill. This prevented it progressing beyond second reading, when it was supported by 232 to 98, but kept discussion of its provisions going, in the end, beyond the general election called in September 1974. The Committee was immediately controversial because its composition had been decided by the Speaker according to the vote on the second reading of the Bill. This was interpreted as giving it an anti-abortion majority, despite the fact that many MPs who supported the existing Act had voted for the Bill because they were anxious to stamp out abuses of it. Anti-abortionists were able to claim, erroneously, that 'the vast majority of MPs, regardless of where they sit and their religious or other convictions, tend to think this Act needs substantial amendment.' Supporters of the Act complained that in 1966, the standing committee examining the original Abortion Bill had not reflected the over-

whelming majority who supported it either. In addition, some women Labour
MPs were incensed at the small number of women on the Committee. Lena Jeger
was principled about the importance of this imbalance, arguing that 'by getting
more women on the Committee, we might find ourselves with, God forbid ...
Mrs Knight' or other anti-abortionists.[61] Government business managers were
under heavy pressure from both sides, with angry claims at a Parliamentary
Labour Party meeting from Labour women MPs that the Leader of the House,
Ted Short, had agreed that two extra women should be added to the Committee.
However, Bob Mellish, the Chief Whip, said that White and Abse had threatened
to resign from the Committee if its composition was changed.[62]

The Churches and the medical profession were also deeply divided on the way
forward. The BMA had remained silent on the Bill until May 1975, when young
doctors staged a sit-in at its headquarters, demanding that the Association state
publicly its opposition to the Bill's restrictive measures. Eventually the BMA capitulated, publishing the evidence it had submitted to the Select Committee, in
which it had questioned the Bill's ability to stamp out abuses of the Abortion Act,
and criticised the clauses seeking to restrict the grounds for abortion.[63] The
Anglican Church was, typically, even more divided. Ongoing efforts at greater
cooperation with a view to possible reunion between the Church of England and
the Methodist Church were hit by the abortion issue. A joint document was
pulled at the last minute by Anglicans who objected to its general support for the
existing Abortion Act. Although the joint group which had written the report,
including the Anglican Board for Social Responsibility, had unanimously backed
its conclusions, 'leading Anglican Churchmen' were said to be unhappy about it.
Of course the Church of England had not gone as far as Parliament in its recommendations on abortion in the 1960s, and now the General Synod accepted a
motion supporting the White Bill, with its sponsor, lay member Robert Edwards,
saying that 'a nation could no longer call itself civilised' when there were 150,000
abortions a year. By the time the Select Committee reported in the summer, it had
predictably failed to reach agreement on fundamental questions, addressing itself
only to minor administrative solutions to some of the abuses under the Act. Nor,
to the annoyance of pro-abortionists, did it tackle what they considered the main
reason for private-sector abuses, the lack of abortion facilities within the NHS.
This reflected the fear of anti-abortionists that extending NHS facilities would
normalise abortion within the NHS, rather than restricting it.[64]

At the end of the parliamentary session, Castle pledged the Government to tightening up the regulation of the abortion system in line with the Select Committee's recommendations, and said that there would be a vote in the new session on re-establishing the Select Committee. Castle, who, as Owen says, was 'untypically nervous of public opinion' on abortion because of the Catholic vote in her Blackburn constituency, decided to show her hand. Having held back during discussion about the first Select Committee, she now decided to use her influence, particularly within the PLP, to resist its reconstitution, having 'made up my mind that it's time to stand up and be counted'. Castle was determined to make a speech to the PLP, outlining her opposition to another select committee at a meeting called by other women MPs who supported the Abortion Act. According to her diaries, she and Owen worked hard on producing a speech that would carry the weight of her convictions without undermining her position as a minister, or alienating too many anti-abortionists. As she records, the pressure on her was immense:

Somehow all this has leaked and in the lobbies this evening I have been besieged by irate Catholics. Jimmy White threatened to resign from the party if there was any tinkering with the free vote. Bob Mellish took me aside to talk to me like a Dutch uncle, though a friendly one. 'I know that with all your savvy you'll realise this issue is dynamite.' I kept my nerve, refusing to answer those who came up to me asking what I was going to say tomorrow. 'You'd better come and listen hadn't you?'

However, the most bruising encounter was still to come. Harold Wilson, her old friend and protector, from whom she had become increasingly estranged since 1970,[65] 'waylaid' her and took her to his room in the Commons, for a display of his delicate mental condition just weeks before he resigned as Prime Minister.

His eyes were baggy and I noted that he was in one of his 'I'll get the hell out it' moods ... Pouring me a brandy he said he had given up brandy himself in order to lose weight, arguing that for some unknown reason he had actually lost weight since switching to beer. 'I drink five pints a day,' he boasted, but proceeded to pour himself some Madeira. The pleasantries over, we proceeded to have a major row. He told me categorically that he wasn't going to have me splitting the party. 'I'm sick of pulling this party back from the brink. If this goes on I shall throw in my hand – and then see how some of you will get along.' 'Like who?' I replied, at which he gave me a hostile look, as if to say, 'You'd go, for one.' Does he realise how little his threats worry me? Harold then laid down the law: I could say how I was going to vote personally, but I must not give any reasons. If I did I must give both sides of the issue, or another minister would have to put the reasons the other way. I quite liked this latter idea, but he did not. 'Perhaps someone else had better speak tomorrow: John Silkin for instance,' Harold went on. I told him John was as much against re-establishing the Select Committee as I was. 'And imagine what will be said if I do not speak now,' I continued. He went on menacing me about how neutral I must be in my arguments, ending nastily, 'Think about it.' I did, going to bed wondering how I could salvage something from this wreck.[66]

The next day Castle redrafted the speech, trying to balance her opinions against the Wilson fiat. Though pleased with it, Owen thought Wilson's ruling would make their life difficult during the debate on the motion to re-establish the Committee. Castle's success at the PLP meeting spilled over into her most bubbly and vainglorious prose:

The meeting of the PLP was exceptionally well attended, for a Thursday night. All the abortion antagonists were there. As Shirley [Williams] slipped into a seat next to me on the platform she whispered, 'I've come to the conclusion that your job is even worse than mine.' [Williams was then Secretary of State for Prices and Consumer Protection] In the debate Kevin McNamara demanded that I should not disclose my own views, as this would inevitably carry the weight of a Secretary of State. Brian Walden, on the other hand, made a passionately eloquent speech, demanding that the party should have the courage of its convictions and I of mine. I sat there calmly, convinced that the speech I had prepared would strike exactly the right note between the two. And so it proved. It was temperate, cunning and firm and it did the trick. 'Ten out of ten,' said Bob Mellish loudly afterwards. Even Jimmy Dunn thanked me, while Shirley said, 'No one could object to that.' And yet it had left the party in no doubt where I stood. 'That is my conviction, Brian,' I had said and he came and congratulated me on it. So did innumerable others, including the women who were delighted that I had not been frightened of the one thing they wanted: a statement of how I intended to vote myself. 'Never in my life have I been accorded such unanimity,'

I said to Norman [Warner, one of her special advisers], back in my room. 'I wouldn't have believed it would be possible on that subject,' he replied.[67]

The confidence was misplaced and Owen's pessimism proved correct. In the vote on 9 February, MPs reappointed the same fifteen members to the Select Committee. The minority who had previously objected to the Committee's imbalance towards anti-abortionists immediately resigned, saying that the Bill could only lead to the return of back-street abortions.[68] The vacancies were filled and two further reports were produced during the year, which similarly failed to satisfy those who wanted to restrict access to abortion, or those wanting to expand its provision within the NHS. As the midwife of the Abortion Act, David Steel commented: 'Considering that the Select Committee this Session consisted entirely of opponents of the 1967 Abortion Act, the report could have been much more destructive.'[69] In December the Committee was wound up. Anti-abortionists rallied their forces once again, staging all-night vigils and mass rallies of up to sixty thousand people across the country, and garnering the public support of the Duchess of Kent (a convert to Rome in the early 1990s), who said termination of pregnancy raised disquieting aspects: 'If there is abuse, it could easily become the accepted standard. Human life is sacred. It is a gift from God, and as such should never be taken for granted.'[70]

In February 1977 another bill seeking to amend the Abortion Act, sponsored by Tory MP William Benyon, won its second reading, this time by 170 to 132 votes, rather closer than the margin on the White Bill in 1975. Nevertheless, supporters of the Abortion Act were again left in a minority on the Standing Committee, and had to fight a long war of attrition, with the Committee sitting up to sixty hours per week with consecutive all-night sittings in an effort by its sponsors to push it through to its final stages before time ran out in the summer. Despite a direct plea to the Prime Minister, and the consideration of the question by the full Cabinet, the Government refused to give extra time to the Bill, saying that it had implemented all the main recommendations of the Lane Committee to tighten the working of the Abortion Act. It denied that it was trying to kill the Bill, with a novel use of language by the new Health Minister, Chris Moyle, who said that 'the Government has a positive attitude, and that attitude is one of neutrality.'[71] Michael Foot, the Leader of the Commons, and number two in the Government to Jim Callaghan, faced a barrage of complaints from MPs demanding the Government give time to finish the remaining stages of the Bill, with an irate Dame Jill Knight claiming that 'an overwhelming number of backbench MPs' had supported such a motion. Bob Mellish, now on the back benches, revealed his own hand, attacking those opposed to the Bill as anti-democratic, and claiming that the first Wilson Government's treatment of capital punishment indicated they should indulge the present Bill in the same way. On the other side, supporters of the Act claimed that the chairmen of the Standing Committee had been biased in favour of the Bill. Other Labour women MPs in the vanguard of defending the Abortion Act, Audrey Wise and Helene Hayman, pointedly asked questions about battered babies and child benefit, implicitly distinguishing between discussion of the rights of the unborn and the plight of living infants. Undeterred, Conservative Bernard Braine reintroduced the Bill in the following session. Although it received a second reading, the margin was so narrow, six votes, that Owen's strategy of playing a long game to thwart legislation had proved successful.[72]

*

If traditionalists were aghast at the prevalence of legal abortion and birth control services in Britain during the 1970s, their most anxious concern was the penetration of these habits into Britain's youth, reflecting and encouraging greater promiscuity. Sex education had been contentious since the beginning of the 1960s, when outraged conservatives objected to official sanction being given to the view that sex outside marriage might not always be taught to be wrong. Although responsibility in Whitehall rested jointly with the Department of Education and the DHSS by the end of the 1960s, the actual availability and content of sex education in schools was strictly a matter for local education authorities and schools themselves. This resulted in a wide variety of provision across the country, which, despite the increasing central control over education and the gradual inclusion of sex education in the national curriculum, persists to this day. However, sex education first became a matter of national controversy in the early 1970s, with the production of new educational materials in print and on film. The most notorious example was the film by Dr Martin Cole in 1971, *Growing Up*. Cole, a lecturer in Genetics at Aston University, was clearly very much of his time, a radical with a rather zealous belief in the benefits of promiscuous premarital sex, who later also advocated lowering the age of consent. The film itself contained separate scenes of a man and a woman masturbating, as well as a couple having intercourse. Conservative MP Sir Gerald Nabarro urged that the Director of Public Prosecutions, Sir Norman Skelhorn, see the film with a view to possible prosecution. Skelhorn declined to act, although he said that if it were viewed by schoolchildren he would reconsider his decision.[73] In Birmingham, where the film was made, the Conservative-controlled Education Committee suspended the schoolteacher Jennifer Muscutt, who was seen masturbating in the film (although she had not been a teacher at the time). The Committee viewed the film and subsequently banned it. Sir Francis Griffin, the council leader, asserted that 'expressions of opinion in the council are often a true reflection of the normal standards which the man in the street hopes to maintain' – sentiments of which Lord Devlin would no doubt have approved. Muscutt was eventually reinstated.[74] *Growing Up* also provided the first opportunity for Mary Whitehouse to lobby the woman who would, by the end of the decade, become such an iconic figure for moral conservatives seeking a return to 'traditional values'. However, on this occasion Margaret Thatcher did not take up the banner. As Education Secretary she criticised Cole's film, and strongly advised against it being shown in schools, but she resolutely refused to consider intervening from the centre in local decisions on sex education provision, or to allow parents the right of withdrawal from sex education lessons.[75] The ready willingness of local education authorities to ban *Growing Up*, including the Inner London Education Authority, perhaps demonstrated the strength of her case that there was no need to interfere.

The early 1970s were also punctuated by a series of celebrated and well-recorded legal assaults against the underground press, first *IT* for printing gay contact adverts, then the *Little Red School Book* (*LRSB*), for its corrupting influence on schoolchildren, and most famously against *Oz* for its 'School Kids' edition. These last two cases sharpened fears that sex education was being hijacked by propagandists for an alternative underground lifestyle, and sexual promiscuity and hedonism ruthlessly peddled to young children. The *LRSB* neatly encapsulated the fears of Whitehouse and others that sexual anarchy was the other side of the coin of political anarchy, with its clear overtones of Maoist propaganda. As Alan Travis notes, the uncontentious advice on homework and other adolescent problems went unnoticed. The link between the effects of permissiveness and the radical left on Britain's youth was underlined by the evidence given in the *Oz* trial by the sixteen-year-old culprit who had authored the infamous Rupert Bear cartoon, Viv Berger, who said:

> *These are the kinds of drawing that go around every classroom, every day, in every school ... Maybe I was portraying obscenity, but I don't think I was being obscene myself ... If the news covers a war or shows a picture of war, then, for me they are portraying obscenity – the obscenity of war. But they are not themselves creating that obscenity, because it is the people who are fighting the war that are creating that obscenity ... For example, I consider that the act of corporal punishment is an obscenity. I do not consider the act of reporting or the writing about corporal punishment is obscene.*

Perhaps not surprisingly Berger's mother was the director of the National Council for Civil Liberties, who also gave evidence at the trial.[76] If Berger's testimony showed the futility of Whitehouse's puritanism, it also provided ample evidence for those keen to portray permissiveness as a tool of the left. These fears were distilled into less partisan advice to ministers on the seriousness of the threat of radicalism spreading from the university student movements in the late 1960s further down into the school-age population. Writing to Robert Armstrong, then Ted Heath's PPS, Thatcher's Private Secretary suggested that there was little cause for alarm:

> *The general outlook of the young has changed and is likely to go on changing. Physically, they are maturing earlier. They have more money to spend. Their attitudes towards authority and conventional rules are more challenging. The causes of these changes are complex, but in part they seem either a reaction to, or an imitation of, the adult world they see around them. External factors, for example the mass media, especially television, and parental attitudes, themselves changing, seem to us more potent factors than education or its institutions in creating this new outlook.*[77]

The *Oz* and *LRSB* trials represented the high noon of the battle between the underground press and the authorities. On one side the underground was fizzling out, or 'sinking giggling into the sea' in Desmond Donnelley's echoing of Peter Cook's phrase, whilst on the other the DPP and the courts were increasingly aware that the hardcore pornography easily available on the streets of Soho, corrupted by the police as much as the pornographers, made *Oz* seem like the real Rupert the Bear cartoon. However, along with educational films like *Growing Up* they sparked a new moral concern about sex education and advice to schoolchildren. When the Conservative Government introduced the NHS Reorganisation Bill, setting up a comprehensive family planning service, Jill Knight attempted to ban contraceptive advice to those under sixteen without parental consent. Sir Keith Joseph, citing existing guidelines that doctors should consult parents, rejected the call. But concerns about contraceptive advice and sex education converged on this Bill, as Baroness Elles, Conservative spokeswoman and barrister, sought to insert a clause making it a responsibility of the social services and education secretaries to approve all sex education material, and prescribe the parameters of its content. When the legislation was reinforced by a DHSS circular to GPs, it stated that any doctor 'acting in good faith' to protect a girl against 'the potentially harmful effects of intercourse' could legitimately prescribe contraceptives. It would be 'prudent' to consult the parents, but only with the child's consent.[78] As with doctors' involvement in referring women for abortion, these guidelines were adhering strictly to the medical, as opposed to the social, reasons for contraception. Such a narrow perspective of abortion angered women who wanted access to termination on social grounds or on demand. Soon this division of the social and moral arguments from the medical, and the principle of doctor–patient confidentiality, were to come under attack from conservatives opposed to the prescribing of contraception to children under sixteen.

In January 1976 Elles introduced an unprecedented debate in the Lords on sex education. Arguing for parental vetting and approval of all sex education classes and materials, she launched a scathing attack on the work of the FPA in sex education, citing information leaflets the organisation had produced some years earlier – 'the finest collection of obscene literature which has ever been displayed in this House'. She personally attacked Alistair Service, the FPA Chairman, for his history of working for abortion and divorce law reform, as well as his more recent work with the BCC, leading to the DHSS 'takeover' of family planning. She wanted the Government to hold fast against any suggestion of lowering the age of consent or relaxing the law on incest, to put failure warnings on packets of non-medical contraceptives and to exercise more control over sex education films. Baroness Gaitskell was, once again, the most fervent supporter of a more liberal policy, defending the FPA and blaming inadequate parental instruction and political intransigence for existing problems:

> [Parents] have left their children to acquire like vagabonds their knowledge about sex. Here were are, in this mature House of Parliament ... perpetuating and adding to the mountain of myths about sex, and not setting about reducing the ignorance and guilt which have been such a legacy from Victorian years.

However, Gaitskell was in a small minority of peers. Even those on the Labour benches who counted themselves supporters of greater individual freedom voiced concerns about the trends in behaviour among young people. Baroness Summerskill, who was fighting a long-running campaign to protect women from the adverse side effects of easier divorce law and the contraceptive pill, was also scathing about the failure of society to give girls the information they needed to protect themselves from pregnancy and venereal disease in the face of the onslaught of the commercial ubiquity of sex. Whilst supporting contraception and more sex education outside the home, Summerskill argued:

> In view of the fact that the media are dictating the mores of the country, I feel that we must give advice which counteracts the powerful propaganda of those interests which portray for ulterior motives the delights of sex. To withhold information on sex is wrong, and there is no justification for keeping adolescents in ignorance when the media provides the very antithesis of how sex knowledge should be disseminated.
>
> The need of the girl for enlightenment on the subject is greater than that of the boy. When a scantily dressed young woman is shown on television romping with an attractive youth in a bedroom, there is never any warning that one act of sexual intercourse alone may result in pregnancy and venereal disease ... if there were a warning it would ruin the story and so affect the commercial interests of the producers, which are paramount and largely determine the policy, which is to please the customer and not at any risk introduce an aspect of the subject which is displeasing.

More than one peer put the argument that sexual promiscuity was the bedfellow, for want of a better word, of left-wing ideology – Lord Clifford claiming baldly that 'the International Socialists and their allies are responsible for many of the more notorious cases of sexual maleducation.' Lord Sudeley went further, managing to encompass Engels' argument that sexual morality existed to safeguard property with the 'disastrous' effects of the implementation of his theories after the Russian Revolution, as well an attack on commercial interests which were 'reminiscent of *Mein Kampf* and sinister folk, who, in keeping their own sheets clean, enriched themselves by dirtying other people's. No party should be so dedicated to capitalism as to avow that profits should be allowed to interfere with the nation's morals.'

Lord Crowther-Hunt, the minister replying to the debate, sympathised with all the arguments made, safe in the knowledge that, as he repeatedly emphasised, central Government had no responsibility for sex education in schools, leading to a fierce row with Elles, who wanted more government intervention. Crowther-Hunt's obvious riposte was that if the Government just happened to take a contrary view to hers, 'she certainly would not be urging that the Government should ensure that values contrary to those which she wishes are taught in the schools of this country.'[79] Ministers led by Shirley Williams tried to rein in some of the perceived excesses of progressive education by establishing a 'core curriculum' of responsible sex education within the context of 'parenting' instruction. Such initiatives were undermined by the local campaigns against some of the more radical left-wing material circulating in London in particular, notably at the William Tyndale School in Islington and in the London Teachers' Association.[80]

By 1978, fears about the greater provision of contraceptive advice in family planning clinics on the basis set out in the DHSS memorandum of 1974 were causing wider controversy, attracting press comment and the close attention of 'pro-family' campaign groups, notably those led by Valerie Riches and Victoria Gillick, who were to be at the forefront of campaigns against contraception throughout the 1980s. These groups sought to 'reassert' parental rights to refuse to allow doctors to prescribe contraceptives to children under sixteen. With a general election fast approaching, some adopted a tactic first used in 1972 in Birmingham, to ask all candidates to complete a questionnaire on their views about sex education and contraception. Mary Whitehouse herself warned during the election campaign that 'one is driven to conclude' that if Labour was 'returned to power, such clinics before very long will become part of a way of life for our children'. The pressure was being piled on to withdraw the 1974 memorandum. Patrick Jenkin, the Shadow Social Services secretary, promised the guidance would be reviewed if the Conservatives won.[81]

*

The growing campaign against the pervasive and pernicious effects of an increasing tide of pornography brought together the equally indefatigable Mary Whitehouse and Lord Longford. The overturning of the prison sentences of the *Oz* defendants led to the launching of a 'Nationwide Petition for Public Decency' in 1972. The previous year the Responsible Society had canvassed support for the more vividly titled Campaign for National Disgust. The reaction of Archbishop Ramsey's staff to a request that the Primate should support the campaign was one of near horror, his Private Secretary commenting that 'I cannot for a moment imagine that the Archbishop would wish to join in anything called a Campaign of National Disgust.'[82] The National Festival of Light (NFoL) was founded in March 1971, and shared its membership with similar grassroots organisations such as Whitehouse's National Viewers and Listeners Association (VALA, pronounced 'valour' by its members), which had developed out of Whitehouse's original 'Clean Up TV' campaign. However, the festival itself was the brainchild of Peter Hall, who had recently returned from working in India for the Christian mission Operation Mobilisation, only to be appalled at the 'moral landslide' which had taken place during his absence. A year after the launch of the NFoL, the London Festival of Jesus, an offshoot, staged an aquatic rally which ingeniously sought to use the national resonance of the evacuation from Dunkirk in 1940 to inspire the nation to moral renewal. One of the leaders of Dunkirk Miracle '72, which numbered twenty-five boats and 3,500 people, identified a link: just as the soldiers on the beaches had been rescued because of the nation's prayers, so help would come through prayer for our social, economic and spiritual plight. However, even the Christian news magazine *Crusade* said that Dunkirk Miracle '72 was 'pointing a loaded pistol of imminent doom at the man in the street to encourage him to face spiritual realities'.[83]

A number of local pressure groups, inspired by these national efforts, took the fight against moral permissiveness to their local authorities where discretion over censorship and arts funding, as well as provision of education services, meant that their influence over the local moral 'climate' was still strong. As national campaigns like NFoL were unable to sustain large rallies beyond 1972, this became important to the survival of the moral-reform movement. London, with its size, its concentration of cinemas and theatres, and the inevitable lead it gave to the rest of the country, was a main focus of activity. In 1972 Whitehouse and festival colleagues prayed in the rain outside a GLC meeting which, whether or not the result of divine intervention, did comply with their demands that the council use its power to view films themselves before granting licences, rather than merely rubber-stamping BBFC decisions. This tactic was adopted in the Bodmin area of Cornwall by the Community Standards Association, which sought to 'awaken the conscience and mobilise the concern of the community over the encroachment of mental and moral pollution with its disastrous consequences for the physical and psychological health of the individual and its damage to society as a whole'. It also monitored the content of sex education in schools and tried to persuade local newsagents not to stock pornography. Another such group, the Bristol Family Life Association, was a specifically Christian and church-based organisation which tried, unsuccessfully, to persuade Bristol City Council to ban a homosexual festival in 1978.[84] The rise of such pressure groups reflected a concern among mainly middle-class conservatives that traditional values were being undermined. In the words of one commentator at the time, 'in the past the orthodox could depend on their values being defended by institutionalised groups such as the church, the Conservative Party, social workers, teachers etc. without having to think about the matter, but in the current world none of these agencies is totally reliable.'[85]

The unreliability of the police in investigating and prosecuting the producers and purveyors of pornography was gradually revealed during the 1970s, as ongoing suspicion about corruption within the Metropolitan Police's Obscene Publications Squad reached a critical mass in the wake of the trials of *Oz* and the *LRSB*, which begged the question why harder material easily available in Soho was not being successfully targeted. As Alan Travis documents in *Bound and Gagged*, very soon Home Office officials were asking just this question of the Metropolitan Police and the inept DPP, Sir Norman Skelhorn.[86] Of course, the Obscene Publications Squad was, in one sense, operating according to the same philosophy as Whitehouse and those who believed that sexual and political anarchy were two sides of the same coin. The radical left 'yippies' behind *Oz* and the *LRSB* were not only an easier and less well-resourced target, but were social and political anathema to conservatives. Whitehouse abhorred commercial pornography barons equally, but their corrupt relationship with some elements in the Metropolitan Police, and the political apathy of many conservatives to commercial, as opposed to social or political, exploitation of new attitudes towards sex, gave pornographers greater protection. It was the hubris of the Obscene Publications Squad and their porn paymasters which brought them down – once Whitehall officials and ministers realised the extent of the corruption.

Britain was in the grip of a moral decline dating back twenty or thirty years, according to Whitehouse. She saw the roots of this decline in communism and the far left, making little or no distinction between the effects of pornography and the rise of industrial militancy. Her confident hope that the Conservative Government would sponsor an international conference on moral pollution in 1972 failed to materialise, but Whitehouse's lobbying had become more successful, and her letters were no longer ignored, as they had been for a time under Wilson. Her main tactic was to humiliate political and religious leaders into listening to, and if possible supporting her campaigns. The greater prominence of moralistic language in the rhetoric of the emerging Thatcherism made such people more instinctively at home within the Conservative Party, but there was still a feeling among some of these groups that the nonconformist tradition in the Labour Party made it as useful to lobby as the Conservative Party, prey as it was to commercial interests, particularly over pornography, gambling and licensing.[87] Criticism was voiced within the Conservative Party about the 'selling of obscenity'.[88]

The spread of pornography and obscenity was increasingly viewed as the single cause of moral decay. This was often ingeniously elided with the threat of blasphemy. As campaigners such as Whitehouse and Longford invested prime importance in moral revival being grounded in Christian principles and teaching, it was in this debate that the Church's voice was at its strongest during the 1970s. Church leaders were inevitably increasingly called on to condemn particular liberal outrages and support various campaigns. Ramsey attempted to give guidance without continually being drawn in:

I believe that the Church's function is best exercised not by passing judgements on particular incidents. It is not for the Church to have an index of prohibited books or films. It is the Church's function to state the Christian moral principles which bear upon present problems and to expose the trends which make for evil. Nudity and sex are not in themselves wrong. What is wrong is the separation of sex from its highest purpose and its exploitation for commercial profit by the entertainment or advertising or any other industry. While pornography is a great evil, a more insidiously dangerous evil is the infiltration of false values through the trivialisation of nudity and sex, and the treatment of them for merely sensuous gratification.[89]

In fact Ramsey and many other bishops were appalled by the apocalyptic language which was often used by the Whitehouse lobby, and objected to their air of moral superiority and the way in which the support and participation of the Church was automatically assumed, often through underhand tactics of informing the media of correspondence before the Church had had a chance to respond. This antipathy really set in with the launch, in the wake of the over-turning of sentences against the *Oz* defendants, of the NFoL, led by Colonel Orr Dobbie, as well as Whitehouse, Longford and Malcolm Muggeridge. Dobbie wrote to Ramsey requesting not only a statement of support, but also that the whole apparatus of the Church of England should be engaged in a national day of prayer for the festival launch in September 1971. Ramsey's Private Secretary, Hugh Whitworth, reporting his conversations with the equally wary Methodist and Catholic hierarchy, replied that 'the 19 September, being our Ordination Sunday, was not a suitable date on which to ask the clergy to pray to be delivered from moral pollution.'[90] However, the news that Cardinal Heenan had consented to give the festival his blessing forced Ramsey into making a gesture of support – not the last time that such 'divide and rule' tactics were to be successful with the Churches, which were obviously anxious not to be seen as less 'moral' than their competitors. Ramsey submitted a short prayer to be used at the festival. This made no mention, however, of morality or obscenity, and perhaps as a result, was relegated to the end of the day's proceedings, receiving no coverage in the media. The festival's organisers then claimed at a press conference that Ramsey had declined to give it his blessing. Writing to Muggeridge about his treatment, Ramsey barely concealed his anger, and revealed some of the underlying reasons why he objected to their tactics:

It really is quite ridiculous to suppose that a Bishop in this country expounding Christian faith and morals needs to wave a piece of paper saying that the Archbishop of Canterbury agrees with him ... alongside things which were well said there was also a good deal of use of what can fairly be called the Billy Graham technique of evangelism. This is something with which I am out of sympathy, for in my experience while it helps some it alienates others ...

The NFoL rally has no monopoly of evangelistic effort, and you rather speak as if it had ... I am aware enough of the failings of my own Church as of other Churches, but I do find your language of denigration extravagant. You suggest that we are preoccupied with 'the letter of ecumenicalism' and are acquiescing in the terrible moral crisis which exists ... I wonder how you suppose I spend my own time ... a good deal more of it is given to trying as best I can to present the Christian faith and its moral corollaries, especially to young people, by speaking and discussion.

I hope the NFoL will succeed in reaching people who are not otherwise reached. I hope I have made my attitude towards it clear to you. Every intense spiritual and ethical movement that I have known is liable to a kind of self-righteousness, and it is not the least surprising if this Festival is exposed to this danger.[91]

The launch itself drew a huge crowd in Trafalgar Square. Not all were sympathetic as women and gay liberation protestors tried to sabotage proceedings. According to the *Guardian*,

there were tomatoes, white mice, stink bombs, and a posse of demonstrators dressed as nuns who ran howling at the platform. Reliable sources said later that some were male homosexuals and others were lesbians. This is real pornography. People in India are dying in their thousands. What about Vietnam? Not this hypocritical bullshit.[92]

The Church of England demonstrated, in the eyes of the festival, its further 'acquiescence' in the terrible moral crisis in Britain when the Dean and Chapter of St Paul's Cathedral consented to a special communion service to mark the third anniversary of the musical *Hair*. Whitworth merely observed that 'my children assure me that *Hair* is neither blasphemous nor obscene but they do not think that I would enjoy it because it was so noisy.'[93] Dobbie and the festival's supporters were outraged, taking no comfort in Ramsey's buck-passing that services in St Paul's were beyond his jurisdiction.

Ramsey, as can be seen from the Lambeth Palace archive, was bombarded with every shade of opinion including a commercial purveyor of naturist publications, Sun and Health Limited, indignant at its wares being seized by Customs and Excise, and helpfully enclosing samples of these, together with comparisons from the *Sun* and of hardcore pornography available on British streets, for the archbishop to judge the relative innocence of its naturist magazines.[94] What influence it thought Ramsey would have with Customs is not clear. Perhaps it had confused the initials CE with C of E.

Ramsey had some reason to be indignant at the suggestion that he and his bishops were standing by while Britain sank into moral decay. Apart from the public statements and initiatives of individual leaders of the Church and priests within parishes and communities, the bishops had begun to formulate their own response, in a characteristically more measured, analytical fashion than Whitehouse or the NFoL. The results of such discussions were then taken to the Government to see where they might help inform administrative and legislative reform. The bishops appreciated the difficulties which legislators and the Home Office faced in any attempt to define more closely the obscenity laws, and saw little point in pressing the issue with no clear way forward. However, religious influence was being squeezed from two directions. On the one hand, the confidence of grassroots traditionalists in the determination of their spiritual leaders to resist, rather than compromise with, permissive Britain was waning. On the other hand, the rest of the Establishment had come to accept that the influence of the Church was now small and shrinking. *The Times*'s 1971 survey of *Who's Who* found that only two per cent thought that the Church was 'very influential' but seventy-eight per cent thought it had 'little, if any influence'.[95]

Though official action against pornography and obscenity at this time was largely restricted to the police and the courts, the parliamentary supporters of moral revival were not inactive. Longford launched his famous inquiry into pornography, which captured the attention and imagination of the press, especially when the newly dubbed 'Lord Porn' and his colleagues visited Denmark to see a more permissive law in action, and he was photographed declining the offers of a club dancer who was brandishing a whip. In the Lords, the length of the inquiry was framed by debates initiated by Longford which, as usual, aroused peers to heights of passionate indignation. Lord Eccles who had been particularly keen to promote moral instruction in teacher-training as Education Minister in the early 1960s, spoke for the Government. Norman Shrapnel's description in the *Guardian* painted a more vivid scene than the Hansard report:

> *Lord Eccles, who in all but name has evidently become responsible for the Department of Ethics and Public Morality, was determined to do what he could to ensure that the permissive tide does not bury us still deeper.*
>
> *'It is faintly possible', Lord Eccles told a startled House, 'that in time the inhabitants of Westminster might get used to copulating in the street like dogs and pigeons.' Peers exchanged nervous glances. Nobody they knew, surely? 'But not tomorrow morning,' Lord Eccles added more reassuringly.*[96]

When peers returned to discuss the product of Longford's Committee, an unusually sanguine Baroness Young, speaking for the Government, commended its support for the family, careful sex education and control of pornography. However, she noted that recent polling revealed that most people felt they personally would not be harmed by exposure to pornography, and that as a result

> *it is peculiarly difficult to frame a law which will impose appropriate restrictions on the material to which we think various groups ... ought not to be exposed without at the same time interfering to an unjustifiable degree with what we ourselves believe we should be free to choose to read or see.*

Perhaps this was delivered through gritted teeth. Rejecting the liberal arguments that the threat from pornography was exaggerated, the Bishop of Leicester, a member of the Longford Committee, quoted a correspondent who demonstrated that not being able to make the choice what to read or see might be an advantage: 'I never thought that I should give thanks to God for being blind, but since my wife has told me what she has seen in the film, *The Devils*, I am genuinely grateful that I at least have been spared that.'[97]

Once again, the Churches were strong-armed into taking part in the public event organised by the NFoL following the Lords debate, partly motivated by the desire to ensure that the festival did not 'steal all the limelight'.[98] This time, however, the Anglican, Catholic and Methodist leaders acted collectively to widen discussion beyond 'pornography' to 'The Family in Society', Cardinal Heenan insisting that:

> It is important that the meeting ... should be regarded as a specifically ecumenical occasion. The Archbishop, the Moderator and myself [sic] will be speaking officially of the Family as the centre of Christian Society. If this meeting is to be worthwhile, it is most important that it should teach positive doctrine. It would fail of its purpose if it were regarded as a protest meeting.[99]

In discussing plans for the meeting, Longford complained that it would be 'very difficult to make any money unless he [the Archbishop] will allow more freedom in rousing public feeling'. The festival's 'fire-eating' chairman, Colonel Dobbie, was equally disappointed by such banality, asking why the spiritual leaders could not 'take more exciting lines in their statements'. Not that the festival organisers themselves were short of ideas to capture the imagination of the public and the press. These included soliciting a message from the Queen Mother and even 'a message from the Queen on her silver wedding to keep in cold storage for publicity purposes'.[100] Despite warm words from ministers, the Government made little effort to implement the aims of Longford or the NFoL, which focused on rewriting the Obscene Publications Act to separate out obscene material from that with genuine literary merit, or to crack down on obscenity in the broadcast media by bringing television and radio with the scope of the obscenity laws.

As the motivation to hold large-scale rallies, whether by land or sea, petered out after a couple of years, and no action was forthcoming on the efforts of 'Lord Porn', there was a gradual change of tactics by Whitehouse, the NFoL and their supporters. Until the mid-1970s they focused on inspiring and encouraging moral revival and personal responsibility among the 'misty millions' who naturally agreed with them, rather than a simple reimposition of state censorship. As this strategy failed to bear significant fruit, more emphasis was placed on legislative and political change, as well as the increased use of private prosecutions.[101] Whitehouse herself dramatically altered the rules of the game in 1976 when she launched her first private prosecution, against the editor of *Gay News*, Denis Lemon, for publishing the dreadful James Kirkup poem 'The Love that Dares to Speak Its Name', which described an assault by a Roman solider on the freshly crucified body of Christ. Lemon was fined £500 and received a suspended nine-month jail term. God's vicarious legal assault on *Gay News* through the good offices of Mary Whitehouse was a marginal *bouleversement* of the obscenity laws. It highlighted the relative strengths of the recent Obscene Publications Acts and the mediaeval common law of blasphemy. When Lemon's appeal against conviction reached the House of Lords, where it failed, Lord Scarman, formerly Sir Leslie Scarman, the first President of the Law Commission from 1965 to 1972, argued that the blasphemy law should be extended to protect other religions from offence,[102] a consistent position which was ignored or rejected thereafter until, in the wake of the attacks on the World Trade Center on 11 September 2001, David Blunkett proposed to introduce a new offence of incitement to religious hatred – although there was no suggestion that the existing blasphemy laws should be altered.

Perhaps of greater significance was Whitehouse's campaign to stop the Danish film-maker Jens Jørgen Thorsen coming to Britain to shoot the self-explanatory *Sex Life of Christ*. The invocation of the Home Secretary's power to exclude people who might pose a threat to 'public order, public security or public health' was threatened by Jim Callaghan, by now Prime Minister, and Whitehouse's machine threw everything it could at the Government to prevent Thorsen's arrival. She even had her secretary and a Danish neighbour translate the film's script into English to present to the Home Secretary, Merlyn Rees, as well as sending it to William Rees-Mogg at *The Times*, who agreed that it was too shocking to quote in print. The public and political opposition to the film was widespread and genuine, and when Thorsen arrived at Heathrow in February 1978, he was arrested and served with an exclusion order from Rees, who explained to the Commons that Thorsen had been carrying a copy of the film script when he was seized, and that his presence was likely to lead to possible breaches of the peace and was not conducive to the public good. At this point, Rees sought to draw a line under these episodes by appointing an official inquiry into the obscenity laws and film censorship under the chairmanship of the philosopher Bernard Williams (who had been divorced from Shirley Williams, by now Education Secretary, since 1974). Predictably this enraged Christian campaigners, who complained that Williams was a humanist who could not reflect Christian concerns about the importance of the family, marriage and chastity.[103]

Undeflected, Whitehouse moved on from combating artistic licence with the Body of Christ, with which many people might sympathise, to a much more emotive criminal practice which was far more likely to persuade people to man the barricades than an obscure Danish film-maker or a mediocre poet. Her attention had been grabbed by the rise in availability of child pornography, or 'kiddie porn' as she called it, mostly produced abroad, but alleged to be circulating widely in the UK. Although the use of children in making pornography was clearly already illegal, the dissemination of such material was not necessarily so. This time, rather than ridicule, Whitehouse invited only praise, with *The Times* commenting with a semi-detached smile that

> *Mrs Whitehouse is often accused of exaggerating the damage that is likely to be inflicted on society by particular affronts to her own set of moral values, and there are indeed instances where she may seem to confuse offences against good taste with something much more harmful in its effects. But the protest she is now making against child pornography is not one of these instances.*[104]

Margaret Thatcher, displaying her acute sense of what would play well with the British public, immediately supported the campaign after discussing the subject with Whitehouse. Whitehouse, milking this support for all it was worth, now saw Thatcher as her political alter ego, crowing after their meeting that the Conservative leader had been 'aware of the problem, and absolutely at one with me in this. She listened as a deeply concerned woman'.[105] From this moment might be marked the beginning of the illusion under which Whitehouse and her fellow campaigners laboured for many years, that a Conservative government under Thatcher would not just champion a rhetorical moral revival in Britain, but would implement the policies which would be necessary to achieve this. The following year Willie Whitelaw, as swept away in the honourable battle against child pornography as everyone else, promised the VALA conference that the Protection of Children Bill and the Tory-controlled Greater London Council's drive to clean up Soho were 'only the forerunners of a more comprehensive reaction' against obscenity.[106] From then on and through the 1980s, the gap between Conservative warm words and the actual achievements in office in this area was to yawn increasingly wide.

In the meantime, Whitehouse and Thatcher were riding the tide of public and political outrage about child pornography. Whitehouse, who during the 1970s seems to have thought she should have open access to the offices of successive Prime Ministers and Home Secretaries, used the Thatcher meeting to embarrass the Home Office for offering her an appointment with a poor Assistant Under-secretary: 'I was not very impressed with that.'[107] Rees resisted the initial calls for him to take action, saying that the DPP had advised him that there were few offences which were not already covered by law, and that there was a danger of catching innocent parents and families with blunt legislation.[108] Undeterred, Whitehouse launched a national campaign for legislation, ignoring the facts of the legal position, saying:

> We know that 200,000 children are involved in the kiddie porn industry in the United States, and legislation to stop it is being discussed there ... and because we are seeing it in this country now, and also because what happens in the United States is bound to come here, we feel that it is urgent to stamp out this trade.[109]

Rees had assured the Commons that despite the ongoing Williams Committee review of obscenity he would be prepared to act sooner against child pornography if necessary. But when Conservative MP Cyril Townsend introduced a Private Members' Bill on the subject in February 1978, the Government said that it was better left to Williams, and that legislation in advance would be bound to have 'unsatisfactory features'. Given the focus of the Bill, this negative attitude was administratively defensible. The Bill proposed to make illegal only the production, or possession with a view to production, of indecent photographs or film of children under sixteen. The Government had not accepted that such production was a problem that the current law was inadequate to deal with. Nevertheless, the Home Office was bulldozed into acquiescing in the Bill's progress, with overwhelming support among MPs across the House, and a second reading being agreed without a vote. This belated acceptance of the populist will of the Commons on the issue did not save the Government from being attacked. The Conservatives used this perceived weakness to paint a picture of a government which was 'complacent' on child pornography, immigration and crime. This was a counter-offensive by Whitelaw against Rees's own attack on a speech by Thatcher weeks earlier in which she said that British people feared they would be 'rather swamped' by immigration. There was clearly far more at stake than closing some theoretical loopholes in the law on child pornography. With a general election possibly only months away, the main parties were scrabbling for the moral high ground. It was also recognised that this was a preparatory assault by Whitehouse in advance of the liberalisations expected in the forthcoming Williams Report. In her autobiography, Whitehouse brands the Labour benches in both Houses as opponents of the Bill, singling out a former Cabinet minister, 'humanist' Lord Houghton, for particular opprobrium.[110] Singling out would be pretty much an accurate description, as only Houghton made any concerted attack on the Bill. In the Commons no voice was raised against it, with Home Office minister Brynmor John daring only to cast aspersions on the claim by the deputy Chief Constable of Greater Manchester Police, James Anderton, that five per cent of the pornography they seized contained children.[111] Anderton, whose crusading role as the truncheon-wielding Mary Whitehouse of the Police was at this point at its height, launched 355 raids against pornography in sixteen months, including against W. H. Smith, seizing material including *Men Only*, *Mayfair* and *Penthouse*.[112] It was to continue for many years, culminating in his notorious comment during the AIDS crisis that homosexuals were swimming in a cesspool of their own making.

Labour was so in awe of the aims of the Bill that, when left-winger Ian Mikardo, himself a supporter of the Bill, thwarted its final stages to protest at Tory filibustering of an Employment Protection Bill, the Government took the extraordinary step of inserting it into government business in order to get it through.[113] MPs were so carried away with the heroism of their championing of the Bill that when it left them for the House of Lords, loud cheers went up on both sides of the House.[114] What really outraged Houghton was not the Bill itself but the complete lack of scrutiny which it had received from MPs. As he bemoaned, so frightened had MPs been of appearing to be in favour of child pornography that they completely skipped the committee stage, when Bills are debated line by line. He complained that the Bill was not based on any hard evidence of the extent of the problem, or an assessment of what the effects of its provisions would be.

*

It has often been overlooked that the legislation which reformed the law governing homosexuality and divorce in the late 1960s applied only to England and Wales. The rest of the UK continued to labour under legislation dating from the nineteenth century. Northern Ireland also clung to abortion law as interpreted in the late 1930s to mean that abortion was only legal to protect the immediate life of the mother or to prevent serious risk to her health. It was not as if this had been, in the case of divorce in Scotland, for want of trying. Between 1970 and 1975 there were no fewer than eight parliamentary attempts to bring the law into line with that in England and Wales, and Scottish members could only look on as Commonwealth countries from New Zealand to Nigeria, and in Europe West Germany, France and Italy, all reformed their divorce law. In Scotland, couples were still bound by the fault-based system which England and Wales had partly shrugged off in 1969, and shed further in 1977 when the Special Procedure was introduced. This allowed for undefended divorce petitions to be heard without legal representation in court, motivated by the alarming rise in the cost of legal aid since the Divorce Law Reform Act. With little parliamentary discussion of this administrative change came, in the words of the foremost historian of divorce in England, 'the only fundamental change in divorce since it ceased to be obtained by private Act of Parliament'.[115] However, when Scottish Nationalist Iain MacCormick came top of the ballot in 1975, his Bill, which was closely modelled on the recommendations of the Scottish Law Commission, did not propose to go as far as extending the Special Precedure to Scotland. There was some opposition from Conservatives such as Tom Galbraith, who had successfully frustrated previous divorce reform bills and continued to argue that conciliation and marriage guidance were preferable to easier divorce. Galbraith, who as a junior minister had been forced to resign when caught up in the Vassall spy scandal in 1962, was not deterred by the fact that his own marriage had been dissolved in 1974.[116] But most Scottish MPs welcomed the Bill, notably a young Robin Cook. He had introduced a similar bill in the previous year, and criticised Galbraith for his obstruction of it and his use of the 'Casanova's Charter' argument which had been such a feature of debates on English divorce reform in the late 1960s. Galbraith, Cook said,

> *drew a vivid contrast between the deserted and lonely wife left at home and the*
> *husband who divorced her after five years, having left her to cohabit every*

night with a younger woman. Frankly, such a situation exists only in fantasy
… [In] England, where there has been such a provision [for divorce after five
years separation], he will find that last year more women than men resorted to
the five year clause. The fact is that women often find themselves in the
situation where they are totally innocent of the marriage breakdown but in the
eyes of the law they are guilty.[117]

Scottish women in general, and some in particular, might be grateful for Cook's persistent support of divorce law reform north of the border. At the same time, Cook was also at the forefront of calls to extend the Sexual Offences Act 1967 to Scotland. The gay liberation movement in the early 1970s had fostered a growing sense of public identity for those homosexuals prepared to 'come out', with a more visible sense of community and more self-conscious claim to equality before the law.[118] Although these grassroots organisations had profound social effects, their more radical activity made little political progress. The only attempt to lower the age of consent from twenty-one to eighteen, again by Boofy Arran, was roundly rejected by peers, many of whom clearly did not accept even the 1967 legislation. With the mood music of Mary Whitehouse's private prosecution of *Gay News*, evidence of the growth of gay organisations presented by Lord Halsbury did not incline peers towards any further relaxation of the law. With a forensic detail which he was to put to use for another two decades until being ejected from the Lords in 1999, Halsbury catalogued, in addition to *Gay News*, '17 assorted monthly glossies priced at around £1.50 each specialising in some form of kinkiness, sado-masochism or white preference for coloured partners'.[119]

Others were similarly uncompromising. The Lord Chancellor, Lord Elwyn Jones, was obliged to reprimand Mr Justice Melford Stevenson, who had disparagingly referred to that 'bugger's charter which enabled perverts and homosexuals to pursue their perversions in private'.[120] However, ministers were able to hide behind a review of the age of consent in train by the Criminal Law Revision Committee and an advisory group on sexual offences, which in the end did propose that it be lowered to eighteen for homosexuals, something which failed to commend itself to politicians for another fifteen years.

In the Scottish context the Government's attitude was open to criticism on more than one front. First, it introduced a bill on sexual offences in Scotland which restated the existing position that all homosexual acts were illegal. This was defended by arguing that in reality, there were no prosecutions for those acts which were now not illegal in England and Wales, and so there was no need to change the law. The Lord Advocate explicitly stated that he did not propose to prosecute such offences in future. This united Labour supporters of reform like Cook with the Conservative spokesman, Malcolm Rifkind, against both the constitutional anomaly of passing a law which there was no intention of enforcing and the offence towards changing social attitudes in Scotland of blocking a change in the law. A private bill introduced by Lord Boothby passed all its stages, adding nothing to the sum of knowledge, save the extraordinary confession by Lord Platt that 'as a musician *manqué* ... I must acknowledge the debt of music and other arts to the largely homosexual Church of the fifteenth and sixteenth centuries, with its various practices including the castrati and so on.' Despite such artistically inspired arguments for a less punitive approach to homosexuality, the Bill was lost for lack of time, and Cook's Commons version fell at the first hurdle.

If fear of the electoral effects of religious opposition to relaxing laws on morality motivated soft pedalling in Scotland, the parliamentary strength of Ulster MPs was even more a cause for caution in Northern Ireland. In July 1976 Merlyn Rees, while still Northern Ireland Secretary, asked the Standing Advisory Commission on Human Rights to report on whether the homosexual and divorce laws should be changed in Northern Ireland to bring them into line with England and Wales. This was partly in response to the case which Chris Dudgeon lodged in Strasbourg that the criminalisation of homosexuality in Northern Ireland violated his right to a private and family life under the European Convention on Human Rights. In the province the law was seen as increasingly difficult to implement. In March 1977 twenty-two charges of homosexuality were dropped by the police. In April 1978 the Government published a draft Order to extend the Sexual Offences Act to the province. Ian Paisley's response was to reactivate a vigorous 'Save Ulster from Sodomy' campaign which had successfully prevented the inclusion of Northern Ireland in the Sexual Offences Bill in 1966. Paisley's campaign reflected deep and continuing disapproval of homosexuality among many Protestants and Roman Catholics, with whom Paisley made an unprecedented alliance in the campaign, attracting 70,000 signatures to a petition. Wider public opinion was actually quite evenly divided on the question of extending the Act to Ulster, indicating the gradual decline in religion's hold over individual consciences and attitudes, if not politics. Nevertheless, Ulster MPs, local councillors and Protestant and Catholic Churches united to oppose the move, forcing the Government to withdraw the Order.

Paisley and his fellow Unionists were, of course, in a paradoxical position. While on the one hand they were at pains to stress their integration with the rest of the UK, including shared history, culture and law, their determination to resist the moral degradation, seemingly endemic on the mainland, further isolated them from British legal and cultural norms. Paisley's fundamentalist defence of traditional Protestantism ranged widely at this time, engendering less public sympathy and even ridicule in some areas. When Cardinal Basil Hume celebrated the first Catholic mass in the Chapel of the House of Commons in 1978, to mark the five hundredth anniversary of the birth of Sir Thomas More, Paisley protested that the mass was 'a blasphemous fable and a dangerous deceit'. A magnanimous Hume brushed aside the protest.[121] More bizarrely, Paisley carried the Unionist suspicion of Catholic insidiousness to a new level by objecting to a production of *The Sound of Music* at a predominantly Protestant school in County Down. A statement said:

> *We see this as yet another inroad of the great ecumenical deception ... The Sound of Music is full of Romanish influences which Protestants abhor. At one point candles are lit on the stage, some of the children have to appear in the garb of Catholic nuns and they also have to bless themselves publicly in the way that the Romans do.*[122]

Whether this was really part and parcel of the 'Save Ulster from Sodomy' campaign is not clear, though it might be argued that the failure to protect impressionable minds from Julie Andrews could have influenced the relaxation of attitudes towards sanctions against homosexuals – or vice versa. When the Government brought forward proposals to bring Northern Ireland into line with British divorce law, it was generally supported during a period of public consultation. In the Commons, Ulster Unionist James Molyneaux admitted that

> *we cannot legislate for righteousness. Simply to preserve a tough and unyielding divorce law will not compel couples to honour their matrimonial*

obligations. We are talking here of far deeper things – of principle, honour, integrity and loyalty. We who are privileged to serve in this House may strive to inspire and encourage these qualities; sad though it may be, we cannot legislate for them.

However, Paisley and his colleagues again opposed the move on religious grounds, saying that attitudes in Northern Ireland cleaved more closely to 'the Christian principles [that] prevail in their minds and in their upbringing':

Christian marriage is a thing of human sympathy and compassion … He [Jesus Christ] set out the only conditions on which the marriage bond could be broken – not with the consent of God's law, but by permission, because of the infidelity of a person who broke the solemn contract. It cannot be true to say that we are unsympathetic because we take the view of the one who was the most sympathetic person of all.

Enoch Powell was equally firm in resisting the move. At enormous pains to demonstrate his intellectual consistency, he pointed out that he voted against the English Divorce Law Reform Bill in 1969, convinced that marriage as an institution would be undermined by easier divorce and that a bad, unhappy or even unfaithful marriage was almost always better for children than divorce. However, his fearsome ire was also deployed to protest against the measure being implemented through a government Order in Council, rather than through a private members' bill, as had been the case for divorce in England and Wales and then Scotland. Pointing out that the House was poorly attended to discuss the Order, he argued that if there had been real demand in Northern Ireland to have the law changed, a Northern Ireland MP could have been found to introduce a bill, as had happened in Scotland:

We have not only infringed what I would have thought was an obvious constitutional and moral principle, namely, that what is a matter of conscience in Great Britain ought also to be a matter of conscience in Northern Ireland, but if we had used Private Members' Procedure we should have engaged the interest and concern and responsibility of the whole House in what we are doing.

The measure was nonetheless carried by 110 votes to 16.[123] Nationalist sensitivities were undoubtedly at their height at the end of the Callaghan Government but were already being swept away by the tide of political debate, which was turning away from the postwar consensus to a more polarised world, dominated politically by Margaret Thatcher's Conservative Party, and in time by a more radical, identifiably Thatcherite *Weltanschauung*, which gave hope to traditionalists yearning to turn back the tide of permissiveness.

6. Stigma and the Sixties: 1979–1990

'I find it difficult to imagine that anything other than Christianity is likely to resupply most people in the West with the virtues necessary to remoralise society in the very practical ways which the solution of many present problems requires.'

Margaret Thatcher[1]

'To prohibit the progress of science in any particular direction may well be tyranny; to seek to shape its course is surely sensible. In doing so we should be careful also to preserve the right of society to determine how the achievements of science are used.'

Sir Cecil Clothier[2]

'Who are these people with the Gannex conscience? You know, the one you reverse according to the way the wind is blowing? ... These are the people who robbed a generation of their birthright ... It's not advice we require from these people, it's an apology. Where did the hooligans, the louts and yobs on the late-night trains learn their contempt for the security of the law-abiding citizen?'

Margaret Thatcher[3]

'The Tory Government had played such an abominably duplicitous trick on us all. "Traditional values ... family stability ... parental choice ..." It was all electioneering humbug!'

Victoria Gillick[4]

There is a common perception that the arrival of Margaret Thatcher in Downing Street, heralded as it was by her quotation from St Francis of Assisi, marked the beginning of political hegemony for a religious moral view of Britain firmly embedded in the 1950s, if not in the 'Victorian virtues' which the Prime Minister was soon praising. As we have seen, during the turbulent decade then drawing to a close, Thatcher, encouraged by political prophets such as Sir Keith Joseph and moral crusaders such as Mary Whitehouse, gave increasing prominence to these views, emphasising the traditional family and combating the disasters of the 1960s and the permissive society. On pornography and obscenity in particular, conservatives rounded on the excesses of an anything-goes society, and suggested, either implicitly or explicitly, that Labour was at least partly to blame, and would further hasten this rush towards the abyss if re-elected. However, as will become clear during this chapter, the translation of this vision into practical policies and legislation during the 1980s at best was mixed, and at worst failed to halt or even further encouraged the very social and cultural trends which had been apparent since at least the 1950s, and against which moral traditionalists railed.

Thatcherism exalted the family above all other building blocks of society, hallowed in Ferdinand Mount's bible as 'the subversive family', resisting totalitarian government as well as nurturing future generations.[5] The formation in 1982 of the Cabinet Family Policy Group was greated by considerable press speculation that it would aim to spearhead a return to traditional family values and form a new blueprint for family policy. The group aimed 'to identify characteristics of behaviour and attitude which the government might legitimately hope to see adults possess, or conversely avoid'. One leaked paper suggested this might include 'what more could be done to encourage families, in the widest sense, to assume responsibilities taken on by the state, for example responsibility for the disabled, the elderly, unemployed 16-year-olds'. It also asked, 'Do present policies for supporting single parents strike the right balance between insuring adequate child support to prevent poverty, and encouraging responsible and self-reliant behaviour by adults?'[6] Ministers were relatively relaxed about these leaks, which was in stark contrast to the previous year, when a paper from the Central Policy Review Staff, the Government's 'think tank' established by Ted Heath, and which Thatcher was shortly to abolish, suggested radical cuts to the welfare state, and the paper was immediately disowned. Members of the new ad hoc group included Joseph, Willie Whitelaw, Geoffrey Howe, Norman Tebbit, Michael Heseltine, Norman Fowler, Baroness Young and the sports minister, Neil Macfarlane. However, there was little evidence of its influence in the 1983 Conservative election manifesto, as critics such as Hugo Young pointed out. According to Thatcher, the title of the group was somewhat misleading, as it ranged across almost the whole of domestic policy, from education vouchers to home ownership, as well as issues more directly related to family policy.[7] Although the group itself fizzled out, the idea of having a Cabinet 'family' group seemed to stick, as succeeding governments found its political symbolism hard to resist.

The Conservative and Labour Parties continued to argue about whether economic liberalism or the welfare state more undermined the responsibility of the individual and the self-reliance of families, and traditionalists and liberals continued to argue about whether more should be done to reinforce the primacy of the traditional nuclear family. Occasionally conservatives such as Whitehouse or Jill Knight would cite some radical feminist or gay liberation nonsense about abolishing the family (though most people within these groups would also have counted themselves among those willingly part of families), but there was almost complete consensus across the political spectrum about the enduring importance of families. As the question of restricting access to divorce receded from political debate, the main field of contention about government's role in protecting the traditional family shifted during the 1980s to the extent to which the tax and benefits system should favour married couples, and whether it should encourage more women with children into the labour market. Here Thatcher was quite firm:

> *There was great pressure, which I had to fight hard to resist, to provide tax reliefs or subsidies for child care. This would, of course, have swung the emphasis further towards discouraging mothers from staying at home. I believed that it was possible – as I had – to bring up a family while working, as long as one was willing to make a great effort to organise one's time properly and with some extra help. But I did not believe that it was fair to those mothers who chose to stay at home and bring up their families on the one income to give tax reliefs to those who went out to work and had two incomes.*[8]

However, in the very hour of her greatest electoral triumph in 1983, Thatcher was brought news which threatened to undermine the Conservatives' status as the party of Victorian family values. The party Chairman, Cecil Parkinson, Thatcher's beloved protégé and possible successor, confessed to his leader an adulterous affair with his former secretary, Sara Keays, and her pregnancy. Divorce and remarriage were likely. Thatcher reluctantly tore up her imminent reshuffle plans which had involved Parkinson leapfrogging most of his older colleagues to become Foreign Secretary, moving him instead to Trade and Industry, but counselled him to stay with his wife, Ann, for whom she showed the most concern. Parkinson pointed out the potential conflict with the party's espousal of Victorian values, but Thatcher retorted, 'What could be more Victorian than keeping the family together?' This neat accommodation on Thatcher's part could be interpreted as a practical lack of prudery and understanding of individual human failings or, alternatively, a cynical display of hypocrisy when traditional family values were traduced by one so dear to her. In any case, Parkinson might have toughed it out, had it not been for Keays' profound sense of betrayal and harsh treatment by Parkinson, not only of herself, but also of their daughter. It was this publicity which eventually forced him to resign.[9]

As Labour tore itself apart during the first years of the Thatcher Government,there was little threat of a leftist radicalisation of policy towards the family and personal morality. When the Labour Party's ruling National Executive Committee (NEC) came to approve the draft of the manifesto' which Gerald Kaufman later dubbed 'the longest suicide note in history', in 1982, there were sharp divisions about the proposal to support reducing the homosexual age of consent from twenty-one to sixteen. According to Tony Benn's diary account, the right, including the party's home affairs spokeswoman, Shirley Summerskill, opposed it, as did Michael Foot. Neil Kinnock suggested a Royal Commission. Only Dennis Skinner, reportedly not very enthusiastically, Joan Lestor, Benn and two others supported it.[10] However, when the proposal returned to the NEC the following week, an event which doesn't make Benn's diary, it had been watered down to include eighteen as the age of consent, tacked on to a seemingly contradictory pledge to introduce equality before the law. It was narrowly carried by nine votes to seven.[11]

However, the break with the Social Democratic Party had shorn Labour of its most eloquent and successful liberal advocates – Roy Jenkins and Shirley Williams. As Labour fractured and its support in opinion polls and at by-elections plummeted during 1981 and 1982, the ascendant SDP became the target for Conservative attacks on the evils of the permissive society. Tories were genuinely rocked by Williams' victory at Crosby in Liverpool, where she overturned their 19,000 majority, so much so that it even rates a mention in *The Downing Street Years*.[12] The following year Jenkins ousted another Tory at Glasgow Hillhead. Jenkins and Williams were almost mythic figures in the pantheon of progenitors of the permissive society as former Labour ministers. This allowed Thatcher and others to make specific references to their past record as part of a wider attack devised by senior Conservatives who believed that a campaign on traditional values would reap electoral dividends.[13] In a speech in May 1983, Thatcher accused them of being responsible for the destruction of grammar schools, the extension of nationalisation (hardly a part of Labour doctrine any of the Gang of Four warmly embraced) and the undermining of 'respect for the family in the name of a misleading permissiveness'.[14] In fact, the SDP–Liberal Alliance benefited from one of the darkest periods in postwar British politics, the notorious Bermondsey by-election in February 1983. Although it came about when the former Chief Whip, Bob Mellish, resigned in despair at the takeover by the radical left of the local party, an undercurrent of homophobia permeated the campaign when the Labour candidate, Peter Tatchell, became the victim of a smear campaign by supporters of the Mellish-inspired Independent Labour candidate, John O'Grady, also on the traditional right of the Party. Tatchell, although he protested vigorously against the smears 'based on bigotry and prejudice', refused to answer questions at the root of them – about his homosexuality. Simon Hughes, the Liberal candidate, was the beneficiary, though as *The Times* pointed out, he was also unmarried, but was 'mercifully' free of similar smears.[15]

Far more damaging to Labour in the long term was what became known in 1987 as the 'London effect'. During the early 1980s a number of the figures who soon provoked so much trouble for the party on the national stage were just emerging from obscurity – notably Tony Banks, Bernie Grant, Ken Livingstone (all MPs from 1987) and Margaret Hodge. The 'London effect' specifically related to policies towards lesbians and gays, and sex education in certain London boroughs and the Inner London Education Authority, where a 'Positive Images' campaign led to protests from some parents. It was these incidents, highly publicised locally and nationally, which fuelled calls from conservatives for a ban on such activity, and for parents to be given the right to withdraw children from sex education classes, both of which eventually bore fruit. Although the party did not drop its commitment to enforcing gay rights and championing discrimination in 1987 or even in 1992, the leadership was clearly on the defensive. Patricia Hewitt, former director of the National Council of Civil Liberties (NCCL) but by 1987 Kinnock's Press Secretary, was tasked with setting up a group to try to counter the 'London effect' in the run-up to the general election. Apart from the general extremism which was the main complaint about elements of the London party, Hewitt's leaked letter revealed concern that 'it's obvious from our own polling, as well as from on the doorstep [that] ... the gays and lesbians issue is costing us dear amongst the pensioners.'[16] Embarrassingly for Hewitt, Benn's talent for tape recording combined with his talent for leaking. As he recounts in his diary after seeing the reports of Hewitt's letter:

> *I remembered that Patricia Hewitt was once General Secretary of the NCCL, and my mind turned to a foreword I had written to their pamphlet Gay Workers, Trade Unions. I found the cassette recording of the press conference at which they launched the pamphlet on 27 January 1981, and, as I had remembered, Patricia Hewitt was also asked to speak and supported the rights of gay people. So I typed it up and rang Richard Gott of the* Guardian.[17]

Even closer to the general election, the *News of the World* first broke the story of Peter Mandelson's homosexuality, in a particularly vile and spurious attempt to damage him, the Kinnocks and the Labour Party.[18]

Labour continued to be dogged by controversy over its policy towards homosexuals. Its initial reaction to the proposal to ban the 'promotion' of homosexuality by local authorities was not to oppose it entirely, although it later stiffened its position and consistently advocated its repeal. Resistance by the party's leadership to growing calls from the lesbian and gay community to support equalising the homosexual age of consent alienated many supporters on the left of the party. Matters came to a head at the 1989 party conference, when angry delegates lambasted the NEC for ignoring the votes of three previous conferences to support sixteen as the equal age of consent. The NEC was also ridiculed for replacing a commitment to 'full equality' with the oxymoronic 'greater equality' for lesbians and gays.[19] After heavy lobbying by gay rights groups, a free vote on the age of consent was conceded by the leadership, thus handing ammunition to the Conservatives, Thatcher and Kenneth Baker publicly condemning any relaxation of the existing homosexual age of consent of twenty-one.[20]

Later on, Labour councils would encounter similar criticism for allegedly rewarding promiscuity by giving housing priority to single teenage mothers. Apart from the increasingly limited areas of policy under the control of local councils, Labour was hardly in a position to make a difference to the public morality of Britain after 1979. Neither, arguably, was the Conservative Government. As Thatcher herself has since said, 'the wider influences of the media, schools and above all the churches are more powerful than anything government can do.' Leaving aside for one moment the question whether government could have any influence over the media or schools, this brings to the fore the centrality of religious teaching and tradition in conservative and Thatcherite philosophy. Interestingly, although she praises in general terms the importance of the social cohesion, discipline and support provided by the Churches and their associated organisations, *The Downing Street Years* makes no other reference to Christian or religious doctrine more widely, or its specific role during the 1980s in fostering the moral renaissance which she and others argued should be the Churches' mission. However, the prequel, *The Path To Power*, is more expansive: 'Near the end of my time as Prime Minister, I became increasingly conscious of and interested in the relationship between Christianity and economic and social policy.'[21] Forecasting a return to an intellectual and moral climate based on the 'traditional virtues', Thatcher takes a sideswipe at the Church of England by quoting Pope John Paul II's criticism of state social intervention:

> *By intervening directly and depriving society of its responsibility, the Social Assistance State leads to a loss of human energies and an inordinate increase of public agencies, which are dominated more by bureaucratic ways of thinking than by concern for serving their clients, and which are accompanied by an enormous increase in spending. In fact, it would appear that needs are best understood and satisfied by people who are closest to them and who act as neighbours to those in need.*

Clearly Thatcher was not troubled by the ulterior motive in the last sentence of the Catholic Church jealously guarding its traditional hold over society. Thatcher and moral conservatives increasingly despaired of the Anglican leadership during the 1980s. This was nothing new. As we have seen, from the 1960s the willingness among many bishops and others in the Church of England to adapt traditional teaching to contemporary mores and to accept the retreat of doctrine from the criminal law infuriated traditionalists. During the Thatcher administration the fissures became more political, as the social consequences of the

Government's policies led many churchmen and women to speak out directly against them. This was not confined to Anglicanism. In Scotland, the strong Catholic socialist tradition led the religious charge against the Government's social and economic policies. These two trends led Thatcher and many other conservatives to prefer the traditionalist teaching of other religious leaders, notably the Chief Rabbi, Immanuel Jakobovits, who comes in for particular praise in the Thatcher memoirs. Later, a similar moral outlook among newer immigrant communities would also find common cause with traditionalists, although during the 1980s such affinities were not clearly enunciated or explored.

The significance of traditional family values and conservative moralism in Thatcherite policy during the 1980s was never as great or as consistent as is popularly thought. However, there is a strong argument for pointing to the period after the 1987 general election victory as the moment when such concerns came to the fore. This is supported by Thatcher's own reflections. There is an astonishing admission in *The Downing Street Years* that she became

> *increasingly convinced during the* last two or three years *of my time in office that ... we could only get to the roots of crime and much else besides by concentrating on strengthening the traditional family.*
>
> *All the evidence – statistical and anecdotal – pointed to the breakdown of families as the starting point for a range of social ills ... The most important – and most difficult – aspect of what needed to be done was to reduce the positive incentives to irresponsible conduct. The question of how best ... to support families with children was a vexed one to which I and my advisers were giving much thought when I left office.*[22]

Given that Thatcher and traditionalists on the right had been blaming the left for the whole gamut of ills afflicting the family and society since before coming to power, this is a rather amnesiac view of her time in office. However, it does reflect the fact that, with the economy on an upward trajectory in the mid-1980s, deeper social problems were coming to the fore. This echoes what happened in the 1950s when, after concentrating on postwar economic reconstruction, social issues which had been left dormant since the 1930s found room for discussion.

Even in 1987, at the point of the historic third election victory, the Thatcher administration's record for rolling back the frontiers of the permissive society was distinctly unimpressive, not least in the eyes of those who were urging a Conservative return to Victorian values. Journalist and left-wing apostate Paul Johnson attacked ministers for adopting rhetoric which there was no prospect of them implementing. Victoria Gillick, foremost campaigner for parental control over the provision of contraception to schoolchildren, later lambasted the Tory record in the 1980s and the Government's decision to take to the Law Lords an Appeal Court ruling that doctors must consult parents about contraceptive advice to under-sixteens:

> *The Tory Government had played such an abominably duplicitous trick on us all. 'Traditional values ... family stability ... parental choice...' It was all electioneering humbug! ... How Mrs Thatcher dared to do such a thing [take the contraception case to the Lords], having ridden into office on the back of 'traditional family values', is a measure of just how hard-nosed politicians can be in defence of departmental policies and strategies of social planning.*[23]

The campaign against 'video nasties' in 1983–4, which resulted in the Video Recordings Act, was a solitary legislative success up until 1987, and one which carried away most of the Labour Party in its fervour as well as Conservatives. The ultimate utilitarian proposals of the Williams Committee on obscenity were easily resisted, but no Conservative improvement of the discredited obscenity laws materialised. As Gillick's bitter criticism reveals, the Government, despite its rhetoric, was not prepared to make the leap of restricting doctors' discretion over informing parents about advice to their children on contraception. If the 1987 Conservative manifesto made clear an intention to clamp down on 'sexual propaganda' in schools and bring the broadcasters under the Obscene Publications Act, there was little else to put flesh on the bones of a conservative moralist agenda. In fact one might be forgiven for thinking it pointed in quite the opposite direction when it said:

> *Particular laws which are not enforced or which are full of obvious anomalies risk bringing the law itself into disrepute. Changing tastes also require the*

reform of outdated laws which govern personal habits and behaviour: such reform should where possible be on the basis of a wide consensus.[24]

Avoiding using the word 'morality', rather than 'taste', displayed a sensitivity about suggesting radical reform. The use of the C-word, anathema to the Iron Lady herself, is perhaps most surprising, even when one realises that this applied only to licensing and Sunday trading. Victorian virtues sacrificed on the altar of commercial interest, or a pragmatic compromise between tradition and contemporary mores? The Government's attempt to deregulate Sunday trading in 1986 fell victim to a massive backbench rebellion among Tory MPs. Despite the new manifesto pledge, it was only after the 1992 general election that a second, ultimately successful, attempt was made.

Perhaps what this illustrates most is the continuing divisions within the Conservative Party about the importance of a shared public morality. Though measures like the prohibition of the 'promotion' of homosexuality or video nasties received almost total support in the Conservative Party, there was not agreement about their significance. Beyond such interventions, a proportion of the party did not support making moral judgements about individual behaviour or behaviour between different individuals and families. Taking another issue, capital punishment, a fissure began to open up during the 1980s between the views of Conservative politicians and those of party activists. MPs increasingly accepted that it was not realistic to seek to reintroduce it, in defiance of grass-roots Tories. A number of ministers with responsibility for criminal justice, who would potentially become the first politicians since Sir Frank Soskice to face the awesome responsibility of authorising an execution, rejected the arguments of deterrence and symbolism which retentionists espoused. Willie Whitelaw was the most significant of these. As he recalls, when MPs voted on hanging for the first time for a decade in 1982, there was the added piquancy of a new Prime Minister publicly in favour, whilst her Home Secretary was equally against. Whitelaw made a powerful speech against reintroduction, which was rejected by 119 votes. In the future this majority would only grow.[25]

Looking at the composition of the Family Policy Group in the early 1980s, it is not surprising that such divisions made it difficult for Conservatives to make much headway in reasserting traditional morality, as moderates were often reluctant to embrace reform. However, by the administration's third term some of the senior figures in the party such as Whitelaw had retired, or in Norman Fowler's case moved away from a social-policy brief, giving greater vent to the more hard-line authoritarian tone of Thatcher herself and younger ministers, such as Kenneth Baker, keen to flex their right-wing credentials. These tensions within the Conservative Party are well exemplified by debate about what the political response should be to family breakdown and divorce. In December 1982 Conservative MP Peter Bottomley led a Commons debate on 'family policy' in which MPs from all parties paraded their devotion to supporting families. Geoffrey Finsberg, the junior health minister responding for the Government dutifully quoted from *The Subversive Family*, but also rejected the idea that the relaxation of the divorce law in 1971 was responsible for the hike in the divorce rate: 'Some people say that easier divorces cause people to put less effort into making their marriages work. That may be true in a few cases, but I suggest that there is a deeper underlying social trend that was not markedly affected by the change in the law.'

Citing his department's own figures, which showed that the increase in claimants of supplementary benefit merely shifted from separated couples before 1972 to divorced couples afterwards – meaning that marriage breakdown had been occurring anyway – Finsberg was even-handed:

> *Even if easier divorce is by no means the main cause of marital breakdown, there is a balance to maintain. We must not use the law to force people to remain in a moribund and stressful relationship; neither must we change too much or too soon the body of law that reflects the community's moral preferences.*[26]

One can hardly imagine Margaret Thatcher making such a speech. When the Government did go on to introduce reform of the divorce law in 1984, it was a minor tinkering with the length of time after marriage before a petition for divorce could be made. It was not in a regressive direction. The Government wanted, and secured, a reduction in the time bar from three years to one year. However, on a free vote MPs, and particularly Conservative MPs, were sharply divided over whether reducing or abolishing the existing three-year bar would increase the number of divorces, harm more children or devalue marriage in the eyes of the public.[27]

*

If Conservatives, despite being the *soi-disant* 'Party of the Family', were divided over how far government could go to support the institution, pornography and obscenity had for a long time been a scene of greater harmony between moral campaigners and the Conservative Party. The Heath Government had not acted on the work of the Longford Committee, which was backed by most Conservatives, but by the late 1970s the arrival of Margaret Thatcher, and particularly her support over Mary Whitehouse's campaign against 'kiddie porn' in 1977, had given hope to those who expected a new Conservative Government to turn the tide against filth and obscenity. As with the attitude of ministers towards the family, youth and sex during the 1980s, however, traditionalists were to be sorely, though not totally, disappointed.

The new administration flunked its first two tests. Bernard Williams' committee on obscenity and pornography, which had been appointed by Merlyn Rees in 1977, reported in November 1979. Since its inception it had been attacked by Whitehouse and other conservatives for being dominated by liberals and utilitarians. Its report did not disappoint. The obscenity laws were completely discredited after two decades – attacked by the literary establishment and liberal juries on the one hand, undermined by the pornography industry with the help of the Metropolitan Police Obscene Publications Squad on the other. The Williams prescription for rescuing them from this state was a two-pronged strategy, neither of which was likely to find favour with conservatives.

Perhaps most importantly, the report constructed a new definition. Material would be obscene if it was 'offensive to reasonable people by reason of the way it portrays or deals with violence, cruelty or horror, or sexual, faecal or urinary functions or genital organs'.[28] Visual material which might give offence to reasonable people should be restricted to licensed sex shops and cinemas where it would not be on public display but could be available to those adults who chose to see it. All censorship of the written word would be withdrawn. This was based on the new principle which the report introduced. The likelihood of harm would be the new test on which all but a small proportion of pornographic material would be judged legal but restricted. Only that using children, physical violence and animals would be completely beyond the pale.

The report's reception was cool to say the least. Williams was even prompted to launch a bitter attack on governments which appointed expensive and time-consuming committees and commissions, only to ignore their findings – what he called 'passports to the pigeon-holes'. Norman Brook would not doubt have approved of these sentiments. The Government's reaction was almost to ignore it.[29] Without even giving Parliament an opportunity to debate the Williams Report, action on one part of it came through the initiative of a Tory back-bencher, Tim Sainsbury, who piloted through a bill banning indecent public displays. The reaction in Soho, according to Alan Travis, was merely for purveyors of pornography to boost their trade by advertising in shop windows: 'Warning: sexually explicit material inside. Do not enter if you are easily offended.'[30]

The second disappointment for those expecting the Government to halt the tide of filth came late in 1980 when a piece of agitprop about the British in Northern Ireland opened at the National Theatre. *The Romans in Britain* saw Mary Whitehouse's most audacious raid on theatrical licence since the abolition of the Lord Chamberlain's blue pencil in 1968, and a brilliant successor to the *Gay Times* blasphemy prosecution of 1977. Whitehouse was appalled that the play, written by Howard Brenton and directed by Michael Bogdanov, which used the Roman occupation of Britain as a metaphor for Northern Ireland, contained a scene of simulated male rape by Roman soldiers of a Celtic druid. Without having seen the play personally, she applied to the Director of Public Prosecutions for permission to launch a private prosecution under the 1968 Theatres Act, which had introduced this precondition in order to prevent malicious or trivial cases undermining the removal of the Lord Chamberlain's censorship powers. Both the DPP and the Attorney General, Sir Michael Havers, turned Whitehouse down. Undeterred, she found a legal loophole in the Sexual Offences Act 1956, which allowed for prosecution for procuring an act of gross indecency – the law normally used against men 'cottaging' in public toilets. Whitehouse's solicitor, Graham Ross-Cornes, was the main prosecution witness, having valiantly seen the play on Whitehouse's behalf. The disingenuousness of this ruse was revealed by Ross-Cornes's admission that he and Whitehouse were disgusted with and offended by the whole play, not just the scene of simulated rape. On the substance of the act he was unable to confirm whether what he had seen was really the actor's penis or his thumb held in an erect position (to which the actor concerned might have taken exception). The defence of Bodganov by Sir Peter Hall, who appeared as a witness, rested on the distinction that the act depicted was obscene, not the depiction of it, which was intended to be shocking in order to carry the argument behind the play about the brutality of colonisation and military occupation – the same defence that young Viv Berger had made during the *Oz* trial. The judges' ruling was confusing. Clearly unimpressed that the 1956 Act was being used in this way against a stage play rather than more usual *al fresco* scenes of indecency, they admitted that it was technically correct, and that it was not inconceivable that Parliament could have intended for stage plays to be covered in this way when it abolished censorship in 1968, although it was not clear. Sir David Napley, a member of the Home Office's ongoing review of sexual offences legislation, condemned the prosecution, and denied that the Act was ever intended to be used in this way. However, the judges also ruled that an act would have to be determined to be grossly indecent in the same way as in other circumstances, although neither sexual gratification or physical contact were necessary criteria. None of this ruled on the facts of the case, however, and Whitehouse's counsel immediately withdrew the prosecution, claiming that her point had been made and that, magnanimously, they did not want to inflict unnecessary punishment on Bogdanov.[31] In fact, the actors involved in the scene of simulated male rape had actually practised the common theatrical device of 'fluffing', or arousing themselves, in order to present themselves in as good a light as possible, or to counteract the inevitable physical stage-fright.[32] If only she had known.

Potentially more damaging for the theatre than Whitehouse's legal challenge was the reaction of Sir Horace Cutler, Conservative leader of the Greater London Council, who walked out of a preview of the play in disgust, threatening the National Theatre with a cut in its grant, saying, 'While I may be accused by some of censorship, there are limits to what I will recommend the spending of ratepayers' money on when it comes to the theatre, and *The Romans in Britain* is the limit.'[33] The GLC Arts Committee subsequently froze the NT grant, although the decision was dramatically reversed the following year when the GLC fell to Labour. The new Arts Committee chair, future Labour MP Tony Banks, pointedly suggested that the NT might need an even bigger rise because of the legal costs incurred during the *Romans* case.[34]

When the rapid spread of 'video nasties' on the new medium of home video cassettes provoked outrage in the press, the political reaction was very different.

The novelty of videos here is important. Though Whitehouse and her allies in the National Viewers and Listeners Association and Christian Action, Research and Education (CARE), the two pressure groups heavily involved in the campaign, were highly effective in their lobbying techniques, perhaps the main reason why politicians were persuaded to act now was that the issue involved the uncertain growth of new technology. This was to prove a similar spur to action when use of the internet became widespread (although not primarily through legislation), and was also the case with scientific advances in fertility treatment and genetic research. Of course, the focus on potential harm to children by 'video nasties' was also, properly, the main cause of concern. Quite how far the Video Recordings Act was successful is hard to tell. Within a decade easy access to extremely violent horror films was once again a cause for public and media hysteria, particularly when the two young boys found guilty of murdering toddler James Bulger were said to have watched one particular film.[35]

Shortly after this victory, campaigners against obscenity returned to the fray with the first effort at a new strategy to define clearly in law what acts would be considered obscene, and therefore banned, rather than just broad categories of material which might or might not fall under this description. Winston Churchill took up the mantle and included in a 'laundry list' such acts as masturbation, sodomy, oral sex, lewd exhibition of nudes, cannibalism and vicious cruelty towards persons or animals. Despite Whitehouse's best attempts to shock MPs with the content of recent Channel 4 transmissions, both the Government and broadcasters were adamant that the watershed system provided adequate protection for children, and there was widespread concern that such restrictions would spell the death of drama and documentaries. Among writers and programme- and film-makers who joined in condemning the implications of the Bill, David Attenborough commented that the praying mantis committed three of the Bill's forbidden acts simultaneously.[36] Another attempt to strengthen the obscenity laws and bring broadcasters within their aegis in 1987 also failed. This tried to reinforce the 'corrupt and deprave' concept with a new term of 'grossly offensive to reasonable persons', though this seemed only a less archaic version of the existing law which would satisfy no one. The Conservative Government was not wholly deaf to these arguments and in its 1987 manifesto admitted that

there is deep public concern over the display of sex and violence on television.
We will therefore bring forward proposals for stronger and more effective
arrangements to reflect that concern. We will remove the current exemption
enjoyed by broadcasters under the Obscene Publications Act 1959.[37]

Not that they showed any great hurry to crack down on broadcasters after the
election, but in 1989 the Government did introduce a broadcasting bill, which
encompassed these changes. The new Broadcasting Standards Council which it
created took a much more holistic approach to monitoring and adjudicating on
complaints, using research and polling to back up its work. Its consensual
approach was, however, to prove extremely unwelcome to Whitehouse. However,
as she had repeatedly shown, the impotence of the Obscene Publications Act did
not preclude more ingenious assaults on cultural depravity. She was not alone in
pursuing these. Customs and Excise during the 1980s and 1990s continued to use
Victorian postal legislation to prosecute importers and vendors of literature
which would not even reach a jury under the Obscene Publications Act. The
most notorious example of this was their raid on the bookshop Gay's the Word
in which works by such depraved authors as Gore Vidal, Henry Miller, Armistead
Maupin and Kate Millett were seized. Only after a long legal battle ending up in
the European Court of Justice were the defendants cleared because under EEC
law it represented a restriction on trade, as the books were not themselves illegal
in the UK.[38]

*

If conservative moral campaigners were having little effect on the commercial
promotion of sexual permissiveness through pornography, the media or advertising, when they focused their pressure on the publicly funded sector of sex
education they arguably had a greater impact.[39] Significantly, conservative critics
of providers of sex education materials often referred to a sex education
'industry', suggesting comparison with the pornography industry. On an even
grander scale, opponents of sex education such as Valerie Riches of The
Responsible Society suggested that the Family Planning Association (FPA) was
'part of a carefully planned international attack upon the nature of the family
and the value of human life'. It was materials produced by voluntary organisa-

tions such as the FPA and Brook Advisory Centres and public bodies such as the Health Education Council for use in schools which became the focus for family values campaigners. One such pack was denounced in the Commons because it 'shows full frontals and goes into considerable detail about sexual intercourse. There is little left the imagination and even less to prayer.'[40]

It should be remembered that in the early 1980s, provision of sex education was still patchy and there were no formal obligations on schools. However, Conservative concern about the infiltration of progressive teaching in schools extended to the personal lifestyles and sexuality of teachers, with one Tory MP demanding that the family be 'safeguarded ... morality instilled in every child [and] sexual deviance within the teaching profession weeded out'.[41] Quite how such a McCarthyite witch hunt was to be effected is not clear. Campaigners began gradually to have some success at forcing ministers to rein in some of the less savoury sex education materials available. At first the Government conceded that schools should publicise the content of sex education provision to parents, but rejected calls for parents to be given the right to withdraw children from sex education classes. In a speech in April 1981 outlining plans for a sex education campaign for sixteen- to nineteen-year-olds, junior minister Sir George Young was extremely even-handed. He agreed that in the previous two decades,

> *traditional family values have been undermined. This Government wants to reassert them. I consider it necessary that any material ... makes it clear that the option of chastity is not a vestigial concept of the nineteenth century but something which has relevance today.*[42]

However, Young was also clear that to attempt this by curtailing contraceptive advice to young people would be an 'irresponsible and blind act of faith'. Attacks by Conservative MPs on various pieces of sex education literature continued with the Government soft-pedalling on the issue of parental right of withdrawal, until in 1986 the issue was forced when an amendment was tabled to the Government's Education Bill by Lord Buckmaster to this effect. The Government would not go this far, but produced a compromise which stated that schools should 'take such steps as are reasonably practicable' to ensure that sex education would be 'given in such a manner as to encourage ... pupils to have due regard to moral considerations and the value of family life'. Kenneth Baker made clear that parents would have the right to inspect teaching materials, and he suggested that by supporting the Government, Parliament could 'give a clear signal reinforcing the institution of marriage as the foundation of a healthy family life and the very bedrock of our civilisation'. Once the semantic possibilities had been digested, it was clear that some Conservatives were not satisfied, and tried once more to insert a parental right to withdraw children from sex education classes. Confusion was compounded when Labour, unsure what to do, initially supported such a move, ostensibly to prevent people like Victoria Gillick from mounting legal challenges against schools' sex education. However, it was suggested by more than one commentator that a fear of adverse reaction from some parents from ethnic minorities was also a motivating factor. The party conference season intervened, giving moral lobbyists from CARE an opportunity to stiffen the resolve of Conservatives, urging them to 'save a generation from the immoral propaganda for promiscuity, homosexuality, contraception, anti-marriage views, fornication, and encouragement of children to experiment with sex, which has passed in too many schools during the past two decades as health education.'[43] This pressure was telling and Baker retreated further, announcing new plans for sex education to be transferred wholly to school governing bodies, which would decide whether parents at their school would have a right of withdrawal. Although those campaigning for an automatic parental veto or even an end to school sex education would not be pacified, Baker had done enough to quell the backbench rebellion.

*

The importance of the debate about sex education was further magnified by increasing concern among traditionalists about the spread of greater tolerance, even equality, for homosexuals during the 1980s. Despite the hopes of moderate liberals behind the implementation of the Wolfenden Report that homosexuals would be content with humane understanding and a limited degree of tolerance, by the 1980s their treatment by the law and society had become even more controversial. The new Conservative Government in 1979 still had to cope with the anomalies in the treatment of homosexuals under the criminal law between England and Wales, where the 1967 Sexual Offences Act had decriminalised consensual acts between two males aged over twenty-one in private, and

Scotland and Northern Ireland. In Scotland, the Government continued to insist that although the law maintained a complete ban on homosexual activity, the law was not enforced. In 1981 the European Court of Human Rights (ECHR) finally ruled in the Chris Dudgeon case that maintaining the ban in Northern Ireland because of the prevailing public mood was disproportionate when set against the breach of the individual's right to respect for private and family life under the Convention.[44] The Government's response was not consistent. It resisted Robin Cook's renewed attempt, by tabling an amendment to its own Criminal Justice Bill in 1980, to extend the Sexual Offences Act to Scotland. However, support ranged across all three main parties (though not the Scottish Nationalists). The amendment was carried by 203 to 80 votes. Conversely, the Government reluctantly followed its obligations under the European Convention and published an Order extending the Act to Northern Ireland. Opposition among Ulster politicians was almost total. Evidently, with a fresh mandate, the Conservative Government was now more fearful of the ECHR than the dying Labour Government had been of Ian Paisley's 'Save Ulster from Sodomy' campaign.

It has become axiomatic to describe the profound effect of the AIDS crisis on society and politics during the 1980s, to see it as a watershed after which nothing was quite the same again, either for the individuals and communities affected, or for politicians and officials, or for the agencies working with victims and potential victims. In some respects this is undoubtedly true. The political reaction was certainly remarkable, but in a way it only heightened the natural responses of different groups. Sir Keith Joseph was reputedly unable to cope when informed about the virus and the way it was transmitted. Some Conservative MPs rode the early wave of draconian calls for notification and punitive measures including compulsory testing and quarantine. However, officialdom, led by scientific advice and the Government's Chief Medical Officer, Sir Donald Acheson, began to shape a consensual, liberal response, drawing on instinctual bureaucratic traditions originating in the response to wartime conditions half a century earlier. The clash between liberal and punitive responses resolved itself initially in a similar way to other areas of policy determined by new science and technology such as embryo research. This was, as Virginia Berridge described it in her dispassionate account of the subject written in the mid-1990s, 'an open policy arena, *tabula rasa*'.[45] The authority of impartial scientific advice to Government was still unchallenged (though this changed in the

1990s following health scandals particularly 'mad cow disease' or BSE). Though there were strong disagreements within Whitehall and beyond about the course which was followed, the preference of Acheson and his Expert Advisory Group on AIDS for an inclusive dialogue with gay groups held the line for a liberal approach for the rest of the decade, though sometimes in the face of accusations of a 'gay' conspiracy. In its effects on the gay community in Britain, AIDS was paradoxical. On the one hand, apart from decimating it, it was grist to the mill of moral traditionalists who loathed the idea that homosexuality might be gaining greater social acceptability. It thus helped to fuel anger in this direction, particularly in the media, but also among public agencies such as the police. However, it also led to the legitimisation of the gay community as part of the public policy consensus in the fight against the disease.

According to one senior civil servant, 'until the end of 1986, ministers would have nothing to do with it ... They thought it would be political death.' A ministerial working group had been inconclusively shuffling along with early decisions on confidentiality and information campaigns. It was chaired by the devout Catholic Barney Hayhoe, who despite initially reacting in a similar way to Joseph, still erred on the side of the scientific advice ministers were receiving. However, other ministerial voices were in spasms at some of the more idiomatic information material which Norman Fowler had approved. Lord Hailsham wrote to Willie Whitelaw: 'I am convinced there must be some limit to vulgarity! Could they not use literate "sexual intercourse"? If that is thought to be too narrow, then why not "sexual relations" or "physical practices", but not "sex" or, worse, "having sex"!'[46]

Fowler and others were frustrated that this working group and the Cabinet committee structure were not sufficiently focused or motivated to react quickly and purposefully enough to the unfolding public health crisis. According to Fowler, the Cabinet Committee on Home Affairs, which was responsible for health policy, was at fault. He, Whitelaw and Robert Armstrong, the Cabinet Secretary, advised by Acheson, and Sir Kenneth Stowe, Permanent Secretary at the DHSS, persuaded the Prime Minister to establish an ad hoc Cabinet committee to deal with the crisis.[47] According to Fowler, this group was far more willing to take tough and potentially controversial decisions. No issues were referred up to full Cabinet, normally the prerogative of any minister who will not accept the decision of a Cabinet committee on which he or she sits. Fowler says that when he and Whitelaw, who chaired the committee, agreed, which they usually did, business went through. The only significant dissent within the committee came from the Scottish Office, headed by Malcolm Rifkind, which felt that the free needle-exchange programme which was proposed was a 'retrograde' step, considering the severe heroin problem in Scotland. The very admission of the existence of the Cabinet committee was itself almost revolutionary, as the Conservative Government maintained the traditional refusal to disclose any details about the Cabinet committee system, including the membership or remit of committees, until this was relaxed under John Major's premiership. The committee was also strongly motivated by the sense of panic sweeping the nation, fuelled by media stories about the banal symptoms associated with AIDS. According to one minister involved, AIDS went from taboo to ubiquity at the dinner table, 'dowagers talking about condoms'.

When Parliament spent a whole day, exceptionally, debating the single subject of AIDS in November 1986, MPs reflected a similar balance of opinion towards a consensual, non-judgemental approach, largely supporting the measured response which the Government had taken. However, there were a significant number of mainly Conservative MPs who were insistent that a firmly moralistic line should be taken to warn people against promiscuity, and that the Government should not be scared of taking firm measures to deal with the problem through fear of offending the gay community. Announcing a nation-wide leaflet drop to all homes, Fowler and Tony Newton, the Health Minister, were at pains to emphasis the lack of risk in social contact with infected people, but did not yet commit the Government to some contentious proposals including free condoms, and needles for intravenous drug users. The Labour front bench supported the Government's actions and took a similarly cautious line. Backbenchers felt the need to be restrained. Leo Abse, making his usual Freudian analysis of the behaviour of the promiscuous among homosexuals and heterosexuals, said they should be assisted, not condemned by Tory moralists. Taking a sideswipe at Cecil Parkinson he said that 'the only people who cannot keep their trousers up are those who are ... right at the heart of the Conservative Party.' He mocked a statement by the Bishop of Birmingham that the only way to avoid the epidemic was to behave in accordance with biblical teaching. That, Abse noted, would mean women becoming committed lesbians – 'an injunction not to be found in my reading of the Bible'. One of Abse's main targets was the Conservative Sir Ian Percival, who launched an attack on Abse's own culpability:

A very material factor in the spreading of this disease and of the misery that it causes is that so many have strayed so far and so often from what were taught as the normal moral values until the 1960s ... There are some who have deliberately set out to destabilise society by corrupting the young with sex and drugs ... I just hope that those who have been involved will ... shake and quake at the thought of the devil that they have unleashed.[48]

However, once the crest of this initial wave of crisis was deemed to have been ridden, contrary instincts began to have their effect on policy towards AIDS and sexual morality. As a heterosexual epidemic failed to materialise, the political response of the 1980s to the disease began to be criticised from all directions. It had been melodramatic; it was motivated by a gay conspiracy to gain attention through linking it to heterosexuals who were not greatly at risk; or, from certain gay quarters, a proper focus on the needs of gay men had been marginalised by the attention given to potential heterosexual infection.

As attention turned from the short-term imperative of combating the spread of HIV infection to the longer-term reduction of AIDS and other sexually transmitted diseases, researchers sought to remedy the almost total absence of reliable information about sexual behaviour and attitudes. Since the Second World War there had, of course, been notable pioneers of sex research. The Kinsey Report was the most famous and the most controversial, with its estimations of the extent of homosexual activity in the US male population. Despite more recent questioning of Alfred Kinsey's methodology, as well as the influence of his personal proclivities on his research and his research team, this was a watershed in sex research.[49] In Britain, Michael Schofield's and Alfred Gorer's studies during the 1950s and 1960s were the first to explore the effect of greater freedom for young people, and the extent of sexually liberated attitudes and behaviour. Gorer's first study was rather coyly titled *Exploring English Character*. They both concluded that less had changed than the common, or media, perception allowed.

In 1988 a group of researchers at London University piloted the most sophisticated survey of sexual attitudes and behaviour in Britain, with the intention of assessing the success of health education campaigns, and planning for future levels of hospital care. Despite support for the research from the Health Education Authority, the Economic and Social Research Council and the DHSS,

Downing Street was reported to have intervened to block Government funding of the full study. Ostensibly the reason behind Margaret Thatcher's veto was invasion of privacy, although the survey was voluntary and anonymous. The *Sunday Times* quoted 'authoritative sources' as saying that 'Thatcher doubted whether such intimate questioning would produce accurate responses, and questioned the credibility of the exercise,' but also that she feared the Government could be 'tainted' by undertaking a survey which could have given rise to 'unseemly speculation' in the popular press. As Fowler concedes, her 'lack of feel' for such subjects could have led her to step in and make a decision, which he considers a mistake.[50] This is also the version supported by Hugo Young in his authoritative, critical biography of Thatcher, *One of Us*. However, other ministers have been less backward in coming forward to claim responsibility for the refusal of funding for the study. Kenneth Baker, in his memoirs, while supporting the cautious approach of the Cabinet Committee on AIDS, dismissed the aims of the researchers, sharing the credit with colleagues:

> *Early in 1989, the two Health ministers, David Mellor and Ken Clarke, proposed that there should be a government-sponsored survey of the sexual behaviour of 20,000 British people in the year 1990 ... George Younger, Douglas Hurd and I opposed this survey and stopped it. We believed that such a survey would become just another Kinsey Report, revealing that Britain had become a more promiscuous society – which we knew – and more experimental in the realm of bisexual relationships – which we also knew. A new survey therefore would neither increase the sum of human knowledge nor do anything actually to help AIDS sufferers.*[51]

Virginia Berridge points to a comment by Acheson that, despite such opposition, the 'door was still open for a while', but that that the publicity surrounding the *Sunday Times* article snuffed out the remaining political support.[52] The move was condemned by Labour's spokesperson at the time, Harriet Harman, who stated that the Government had 'shown itself to be no respecter of privacy anywhere else. This survey must go ahead on scientific and medical grounds.' The survey, published in 1994 as the *National Survey of Sexual Attitudes and Lifestyles*, was rescued by the Wellcome Trust, and has been much quoted since, although not without its critics, including those who argue its methodology was flawed, leading to underreporting of male and female homosexuality.[53] According to Berridge, the very fact that the Government had considered funding such a survey was unusual, reflecting the level of concern about AIDS within official circles. Although the national sex survey received an unprecedented amount of publicity, no doubt due to its subject, other similar research did not, such as one on illicit drug use in the mid-1980s, at the height of the Government's 'Just Say No' war on drugs, which was also rejected for public funding.[54] Even if the statistical evidence which such research supplied was not perfect, this reluctance to enquire into the private morality of citizens in order to inform public policy responses to social problems, anachronistic at the time, would seem absurd a decade later under New Labour. However, all traditionalists needed to know was that immorality was prevalent and spreading. Those less fearful of a more liberated society, whilst wanting to make empirical judgements, would not always be comforted by the evidence of trends in behaviour and disease.

*

The emerging AIDS crisis quickly fed into the ongoing battle by conservative moralists against the spread of permissive sex education, which was increasingly being given a new edge as the place of homosexuality in sex education gained greater prominence during the mid-1980s. The story of the passage of Section 28 of the Local Government Act 1988 has subsequently been seen as a seminal moment in a number of ways: as a response to the AIDS crisis and increasing social visibility of gay men and women; for the course of sex education in schools; as part of a wider response within public services towards issues of sexuality; and as the second motivating force in mobilising the gay community and gay rights movement in Britain into distinct strands of traditional lobbying and more radical direct action. It remained a touchstone issue for both conservatives and liberals for fifteen years until its repeal in 2003. However, at the time, many people saw it simply as a reaction, or overreaction to some highly publicised incidents, mainly in a few London boroughs. As Gillian Shephard, then a new MP in her first parliamentary term, but a future Education Secretary, recalls, there was simply no suggestion that it would become such a symbol of discrimination against homosexuals.[55] Moves to ban the 'promotion of homosexuality' developed incrementally out of dissatisfaction among moral lobby groups at the compromise reached on parental control over their children's sex education. The political furore and protest which accompanied the passage of the Bill during the winter and spring of 1987–8 might never had happened, had the measure prohibiting the 'promotion' of homosexuality slipped quietly on to the statute book in the previous session as part of a Private Members' Bill introduced by the redoubtable Lord Halsbury and taken up by Dame Jill Knight in the Commons.

In the spring of 1986 a few Labour-controlled councils in London began to propose that children should be taught positive images of homosexuals. The black leader of Haringey in London, Bernie Grant, made particularly good copy for those in the press who wanted to portray this as part of the end of civilisation. Local branches of the Parents Rights Group (PRG) and others opposed to such policies began campaigning against their councils, collecting thousands of signatures in the process. Nationally, morality groups, including the Conservative Family Campaign, the Committee for a Free Britain and the Unification Movement, commonly known as the Moonies, actively supported such local efforts. Returning to the alleged nexus between sexual permissiveness and political extremism, the PRG enlisted the help of individuals involved in the recent Union of Democratic Mineworkers' (UDM) fight against Arthur Scargill's National Union of Mineworkers for the rights of miners to keep working. John Liptrott, the UDM's General Secretary, proclaimed that the battle in Haringey, that notable mining community, was 'a battle over who controls the country. There's a saying: corrupt the morals and you defeat the people.'[56]

Soon the press was clamouring over a number of books which, it was alleged, councils were making available to schools. Though it is clear that they never received anything like the distribution or influence which critics claimed, interventions against them were highly successful. Kenneth Baker attacked the infamous *Jenny Lives with Eric and Martin*, a Danish book about a girl living with her father and his male partner. Another was *How to Become a Lesbian in 35 Minutes*, which, displaying an almost endearing naïveté, conservatives thought was literally a manual for turning girls into lesbians in little more than half an hour. Some of these books had been around for some years, with little or no publicity. One such was *The Playbook for Kids about Sex*, published by Sheba Lesbian Press. This was now seized on by those anxious to prove the evils to which schoolchildren were being subjected. One member of Sheba, Sue O'Sullivan, recalls how they were paid by an unlikely source to distribute copies more widely than ever before:

Leading up to the '87 election we got a call from somebody who it turned out worked for the Conservative Government, or he was a sort of gofer for the Conservatives, and he wanted to order a large number of The Playbook. *We thought about it for a while, and then we decided, well why not? I mean they obviously had the book, why not sell them more? So a large car drove up outside our offices in grungy Bradbury Street in Dalston, the street of many co-ops, and this guy got out – very stony-faced, in an overcoat – he almost looked like a gangster. Anyway, he came in, he took away over a hundred copies and left us with a large amount of money. And we wrote a letter to Mrs Thatcher and thanked her very much for supporting our publishing venture and for giving us so much free publicity as she did.*[57]

At this point the parliamentary supporters of the PRG, led by Knight, intervened. A Bill sponsored by Halsbury proposed to ban the promotion of homosexuality by local councils as an 'acceptable family relationship'. Awareness of the implications of this Bill was extremely low both inside and outside Parliament, and its Lords stages proceeded almost without comment. In the Commons, with the standard now held by Knight, the Bill's committee stage was due to be taken on 8 May, but with Margaret Thatcher expected to call a general election within days, and stuck behind a queue of other contentious bills, it was not expected to complete all its stages. However, as Alf Dubs (now Lord Dubs) remembers, with the Commons virtually deserted the day after the local elections and in anticipation of a dissolution, the Conservatives sprang a surprise, curtailed debate on the bills at the head of the queue, and reached Knight's Bill with over two hours to spare. Stuck on the front bench alone, with no assistance, unsure of the Labour Party's position on the measure, but clear of his own, Dubs attempted to talk the Bill out himself, though this tested his own knowledge of homosexuality and sex education to its limits. However, he finally managed to get a message to a whip that he was going to call a vote, calculating that there were fewer MPs present than the quorum of forty. Telling Labour colleagues 'for socialism go and have a cup of tea and forget this one',[58] an interpretation of socialism which some of less liberal disposition might dispute, the division was called. The result, twenty to nil in favour of the Bill, meant that it fell as the quorum was forty. The Government's official position in both Houses had been sympathy with the aims of the Bill, but a firm insistence that it was unnecessary, or at least premature, given the very recent introduction of stricter guidelines from the Department of Education, and even potentially harmful, because 'the distinction between these, and what I have described as proper teaching about homosexuality, cannot be drawn sufficiently clearly in legislation to avoid harmful misinterpretation. This is a risk we cannot take.'[59]

However, at the final Prime Minister's Questions before the general election Thatcher willingly responded to Knight by giving the Bill her personal support for the following session.[60] During the election campaign, the 'positive images' policies of Labour-controlled councils in London became a significant issue in the capital, but not more widely. The Conservative Party itself, and the PRG, played on fears that such policies were only the thin end of the wedge. Despite the fact that the general election had no bearing on local councillors, one member of the PRG warned:

I live in Haringey
I'm married with two children
And I'm scared.
If you vote LABOUR they'll
Go on teaching my kids about
GAYS AND LESBIANS instead of
Giving them proper lessons.[61]

Following the election there was an attempt by the Department of Education to harden further its guidance on sex education in favour of teaching about marriage and stable family life, and 'no place for teaching which advocates homosexual behaviour, which presents it as the norm or which encourages homosexual experimentation by pupils.'[62] This, however, resolved nothing for either side. In October the Prime Minister bolstered support for the measure in her triumphalist post election conference speech in Blackpool, when she attacked the 'positive images' campaign among left-wing local authorities, saying that 'children who need to be taught traditional moral values are being taught that they have an inalienable right to be gay.'[63] According to one interpretation by Allan Horsfall, such rhetorical attacks on gays and lesbians did not mean that the Government was committed in policy terms to a legislative prohibition. He suggests that the acceptance of an amendment to its Local Government Bill was a concession given in return for Knight acquiescing over one of the Government's most controversial policies of that year, introducing prescription charges for eye tests. Knight, whose late husband had been an optician, was fighting a lone battle in the Conservative Party against this.[64] There were other reports at the time that the Cabinet was divided over whether to accept the amendment, but that the Prime Minister gave it her personal fiat.[65]

In December, when the Government's new Local Government Bill was being debated in committee, Tory MP David Wilshire tabled an amendment giving effect to the provisions of the Knight Bill.[66] The main difference between the two was the substitution of 'pretended family relationship' for 'acceptable family relationship', arguably an even harsher view of the validity of homosexual partnerships. The Government, in the ministerial guise of Michael Howard, future party leader, gave the Bill its full support, saying that recent examples proved that action needed to be taken to prevent local authorities from glorifying homosexuality and to 'encourage youngsters to believe that it is on an equal footing with a heterosexual way of life'. It introduced one caveat, that the clause should not prohibit 'the doing of anything for the purposes of treating or preventing the spread of disease' – aimed at protecting the fight against AIDS. Howard later claimed that the clause would not prevent the objective discussion of homosexuality. None of the supporters of the clause made any attempt to define or justify the key phrase 'pretended family relationship'.

Labour was suddenly caught in a dilemma by the new clause. The leadership, sensitive to anger expressed by some working-class supporters in London about the activities of their Labour councils in relation to gay rights, was fearful of being seen to condone 'proselytisation' of homosexuality, but believed that the proposal would encourage discrimination against lesbians and gays. Along with the Liberal Democrat MP Simon Hughes, Labour was prepared to see a bald prohibition on the promotion of homosexuality, but wanted to remove the rest of the clause which related to 'the acceptability of homosexuality as a pretended family relationship'. When the Bill came before MPs again, Labour tried to mitigate the potentially harmful effects of the measure with amendments protecting work in sex education and anti-discrimination.[67] Labour's spokesman, Jack Cunningham, was also insistent that the proposal was excessive because the alleged or real abuses by local authorities amounted to a handful of instances in London, notably in Haringey and the Inner London Education Authority, but also on one occasion in Ealing, which, he pointed out, had been endorsed by Conservative councillors. However, the new clause was not opposed, nor did Labour try to delete it from the Bill when it came back before the full House. As a result, as Cunningham later admitted to Labour's ruling NEC, the media were able to portray their position as supporting the clause.[68] Chris Smith, the only openly gay MP at the time, criticised his party's tactics for not voting against the clause immediately. According to the lesbian activist Lisa Power, Cunningham told members of the lesbian and gay community immediately after Section 28 was passed that they were wasting their breath calling for repeal because Labour would never do it.[69] However, it is difficult to support the counterfactual suggestion by some gay activists that had Labour opposed the clause from the outset, the Government might not have defended it. What Labour did try to do was mitigate the effects of the clause by supporting amendments to protect sex education and counselling or prevent discrimination on grounds of sexuality. These were opposed, and defeated, by the Government.

Bernie Grant made a vociferous defence of the 'positive images' campaign and as Hughes and a number of Labour MPs suggested, wider sexual influences on young people might also be considered dangerous:

> If the clause's aim is to protect the young, why are we not doing something about soft porn magazines, which are on sale in newsagents? Why are we not doing something about ... page 3 pictures in the popular newspapers? If we are trying not to promote different forms of sexuality, why do we not deal with television advertising, which often tries to sell products merely by appealing to people's sexual nature and motives? Why do the Government suddenly select this target, rather than another?

The tempers of opposing sides erupted fiercely when, as Smith condemned attacks on gay people and property, in particular the recent arson attack on the newspaper *Capital Gay*, Elaine Kellet-Bowman enraged Labour MPs by condoning such arson attacks, repeating this by saying, 'I believe that intolerance of evil *should* grow [emphasis added].' Applause broke out in the public gallery in support of Smith, and the Speaker threatened, not for the first time, to suspend the sitting. When the Bill passed its final stage shortly before midnight, the gallery erupted in anger again and protestors had to be bundled out by attendants as the Speaker suspended the sitting.[70]

Until this point there had been little extra-parliamentary discussion of the clause, which had been restricted to two debates of less than three hours in the Commons. However, with the Bill now on the way to the Lords, gay rights campaigners began to mobilise. During January and February the largest demonstrations held to date for lesbian and gay rights, and in support of people suffering from AIDS, were held in London and across the country. Neil Kinnock was stung into condemnation of the clause. Speaking at a party conference in Scotland, he said that the clause was

> *crude in its concept, slanderous in its drafting, vicious in its purpose. It is an assault on the civil rights of thought and expression in its catch-all provision against 'promotion', and no limpid assurances from ministers can change the fact that the output of geniuses – some of whom happen to be homosexuals – like the mundane work of teachers – who want to prepare and counsel pupils for the realities of life – can fall foul of this pink triangle clause produced and supported by a bunch of bigots.[71]*

Howard, denying that arts and other public services would exclude homosexuals in this way, was able to launch an attack on Labour's earlier prevarication, led by Cunningham:

> *In my innocence, I always supposed that if one was totally opposed to a clause the appropriate thing to do was to vote against it. However, the Labour Party takes a far more sophisticated approach to such matters. In the new Labour Party, if one is totally opposed to something, the thing to do is to say that one supports it and will vote for it, refuse to divide, force a vote in Committee and, when one's leader has declared one a bigot, to put out a piece of paper saying one is totally opposed to it.[72]*

Perhaps the most famous incident came when peers approved the clause in February 1988. Just after the result of the vote was announced, three women let down ropes from the railings at the front of the public gallery and abseiled into the chamber, shouting 'Lesbians are out'. They were ushered out by Black Rod, though not charged by police.[73] One unforeseen consequence of this episode may have been to sway MPs against voting for the televising of Commons proceedings only days later – the protest had occurred in front of television cameras – although it was pointed out that such incidents would happen anyway, as they had as long ago as the era of the Suffragettes.[74]

If the legal consequences of Section 28 proved in the end to be nil, the wider repercussions were far more profound. The Section was arguably highly successful in the narrow terms in which it was framed – many lesbian and gay initiatives run by local authorities were curtailed and other public bodies, for example the British Film Institute, became far more reluctant to support such work, whether or not the Section applied directly to them. More importantly there is evidence that the Section did have an effect on the attitude which schools took towards sex education, counselling of pupils about sexuality and homophobic bullying, with considerable misunderstanding that it did apply to teaching in schools. However, almost as soon as the Act was passed, the Department of the Environment pointed out that, since the 1986 Education Act, sex education was the responsibility of school governors, and that local authorities had only an advisory role. Dame Jill Knight was outraged.[75] It has also been argued by gay rights campaigners that the atmosphere of a conservative political 'victory' against homosexuals fuelled the increase in police activity against gay men, which had already been evident since the advent of AIDS.[76] It is interesting to note that a large group of parents campaigning against the 'positive images' policy in London went to Manchester to show their support for Chief Constable James Anderton, following his notorious speech on AIDS.[77] The number of arrests of gay men for consensual sexual offences including cottaging and procuring rose to a record level in the late 1980s.

*

Just as the 1970s opened with immediate attempts to restrict the operation of the Abortion Act, so the new Conservative majority in the Commons at the end of the decade fuelled the hopes of pro-life groups. However, divisions within their ranks over the best way to make radical inroads into the present extent of abortion soon began to appear. Some favoured a reduction in the time limit for abortion from twenty-eight to eighteen weeks, others an insistence on stricter implementation of the 1929 Infant Life Preservation Act, which protected children 'capable of being born alive' – the argument running that if medical opinion said that babies could now regularly be born alive before this time, they could not be aborted. Even more importantly, their advantage gained by the large Tory majorities, which from 1983 until 1992 were in three-digit figures, proved to be ephemeral, as moderate opinion in favour of some revision of the Abortion Act increasingly proved not to support the aims of LIFE, the Society for the Protection of the Unborn Child (SPUC) and their parliamentary supporters to return to the position before 1967. However, a growing consensus in favour of a modest reduction in the time limit for abortion was based on the medical evidence of the increasing viability of babies born before the twenty-eight weeks in the Abortion Act, rather than on the moral issue of affording greater protection to the unborn child. A bill in the first session of the new Parliament to reduce the time limit to eighteen weeks reached its report stage, but even with four days devoted to it, could not overcome objections. Then when the Liberal Merseyside MP David Alton, a Catholic, made his first attempt at a moderate reduction to twenty-four weeks, he provoked opposition from defenders of the Abortion Act and pro-life groups who clung to the argument that improvements in neonatal care made such a limited reduction almost pointless. Though legislative challenges to the Abortion Act continued to prove fruitless during the 1980s, there were other avenues open to pro-life campaigners. In 1981 the certification form which doctors had to complete after approving an abortion was revised, removing non-medical grounds. Also, in 1985 clinics were restricted to carrying out abortions until twenty-four weeks. Yet the overall figures for abortion did not fall. An attempt by an Oxford student in 1987 to stop his former lover from having an abortion on the grounds that the foetus could mount a legal challenge through the father also failed, though the right of fathers to veto abortions was subsequently taken up by pro-life campaigners.[78]

Following a general election campaign in which pro-life campaigners attempted to make abortion a significant issue, Alton introduced another bill, this time aiming for a more radical reduction in the time limit to eighteen weeks. Margaret Thatcher allied herself firmly within the moderate camp when she made known publicly that she could not support the Alton Bill, a decision described by LIFE as 'disgraceful'. Gillian Shephard warned colleagues that those like herself and the Prime Minister who supported a reduction to twenty-four weeks were 'appalled that a lot of people who have not thought too carefully will vote for Mr Alton in the belief that the bill will be amended. Twenty four weeks is not on offer. This bill is a stop on the way to abolishing the Abortion Act.'[79] This strategy was confirmed by Alton's own statement:

> *The only way to tackle the abortion issue is through numerous small measures, nibbling away at one area after another. If we fail on the question of disability this time, then that is the thing we tackle next. Then we must look at the private clinics and the grounds for abortion.*

Although the Bill won a second reading by 296 to 251 votes, a combination of tactical manoeuvres by its opponents, and intransigence in the face of appeals from Alton for government time, meant that it failed.

The continuing battle between defenders and opponents of legal abortion became increasingly entwined during the 1980s with a rather different ethical dilemma – how society should respond to the rapidly developing technologies involved in fertility treatment, medical research on human embryos and genetics. The first 'test-tube baby' had been born by in-vitro fertilisation (IVF) in 1978, leading to widespread concern about the moral and medical implications for children born through such techniques. From religious groups there was growing opposition to the production of 'spare' embryos which could be either destroyed or used for research, and they began to campaign for such research to be ruled illegal by the courts or banned by Parliament. This led the Conservative Government in 1982 to appoint a committee to negotiate this complex, and to the public baffling, ethical minefield. Norman Fowler's choice to chair the committee was Mary Warnock, Oxbridge philosopher and former headmistress of Oxford High School, who had recently chaired inquiries into the education of disabled children and then vivisection.[80] Fowler says that the decision of this 'wise woman' to chair the committee was vital. It was also supported, perhaps surprisingly given Warnock's liberal reputation, by the Prime Minister, although Thatcher's attitude in the area was consistently more pragmatic and liberal than that of many in her party. Warnock's recent memoir, *People and Places*, contains an attack on Thatcher's philistinism, personal rudeness and, more substantially, what she considers the damaging effects of her education policies, particularly in higher education and special needs. It is also a reminder that Warnock was by no means left-wing, both she and her husband having joined the drift from Labour to Conservative of many of their generation during the mid-1960s. Considering the not unhelpful role Thatcher was to play in seeing this particular Warnock Report enshrined in legislation, such vitriol might be described as ungracious.[81]

Warnock's remit, to 'consider recent and potential developments in medicine and science related to human fertilisation and embryology; to consider what policies and safeguards should be applied, including consideration of the social, ethical and legal implications of these developments; and to make recommendations', gave her committee a long philosophical leash but in the harness of producing a legislative framework. What is most striking about the committee's deliberations is the process of learning and 'cross-fertilisation', excusing the pun, between members from scientific, professional, philosophical and lay backgrounds. Warnock recounts in another memoir the process by which Dr Anne McLaren explained the process of fertilisation and embryonic development to her fellow committee members:

> It is astonishing to me now to realise how totally ignorant of this complex developmental story I and most of my colleagues were. Anne never despised our ignorance … Most people thought of the early embryo as a tiny homunculus, recognisably human. We were now learning to think of the gradual development of the embryo in a completely different way.

However, this learning experience was a two-way process. McLaren later confessed to having been an 'ethical illiterate' when she joined the committee: 'It had simply never struck her that, while she thought of herself as simply working on the division of cells in early mammalian development, with a view to relieving, as she said, some young healthy women from the burden of infertility, other people saw her as a murderer.'[82]

Here was a succinct depiction of how the working of a broadly drawn committee of inquiry could act as a microcosm for groping towards a wider public consensus on highly controversial ethical issues. Many people were more exercised about the long-term consequences of new technologies for children and families than their theoretical moral implications. Warnock said that neither a 'superficially attractive' utilitarian balance between present and future benefits and harm, nor an obedience to strict rules, would suffice. The strict rules did not yet exist in this area, and a decision on the wide range in sentiments about the status of the embryo had to precede a utilitarian calculation of potential harm and benefit. What would work and what would be generally acceptable were two sides of the same coin. Negotiating the difficult waters between a traditionalist position of religiously based public morality and no shared public morality, Warnock said that

> *within the broad limits of legislation, there is room for different, and perhaps much more stringent, moral rules. What is legally permissible may be thought of as the minimum requirement for a tolerable society. Individuals or communities may voluntarily adopt more exacting standards.*[83]

The committee easily came to the conclusion that IVF should be allowed to continue, subject to regulation by an independent authority. The crunch issue, as Warnock makes clear, and as the subsequent arguments have shown, was to be the question of whether research should be permitted on 'spare' embryos in the laboratory, and if so, until what stage of development. The production of such spares was necessary not only to produce enough embryos to make implantation viable, but also to improve IVF techniques, making them acceptable to women, and hopefully reducing the need to overproduce embryos in the first place. There was also the question of whether spare embryos should be used for medical research into genetic diseases such as muscular dystrophy and cystic fibrosis. It was the potential of gene therapy, in fact, that drove the increasing levels of support for embryo research, rather than issues to do with IVF. Religious opponents of embryo research obviously applied the same argument as they did against abortion – human life begins at the point of conception and should be legally protected from that point. 'Pro-life' campaigners (a tag which was offensive to supporters of embryo research, who thought this position inhibited life in different ways) did engage with arguments about the point at which any limit should be placed on embryo research, just as they did with the time limit for abortion, but their fundamentalist position was based on warning about a slippery slope towards Nazi eugenics. In Warnock's tart phrase, they should not even have got on the slope in the first place. The majority of the committee agreed that a public consensus could be reached only by deciding at what stage human life became so valuable that it must be protected. Again, following the explanations of early development from McLaren, they decided on a fourteen-day limit. This would prevent research before the point when the 'primitive streak', which is the precursor to the central nervous system, begins to develop – thus precluding research on an embryo which could potentially feel pleasure or pain.[84]

Five years elapsed between the publication of the Warnock Report and the publication of the Government's own Human Fertilisation and Embryology Bill in 1989 after consultation on a White Paper – a brief hiatus next to the ten years it took for the Wolfenden Report's recommendations on homosexuality to reach the statute book, but given the greater urgency of unregulated scientific advance in this new area, it was a significant delay. However, it also made a material difference to the level of consensus which could be reached for legal, regulated embryo research. In the year following the Report's publication there was considerable support for a bill, sponsored by Enoch Powell, to outlaw embryo research. An enormous lobbying operation by pro-life groups against what it told MPs was 'human vivisection' was launched. Just as anti-abortionists were eternally confident of the support of the Prime Minister, so opponents of research on human embryos assumed Thatcher would be in favour of more exacting standards applying all round.[85] In fact, she remained studiedly neutral, refusing to accede to demands for a moratorium or a ban on embryo research, whilst making clear she understood people's concerns and shared some of them, particularly on genetic engineering. The Powell Bill won its second reading by 238 to 66, a majority of 172. The Tory MP Ann Winterton declared that MPs had made 'an attempt to step where the Government have been too slow or lacked the moral courage to tread'. Given that the Warnock Report itself had argued against a rush to legislation, ministers might have taken exception to that, but they were also divided. While Fowler and his Health Minister, Kenneth Clarke, voted against the Bill, many other ministers voted for it, including John Major. On the Labour side, the future leader John Smith also supported it. For this Smith was subsequently criticised by Leo Abse, who had tried to persuade him of the difference between the destruction of human life caused by abortion, which they both opposed, and new technology which promised the possibility of creating life by IVF.[86] The Prime Minister remained uncommitted.

A consultation document published in 1986 was roundly attacked by pro-life groups, who saw it as a delaying tactic to push the question past the next general election. As repeated attempts by their parliamentary supporters to introduce another bill met without success, pro-life campaigners stepped up previous attempts to bring the issue into play during the election campaign, along with abortion. SPUC and LIFE claimed they were instrumental in boosting the vote for pro-life candidates of all parties. Following the 1987 general election, the Government published a White Paper along Warnock lines, but with alternative clauses on embryo research, on which there would be a free vote in Parliament. Only in 1989 did the Government bring forward a bill. At this point the Warnock proposals became entwined with abortion. Both debates clearly involved moral judgements about the status of the human embryo. The linkage meant that this became the central question around which different opinions ranged, potentially increasing polarisation between those who believed in the sanctity of life from the point of conception, and those who felt that legitimate protection of the embryo became paramount only later and was balanced against other interests. However, some pro-life groups objected to the two issues being decided in the same legislation, fearing that a deal had been done by more moderate colleagues that embryo research would go through in return for easing the passage of a modest reduction in the time limit for abortion. This was confirmed by Ann Widdecombe's suggestion that such an outcome would mean they would back off on further restrictions on abortion for a while. It has also been seen as a 'tokenistic gesture ... safe in the knowledge that the probable outcome ... would be the confirmation of already established medical custom and practice'[87]. In fact, Thatcher gave her strongest support for this position when trailing the possibility of a vote on the two issues in February 1989, when she said that she favoured a 24-week limit for abortion, that this was the considered view of most of the medical profession and was, in any case, the established norm in most hospitals and clinics.[88]

When the Human Fertilisation and Embryology Bill was debated in the Lords, peers approved embryo research by 234 to 80 votes.[89] When the Bill reached its committee stage in the Commons, it was debated on the floor of the House, rather than upstairs, to give all MPs a chance to take part. Clarke confessed to the Government's and his own uncertainty about the wisdom of linking abortion and embryo research, saying that 'even in the past month or two I have genuinely changed my mind.' The Lords decision on embryo research was confirmed by MPs by 364 to 193.[90] Voting for research were previous supporters of the ban proposed by Powell in 1985, including Major and Smith (a conversion for which Abse gives Smith no credit). Thatcher also voted in favour. The following day MPs also accepted a reduction in the time limit for abortion to twenty-four weeks, rejecting all the lower figures for which anti-abortionists were campaigning. Even this modest revision of the 1967 Act was marred for them by further measures excluding disability from this time limit and putting abortion outside the scope of the 1929 Act, which anti-abortionists claimed afforded protection to the unborn child.[91] This was to be the last significant outing for the abortion issue in the twentieth century. The heavy emphasis placed during this debate on the current medical consensus regarding twenty-four weeks by government ministers and pro-abortion campaigners like David Steel has led some people to suggest that abortion was becoming treated less as a moral issue or even one of conscience, and more as a neutral, scientific matter. This would be to go too far. The 'medicalisation' of debate about abortion, something which had been a feature since the 1960s, reflected the growing consensus, as suggested so recently by Warnock, that personal sentiment, however strongly held, could not be sufficient to give legal effect to moral choices. But it also reflected an acknowledgement of where the moral consensus lay. Few people were defending late-term abortions except in extreme circumstances, given the state of medical science, and the reduction to twenty-four weeks might have happened much earlier, with widespread support, had pro-lifers not alienated so many people because of their attempt to restrict abortion further.

*

Although the Government proved itself capable of pragmatism on issues of conscience such as abortion and embryo research, the last two years of Margaret Thatcher's administration, as she recalls in her memoirs, did indeed see an intensification of political debate about the family, its problems and potential solutions, and, unsurprisingly, where the blame lay for its present woes. This was led by the Prime Minister, who in March 1989 launched a fierce attack on the legacy of the 1960s Labour Governments, referring contemptuously to the 'prophets of the permissive society' who had blurred the distinction between right and wrong and wrecked the education system. She linked them to one of the personal symbols of Harold Wilson's premiership – the Gannex raincoat:

> *Who are these people with the Gannex conscience? You know, the one you reverse according to the way the wind is blowing? ... These are the people who robbed a generation of their birthright ... It's not advice we require from these people, it's an apology. Where did the hooligans, the louts and yobs on the late-night trains learn their contempt for the security of the law-abiding citizen?*

To the last question the answer might easily have been, as one journalist noted, 'at school since 1979'.[92] Focusing on the causes and consequences of family breakdown, while single mothers and the burden they placed on the social security system remained an easy target for conservatives, the financial and emotional responsibilities of errant and absent fathers became a new preoccupation. Ministers, again led by the Prime Minister, advocated tough action against men who did not face up to their responsibilities, pointing out that four out of five single parents received no maintenance payments. Simultaneously Tony Newton, Social Services Secretary, launched plans which foreshadowed the bungled establishment of the Child Support Agency – the principles behind which had widespread support. Recounting an anecdote in which an estate where children of two-parent families were in such a minority that one child asked her father not to embarrass her by coming to school, Thatcher said that this was 'a new kind of threat to our whole way of life, the long-term implications of which we can barely grasp'. Refusing to concede that economics was at the root of the problem, she looked once again to the past:

> *I believe that in the 1960s far too many young people were ridiculed out of their true beliefs by the proponents of the permissive society, who believed in precious little but themselves. They talked a lot about rights, yet they gave away the fundamental right of a child to be brought up in a real family. And now we are reaping the harvest ... Don't blame freedom and prosperity for the faults ingrained in human nature.*[93]

This lead was followed in swift fashion by the Party Chairman, Kenneth Baker, making the rather fatuous claim that since the false theories of the 1960s, 'more people now recognise that parents have duties to children that involve sacrificing some of their own wants for their children. Having children creates duties and obligations.' But he prescribed that the only way to spare children the pain of divorce was to stop it happening by teaching boys at home and in school about fatherhood and the stability of marriage.[94] Rhetoric aside, quite what the policy implications of these animadversions against family breakdown were remained obscure, as there was no political consensus about the extent to which state intervention could, or should, try to shape family life. Conservative divisions on the issues were once again laid bare at the party conference in October 1990, shortly before the defenestration of the Blessed Margaret. This showed the gap between many of the activists, who railed against gays, perverts and sexual deviants undermining the family, and ministers such as Angela Rumbold, who attempted to placate the baying mob while resiling from any policies likely to be described as radical in any direction. Thanked by the conference chairman, Dame Margaret Fry, for a wonderful speech and 'most of all for being normal', the Education Minister insisted that Government should seek to help all mothers who wanted to stay at home, as well as those who wanted to go out to work.[95] Rumbold was condemned in the most acute analysis of the present state of the debate about the family by Melanie Phillips, still at the *Guardian*, but already with a sharp message for rampant liberal individualism as well as the failings of the right. Thatcher, she argued, was

> *caught within her own ideological contradictions, trapped between her belief that individuals must be free to make their own choices and her equal belief that she must do something about it when those choices are in her view wrong. The mother of the nation washes her hands of any responsibility she might be expected to shoulder for her constitutional offspring; instead, the individual family unit is Mrs Thatcher's little state.*

Despite the rhetoric about moral responsibility, the Thatcher administration was, Phillips said, only interested in economic circumstances:

> *The causes and effects of family breakdown are rarely even mentioned by this self-proclaimed party of the family. Where is the money for family conciliation services to enable children to benefit from their fathers' corporeal contact as*

well as their money? Where is the support for counselling and other child care services to provide education in parenting and prevent families from ill-treating their children? Where are the political initiatives to civilise the 'me' society and teach people not to expect instant gratification and personal fulfilment at all costs, surely one of the contributory factors to the high rate of marriage breakdown?[96]

As she suggested, these were questions equally apt for a Labour Party crawling its way back towards government. Though neither party would ever satisfy Phillips' increasingly strident moralistic demands, the decade after the fall of Margaret Thatcher would see the relationship between the state and the moral responsibility and rights of individuals, families and the wider public good develop even further under the Governments of John Major and Tony Blair.

7. Basics and Bastards: 1990–1997

'We must go back to basics ... And the Conservative Party will lead the country back to these basics right across the board: sound money; free trade; traditional teaching; respect for the family and the law. And above all, lead a new campaign to defeat the cancer that is crime.'

John Major[1]

'The infamous sixties have something to teach Britain about tolerance, about understanding, and about the conditions in which crime breeds. But the nineties, I believed, had something to teach about personal responsibility and individual values. These were my beliefs, and that is why I was content that our approach to these matters should be called "back to basics", for that is precisely what I meant.'

John Major[2]

'My "back to basics" was not about bashing single mothers or preaching sexual fidelity at private citizens. I knew only too well the problems of single parenthood: both my sister and Norma's mother had brought up their children alone ... I wanted nothing to do with a moral crusade under the title "family policy". I had always been extremely wary about politicians trespassing into the field of sexual morality, and hostile to any campaign which appeared to demonise any group.'

John Major[3]

'It is the one event [sic] of my life of which I am most ashamed.'

John Major[4]

John Major's premiership began in a state of paradox. He was Margaret Thatcher's anointed successor, and supported by many on the right determined to prevent Michael Heseltine completing his revenge by assuming the leadership of the Party and the country. Yet Major gained wider trust in the Party and among the electorate precisely because he was the antithesis of the Iron Lady in both personality and political style. Coming from a very different social back-ground to that of his predecessor, Major's outlook was immediately and consistently reflected in his attitude towards social policy and the means by which he wished to create a 'society at ease with itself'. Major identifies this difference very clearly and proudly in his memoirs, as a fresh injection of 'tolerance' into government policy, a traditional Conservative value according to Major, which some around Thatcher, though not the Prime Minister herself, had 'overlooked'. He marked this break with a more 'shrill and censorious tone' by ordering Norman Lamont to unfreeze child benefit in the 1991 Budget and the awarding of compensation to haemophiliacs infected with HIV during blood transfusions. He also signaled his Government's new tack by referring to a more relaxed attitude towards race and homosexuality. It was indeed Major's willing-ness to listen directly to the interests of gay rights campaigners represented by the actor Ian McKellen which contributed towards the parliamentary climate necessary for the lowering of the age of consent from twenty-one to eighteen in 1994 to be accepted.

Major also trumpets new initiatives for women, particularly for greater political representation and against discrimination in the workplace. Launching the Opportunity 2000 campaign in 1991 with a typically incongruous (and unflattering) metaphor, the Prime Minister asked rhetorically, 'Why should half [*sic*] of our population go through life like a hobbled horse in a steeplechase? The answer is that they shouldn't – and increasingly, they won't.'[5] Such anti-discrim-ination initiatives were backed up by an acceptance of other battles which feminist campaigners had been fighting for years, for example the removal of the insidious legal anomaly that a married man could not be convicted of raping his wife. Major was, however, much criticised for failing to appoint a woman to his first Cabinet, though Gillian Shephard became Employment Secretary, and Virginia Bottomley was promoted to run Health, following the 1992 general election. His *pièce justicative* in his autobiography, claiming that he was aware of the problem and sought to prepare these and other women at middle-ranking level, succeeds only in sounding more patronising.

The limits of this social *glasnost* were evident nowhere more clearly than in debate about the family. As Major acknowledges, with evident irritation, at the same time that he was allowing the fatal words 'back to basics' to fall from his lips at the 1993 party conference, some of his ministers were engaged in a concerted effort to demonise single mothers. If Major's own support for the traditional nuclear family was also informed by his own family history, in which both his sister and his mother-in-law had brought up children on their own, his failure to impress his own reading of 'family values' on colleagues such as Peter Lilley and John Redwood reflected the persistent weakness from which he suffered in many areas of policy, most fatally Europe. Though government legislation, most controversially the Child Support Act passed in the dying days of the Thatcher regime, sought to reassert the importance of the responsibility of absent parents, usually fathers, for their natural offspring, this was motivated as much by the aim to reduce spending on social security as by concern for the children of single mothers.

The 1994 Criminal Justice and Public Order Act was one of the largest pieces of criminal justice legislation ever enacted, and its mammoth proportions reflected the breadth of scope with which the Government, and then back-benchers during its passage, sought to tackle a variety of social problems which had been building up, many of them involving controversial issues of morality. The Act became most famous for its restrictions on 'raves' and Edwina Currie's successful amendment to lower the homosexual age of consent from twenty-one to eighteen, but it also covered pornography and obscenity, rape and buggery, stem cells and fertility treatment, obscene telephone calls and racially motivated offences. Conservative hangers also made another vain attempt to reintroduce the death penalty during the Bill's committee stage. Debate on the broad principles of the Bill was framed explicitly on the relationship between crime, individual responsibility, public morality and social changes since the 1960s. When Tory MP Michael Stephen suggested that 'today we are reaping the consequences of the breakdown of respect which occurred in the 1960s … successive governments have listened far too much to left-wing socialist reformers', Tony Blair, the Shadow Home Secretary, was ready with a rejection of this standard attack on the liberal 1960s, which was to sit rather uneasily with his later distancing from the liberalism of that decade:

What makes [the public] angry … is that he stands there after almost 15 years of government, with crime rising in the way that it has, and will not take any blame or responsibility but puts it on the 1960s or the trendy liberal establishment … What people dislike about the Government more than anything else is that they will preach to everybody about taking personal responsibility, but they do not have the guts to take any responsibility themselves for the situation that they created ... Have the Government just woken up? What was happening in the 1980s? When that great fan of the liberal establishment, the noble Baroness Thatcher, was presiding over the Government, why did they not try to take things on and deal with them? ... The truth is that history cannot be rewritten in that way.[6]

The hardline right-winger, Ann Winterton, pointing to the Prime Minister's recent fateful party conference speech, attacked her Government's weakness in the face of liberal hegemony, saying:

They have failed to pay anything other than lip service to the concept of supporting the family and strengthening the bond of marriage which is its very foundation ... Divorce laws have been relaxed, homosexuality is actively promoted, Government-funded agencies peddle powerful contraceptives to young children, and sex education classes for primary school children and upwards concentrate on a mechanistic and unnecessarily explicit interpretation of sexuality ... The House might also reflect that 4 million abortions have done nothing to encourage respect for human life. In addition, bleating agnostic bishops have bitterly failed their flocks by giving no clear lead on moral matters.

If 'back to basics' is to be anything other than a snappy soundbite, it must mean, first and foremost, a return to the acceptance and reflection in public policy of those Judaeo-Christian moral standards which for so many years have bound society together, and which have proved so practical as well as so spiritually preferable. ...

Unless they [the Government] distance themselves from the outdated liberal nostrums that have underpinned public policy since the 1960s, the tide of crime will continue to rise until it rots the very heart of our society.[7]

As we saw in the last chapter, the later focus of the Thatcher Administration on underlying problems facing the family was an echo of the shift in political attention which had occurred in the mid-1950s, when the Conservative Government began to examine social questions which had been overshadowed by postwar reconstruction. To take the parallel one stage further, the Major Government framed the answers to some of these questions in a more liberal direction, reflecting changing contemporary attitudes towards issues of morality, as the Macmillan Government had, largely under the influence of 'Rab' Butler in the late 1950s and early 1960s. Similarly, by the early 1960s the same party had been in government for over a decade, giving rise to accusations of arrogance, corruption and staleness. Pressure had been growing for discussion and reform of a number of laws which the right of the Conservative Party was not prepared to countenance. Just as Butler and Macmillan understood the limits of tolerance within the Party, so did Major and his more liberal-minded ministers. However, the embarrassing fiasco over disability rights in 1994, in which the minister for the Disabled, Sir Nicholas Scott, was humiliated by disability rights campaigners including his daughter Victoria, demonstrated a distinct loss of sensitivity to the wider political and public atmosphere for change. Other failures, despite Major's own protestations, included the Government's and particularly the police's attitude towards race relations and the investigation of complaints by people from black and minority ethnic communities.

*

During the mid-1990s the personal morality and behaviour of individual politicians became a greater focus for public debate than at any time since the Profumo scandal, which brought down Harold Macmillan in 1963. As on that occasion, the actual sins which were committed by a parade of Conservative MPs were minor, and if a similar standard were imposed rigorously in politics, the cramped green benches of the Commons would be distinctly roomier. John Profumo's real sins were two-fold – to have been caught lying, and to be unlucky enough to symbolise a general public feeling that the governing party was in some way dishonest, hypocritical or morally degenerate, depending on your viewpoint. Under John Major, errant MPs were less guilty of the first offence, more often looking ridiculous or pathetic in the glare of tabloid press intrusion into their lives which made coverage of the Profumo scandal look distinctly amateur. However, they were certainly more guilty of the second. The more Major tried to construct a philosophically coherent social policy around the admittedly 'trite' theme of 'back to basics', or later 'traditional family values', evidence of his own foot-soldiers undermining him, and traditional family values, through adultery, illegitimacy, homosexuality or financial skulduggery would emerge to tar the whole administration with the brush of 'sleaze'. Such allegations looked all the more damning juxtaposed with the increasingly blatant attack by some ministers on 'feckless' single parents and teenage mothers in particular. Small wonder that, as the crisis broke around the Prime Minister's head, the man whom for two decades moral conservatives had blamed as much as any for the permissive society, Roy Jenkins, struck back:

> *The Conservative Party ... is like an injured animal on a road which ought to be allowed to creep away from the headlights into the undergrowth, where it can perhaps hope to recover from its wounds. Until it is allowed to do so, there seems only too great a likelihood that its nastier elements, encouraged from within the Cabinet, will exercise increasing sway.*[8]

The sudden death of John Smith and the election of Tony Blair as Labour leader saw the tide of new philosophical ideas flow up the estuaries of the party's thinking, as Blair and others sought to enrich the concept of New Labour and distinguish it from Kinnock's and Smith's modernisation, rooted more in the Labour movement. Jenkins was one personal influence on Blair. Smith, often portrayed unfairly as dour and old-fashioned was, in fact, a social liberal, though one staunchly opposed to abortion. As Leo Abse recalls, such views allowed New Labour to paint Smith after his death as 'rigidly conservative', though the public shared a view of him as a 'bank manager' type with 'high moral standards'.[9] Blair and the other leaders of 'the Project' attempted to distance New Labour as far as possible in the minds of floating voters from this old-fashioned image, and still further from the philosophy or achievements of previous Labour Governments in which Jenkins had served and promoted the 'civilised' society. Though they might have winced at the comparison, New Labour's rhetorical style in fact owed as much to Harold Wilson (who had copied John F. Kennedy) as it did to Bill Clinton (who had also modelled himself on Kennedy). The 1964 Labour manifesto had even been titled *New Britain*, and repeatedly referred to 'community'. The Wilson Government had embraced the vitality of a more liberated society in the 1960s and fostered wider social acceptability of greater liberation without abandoning an attachment to traditional social solidarity. The creation of a 'young country' was not, therefore a new ploy. The Blairite 'Third Way' sought a similar accommodation between the individualistic claims of contemporary life and traditional forms of social cohesion.

Prime among the influences on New Labour was the 'communitarianism' of the American sociologist Amitai Etzioni. Etzioni's philosophy was famously adopted by the Clinton Democrats as well as moderate Republicans. A similar fondness for its warm words swept both sides of the political divide in the UK in the mid-1990s. When Etzioni visited London in March 1995, spending time with Blair as well as doing the circuit of think tanks and academic lectures, communitarianism seemed to offer New Labour a truly Third Way philosophy. Equally critical of the effects of free-market economics on the moral fabric of communities and of liberal individualism and the welfare state on personal responsibility, communitarians argued for a renewed emphasis on strengthening the autonomy and responsibility of families and voluntary associations to rebuilt shattered communities. Such aspirations were enshrined in the new Clause 4 of the Labour Party constitution, which Blair wrung out of a recalcitrant party after becoming leader, substituting the meaningless for the irrelevant.

Blair's comfort with communitarian prescriptions seemed inexhaustible. In January 1996 he declared: 'We are social beings, nurtured in families and communities and human only because we develop the moral power of personal responsibility for ourselves and each other. Britain is simply stronger as a team than as a collection of selfish players.'[10] Keeping in mind that the context for this remark was a speech to mark the tenth anniversary of the Anglican 'Faith in the City' initiative, even the use of the word 'moral' was banal. Such prosaic social comments, which could have been uttered by any postwar politician to the left of Margaret Thatcher, were contrasted in the Blair oratory with historical caricatures of the post-1960s social outlook of the left:

> *In the 1960s the pendulum swung towards a more individualistic ethos. For a generation or more, the dominant model of behaviour on left and right was highly individualistic. This was true in the liberation of private life and in intellectual debate.*

Interestingly, this accepted the standard conservative view of the results of the 1960s and the views of social liberals, that 'permissiveness' was commonplace both in personal behaviour and social philosophy. Where New Labour tried to distance itself from this caricature of liberal human-rights thinking was by accepting the dichotomy, also expounded by Etzioni and others, that rights could only be enjoyed because of reciprocal responsibilities which individuals owed to others and society at large. This was also enshrined in the new Clause 4. The idea of 'no rights without responsibilities' became a shibboleth of New Labour. Some, like Jack Straw, went even further, arguing that 'a decent society is not actually based on rights. It is based on duties. Our duty to each other.'[11]

These were not just semantic arguments. Rulings against the UK at the European Court of Human Rights in Strasbourg continued under the Major Government, which accepted such rulings while resisting calls to bring in a UK Bill of Rights in any form. The arguments used continued to be a combination of quotations from Dicey about parliamentary sovereignty and the contradictory claims that a Bill of Rights would either be too inflexible to take account of changes in social values, or too vague to be of any use. However, the Government was now having to make a positive case for the status quo. Although Labour increasingly nuanced its understanding of human rights, it did adopt a Bill of Rights as policy from the 1992 election manifesto onwards. The Home Office minister Charles Wardle, in answering parliamentary debates on the subject, gave Conservative legislative initiatives as examples of extending human rights without enshrined constitutional rights, from the Data Protection Act, through the 'narrow' Official Secrets Act, to the Police and Criminal Evidence Act.[12] If the Major Government resisted attempts to revolutionise British law by conferring positive rights for the first time, the quintessential initiative of the Major years did attempt to make public bodies focus more clearly on the perspective of the users of public services, improving the quality of services and reducing the levels of dissatisfaction which, in the last resort, could lead to legal action and, conceivably, claims at Strasbourg. The Citizen's Charter was a fusion of the Thatcherite effort to inject greater efficiency into public services, which dated back to the Rayner Unit of the early 1980s, and a more Majorite feeling that ordinary, working-class people should receive the same quality of service that educated middle-class people could find, or that people more generally expected from the private sector.

*

Looking back in 1998, John Major categorised his approach to the myriad allegations which constituted the other defining theme of his administration, the millstone of 'sleaze' which was hung around the Conservatives' neck from 1992 until defeat in the next general election in 1997:

> *I took a puritanical view of financial misbehaviour, a tolerant view of personal misdemeanours, and was frankly indignant and angry about the charges over Iraq ... My open approach also led me to respond with fury to the paper-thin claims that personal misdemeanours by a handful of Conservative MPs counted as sleaze by the Government. In this regard we fell victim to an opposition without scruple and to a press without sympathy. The Conservative Party did not invent sin or sex, but it suffered from a great appetite to uncover – in some cases almost to initiate and to encourage – scandals about personal morality.*[13]

The Conservatives under Major may not have invented sin or sex but the comparison between press and public satiability for scandal before and after 1997 is a stark one. They were especially attacked for hypocrisy over conflicting standards of personal sexual morality and preaching of traditional family values. However, the significance of such hypocrisy for all but the media was also questioned. Writing towards the end of the sorry saga in 1996 Melanie Phillips attacked the culture which denigrated individual hypocrisy more than failure to promote stability through family policy:

> *Politicians should say unequivocally that marriage is an important civic and social good and that it is better for individuals and for society if, wherever possible, children are brought up by both their natural parents. They should not be knocked off this course by ministerial scandal, any more than the Church would feel obliged to stop preaching its doctrines if individual priests were discovered to be paedophiles. Hypocrisy has been promoted as the worst vice of society but it is not. Its is essential that public ideals are promoted despite the frailties of individuals.*[14]

Few, if any, of the ministers whose personal lives were splashed across the newspapers and television screens were among those most closely involved in the exhortation of a return to traditional family values in 1993 that culminated in the 'back to basics' episode. Whilst Labour did indeed take advantage of the Government's discomfort by attacking them for 'hypocrisy' and for preaching, some, such as David Blunkett, agreed with the prescriptions of those who were worried about teenage mothers living alone in council housing, if more for the effect on the children than for the implicit encouragement to immorality and illegitimacy. David Mellor's affair with an actress might not have led to his resignation except for his complete inability to avoid annoying the press and public, notably his comments about the press 'drinking in the last-chance saloon' over invasions of privacy. As Mellor was the minister responsible for media regulation, such warnings understandably stuck in the maw of journalists. It was widely felt that Mellor's parading of his 'traditional' family, including parents-in-law, wife and small children, in front of the cameras was perhaps his worst offence, though none of these delivered the *coup de grâce*, which came from another quarter altogether.

Once the fateful 'Back to Basics' speech had been delivered and stupidly spun as including personal morality by Tim Collins, the right-wing press officer at Central Office, the press gloves were off. In the words of one member of the Cabinet at the time, the result was not surprising if you left an 'adolescent' in charge of communications.[15] Tim Yeo, Junior Environment Minister, was the next MP to be caught, this time having fathered a child by his mistress, an 'offence' which Major was again anxious to ignore, as was Yeo's boss at Environment, the morally upright Anglican lay preacher John (Selwyn) Gummer, author of the 1971 polemic *The Permissive Society: Fact or Fantasy?*. Major excused Yeo on the grounds that his wife had been forgiving and that he was supporting the child. Why a minister should have to resign just because his wife was not forgiving is unclear. Yeo, not associated with the moral traditionalist wing of the party was, nonetheless, quoted in the press as saying, 'It is in everyone's interests to reduce broken families and the number of single parents; I have seen from my constituency the consequences of marital breakdown.'

Having ridden out the initial storm, Yeo fell victim to press insatiability during the quiet news period over the Christmas holiday. Shedding some of his own dignity by trying to hide from the press in his car, pressure from his constituency association, fellow Tory MPs and finally Downing Street led him to fall on his sword.[16] At almost the same time, Margaret Thatcher's successor in Finchley,

Hartley Booth, a 47-year-old Methodist lay preacher and married father of three, was forced to resign as a ministerial aide because of an affair with his 22-year-old female former Commons researcher. A frustrated and bemused Finchley Conservative Association chairman commented, 'I think he has been a fool. He knows he has been a fool ... It is a lapse that is completely out of character and that is the end of it. I don't know why he had to resign over this: everybody flirts, don't they?'[17]

As Major recalls, there followed press intrusion into any possible personal scandal involving politicians' families and sex lives, including two tragedies in quick succession – the suicide of the wife of Lord Caithness, and the accidental death of MP Stephen Milligan during an auto-asphyxiation session. Major was particularly indignant at the time, and in his memoirs, about accusations which had surfaced in *Scallywag* magazine, which were then repeated in the more mainstream *New Statesman*, that he had been having an affair with society caterer Clare Latimer. Major threatened to sue. As he writes in his memoirs:

> *Rumours had been swilling around Fleet Street for some time, I learned. They had no basis in truth. There being nothing to find, reporters found nothing, and only innuendo appeared in the mainstream press. Nevertheless, I gained the impression that it contributed to an insolent undercurrent in press reports ... I was not prepared to put Norma, Clare Latimer, my children or myself at risk in this way, and decided to knock the story on the head. The matter was eventually settled out of court.*[18]

This passage perhaps betrays Major's more ruthless side, which enabled him to climb to the top of the greasy pole. Schooled in the black arts of the Whips' Office with their minute knowledge of MPs' personal peccadilloes, Major understood that the best form of defence was attack, invoked the feelings of his family and Latimer, and wielded the axe of the libel law against the rumourmongers. The strategy aroused the famously protective cloak of Commons clubbiness. The *New Statesman* was attacked from all sides, its parties boycotted even by Labour, and MPs voted by 119 to 15 to introduce statutory curbs on press intrusion into privacy, with many privately citing the *New Statesman* story as an added impetus. One minister was quoted as saying of Major's libel action, 'Thank God someone's had the guts to take you lot on.'[19] The *New Statesman* hit back, accusing Major of

Maxwellian tactics,[20] a reference to Robert Maxwell's notorious litigiousness in the face of questions about his business practices, a comparison which, in the light of the Currie revelations, was not quite as offensive as it must have seemed in 1993. Latimer settled the action with *Scallywag* first in July,[21] though not before giving an interview to the *Mail on Sunday* which reportedly caused more grief to the Prime Minister, in which she described the closeness of her Downing Street contact with Major.[22] The action with the *New Statesman* was settled in September 1993, with the magazine paying symbolic damages of £1,001, but having to be bailed out of its legal costs by Labour millionaire and MP Geoffrey Robinson.[23] Perhaps most damagingly for Major, when knowledge of the Currie affair surfaced, Latimer lashed out at her treatment at the hand of the Majors, saying, 'He allowed my life to be trashed because he knew this allegation was not true and to hide the real scandal he was terrified might come out.' According to Latimer, her friendship with the Majors had been abruptly terminated when the original allegations surfaced.[24]

It was in this context that Major gave his 'Back to Basics' speech in October 1993 – a Prime Minister vindicated over rumours of an adulterous affair, drawing some broad lines of policy about basic values underlying public services. Many of his colleagues, themselves perhaps personally blameless in the bedroom department, used the speech to justify their desire to return to tradi-tional family values and condemn feckless teenage mothers on council estates. In retrospect Major understood the implications:

> *I had always been extremely wary about politicians trespassing into the field of sexual morality ... On reflection, I should have seen the risk. The media interest was strong – the hounding of David Mellor bore testimony to that. Editors, ever hungry for human interest stories, still require a 'peg' on which to hang them, and one is the claim that the disclosures are being made in the public interest. I, they decided, had now given them the opportunity to use this line of defence. From that day forward, any tittle-tattle about a parliamentary colleague could be published as a serious political news story.*[25]

Of course, also in retrospect, the sexual scandal which could have been most closely associated with the 'back to basics' message was the adulterous affair which Major had been conducting for four years during the 1980s with Edwina

Currie, which emerged in September 2002 when Currie published her own diaries. Currie, although clearly with a position to defend, claims that watching Major give the 'Back to Basics' speech immediately set off alarm bells, and that the 'campaign' cruelly treated ministers, MPs, women and single parents.[26] Although she conflates the speech itself with the wider utilisation of it by the 'bastard' tendency in the Government, other more liberal-minded ministers, such as Douglas Hurd, Kenneth Clarke, Virginia Bottomley and Gillian Shephard were also wary of the implications of a 'back to basics' agenda. Even the right-wing Education Secretary, John Patten, admitted that it could be unpopular given that some MPs were 'not the best advertisements for family values'.[27] Currie compares Major's style unfavourably with Margaret Thatcher's, claiming bizarrely that 'Margaret Thatcher never laid down the law on morality. She simply tried to live as well as she could.'[28] But the retrospective judgement that Major was unwise to launch a campaign on morality ignores the fact that he clearly did not intend it to be applied to sexual morality. Major's repeated clarifications of this in 1993–4 and in his memoirs are made only more tragic by the knowledge that this was informed by fear of discovery as much as by his genuine distaste for preaching. Nevertheless, there was a fundamental self-contradiction even in Major's own pronouncements about the policy. Contrasting the lessons about 'tolerance' from the 1960s with a 1990s emphasis on 'personal responsibility and individual values' points to a continuing confusion in his own mind about the application of a 'back to basics' philosophy. If Major thought issues of morality could be so simply compartmentalised he misunderstood the debate about the relationship between individual morality, the family, society and crime, while also underestimating the capacity of opponents in the Conservative Party, Labour and the press to scent blood in glib sloganising.

Major reserves his strongest indignation in his memoirs for the elision by the press and opposition of sexual scandal with allegations of financial impropriety and an attempt to tar the whole Government with such a brush during the arms-to-Iraq inquiry. This led to the Scott Report, from which Labour, led by Robin Cook, made such mileage in the run-up to the 1997 general election. The futility of making such distinctions was another symptom of a government on the ropes more generally, where otherwise minor sins were magnified by their ability to cause further damage and embarrassment to an unpopular party. However, there was a degree to which this was also of the Conservatives' own making. David Mellor was not, in fact, driven from office because of his affair with Antonia de Sancha, but for the subsequent revelations about his family holiday courtesy of Monica Bauwens, daughter of a major funder of the PLO, one of the few supporters of the Iraqi invasion of Kuwait. Having used up all his credit with the media, his colleagues and the Prime Minister over the details of his affair, this minor financial irregularity was fatal. The same year that Mellor was forced to quit, the public purse was used to fund the costs incurred by Norman Lamont's solicitors in handling the eviction of 'Miss Whiplash' from a tenancy in his central London flat, on the basis that his public reputation as Chancellor of the Exchequer was involved. The coincidence of the whiff of sexual scandal with such episodes was a gift to the lazy and malicious in creating the generalised image of sleaze which Major so resented. Did the press and public comment about the sexual philandering of Conservative politicians reflect a perverse atmosphere in which, in Matthew Parris' words, 'not getting divorced seems to be the modern sin'?[29] That might confer too great a sense of morality on a tabloid press in whose eyes politicians were damned whatever choices they made in difficult personal circumstances. The issue of the sexual conduct of individual MPs spiralled out of control in an *auto-da-fé* of Conservative MPs caught for increasingly innocuous and obviously private acts the reporting of which could not be in the public interest. The tabloid press seemed increasingly to need no public-interest justification for such reports. Nevertheless the Prime Minister helped to supply one. In stark contrast to the smack of firm leadership implied in his memoirs towards such irrelevancies, he ended by imposing an effective rule of self-immolation on any minister caught in non-marital sex.

*

If the 'back to basics' policy had disastrous implications for individual politicians and the Tory Party, its broader effect was on debate about the family. Long before John Major's fateful 1993 conference speech, right-wing ministers had been growing more vocal about the moral causes and implications of a growing population of single mothers, and their economic effect on a social security budget which was judged to be spiralling out of control. As we have seen, in the last years of Margaret Thatcher's premiership, her Government began to focus on ways of supporting traditional families. Thatcher and Kenneth Baker, the Home Secretary, had made speeches on the dangers of lone parenthood in 1990. In the summer of 1993 there was a new, concerted effort, by an alliance of right-wing ministers led by the Social Security Secretary, Peter Lilley, and John Redwood, the Welsh Secretary, to spark a new wave of outrage at the moral and financial effects of lone parenthood. It began when Redwood visited a deprived council estate in Wales, St Mellons, following which he declared:

> *I want society to exert pressure on teenagers once again to form suitable rela-*
> *tionships before having children ... I'm surprised this is a radical suggestion.*
> *Any politician saying otherwise 30 years ago would have been hounded out of*
> *public life ... The problem is not adults in stable relations who are as good as*
> *married. We have 16 to 17-year-olds with no intention of having a permanent*
> *relationship.*[30]

Redwood and Lilley then made coordinated pronouncements about single-parent families being 'one of the biggest social problems of our day'. Redwood, with no particular brief for family policy beyond Wales, was the outrider for a policy more radical than Lilley, custodian of the Social Security budget, could openly champion. While Lilley was wary of suggesting that the Government could have a major impact on attitudes which led to single parenthood, particularly among teenagers, he and others were clear than the burden on the state was too great, and, following Redwood's harrowing experience at St Mellons, the implications for the children of single mothers on sink estates and for levels of crime were also too grim to accept. Whilst the rhetoric concentrated on teenage mothers, the reality was rather different. Divorced mothers had made up the overwhelming majority of lone parents throughout the 1970s and 1980s. Only in the early 1990s was this group outstripped by mothers who had never been married. However, most of these were still separated from long-term cohabiting partners. The proportion of lone mothers who were single began to increase sharply around 1986 when the number of births outside marriage began to increase at a higher rate.[31] The hard-right Conservative No Turning Back Group attempted to address this wider problem by suggesting a more rigorous means-testing of benefits to remove them from prosperous lone parents,[32] perhaps with the recently divorced Princess of Wales and Duchess of York in mind. Redwood and Lilley were echoed by John Gummer and the Junior Health Minister Tom Sackville. In August Major gave succour to these ministers, whom he had dismissed as 'bastards' over their attitude towards his Europe policy, by saying in a column in the *News of the World* that

> *our spending on social security is rising too fast. More and more people are claiming benefits. We must ensure the really needy get all the help they deserve. But we also need to make sure we aren't giving taxpayers' money ... to people who don't need it ... This will involve some tough decisions. But governments are there to do just that, take the responsible long-term view.*[33]

Joining the fray in September, the Chief Secretary to the Treasury, Michael Portillo, supported the Redwood–Lilley line on single parents, uttering a classic Thatcherite doctrine of the relationship between the state and the citizen in a speech to Church leaders: 'The Christian message is not about taxation, public spending and collectivised charity. The call to do good that lies at the heart of Christianity demands an individual response.' Portillo suggested that high benefits were the cause of a high rate of teenage motherhood, and pointed to a range of possible reforms which would reorient the welfare state away from a morality-sapping dependency culture.[34] However, this brought him into indirect conflict with his boss, Chancellor Kenneth Clarke. Clarke, declaring he was not in favour of the 'minimalist state', agreed that family values were important, but stressed that because of the day-to-day practicalities of politics, he did 'not think we should use things like the welfare state as an instrument for trying to move those changes in any particular direction'.[35] Donald Dewar, Labour's social security spokesman, described the Redwood approach as 'a combination of Victorian morality and bully boy tactics'. Conservatives now condemned feckless teenagers who had babies in order to take advantage of council rules which would allow them to queue-jump the housing lists. Such concerns were shared by David Blunkett, Labour's Shadow Health Secretary. As Major was only too painfully aware, if a little belatedly, his 'Back to Basics' speech resonated particularly well amid such debate about single-parent families. Even as he was preparing his leader's speech for the Conservative Party conference, Redwood and Lilley were using their place on the conference platform to get activists' juices flowing with comments about personal morality, comments which made the Prime Minister feel 'faintly uneasy'. With the right running away with the gift of a Prime Ministerial fiat to condemn immorality, while much of the rest of the Cabinet was counselling caution, Major attempted to refocus the 'back to basics' approach in a Cabinet paper and in speeches on core themes of responsibility in relation to crime and education.

Happily, or otherwise, 1994 was the United Nations International Year of the Family. In Parliament, debates to mark the year were tabled by former Labour minister Joan Lestor and Baroness (Brenda) Dean of Thornton-Le-Fylde. That gave Health Secretary Virginia Bottomley a platform to promote the most banal family policy possible, though it was prefaced by a Thatcherite attack on Labour welfarism, saying, 'Labour's answer to every problem remains the general application of someone else's cheque book – not an approach that would survive long in any family.' Bottomley presented an earth-shattering endorsement of the family by insisting:

The Government's commitment to the family as the cornerstone of our society is unshakeable. That commitment is founded on two convictions: first, the family is the essential source of love and respect between individuals and of their development as citizens. Secondly, family relationships and family values are and must be essentially private. The public interest is to support the family, not to substitute or to undermine it.[36]

Speaking of the possible damaging effects of divorce on children and families, Labour social-policy expert Malcolm Wicks argued that increasing changing postwar family structure was not a 'bloodless revolution' but that

we should not imagine that that trend has something to do with a specific period in our history, such as the 1960s or whatever decade we are against this week. It is happening around the world. We must recognise that the forces are complex and fundamental. That does not mean that we always give in to them. We try to resist some of them.

In a soundbite worthy of his incipient leader in style if not in substance, Wicks accused the Government of spending billions of pounds 'not on a family policy, but on a family breakdown policy', and that measures to allow parents to combine work and family responsibilities should have a higher priority.[37]

In the Lords, peers refrained from using the 'back to basics' policy to attack the Government until the end of the day, when Lord Longford led a second, repetitious debate on 'traditional family values'. Lord Porn dismissed 'back to basics' as meaningless. His purpose, though it was not made clear why it could not have been achieved during the preceding debate on the family, was to ask how the Government interpreted the phrase 'traditional family values'. The Junior Social Security Minister Lord Astor stressed the steps which the Government was taking to support all families and overhaul family law, from the Children Act to the Child Support Act, and he refuted some of Longford's more black-and-white judgements about the family and sexual morality, denying that there was evidence to support his claim that premarital sex made divorce more likely. However, challenged again by Longford to justify the 'back to basics' theme, Astor loyally quoted from Major's latest defensive explanation in the press that 'it is not a moral crusade on personal morals in private. But it does have a moral dimension. It is concerned about responsibility for others and obligations to others.'

One of the common themes during these debates, whether or not politicians blamed the 1960s or economic liberalism for increased family breakdown, was that the effects of divorce were generally assumed to be bad for children in particular, but also for mothers. Alongside growing demands for divorced men to take more financial responsibility for their families, divorce was also now seen as being unfairly damaging to men, and failing to recognise their concerns about access to children after separation or divorce. Even liberal-minded politicians continued to accept the conservative line that there was a causal link between divorce law reform and an increase in family breakdown and specifically the rate of divorce. This proposition, although an attractive one, is not necessarily supported by the historical evidence from postwar Britain. Rates of divorce were increasing in most Western countries, regardless of liberalisation of divorce laws. In Britain, as Philip Cowley points out, the rate of divorce was increasing in the 1960s before the landmark 1969 Act, which broke the principle of fault-based divorce for the first time. Had the increase continued at that rate, divorce would have reached a higher level than it did following the reforms which came into effect in 1971. However, it is undeniable that couples who had decided to divorce found it much easier to do so from this time onwards, and even more so after 1984 when the Conservative Government's Matrimonial Proceedings Act reduced the time before a divorce petition could be made. Debate in the 1990s focused on whether this decision could or should be delayed, accelerated or reversed by alterations to this time limit for which couples have to wait before divorcing. In Cowley's words there was a widespread 'touching faith' among parliamentarians in their ability to influence cultural behaviour like marriage and divorce through legislation, though they disagreed intensely about the detail of what could and should be enshrined in legislation.[38] The disagreements on divorce during the 1990s were as stark within the Conservative Party as between the two main parties. It is true that Conservative MPs supported a range of attempts to erect higher barriers to no-fault divorce in debate on the Family Law Bill in 1995–6, and Labour MPs were more relaxed about the no-fault provisions which the Government put forward, but due to the hostility of many Conservatives, the Government had to rely on support from Labour to get the Bill on the statute book, a culpability which did not prevent Labour ditching the proposals when in office.

The fact that the divorce law had become the subject of likely further reform did not reflect significant pressure for radical reform to restrict divorce or expedite it as in previous decades. Rather like the operation of the abortion law or obscene publications legislation, the provisions of the 1969 Divorce Law Reform Act had not operated in the way envisaged; rather than using the no-fault provisions, people preferred the quicker route of the existing fault-based grounds to prove 'irretrievable breakdown'. Parliament had recoiled from a simple solution to this problem in the 1980s, but the system's critics were increasingly worried about the effect that the process involved was having both on couples and on their children. It also perpetuated the incentive to dishonesty in applying for divorce, and the bias towards more educated people with the knowledge of how to work the system, which were the main reasons for reform in the 1960s.

The Government's proposal, based once again on the work of the Law Commission, was to replace the traditional fact-based proceedings, which had been being steadily weakened since 1969, with time-based ones and to grant a divorce after twelve months, as opposed to the existing seven-month average. Conservative 'defenders' of marriage were outraged, claiming that this meant divorce would be easier, despite the actual longer time period which would elapse in most cases. The Bill's proceedings saw the most serious rebellion by

MPs on an occasion when their party had actually adopted a line on an issue of morality or 'conscience' in the postwar period, as opposed to remaining offi- cially neutral. Not that the Major Government could have been accused of acting hastily. Green and White Papers on the proposals were published in 1993 and 1995 before legislation was introduced. Opposition to the Family Law Bill was led by John Patten, only recently resigned as Education Secretary, and Baroness Young in the Lords. Many Labour MPs, rather than intruding on the private grief of a bitterly divided Conservative Party, took the opportunity of a free vote to stay away. This meant that once Conservative rebels got their act together by supporting an extension of the mediation period before divorce could be granted from twelve to eighteen months, the Government was defeated. Rather than tear up the whole Bill, the Government accepted this arguably cosmetic change. However, in order to get the Bill through at all, the Government still had to rely awkwardly on the official support of the Labour Party. If Labour took a back seat over the move from fault-based to time- limited divorce, it was more adamant about amending the Bill to give greater protection to women. Baroness Hollis secured an amendment in the Lords, in the face of Government prevarication on the issue, so that pension funds should be split equally on divorce. Meanwhile, plans to strengthen the law on domestic violence, which had been dropped by the Government after protests from its own MPs and some elements of the press, were brought back as a further concession to Labour.[39]

Despite Labour's own role in securing passage of the Bill, Conservative division over the Family Law Reform Bill was a target which Tony Blair could not resist, as he sought during 1996 to enhance New Labour's image as the party of the family. Following the Commons votes in which four Cabinet ministers voted against the Bill, he elided the issue with divisions within the tottering Government over Europe, saying:

That was a Government bill, proposed by his Lord Chancellor. Last night's vote was not only about the amendment [to introduce no-fault divorce] – it was fundamentally about the ethos of the Bill and about the direction of the Conservative Party. Does not that vote show the advanced state of decay of his Government – that he now has to rely on opposition support to carry that messed-up measure through the House of Commons?

Blair made no attempt to explain what he meant by 'the ethos of the Bill and the direction of the Conservative Party', and this seemed particularly cynical given Labour's support for its provisions. Major was understandably incandescent, defending his consistent policy of allowing a free vote on a subject traditionally a matter of conscience.[40] This marked the beginning of a deterioration in relations between the two leaders in the run-up to an increasingly bitter general election, reportedly leading Major to describe Blair as an 'Elmer Gantry' character, after Sinclair Lewis's fictional fire-and-brimstone evangelist, a charlatan who used the American Christian revival and his talent for preaching to his own ends.[41]

*

If the Conservative Government was reluctant to extend the law on domestic violence because of opposition within its own ranks, sexual violence against women belatedly gained a new legal recognition in the 1990s. Though in retrospect it seems astonishing, until 1992 it was doubtful whether a man could be convicted of raping his own wife. The persistence of this sexual life sentence for women originated in an eighteenth-century common-law principle, upheld almost intact until the middle of the twentieth century, that 'the husband cannot be guilty of a rape committed by himself upon his lawful wife, for by their mutual matrimonial consent and contract the wife hath given up herself in this kind unto her husband which she cannot retract.'[42]

From 1949 onwards it was recognised that legal separation constituted withdrawal of implied consent to intercourse. However, the insertion in the Sexual Offences (Amendment) Act 1976 of the phrase 'unlawful sexual intercourse' only compounded the confusion, and was interpreted by the courts very narrowly and relating only to extramarital sex. It was only when the case of R v. R reached the House of Lords in 1992 that a court upheld the conviction of a man for such an offence. The uncertainty surrounding the common-law position on rape in marriage reflected not only judicial conservatism about the sexual relationship between a married couple but also parliamentary failure to define rape accurately over more than a century, dating back to the 1861 Offences against the Person Act, which was the first legislative attempt by the Victorians to regulate sexual activity. In the words of one academic lawyer, *the 1861 Act served to perpetuate the mystification about whether rape was a property crime, infringing a man's rights over a woman's sexuality, a physical crime of violation or a 'moral' crime undermining female sexual chastity. But the real tragedy was that the Act failed effectively to hold men to account for their actions and encouraged the courts to maintain a suspicious attitude towards female victims requiring they prove themselves beyond reproach.*[43]

A number of cases during the 1980s had ruled that consent should not be held to be indefinite or absolute on marriage, and that separation could be held to denote the withdrawal of such consent. However, the Law Lords went much further in R v. R, ruling unanimously that there was 'now no justification for the marital exemption in rape', despite the fact that once again, the facts of this case involved a couple who had already separated and had both indicated that they would seek a divorce, and the rape occurred at the home of the woman's parents, not in the marital home. Interestingly, the case partly turned on the interpretation of the phrase 'unlawful sexual intercourse', which the appellant claimed meant 'outside marriage'. Dismissing this suggestion, Lord Keith of Kinkell said that 'in modern times sexual intercourse outside marriage would not ordinarily be described as unlawful.' Mindful of Parliament's role in setting legal parameters, particularly in controversial areas involving sex or other moral issues, Lord Lane had raised the question in the Appeal Court of how far the courts could legitimately go:

It is said that it goes beyond the legitimate bounds of judge-made law and trespasses on the province of Parliament. In other words the abolition of a rule of such long standing, despite its emasculation by later decisions, is a task for the legislature and not the courts. There are social considerations to be taken into account, the privacy of marriage to be preserved and questions of potential reconciliation to be weighed which make it an inappropriate area for judicial intervention ... We take the view that the time has now arrived when the law should declare that a rapist remains a rapist subject to the criminal law, irrespective of his relationship with his victim.

This is not the creation of a new offence, it is the removal of a common law fiction which has become anachronistic and offensive and we consider that it is our duty having reached that conclusion to act upon it.[44]

The Law Lords also relied on the clarification of the position in Scotland which had occurred in 1989, when the High Court made a similar ruling that the maintenance of partial exemptions when a couple were still living together were no longer tenable.[45] A further appeal to the European Court of Human Rights on the grounds that this retrospectively changed the law was dismissed because the Government and Law Commission had already recommended that the law be changed.[46] The Criminal Justice and Public Order Bill clarified the position and enshrined the ruling in R v. R. To quote Kim Stevenson again, 'some attempt at formal expression in the previous century might … have improved the position of female complainants and made convictions easier to secure by providing clarification of what actually constitutes the crime of rape.'

*

If the rights of women were gaining increasing recognition during the 1990s, the social responsibility of young people remained of paramount concern. The murder in 1993 of three-year-old James Bulger by ten-year-old boys provoked a new wave of concern about possible effects of violent films on children. The two boys who killed Bulger were reported to have seen the horror film *Child's Play 2* and the judge in the trial linked this with the killing, leading to inevitable calls for a clampdown on such films. Ironically, the British Board of Film Classification (BBFC) received more complaints about the news coverage of the trial than any previous news programme.[47] The immediate impact was to prompt Michael Howard to attempt to tighten the BBFC's certification criteria for violent films and increase the penalties for renting an adult-certificated film to a child. The other political parties were not prepared to let Howard make all the political capital out of this new wave of public concern, fuelled by lurid tabloid revelations about the significance of the effect of films on juvenile crime. The Liberal Democrat MP David Alton, a Roman Catholic, sought to amend the Criminal Justice Bill – an increasingly Heath Robinson contraption – to ban the rental of psychologically damaging or inappropriate films to children. He received strong cross-party support and Howard was forced to seek agreement with Tony Blair, Alton and the BBFC for a compromise which in the eventual legislation required the BBFC to pay particular attention to the harm a video might cause to any person likely to see it. Although this kept to the 'harm' principle embodied in the Williams Report, rather than the more subjective and traditional 'deprave or corrupt' construction, it represented a victory for Alton and his Movement for Christian Democracy, which sought to increase the influence of Christian values in politics, and its intense lobbying of parliamentarians over the issue. Perhaps more significant, though, was Howard's role in resisting pressure from moral conservatives to go further, lest, according to one Home Office source, 'the censors would ... be forced to ban everything which would not be acceptable for children,' rather in contrast to his hardline right-wing image.[48] In addition, new research appeared which supported both the proponents and sceptics of a causal link between violent films and violent crime. The most influential such report was commissioned by Alton himself. Professor Elizabeth Newsom concluded that violent videos amounted to a form of child abuse and should be restricted. On the other hand Dr Kevin Brown of Birmingham University concluded that the most important influence in the development of anti-social behaviour among youngsters was a violent family background, though some, including the most potentially dangerous, could be influenced by watching violent videos.

It was not as if the BBFC under James Ferman was unresponsive to waves of concern about violent films. In the wake of the Bulger murder, Ferman vetoed the release on video of Quentin Tarantino's *Reservoir Dogs* and Abel Ferrara's *Bad Lieutenant*, because they 'simply happened to be around' at the time. However, the Board came in for its severest political mauling of the 1990s following its decision to pass David Cronenberg's film *Crash*, about a group of people seeking sexual gratification from car crashes. The right-wing press and the National Heritage Secretary, Virginia Bottomley, called for Ferman to act, regardless of whether they had actually seen the film. For Ferman this exemplified the need for a stronger test of a film than its ability to shock or offend. He was supported in this by the Board's Vice-President, Lord Birkett.[49] Their line was increasingly at odds with ministerial sensitivity to press and public concern about violent films, conflict which came dramatically to a head when Howard was succeeded at the Home Office by his Labour shadow, Jack Straw, in 1997.

The victory for the National Viewers and Listeners Association in bringing broadcasting within the scope of the Obscene Publications Act and establishing an independent body to monitor television and radio for taste and decency proved pyrrhic. The Broadcasting Standards Council (BSC), the body established under the 1990 Broadcasting Act to mollify conservative critics of television's exemption from tighter regulation, had proved a disappointment to Mary Whitehouse and her supporters.[50] She was outraged that programmes, particularly some broadcast by Channel 4 such as the adaptation of Mary Wesley's wartime novel *The Camomile Lawn*, with sexual explicitness and swearing, continued to be shown just after the nine o'clock watershed. Not that the BSC was silent over such programmes. Channel 4 was censured over that particular series and forced to print an apology in the national press for broadcasting a repeat showing, although such repeats only served to underline the restricted powers of the Council.[51] With delicious irony the BSC also responded to a large number of complaints about the sex scenes in the Ken Russell adaptation of *Lady Chatterley's Lover* for the BBC. Despite toning down the novel for the small screen, the BBC justified portraying the physical side of the relationship between Chatterley and Mellors to stay true to the story, but the Council found that the sex scenes were 'unduly protracted'.[52] However, according to one of the Council's founder members, former Labour MP Alf Dubs, the Council quickly succeeded in creating a new atmosphere of openness and empiricism in discussion about taste and decency on television which was encouraged, perhaps again to Whitehouse's chagrin, by its First Chairman, former editor of *The Times* William Rees-Mogg. Whereas previously decisions had largely been taken behind closed doors by people in the industry, on a largely political basis, the Council tried to be more open in reaching decisions, and to do so informed by a new body of research about public attitudes and the effects of programme content and scheduling decisions.[53]

*

In 1996, as the general election grew closer, personal moral values and their influence on social cohesion and crime became increasingly controversial between the main parties. Incidents which dominated the political scene included a schoolgirl stabbing, the massacre of children at a primary school in Dunblane and the murder of London headmaster Philip Lawrence. Specific calls for action on guns, knives, stalkers and paedophiles were tossed around with alacrity, while the broader question of the moral values which were imparted to children became an overarching framework for this debate, particularly when

Lawrence's widow Frances called for a new moral crusade to focus on the teaching of children, saying that 'the nation is engaged in a process of reduction of values and principles. Thinking almost seems to be out of the equation.'[54]

This was all grist to the mill of electioneering politicians. All the party leaders, Church leaders and teaching unions endorsed Mrs Lawrence's comments. Tony Blair committed Labour to the citizenship classes for which she argued and John Major pointed to the tightening of broadcasting regulation as a measure to tackle the excessive violence on television which she denigrated.[55] Such political harmony lasted barely a week as Labour seized on Home Secretary Michael Howard's decision to leave legislation on paedophiles and stalkers to back-benchers rather than incorporate it within the Government's own criminal justice measures in the final parliamentary session before the election. The moral implication was made explicit by Peter Mandelson: 'In the week that the Government has claimed to support Frances Lawrence's worthy campaign, their actions have spoken louder than their words ... When it comes to morality they talk tough and act weak.'[56]

This heady mix exploded in debate on the Queen's Speech. As Blair reiterated a Labour pledge to support any Government legislation on these two issues, Major dramatically accepted the offer after consulting with colleagues on the front bench, with both sides accusing the other of playing party politics with morality, the Prime Minister warning Blair:

> *Any politician should be cautious about cloaking himself in righteousness. I do not know how the right hon. gentleman [Blair] can disclaim, as he has just done, any responsibility by the Labour party for faults in this society when his Labour Party has, over the years, consistently championed every fashionable, politically correct cause that has undermined our traditional way of life, and has opposed every measure that we have taken to correct the balance.*[57]

Buoyed by polling evidence that the public trusted Labour far more than the Conservatives to act on such issues,[58] Blair continued to press the moral buttons, and talked of 'a new social morality'. As with much New Labour rhetoric, this phrase on closer inspection appears meaningless, even in Blair's own terms. He was not calling for a rejection of traditional morality in his responses to Frances Lawrence – in fact the reverse, thought Blair was careful to avoid the pitfalls of

Major's 'back to basics' campaign. He was not arguing for 'a lurch into nostalgia or Victorian hypocrisy. We do not want to return to prejudiced attitudes on sex, sexuality or the role of women. Neither do we believe that supporting the family means attacking lone parents, the vast bulk of whom have endured pain through divorce or separation.'[59]

Blair also gave the appearance of responding positively to renewed calls for a reintroduction of corporal punishment in the new Education Bill, though not actually supporting such a move. He led a charge of senior figures defending the parental right to smack their children in a glossy three-page spread in *Parent* magazine devoted to the Blairs' espousal of family values, in which the Labour leader said that 'there are lots of ways of disciplining a child and I don't believe that belting them is the best one... [but] I was caned as a schoolboy and it probably did me no harm.'[60] The Liberal Democrat leader, Paddy Ashdown, also confessed to admonishing his own children by smacking, though he felt that he had sometimes smacked his children when he shouldn't have. The Archbishop of Canterbury went further, saying that 'you gently slap them if they do transgress and there is nothing wrong with that as long as it is done with love and with firm discipline.'[61]

Although a case challenging a parent's right to smack his or her child was pending at the European Court of Human Rights, a proposal to reintroduce corporal punishment in schools, wildly popular among Conservative activists as well as with Home Secretary Howard, had been ruled illegal repeatedly in the 1980s, following a Commons vote to ban it, by a majority of just one, in 1986. However, pressure was mounting on Gillian Shephard and the Department for Education and Employment from Tory right-wingers, including some on the Commons Education Select Committee, to use the opportunity of the Education Bill to force a vote on the issue. However, it was not government policy, and when Shephard announced her personal support for corporal punishment on Radio 4's *Today* programme, despite the practical and legal difficulties of reintroducing it, Downing Street's reaction was apoplectic. Whilst visiting the new wing of a school in Surrey, Shephard was interrupted in the course of her unveiling duties by an 'overawed' school secretary to say No. 10 was on the phone. It turned out to be the Prime Minister calling to give his minister a dressing down. Given that Major had himself voted to retain caning in 1986, his tetchiness might be characterised as ungenerous. The press inevitably had a field day, and the opposition and teaching unions, all opposed to caning, gave Shephard a verbal lashing.[62] Right-wing Tory MPs were emboldened to try to force the reintroduction of caning through an amendment to the Government's Education Bill. The growing rebellion forced Major to concede a free vote on the issue, despite the legal obstacles. When the vote came in January 1997 it was once again Labour who rescued the Government from its own backbenchers, ninety of whom voted for corporal punishment. Shephard, conspicuously absent from the debate, abided by collective responsibility and voted for the status quo.[63]

*

As with corporal punishment, government policy on sex education was a revealing indicator of the tensions within the Conservative Party following the fall of Margaret Thatcher regarding the adaptation of traditional family values to the demands of contemporary society. The publication in July 1992 of a new ten-year national health strategy, *The Health of the Nation*, put a greater emphasis than ever before on preventive health care. Most strikingly it also included targets to reduce teenage pregnancy, gonorrhoea among men as an indicator of HIV infection rates and, one of the main causes of the spread of HIV, needle-sharing among intravenous drug-users. The document said that 'the Government attached a high priority to obtaining better information about the incidence and prevalence of HIV in the population and had initiated surveys in 1990.' This was, perhaps, a reaction to the furore in 1989 when Downing Street had vetoed the National Survey of Sexual Lifestyles and Attitudes, with Thatcher and other ministers apparently of the view that such research was of no value. Clearly something had changed. *The Health of the Nation* raised concerns about the anecdotal evidence of the level of HIV infection in London, particularly among homosexual men, and the Chief Medical Officer's estimate in 1990 that about fifty per cent of all conceptions each year were unplanned or unwanted. Overall the White Paper concluded that 'there needs to be a willingness to address and discuss attitudes and behaviour in what are very sensitive areas.' It listed five main areas where the Government would work to combat HIV and AIDS: prevention; monitoring, surveillance and research; treatment, care and support; social, legal and ethical issues; and international cooperation. It promised to develop further NHS facilities for sexual health, including the establishment of easily accessible clinics in every area as a priority. It also emphasised that sex education including HIV and AIDS was now part of the national curriculum, with 'flexibility' beyond this statutory requirement for school governing bodies to provide additional education on the health risks of promiscuous behaviour as well as moral considerations, the value of family life and the responsibilities of parenthood. The Government also aimed to expand the full range of family planning services to make it 'appropriate, accessible and comprehensive'. However, nowhere was any mention made of access to abortion advice or operations within the NHS.[64] Robin Cook, Labour's health spokesman, and his successor David Blunkett both criticised the lack of resources to back up the admirable strategy set out in *The Health of the Nation*.[65] Blunkett was particularly scathing about the running down of family planning and sex education services, and the 'appalling' statistics on teenage pregnancy and abortion, saying that better education which included 'love and relationships' would have an effect.[66] However, Virginia Bottomley was the victim from her own side of some patronising sexism as well as criticism. Suggesting that she would make the best possible nanny, if one were necessary, Michael Trend advocated a more laissez-faire approach:

Individuals are free to make their own decisions and ... they will often involve moral choices – such as whether or not to bring a child into the world without the benefit of marriage ... the present evidence will not allow the proposition that more sex education equals fewer teenage pregnancies. The reasons for such a development lie elsewhere. What is most needed is a stronger emphasis on the individual and more stress on the limits of the Government.

However, he then immediately contradicted himself by saying that 'health education is all-important.' Quoting Disraeli's maxim '*Sanitas, sanitatum, omnia sanitas*', Trend seemed to make a distinction between sexual health education and sanitation: 'Legislating for individual behaviour is, however, a very different matter. Sensible people will behave sensibly about their health, and when they do not they will know that they are not behaving sensibly.'[67] Presumably, unsensible people, including children, would be left to their own devices.

The new willingness to promote HIV awareness within sex education had been facilitated by a more liberal approach from Kenneth Clarke, who, before he moved to the Home Office following the general election, had said in a speech to the National AIDS Trust: 'Education about HIV and AIDS will be effective only if all

those who work in or with the education service accept their share of the responsibility and are sending out the same messages.' However, even this modest
encouragement for sex education as part of a coherent strategy to prevent poor
sexual and reproductive health among young people was pole-axed by the main set
of education proposals running concurrently with *The Health of the Nation*.

The same month, Clarke's more reactionary successor at Education, John Patten,
also published a White Paper, *Choice and Diversity: A Framework for Schools*, the
main aim of which was a further dismantling of the comprehensive system, under
the control of local education authorities, by allowing all schools to opt out of
council control following parental ballots. This White Paper, and the mammoth Bill
which followed that autumn, contained an important section on the 'spiritual and
moral development' of pupils. This was the result of growing concern among the
Churches and conservatives that many schools were not fulfilling existing statutory
obligations to provide Christian collective worship and Christian-dominated
religious instruction or, in some cases, subverting the provisions by teaching
theology of any but a Christian nature. There was no mention of sex education or
the newly revised national curriculum science provisions. The exemption for
parents to withdraw their children from any sex education classes which had been
inserted into the 1986 Education Bill following a vociferous campaign was still in
place, and the Education Minister Baroness Blatch had said that these safeguards
were sufficient as late as the spring of 1993. The policy was amplified by new
guidance from the department in April 1993. However, when the Education Bill
reached its report stage in the Lords, the Labour peer Lord Stallard attempted to
remove the limited references to HIV and sex education from the science part of the
national curriculum. Blatch accepted the principle of the amendments but criticised their drafting.[68] At third reading, the final parliamentary stage before the Bill
returned to the Commons, Blatch tabled the Government's own amendment to this
effect, uttering barely veiled criticism of Clarke that it was 'extraordinary' that sex
education had been 'slipped into' the national curriculum. Despite protestations
from the Labour spokeswoman Baroness Jay, a prominent figure in the AIDS
community, as well as the former Conservative Health Secretary Lord Jenkin, the
amendment was carried by 131 to 33.[69] When the Bill returned to the Commons,
another cross-party pair of MPs, Labour's Ann Taylor and Conservative Alan
Howarth, protested at the guillotining of debate on this and other important Lords
amendments. Taylor calculated that there would be fifty-three seconds to debate

each one. Howarth, a former education minister responsible for sex education, claimed it was incredible that 'ministers responsible for health should have connived' at this *volte-face*.[70] In the event, Taylor's calculation was wildly inaccurate. The Lords amendment went through with no debate or vote.[71] Arguing for the move, Blatch had insisted on the Lords' rights as 'a revising chamber'. This was a rather Jesuitical reading of the 'revising' role, given that no provisions on sex education had been in the original Bill, and that elected MPs were given no opportunity to debate or vote on the amendment. It was to prove a particularly ironic argument in 2000 when Blatch, Young and other Tory peers were to argue that the Commons had no right to insist on changes to adoption rules to make unmarried couples eligible because the reform had been inserted by a backbench Commons amendment. A twin emphasis on giving information to help young people protect themselves, alongside encouraging responsibility, was re-emphasised by Virginia Bottomley during the Commons debate to mark the International Year of the Family in 1994 when she said: 'Ensuring effective sex education is vital in helping to meet "The Health of the Nation" targets on under-aged pregnancy and sexually transmitted diseases. However, there must also be a proper emphasis on stable relationships and individual responsibility.'[72]

A continuing shadow hung over the debate on sex education under the Major Government in the shape of Section 28 and its effect on schools. The guidance which was issued in 1994 on sex education confirmed that Section 28 did not apply to schools, but evidence continued that the presence of the Section on the Statute Book was having an effect on teachers' willingness to discuss issues of sexuality or combat anti-homosexual bullying. While anecdotal reports abounded about self-censorship by teachers, an Institute of Education report in 1997, which covered 307 schools, found widespread uncertainty about, or criticism of Section 28. Over a quarter of respondents either wrongly believed that, or were not sure whether, Section 28 made discussion of homosexuality in schools illegal. Forty-four per cent said that Section 28 made it more difficult to meet the needs of gay pupils. Eighty-two per cent said that there should be clarification of the implications of the Section. This was against a background of the same proportion of respondents who were aware of verbal homophobic bullying and twenty-six per cent who were aware of physical homophobic attacks on pupils.[73]

*

Conservative MPs and their Government showed no inclination under John Major to address complaints about the prejudicial effects of Section 28. However, as with issues like capital punishment, the more finely balanced House of Commons from 1992 showed itself more liberal than its predecessor towards the question of the age of consent for homosexuals. It became clear soon after the general election that Major was sympathetic to reviewing the existing age of twenty-one, set by the Sexual Offences Act in 1967. Then MPs had been forced to accept twenty-one in the face of fears among some about the corruption of young men between eighteen and twenty-one whose sexuality was not yet fixed. By the early 1990s, the number of people clinging to such a view had sharply declined. Major was prepared to listen with greater sensitivity than any previous prime minister to the arguments of gay rights campaigners such as Stonewall, inviting the actor Ian McKellen to Downing Street to discuss the issue – much to the shock of some of the more *recherché* elements in the Tory Party. Major vigorously defended his approach to the issue in his memoirs:

> I [did not] see homosexuality as a social evil. Many people are gay, and I saw no reason to cast them into outer darkness for that reason ... I was shocked at the attitude of mind that seemed to think I should not have spoken to Ian McKellen. [I] found him a courageous advocate for the cause of equal treatment of gays before the law. I did not agree with him on every point – nor, I think, did he expect me to – but he had a case that deserved a hearing.

Again wielding the historical airbrush against his former lover, Edwina Currie, Major accepted the credit for the subsequent decision by MPs to lower the age of consent to eighteen:

> With my encouragement, in February 1994 Parliament voted to lower the age of consent for gays from 21 to 18 (although not to 16, which McKellen wanted). By tradition this was a free vote, of course. But it is more than an ex-whip's cynicism to observe that free votes do not just happen.[74]

The occasion for the vote was the committee stage of the portmanteau Criminal Justice Bill in February 1994. Whatever Major's encouragement behind the scenes, it was indeed Currie who tabled the clause on the age of consent, and led the debate. The House of Lords' response to the Commons' decision to lower the age of consent to eighteen was distinctly muted. A number of peers were mindful of the MPs' decision, and although Baroness Young voiced the 'slippery slope' argument there was no attempt to remove the clause. However, peers voted against the equalisation of the age of consent at sixteen by a greater margin that had MPs, defeating a Labour amendment by 71 to 245 votes. Unusually, the Archbishop of York, Dr John Habgood, was left to speak and vote alone for the combined moral authority of the twenty-six Lords Spiritual. Arguing in favour of eighteen, Habgood suggested that, as with speed limits, there would be a grey area in which young people below the age of consent would indulge their passions, without there being a need for the law to intervene. He defended a differential in the age of consent between heterosexual and homosexual sex partly on the rather cryptic premise, not born of personal knowledge, that 'homosexual relations of a certain kind between young boys must entail a good deal more physical commitment than homosexual relationships between young girls'.[75]

Many peers were exercised about the effect of law reform on private behaviour, and whether repealing unenforceable laws would lead to a spread of practices which were considered undesirable. Lord Mayhew drew an interesting comparison between the differences in treatment of homosexual practices and drug-taking, saying that maintaining extra legal sanction against buggery would provide a discouragement from a particularly dangerous practice. Several Conservative peers attempted to insert an amendment banning homosexuals from being allowed to care for any children under eighteen, arguing that homosexual relationships were too short-lived and that a network of homosexual men was using safe houses across the country to entice young boys into homosexuality. Baroness Ryder, tabling the amendment, concluded by saying that 'the Bible makes it very clear that it is unrighteous for a so-called homosexual couple to be given the care and custody of a child.' While several peers rejected these arguments from practical experience of placing children in foster care and adoption, two peers spoke from personal experience of gay couples bringing up children in their own family, in the case of the Labour peer and GP Lord Rea, being brought up happily by a lesbian couple himself.[76]

The idea that private, consensual homosexual acts were private, a happy fiction endorsed by politicians of all parties, was dispelled in 1993 by the case of R v. Brown, in which a group of gay men were convicted of actual bodily harm, and imprisoned, for acts of sadomasochism. While any acts in private involving more than two men were still technically illegal until the Sexual Offences Act 2003, and liable to prosecution, these were rare, and the Brown case hinged on the acts of harm which were involved in the practices which these men enjoyed. Michael Howard also emphasised in a radio interview after the vote to reduce the age of consent to eighteen that the law would be enforced against those aged between sixteen and eighteen – echoing the clampdown which occurred after the 1967 Act was passed.[77]

The other area of policy in which sanctions against homosexuals were to be maintained was the ban on homosexuals in the armed forces. A number of former service personnel were fighting court cases against the Ministry of Defence for being dismissed under the ban, and, despite upholding the legality of the ban, British judges, including the Master of the Rolls, Sir Thomas Bingham, voiced their sympathy with the men and women involved, urging the MoD to review the ban.[78] Over the horizon loomed the prospect of a ruling by the European Court of Human Rights. The Government announced a review in October 1995, and the military establishment swung into action to defend the ban, with research in the Navy and then among all three services revealing, respectively, ninety and seventy-five per cent support among personnel for the ban. Whatever the substance of the review, ministers made it clear that there was no chance of it being lifted, the Armed Forces Minister, Nicholas Soames, declaring that 'the view of the service chiefs and of ministers is not based on any moral judgement but on the impracticality of homosexual behaviour, which is clearly not compatible with service life.'[79]

MPs conducting a quinquennial armed services review held hearings into the question, including from former service personnel discharged under the ban. One lesbian former Wren told how she had been too scared to report being raped by a male colleague because her sexuality would become an issue. She had been discharged later when her homosexuality became known. Labour defence spokesman John Reid responded:

If the description you gave was accurate, and I have no way of knowing but I have no reason to doubt what you say, then notwithstanding any regulations I am revolted and disgusted by – it may sound old chauvinist – any man who could treat a woman in that fashion after a rape.

Nevertheless, Reid would not accept evidence from such former personnel or Stonewall that lifting the ban would not have unfair consequences on heterosexual personnel living intimately with homosexuals, or that equal opportunities in other countries or similar conditions had not caused such problems. Reid continued to support and vote for the retention of the ban.[80]

Debate about the treatment of homosexuals began to move beyond the 'promotion' of homosexuality, sexual activity, buggery and the age of consent. Although still widely despised, at least outside metropolitan areas, a more general social acceptance of homosexuals encouraged gay rights campaigners such as Stonewall and their supporters to promote the wider social rights of homosexuals, particularly of homosexual couples and their treatment by public services. The area in which this was most advanced was housing. In 1996 Glenda Jackson, Labour MP for the proverbially liberal seat of Hampstead and Highgate, tabled an amendment to the Housing Bill to extend succession rights to secured tenancies to same-sex couples. Such amendments are rarely carried in standing committees, on which MPs normally toe the party line, but on this occasion the Government whips had not reckoned for the conscience of Conservative David Ashby, who was at the time caught up in allegations of an adulterous affair with a young man. Despite the consequences of adding to his troubles by supporting such a measure, Ashby did exactly that, and finally provoked the wrath of his constituency association, which deselected him.[81] The vote caused the Government acute embarrassment, despite the emollient attitude of the Local Government Minister, David Curry, who insisted that new guidelines would mean that same-sex couples would have rights to succession as good as under the Jackson amendment, which was duly overturned in the Commons.[82]

*

If the 'floggers' in the Tory Party were thwarted by prevailing fashions and the ECHR, this was doubly so for the 'hangers'. The question of restoring capital punishment returned to Parliament, piggy-backed on to criminal justice bills only three years apart in the 1990s, on both occasions led by a former police officer, Conservative MP John Greenway. The first occasion came just weeks after John Major had replaced Margaret Thatcher in No. 10, and only two years after the previous vote in 1988 when hanging had been rejected by 123 votes. On the same franchise there was little reason to suppose that opinion could have changed dramatically. In the event, the majority against restoration for murder of a police officer was substantially larger at 185. The change of regime was underlined by Thatcher and Major supporting and opposing the retrograde step respectively. Only Ian Lang, Michael Howard and David Hunt among the Cabinet joined the former Prime Minister in the 'aye' lobby. MPs rejected a series of other attempts to restore the death penalty for a range of homicidal and terrorist offences, but were also swayed by the new Home Secretary, Kenneth Baker, from approving a Labour amendment to abolish hanging for the remaining offence of treason. Baker argued that this would unwisely prejudge a Law Commission report on the issue. Peter Archer, the former Labour Attorney General who tabled the additional repeal proposal, had wrong-footed the Government, who had not expected to have to face a further extension of the abolition of hanging, and ministers were divided on how to proceed. In the event, enough Tory abolitionists were persuaded by Baker's argument, leaving Archer to protest that the pay-roll vote of ministers and their aides had saved the Government from embarrassment at the expense of compromising a free vote on a fundamental issue of conscience. Ignoring the trend of voting since 1965 and the disproportionate effect of a large, ageing Conservative majority, the hanging devotee Teddy Taylor claimed that 'eventually, the sheer logic of the killing figures, together with public opinion, will have an impact.'[83]

Just three years later, right-wing Conservative supporters of hanging were again arguing that life imprisonment was no longer a sufficient deterrent against murder, particularly of police officers and elderly people in their homes, though Taylor's hopes proved ill founded. The monolithic 1993 Criminal Justice Bill was, once again, the vehicle for addressing an issue of conscience which ministers were not inclined to tackle on the face of their own legislation. Howard, now Home Secretary, who had voted for restoration only three years earlier, said that his mind had been changed by the series of notorious miscarriages of justice, particularly the Birmingham Six and Stefan Kiszko, a mentally handicapped man convicted when he confessed to the murder of a schoolgirl and released after fifteen years' imprisonment when forensic tests proved he could not have been her killer. Howard described these as a 'blot on civilised society', and Tony Blair, still Shadow Home Secretary, concurred with this as the strongest argument against capital punishment. MPs rejected restoration by the widest margin ever, 403 to 159, a majority of 244.[84]

*

The case of disability rights in the mid-1990s exposed the limits of Majorite social reform and was an extremely damaging example of how the Conservative Party misread the mood of the public, preferring to protect the interests of business and employers against the rights of a large minority of people to participate more fully in society. It also emphasised that public policy towards disabled people, even more than attitudes towards women and abortion, was still hidebound by a medical view of the problem. Disabled people were seen at best as unfortunate victims, rather than citizens with equal rights and a political voice. This gradually changed through the efforts of campaigners for disability rights during the 1980s and 1990s, including prominent MPs and peers such as the former minister for the disabled, Alf Morris, Jack Ashley, Betty Lockwood and Roger Berry, and a growing disability rights lobby. Proposals to establish a statutory framework of protection and enforcement similar to those on sex and race discrimination were resisted by the Conservative Government on the grounds of cost and a lack of evidence of discrimination. The Government's refusal to acknowledge changing attitudes was compounded by the ineptitude of ministers and whips in trying to defeat parliamentary attempts to legislate for enforceable rights for disabled people after 1992. Equally, the Government's claim that the cost to employers would come to £17 billion was greeted with scepticism. The Minister for the Disabled, Nicholas Scott, was personally liberal-minded, and acknowledged that discrimination was real and should be tackled. But by 1994 he had held his portfolio for six years, during which time attempts by disability rights campaigners to force legislation on to the statute book were smothered with a warm blanket of voluntary initiatives and codes which had failed to provide sufficient incentives or sanctions in order to tackle discrimination.

During the 1980s, Conservative MPs largely backed their Government's position against statutory protection for disabled people. The 1992 election proved a significant watershed. Scott's admission of the reality of discrimination, and a successful Private Members' Bill in the House of Lords, led to Berry tabling a motion which attracted 311 signatures. When Berry introduced a bill, it was supported by thirty-three Conservative MPs, the highest number to support such a measure. The extent to which public attitudes had changed was demonstrated by the enormous success of parliamentary lobbying on the Bill by disability groups, who descended with a force of two thousand on the Palace of Westminster, ironically one of the least well-equipped buildings in terms of access for disabled people (or for that matter any members of the public). A quarter of a million postcards were sent to MPs encouraging attendance at the debate on the Bill. The Government's resistance to legislation began to look increasingly threatened, not helped by the revelation that Scott's own daughter, Victoria, was a leading campaigner for disability rights legislation. The Government began to resort to more desperate, even underhand, measures to thwart disability campaigners. Anonymous briefings on the cost of implementing Berry's proposals appeared in the Commons Press Gallery, followed soon afterwards by an official government analysis of the £17 billion, with £1 billion annual additional costs. This succeeded in making the financial implications dominate coverage of the issue, despite the fact that the figures were highly suspect, and ignored the savings which could be expected from social security spending on disabled people. This showed the narrowness of the Government's view, as discussion about supporting single parents increasingly focused on economic activity and efforts to reduce welfare spending.

The Government did not oppose the Bill at second reading, assuming that it would be easy to defeat it later on. In committee, ministers sat back and allowed MPs to discuss amendments to improve its provisions and address concerns, without tabling any amendments themselves. Then, just before the Bill returned to the full chamber for its report stage debate, no fewer than eighty amendments were tabled in the name of a claque of Conservative MPs including Dame Olga Maitland, despite her being unable to explain them in the debate. Despite explicit denial by Scott, it was clear that the Government had drafted them. These two were forced to apologise for essentially lying to the House when Scott's colleague Tony Newton, Leader of the Commons, revealed that it had indeed been Scott's department which had asked Parliamentary Counsel to draft the amendments. This was particularly galling because access to the parliamentary draftsmen for private members' bills was restricted to £200-

worth of time, and the implication was clearly that Counsel had spent rather more than that on drafting amendments to scupper the Bill which were tabled by Conservative backbenchers, rather than the Government itself. During the crucial Commons debate on Roger Berry's Civil Rights (Disabled Persons) Bill, Scott and Edward Leigh, a less emollient opponent of the Bill, were clearly conscious that to talk the Bill out would invite condemnation from disabled people and their supporters. However, Berry had already agreed to accept all the government amendments in order to keep the Bill alive. Scott and Leigh still insisted on debating the amendments and delaying a vote rather than simply moving to the final Commons stage. Faced with this dilemma the Government took advantage of a happy co-incidence, the funeral of John Smith, who had died the previous week. With many Labour MPs in Scotland for this occasion, government whips ensured that twelve Tory MPs who were present did not vote on the Bill. The result, twenty-eight to one, fell eleven short of the required forty voting to be quorate.

Not only the Government, but also Parliament itself was brought into disrepute when disabled activists, invited by Labour MP Dennis Skinner, were denied access to the Palace of Westminster for five hours. Some wanted to crawl symbolically into the building, bearing the slogan 'Piss on Pity', but were refused entry by the deputy Sergeant at Arms, leading to further protest and attempts to haul themselves across the threshold. Only intervention from the Speaker resolved the stand-off, or sit-off.[85] The following month the Bill was again blocked by a coordinated effort from Conservative ministers and Jacqui Lait, a ministerial aide, who spoke for almost a whole hour on competitiveness, ensuring that no time was left for the disability bill. Skinner attacked the Government with a characteristically vivid accusation, that, having just returned from the annual D-Day commemorations in northern France paying tribute to war veterans, ministers were now 'kicking their crutches away'.[86]

Following this pyrrhic victory for the Government, Scott was replaced as Minister for the Disabled by William Hague.[87] He moved swiftly to rescue the situation, and in the autumn of 1994 the Government published a consultation document proposing a Disability Rights Act, though crucially without powers of enforcement or a body to oversee its provisions, as proposed by disability groups and the failed Private Members' Bills. The Act was a significant extension of protection for disabled people from discrimination, which had been started with the Chronically Sick and Disabled Persons Act in 1970. However, its restrictions gave Labour room to promise more extensive reform in its election manifesto.[88]

*

Debate about the continuing restrictions on Sunday trading continued to provide one of the most interesting examples of the competing moral claims of economic liberalism, individual freedom, religious tradition and the prevention of exploitation of labour. In addition, the involvement of the European Court of Justice in pointing out that, although some measure of regulation was permissible the law should be changed, highlighted the relative influence of legal regulation compared to cultural attitudes and norms. Ironically, the Luxembourg court said regulation was permissible in order to protect workers' rights – the one argument which the UK Government rejected. The social pressures which in Britain gradually undermined Sabbatarianism and its legal protection worked in the opposite way in many countries on the continent, where regardless of the legality of Sunday trading it remained highly restricted through cultural pressure rather than regulation. In the 1950s and 1960s discussion about Sunday observance centred on the restrictions on cultural and social recreations, notably Prince Philip's polo playing. The Committee set up by the Conservatives had recommended a relaxation of these restrictions, though with protection for workers from being compelled to work on Sundays. Such reform had been popular with most Labour MPs and many Conservatives, but had been thwarted by a vocal minority of nonconformist Welsh MPs led by George Thomas. Sporting and cultural liberation was, nonetheless, achieved piecemeal during the 1970s.

The idea of relaxing Sunday trading laws was beyond the scope of these debates, but by the 1980s, with Thatcherite Conservatism dominating British society and politics, the demands of the free market threatened the peace of the Sabbath as cultural freedom had done in the Swinging Sixties. The Government's own attempt to implement free-market ideology and remove all restrictions failed in 1986 when Conservative MPs rebelled against a three-line whip. But by the early 1990s, Government, Parliament and the courts were becoming increasingly ineffective against the open flouting of the law by retailers prepared to absorb the small cost of fines for Sunday opening, public attitudes which supported partial deregulation, and the increasing willingness of employees to work on Sundays. The inability of backbenchers to force the issue on their own initiative, and the threat of being overtaken again by European law, caused the Government in the shape of Kenneth Clarke to announce that it would introduce legislation to allow Parliament to come to a decision on three options for reform. By the time it was introduced he had been succeeded at the Home Office by Michael Howard, reputedly a less avid supporter of total deregulation. In addition members of the Cabinet with strong religious objections included the former senior elder of the 'Wee Frees', Lord Chancellor Mackay, and a recent ultramontane convert from the Church of England, John Gummer.[89]

Labour's opposition to the 1986 Bill on the grounds that it infringed workers' rights was mollified by the conversion of the shopworkers' union, USDAW, to partial deregulation. Labour's own religious minority who continued to oppose Sunday working was obviously less significant than it had been in government in the 1960s, though senior Welsh figures such as Donald Anderson were still in Parliament. Despite the fact that Tony Blair insisted that workers' rights must be protected, a third of the parliamentary Labour Party and some of the leadership, including John Smith and Blair, voted for partial deregulation, allowing for six hours of trading on Sundays. Among the Shadow Cabinet, John Prescott, Frank Dobson, David Blunkett, Ann Taylor, Michael Meacher and Jack Straw continued to support the 'Keep Sunday Special' campaign. The Government won a majority for reform but was then backed by its MPs against including protections for workers, the very precondition which Blair had cited before reform could be agreed. Labour divisions were in the end as serious as those in the Conservative Party.[90]

*

In July 1996 the House of Lords debated 'society's moral and spiritual well-being'. The debate echoed a Commons debate in May 1970 on 'the permissive society'. On this occasion it was George Carey, Archbishop of Canterbury, who tabled the less divisively worded motion. As in 1970 the debate came as parliamentarians knew that the Prime Minister could go to the country at any time.

The atmosphere of moral stock-taking in advance of the poll, combined with a good dose of conservative doommongering, was unmistakeable.

There were some vintage performances. Amidst all the predictable posturing from liberals and conservatives there were some important points of moral philosophy discussed. Perhaps most notable were the opposing perspectives of Archbishop Carey and Richard Marsh, Cabinet minister under Harold Wilson in the late 1960s. Marsh quoted a newspaper article by Carey in which he stated that 'the politicians seem to think that what essentially matters is economic order and prosperity. The real fabric of society is the spiritual and moral fabric. This is the currency that makes civilisation function.' Marsh challenged him by saying that a 'civilised society in the modern world depends on the ability of politicians to meet ever-increasing aspirations for increasingly expensive material benefits', and suggesting that economic deprivation led to ignorance, immorality and, in the last reckoning, such atrocities as occurred in Nazi Germany or Stalinist Russia. He went so far as to say that 'only industry and commerce can finance the solutions.' Carey took issue with this argument, denying that good economics would inevitably lead to good morality. Carey and Marsh also had the best of the argument about a decline in shared moral values themselves. Marsh again quoted Carey as saying that 'we have lost a sense of community ... and a loss of shared values that used to bind us together.' He denied that this was the case, suggesting that it was in the interests of religious figures to make such claims. In defence Carey responded that he was inviting people of all faiths and none to discuss the issue of society's moral and spiritual well-being. However, he supported his argument by quoting the view of the Chief Rabbi, Jonathan Sacks, that there was a loss of a public sense of moral order and that increases in one-parent families, deserted wives and child abuse were the fault of moral relativism. Carey seemed confused. He suggested that people did not agree with total moral relativism, and were rebelling against it to express their shared moral values, but that there was a 'pervasive notion that nothing is ultimately good, noble, true or right'. But if such a socially damaging notion was really that pervasive, could it still be true that most people agreed on shared values, or would be in a position to challenge them?[91] Of course, this debate came at the end of eighteen years of Conservative government, a period in which moral traditionalists continued to believe, *pace* Sacks, that changes in the 1960s had at best allowed moral standards to slide, and at worst had caused that slide. During the period of Conservative hegemony, Labour politicians had continuously had to parry criticism of their liberal 1960s record as it faded into history. Soon, however, it would be their turn to demonstrate how a different approach in the 1990s would support social cohesion and individual responsibility.

8. A New Moral Purpose for a New Millennium?

'We need to find a new national moral purpose for this new generation. People want to live in a society that is without prejudice but is with rules. Government can play its part, but parents have to play their part. There's got to be a partnership between Government and the country to lay the foundations of that moral purpose.'

Tony Blair[1]

'Symbolism in politics can be important. Statutes enshrining symbols can be a perfectly acceptable way of proceeding. If we believe that symbolism is not based on any sensible appreciation of the truth about a particular matter, we engage in putting forward not symbols, but postures. We should not be engaged in that action.'

Tony Blair[2]

Chief Whip: Are you happy in the Cabinet? Do you want to stay in it?

Hacker: I'm sorry, Vic, but there is such a thing as duty. There are times when one must do what one's conscience tells one.

Chief Whip: Oh, for God's sake. Must you go round flashing your petty private individual little conscience? Don't you think anyone else has got one? Haven't you got a conscience about the survival of the Government? … And you want to blow it all in a fit of moral self-indulgence.

Yes Minister[3]

The approach of the new Labour Government (elected under Tony Blair in May 1997) towards the family and sexuality represented a radical development of four trends which had been evident since the late 1950s. The first was a growing acceptance within Labour that social stability was not to be shored up by a reinforcement of traditional 'family values', Christian morality or a return to Victorian attitudes towards authority. Although British society was still dominated by the 'nuclear' two-birth-parent family, the proportion of second families, single-parent families and other more unconventional households was growing steadily. Labour's new approach, strongly resisted by the right, believed that social justice, not blind support for traditional family structure, was the most effective means of reinforcing individual responsibility and shared moral values. Second, Labour's attitude towards human rights represented a real break with previous postwar governments. Rather than belatedly and grudgingly accepting the decisions of the European Court of Human Rights, as governments had done since the end of the 1960s, Labour embraced the European Convention for the Protection of Human Rights, incorporated it into UK law, and began adjusting policies and practices across the public sector to accord with the rights under the Convention. This raised the possibility of fostering a culture of positive rights in the UK for the first time, potentially offering a set of 'values for a godless age'. Thirdly, the historic differences in legal and cultural traditions at national, regional and local levels assumed an unprecedented significance. Labour's devolution policy accentuated the differences between England, Scotland, Wales and Northern Ireland, even with Labour in power either alone or in coalition across the whole of the United Kingdom. Cutting across this was a greater uniformity of standards which human rights legislation conferred at a UK level. Within England there was also a concern among liberals to standardise levels of access to services, for example abortion and sex education, which previous legislation had left to the mercy of individual health authorities, local councils or individual schools. Fourthly, and perhaps most importantly, the political class, dominated by the electoral success of Labour, held attitudes and beliefs radically different from those of their predecessors. There was also painful debate within the Conservative Party about how to respond to New Labour's success and the clear shifts in public opinion towards a more open, tolerant and diverse response to moral issues at the end of the twentieth century. The seemingly relentless trend towards greater permissiveness and tolerance through each successive generation was starkly depicted by the 1999 Social Attitudes Survey. It concluded:

> *On moral matters, such as religion, sexual mores and abortion, we have found little evidence to suggest that an ageing society will be either more pious or less permissive. On the contrary, attitudes are likely to shift away from those currently held by older groups ... the attitudes currently held by younger gener-*

ations will largely be carried with them into older age, replacing the more
conservative values currently held by older generations.[4]

None of these trends was absolute or irreversible. Many people on the right continued to strive eagerly for a return to more traditional values, and many on the left agreed with the need for a reassessment of some of the consequences of greater individual freedom. New Labour, and Tony Blair in particular, made a firm distinction between 'Victorian' family values, which they rejected as archaic, and wider social values, particularly in relation to education, crime and anti-social behaviour, where they increasingly sought a return to 'traditional' values of personal responsibility. However, these trends did set the scene for a very different national conversation about how issues of morality should be dealt with by the law, public life and even relationships between individuals.

The 1997 general election campaign had seen a good deal of animus about politicians' behaviour in the sense of the financial and sexual 'sleaze' which had mired the Conservatives for five years – in some cases highly personalised. This was most acute in Exeter where the openly gay Labour candidate, Ben Bradshaw, was up against the director of the Conservative Family Campaign, Dr Adrian Rodgers. Not since the Bermondsey by-election in 1982, in which Peter Tatchell's undisclosed sexuality had become an issue, had this been such a focus. Rodgers' use of anti-gay propaganda and doom-mongering about the perceived consequences of electing a homosexual as an MP, including the danger to schoolchildren, was uninhibited. This was also reminiscent of the campaign against Patrick Gordon-Walker in Smethwick in 1964, in which the Conservative Peter Griffiths used the slogan 'If you want a nigger for a neighbour, vote Labour'. Whilst 'bugger' could have been substituted for 'nigger' in this case, Rodgers could hardly have been less successful than Griffiths. Bradshaw won with a majority of eleven thousand and a swing of twelve per cent. Even in defeat Rodgers could not help himself, saying the result was 'a nightmare for Exeter and a nightmare for Britain'. As in Harold Wilson's near landslide of 1966, the rush of new blood into the Commons in 1997 radically changed the social outlook of the Government benches. Labour's policy of all-women shortlists, though it had subsequently been ruled illegal, ensured that there were 124 women MPs.[5] Nine black and Asian MPs took their places on the green benches, six more than in the previous Parliament.

Blair exhibited elements of both traditional and liberal responses to issues of morality. Generally held to be the most religious prime minister since Gladstone, with close ties to the Roman Catholic Church through Cherie Blair's own faith and the education of their children at Catholic schools, Blair's religious convictions infused his political outlook. This was not, however, a puritan, Victorian morality, at least relating to sex. Despite this, his fondness for religious rhetoric sometimes jarred with the increasingly secular demands of political debate in Britain, for which he was satirised as the Vicar of St Albion's by *Private Eye*. He invoked a language of moral concern most earnestly in 1999 when, in an interview with the *Observer*, he called for 'a new moral purpose for this new generation'. All those in the Labour Party with a memory stretching back six years read in disbelief as echoes of John Major's fatal 'Back to Basics' speech in 1993 sprang immediately to mind. Many Conservatives were content to smile knowingly at the risks implicit in using such language. Not that Blair was likely to be caught having an affair with a extrovert female parliamentary colleague like his predecessor, but then that was what people had said about John Major until 2002. When, in July 2004, Blair delivered his speech attacking the '1960s liberal consensus on law and order', he again seemed to revel in offending liberals within the Labour Party. But he also claimed consistency in his views. Referring to one of a series of articles he wrote for *The Times* after the 1987 general election, when still a lowly junior opposition spokesman on trade and industry, he claimed a long history of concern about 'anti-social behaviour' among young people, even implying he had coined the phrase in 1988. This series of articles repays close examination for its evidence of the areas of consistency and change in his views. The article he referred to sixteen years later was indeed a passionate condemnation of gang violence in rural County Durham, and gave little quarter to the traditional Labour argument that such behaviour was the result of social deprivation. Nor does it seem to support the common notion that his later appeal to be 'tough on causes of crime' spoke to these traditional concerns of the left:

This new lawlessness cannot be blamed on deprivation of a material sort. Many of the youths involved are still at school or employed and, in any case, unemployment usually acts as a depressant turning a person inwards, not as a stimulus to group activity.

Nor will it be remedied only by stiffer penalties, though some sentences for

violent offences seem absurdly light. The main difficulty is catching and iden-
tifying the criminals, not in sentencing them.

In any event, that deals only with the symptoms. To perceive the underlying
causes for this violence is more exacting and more troubling in its message. But
it surely has something to do with the decline in the notion of 'community', of
the idea that we owe obligations to our neighbours and our society as well as
ourselves.

... None of us should escape responsibility. For we, collectively, determine the
values of our society. When a sense of community is strong, that adds its own
special pressure against anti-social behaviour. Instead, we have learnt to
tolerate what should not be tolerated. A victim can be assaulted violently in a
public place and ignored by others present.

We are living in a society where increasingly the term is itself becoming
meaningless, where social responsibility and the duties that come with it are
seen simply as a drag anchor on our private pleasure.

For the better off, their wealth may increase, but they will pay an ever larger
price for their security from the world outside. The victims – the young, the
poor and the elderly – will be those that cannot or will not, hide away. This is
Britain 1988 style and it is time we woke up to it.[6]

However, a few months earlier his instincts were rather more in tune with the
rest of his party when he had seemed rather more closely allied to Clare Short's
campaign against sex in the tabloids. Calling for statutory regulation of the press,
something at which he might later blush, he railed against the moralistic
hypocrisy of the Conservative Government and its supporters in the right-wing
tabloid press who were, at the time, attempting to rein in the liberal 'pinkos' in
the broadcast media:

It is strange that Mrs Thatcher should be pursuing with such vigour the elim-
ination of the more steamy sex scenes from our television screens, while
apparently tolerating the same, if not worse, in the pages of newspapers. The
'morally unstable', Mrs Thatcher's phrase, are to be denied moving pictures
and speech, but stills with stories are acceptable and even 'fun'.

... This is the same Tory party that has repeated ad nauseam *indictments of*
the 'permissive society' of the 1960s and how that society led to our moral

decline. It has been blamed for everything from sexual perversion to trade union militancy.

… Perhaps, however, the real reason why Mr Tebbit, the opponent of the open society, becomes defender of one of its worst abuses, is the resonance between the values of the tabloids and of the Thatcherite Tories. It is not just the frequent venomous attacks on 'liberal' politicians … It is the ethos of 'grab what you can, when you can' that pervades each and every page, together with an open contempt for those who do not share it. Like the new generation of city slickers hankering after the latest BMW, it is all about self, greed, acquisition, whether of people or of things.[7]

The Conservative Party's defeat in 1997 left it more shell-shocked than at any election since 1906. Economic mismanagement following the humiliating ejection from the exchange rate mechanism in 19921, the deterioration of public services, and financial and sexual sleaze had all taken their toll. As well as being divided over Europe, the direction of its social philosophy now took centre stage. Former ministers responsible for some of the harshest policies and postures under Major began repenting of previous cruelties, notably the defeated MP and Defence Secretary Michael Portillo. Other former young turks of the hard right joined this soul-searching march towards more inclusive politics. With the spectre of Europe less problematic as pro-Europeans in the party became an endangered species, whether to modernise and reach out or galvanise the core Tory vote became the political test for the Party under William Hague, the youngest party leader since Pitt the Younger. He began to make gestures towards modernisation and inclusiveness by attending the Notting Hill Carnival wearing a baseball cap, which invited howls of derision. At the same time, ignoring the preference of the electorate so recently expressed for more investment in public services (even if Gordon Brown had not yet loosened the purse strings), Hague also made speeches extolling the morality of low taxation of which Margaret Thatcher and Friedrich von Hayek would have been proud.[8]

Hague attacked the concept of 'institutional racism' defined in the Macpherson Report into the police investigation of the murder of the black teenager Stephen Lawrence, stoutly defended Section 28 in the House of Commons and led Conservative attacks on asylum seekers. As the 2001 election approached, tensions between modernisers and traditionalists within the

Conservative Party became heightened over what image it should be presenting to the electorate and on what policies it should focus. Noises off from Thatcher acolytes such as Norman Tebbit continued to haunt the new generation, reminding them of certain boundaries which they must not cross. For example, during debate about the repeal of Section 28, Tebbit, clearly ignorant of departmental responsibilities, opined that 'no gay minister should be Home Secretary … The Home Office is responsible for laws affecting society – the adoption of children [*sic*] and the strengthening of the family. It is better not in the care of someone who does not feel for those issues.'[9]

With the party's poll ratings flatlining, except for a brief lead during the fuel protests of September 2000, defectors with some pretty colourful backgrounds began peeling off, mostly to Labour, complaining that the Tories were stuck in a 1950s nostalgia trip, excluded women and minorities from their ranks, or were overtly sexist, racist and homophobic. Most spectacularly the MP for Witney, Shaun Woodward, who had played rather a big role in the vicious 1992 election campaign as head of communications at Smith Square, crossed the floor of the House over the party's attitude to almost everything, from an obsession with the private sector and to its Europhobia to its hatred of women and minorities.[10] At the beginning of December he had been sacked from the front bench for failing to agree to support a three-line whip on Section 28. Norman Tebbit, in a classic Tebbitism, dismissed the move by saying Woodward was 'not a Conservative because he appears to be more attracted to europhilia and homosexuality than to Conservatism'.[11] The reaction from the Tory Party, apart from Tebbit, was predictably scathing and vicious. Rumours about homosexual misconduct surfaced in Woodward's constituency in Oxfordshire, and his transgender sister was hunted down and attacked by the tabloid press. It was left to more sanguine Tory grandees, such as Woodward's predecessor in Witney, Lord Hurd, to warn:

> *If everybody who shares the kind of concerns and anxieties that Shaun Woodward had left, then the party would never be elected to govern. The leadership must find a way to keep these doors open for people who have anxieties about issues like Europe and homosexual rights, but who nevertheless feel more Conservative than Labour.*[12]

Whatever notice the party took of such advice it failed to stop some others flaking off. The gay millionaire Ivan Massow, who in 1999 criticised Woodward for defecting, and as late as 2000 was toying with running to become Tory candidate in the London mayoral race, left the party citing similar unpleasantness. Despite making various overtures of support to Labour, Massow has since found it possible to rejoin the Tories. It was a delicious irony that the opportunity for the reconstructed Portillo to return to front-line politics was created by the death in 1999 of Alan Clark – serial adulterer and hardcore Thatcher disciple. During his quest for what was understandably a sought-after seat in Kensington and Chelsea, Portillo both challenged the party to change its image and policies, and confessed to a homosexual past. Such candour split opinion within the party along predictable lines. Although some Thatcherite traditionalists including Tebbit were prepared to discount such youthful dalliances as were admitted to by Portillo, continuing speculation about the extent of his homosexuality led many, feigning indifference to sexuality, publicly to condemn Portillo's 'parading' of such issues or lack of complete candour.[13]

When Iain Duncan Smith took up the seemingly poisoned chalice from Hague in 2001 he proved little more successful at bridging this new divide within the Party. See-sawing between modernisers and traditionalists, Duncan Smith faced embarrassing questions over his handling of Section 28, adoption and his front-bench and back-room teams, with rival camps jockeying for position. In 2002 Teresa May, the first female Chairman of the Party, a sign of how far it had come, but still how far it had to go, berated conference activists for being seen as the 'nasty party', an attack which only intensified division without actually deciding direction. The voluntary 'coming out' of the first gay Tory MP in 2002 caused little controversy, even within the party. Although religious right-wingers such as Ann Widdecombe complained about an obsession with 'ideological purity' on matters of personal morality, Alan Duncan received widespread support for the move and the manner in which it was achieved. Duncan Smith and party leaders supported him, recognising the advantage to be gained in assisting an image of inclusiveness. Previous generations of gay Tories willingly accepted closet status like Norman St John Stevas, once described by the *Guardian* as 'the thinking man's Larry Grayson', or less comfortably like Matthew Parris and Michael Brown.[14] Perhaps the most significant effect of Duncan's announcement on his party was to enable other Conservative running as prospective parliamentary candidates, like Westminster Councillor Nicholas Boles standing in Hove, to declare and discuss their sexuality openly before their election. An attempt by the Falmouth and Cambourne Constituency Party to deselect its gay candidate, Ashley Crossley, who was openly supported by Michael Howard, was overwhelmingly defeated.

The Liberal Democrats, still without an openly gay MP despite their pro-gay policies, were not without their own problem defector. Labour MP Paul Marsden switched sides following a bruising encounter with the Chief Whip, Hilary Armstrong, in which his opposition to the war in Afghanistan was supposedly dismissed as not an issue of conscience. However, Marsden's defection was soon seen as a blessing in disguise for Labour, as the turncoat MP was revealed to have rather different moral standards in relation to marital fidelity. To add insult to injury, he justified his adultery by implying that MPs were irresistible to others at Westminster:

It's that magnet of power ... You find reporters and researchers overtly flirt ... Lots of researchers want to be MPs and will be a little bit loose with their morals. It's not unknown that because someone has slept with someone they get jobs.[15]

One American intern asked to be moved from Mardsen's office, though declined to make an official complaint about alleged 'inappropriate behaviour'. His new party must have been relieved when he announced he would not attempt to hold his seat at the next general election.

*

Labour's first Queen's Speech in June 1997 included a bill to implement their manifesto commitment to incorporate the ECHR into UK law. The characteristic industry of the civil service in preparing for what was a widely anticipated change of administration allowed a bill and a White Paper to be published in autumn 1997, for which Jack Straw pushed hard.[16] The White Paper crafted the options which Labour had set out in 1996 which incorporated many of the principles within the Convention, creating the first 'higher' law which would protect fundamental rights, without completely undermining parliamentary sovereignty by allowing judges to overturn primary legislation. Importantly, the purpose of the Bill within the lexicon of New Labour rhetoric had broadened from a technical legal improvement in access to existing justice to one about enshrining New Labour's philosophy of rights and responsibilities in law.

The Conservative Party was, in its bones, opposed to incorporation and the Human Rights Bill. Although some senior figures, including even Margaret Thatcher, had toyed with a Bill of Rights during the 1970s, experience of government and the increasingly inconvenient decisions of judges both in Strasbourg and in domestic courts stiffened resistance. The Tories' official position during passage of the Bill was to attack the erosion of parliamentary sovereignty as well as the potential cost of a huge number of cases being brought. However, this was mollified by the limited protection given to parliamentary sovereignty by the Bill, and the party did not oppose its third reading. In winding up the debate the Conservative spokesman and former Attorney General Sir Nicholas Lyell said:

> *I believe profoundly in the European Convention on Human Rights, but it is a backstop. It must always be remembered that the convention was created after the war to prevent some dreadful things from ever happening again, and it should not start to reach into the nooks and crannies of the private lives of the citizens of these 30 or 40 countries. I hope that the courts will bear that in mind.*[17]

During the earlier second reading debate government and opposition MPs had wrestled over the question of parliamentary sovereignty, with Conservatives continually raising concerns about the implications of a judicial decision to overturn principles or policies debated and agreed by Parliament or approved by the people at a general election. Interestingly, the first hypothetical situation concerned abortion. Drawing on the contentious and symbolic arguments in the USA between the Supreme Court and state legislatures over abortion, Lyell questioned whether the Bill would create similar uncertainties in the UK, distressing women trying to decide whether or not to have an abortion. Straw shared such concern for the protection of ethical principles which had parliamentary and public approval from judicial interference.[18]

The subject was extremely topical. During the 1992 election, the Society for the Protection of the Unborn Child (SPUC), led by Phyllis Bowman, had deluged pro-choice Labour MP Alice Mahon's Halifax constituency with leaflets aimed at influencing voters to vote against Mahon and other pro-choice candidates. She was convicted under the 1983 Representation of the People Act of exceeding the five-pound limit on spending. Bowman took her case to Strasbourg where the court ruled that her right of freedom of expression had been infringed by the conviction. However, MPs were concerned that a similar Lords ruling would leave electoral law in limbo while the Government decided what course to follow. Much to the consternation of anti-abortion campaigners, the Strasbourg Court did not award Bowman damages.[19] Taking its cue, the Government resisted the clamour from Bowman's parliamentary supporters such as the former Tory MP and veteran anti-abortionist Lord Braine to refer the case back to the Court of Appeal. In the review of electoral law and party funding which resulted in the Political Parties, Elections and Referendums Act 2000, a balance was struck which recognised the Strasbourg ruling that the five-pound limit was too low to allow for freedom of expression by setting spending limits at a much higher level. By insisting on a limit this would also protect against manipulation of the democratic process, also accounted for in Article 11 of the Convention.

The capacity of the courts to be sensitive to the importance of Parliament deciding fundamental issues of ethics, rather than new legal principles being handed down piecemeal by unelected judges, was perhaps most evident in the tragic case of Diane Pretty. In 2001, Pretty, dying from motor neurone disease, applied to the courts under the Human Rights Act (HRA) to allow her husband to assist her suicide, invoking her right to respect for private and family life. Opponents of euthanasia were appalled, and critics of the HRA warned of dire consequences if such a right were conceded, claiming that the Act allowed a 'right to death' because all rights under the Act were balanced by their opposite. Such caricatures of the Act were shown to be palpable nonsense by the courts, who, to the distress of Pretty and her husband, consistently ruled that they could not grant her request under the Act, making it clear that if the law were to allow assisted suicide, Parliament must so decide. This became the first human-rights case to go to Strasbourg since the Act had been introduced. Strasbourg, ever mindful of the principle of the 'margin of appreciation', that the ECHR had to take account of national traditions and culture, also ruled against Pretty in 2001. She died shortly after the judgment.

Before, and indeed following, the implementation of the Act in 2000, the jeremiads on the right were of a nightmarish avalanche of claims under the Act which would paralyse the courts and undermine a thousand years of British legal history and culture. In reality its effects, at least in its first few years, were far less dramatic. In fact, for many supporters of the Act they were far less dramatic than had been hoped, thus perhaps justifying the nature of the compromise which had been enshrined in the Act itself. According to Lord Woolf, Lord Chief Justice, 'applications based on the HRA have been moderate in number and usually fully justified. So much so, that in relation to the lower courts, the impact has been described as a "damp squib".'[20]

If the caution of judges in interpreting legislation and ruling on claims under the Human Rights Act revealed a sensitivity to political and parliamentary jurisdiction, the direction of Home Office policy under David Blunkett tested this reticence to its limits and beyond. Blunkett's policies in relation to criminal justice, particularly sentencing, anti-terrorism and asylum and immigration were found to breach the Convention on several occasions. Hostilities between the two were barely concealed. Following the tensions between such legislation and the battering which new proposals from the Home Office received from judges, it was clear that the status of the HRA within the Government was already beginning to be questioned. Division among ministers surfaced, with Yvette Cooper, junior minister under the pro-HRA Lord Irvine, penning a timely defence of the Act which could be read as a thinly veiled attack on its critics in the Home Office as much as those in the *Daily Mail*. Rejecting the enduring charge that it promoted individualism, Cooper insisted that the Act

helps sustain the delicate balance between respect for the individual and support for the communities on which we depend. Many of its provisions protect our ability to form the relationships that hold society together – be it family life, freedom of assembly, or collective worship.'

In a rather more emollient spin on this fundamental principle of the Act she warned those who were implying that the Act was inflexible in dealing with the current threats from terrorism and organised crime that 'most rights are qualified by community considerations, such as national security, protecting others' rights, or public health. Indeed, the courts have endorsed measures to protect people against terrorism, crime and harassment which some civil liberties groups opposed.'[21]

However, despite this robust defence of the Act, the principles underlying it continued to be left largely at the mercy of the media and ministerial whim. The HRA and the growth of judicial review may well have had another adverse consequence on politicians – that of exacerbating the existing lassitude among government MPs to challenge legislation. Just as many Labour MPs backed down over their concerns about the anti-terrorism legislation introduced in the wake of the September 11th atrocities in 2001 because 'peers would sort it out', so their consciences could increasingly be comforted and any guilt assuaged by the thought that judicial review would sort out any injustices in new laws.[22]

The Human Rights Act laid on all public bodies the duty to promote, as well as protect, human rights, and it was in this way that it was hoped that a wider culture of respecting human rights would evolve. Yet the Government continued to resist the creation of a national body, a human rights commission, which could effectively perform this role, as it had with issues of equality in relation first to race in the 1960s, then sex in the 1970s and disability in the 1990s. With new legal protections in the pipeline, against discrimination on grounds of sexual orientation, age and religion, the Government accepted the logic of creating a single Equalities Commission, meshing work on all these aspects of anti-discrimination. Human rights would be incorporated into this new body. In Northern Ireland a Human Rights Commission had long been in existence, and a new statutory version was part of the Good Friday peace agreement. In Scotland, the devolved Government actively pursued establishing a commission covering devolved matters in Scotland. Back in London, the Joint Parliamentary Committee on Human Rights, which ministers had seen partly as a means of avoiding creating a commission, strongly supported creating one. It saw the work of a commission in relation to the promotion of a culture of human rights as two-fold. The first was 'institutional', in that the human rights principles should be seen as fundamental to the 'design and delivery of policy, legislation and public services'. The second area was 'ethical: people should be encouraged to understand that they enjoyed certain rights 'as an affirmation of their equal dignity and worth, and not as a contingent gift of the state'. However, the Committee emphasised:

A culture of human rights is not one which is concerned only with rights, to the neglect of duties and responsibilities, but rather one that balances rights and responsibilities by fostering a basic respect for human rights and dignity, and creating a climate in which such respect becomes an integral part of our dealings with the public authorities of the state and with each other. Such a culture of respect for human rights could help create a more humane society, a more responsive government and better public services. It could help to deepen and widen democracy. It is a goal worth striving for.[23]

Nobody, however, pretended that government, a human rights commission, or any other public body could magically spread a culture of understanding and respect for the values underpinning human rights. In addition to such work, the ethical principles on which the HRA was based were also to be promoted in schools as part of the new citizenship education which was being introduced as part of the national curriculum by Blunkett when he was still Education Secretary.

If the ethics of human rights were seen by some as 'values for a godless age', this was by no means a generally accepted idea. However, there was a paradox at the heart of debate about the shared values which should continue to underpin society, government and the law. Organised religion had, by the end of the twentieth century, collapsed as an active force of inculcating moral values. Despite this, the proportion of people who maintained some form of religious belief remained relatively high. The 2001 census revealed that seventy per cent of people still considered themselves Christian, although the religious tended to be older than the general population. However, given the growth of agnosticism and atheism, and the multicultural nature of religious belief and practice in contemporary Britain, could people still simply rely on a vague conception that values were based on 'religious' principles or even 'Christian' teaching? Many commentators, including secularists, remained unconvinced that human rights principles could replace the whole value system which people previously learned from religion, particularly the 'spiritual' dimension. Should religious teaching continue to be valued, and handed down to later generations, despite increasing lack of religious, or a single religious, belief? If not, how could the ethical principles underpinning human-rights legislation be fostered as an alternative? Clearly the historical relationship between religion and human rights was a strong one, and the most that could be said would be that the two would continue to be strongly linked, though not without tension about which should take precedence in a secular society.

Religion had certainly not given up the ghost in public life in Britain under New Labour. Despite Alistair Campbell's protestation to a journalist interviewing Tony Blair that 'we don't do God,' the evidence from certain parts of the Government, and elsewhere, was that we very much continued to 'do God'. If Campbell was sometimes successful in restraining Blair's impulse to wear his religious beliefs on his sleeve, and to use them to underscore political principles and policies, at other times the Prime Minister slipped this secular leash. In fact Campbell was, on occasion, complicit in this, most notably when Blair used an address to a south London school to announce the date of the general election in 2001. Pictures of Blair at a Church school, hymn book in hand beneath a stained-glass window, singing hymns with the children, brought howls of derision from the press. Campbell, rebutting accusations of cynical manipulation of the visit, said that it had been chosen months before to launch the election, thereby compounding the offence. In his speech at the school Blair implored the children, and the electorate who were his real audience, that 'every vote is precious', as ludicrous a statement as 'Every Sperm Is Sacred' in Monty Python's *The Meaning of Life*.[24] Probing the Prime Minister on the influence of his religious belief became a stock in trade of interviewers. In 2002, Jeremy Paxman rather ham-fistedly broached the subject, eliciting a tetchy response:

> *I am a Christian. I believe in it. But I don't think it is very sensible to start trying to view every decision you take as if it were a religious, rather than a political, decision ... Yes, of course it has an influence on my life and the values I believe in, but I don't wear it on my sleeve.*[25]

One of the most long-standing meeting points between religion and politics, education, assumed a level of controversy not seen since the beginning of the twentieth century. In the same Paxman interview quoted above, Blair made a robust case for faith schools, arguing for the extension of the principle to Muslim schools, on the basis that it was 'indefensible' to fund Christian or Jewish schools alone. Blair, and Blunkett as Education Secretary, were clearly convinced by evidence that faith schools not only inculcated strong moral values in their pupils, but also achieved better exam results. Opponents such as the journalist Polly Toynbee vehemently denied this, arguing that such evidence was merely a demonstration that religious schools attracted the children of middle-class parents better informed about how to exercise choice in the state system, boosting their performance, and that there was nothing intrinsic to their ethos or methods which better equipped children for economic or social citizenship. Although Toynbee perhaps blunted the force of her argument with too much sarcasm and derision about faith schools, she was able to point to a correlation between religious schools and low 'assessment eligibility', meaning the number of children receiving free school meals. Her conclusion was that the 'religious rigmarole' whereby ministers were now encouraging the spread of faith schools was a 'fig leaf' for introducing greater selection.[26] At the same time that the Judaeo-Christian monopoly of state-funded schools was being broken, the Church of England was proposing to open one hundred new Anglican schools, which the Government welcomed as part of the 'diversity' of provision, although within that diversity around a quarter of schools were already Church-run, despite an Anglican church-going population of less than one and a half million. How institutionalising hypocrisy by forcing parents to lie about their religious belief and practice in order to shoe-horn their children into schools which selected on the basis of faith would promote sound morality in children was not clear.

Not all aspects of religious teaching in schools were viewed in such benign terms, even by secularists who believed in the continuing value of faith-based education for teaching moral values. During the passage of the Education Bill through the House of Lords in 1999, peers discussed an amendment to provisions to give extra 'earned' autonomy to certain schools which sought to prevent the spread of the teaching of creationism in science. This had, unbelievably, as the sponsor of the amendment, Lord Peston, declared, been brought to public attention by the recent publicity surrounding a technology college in Tyne and Wear which was teaching creationism alongside evolution in science classes. Richard Vardy, a millionaire evangelical Christian and private donor to the college, pledged to support other schools to do the same, and religious groups from the United States began exploring the possibility of bringing further American-style creationist educational initiatives to Britain. By 2002 the issue had become even more heated as the foundation behind such schemes fleshed out proposals to establish further schools in England. In his grilling by Paxman, the Prime Minister dismissed the issue as 'hypothetical'. In the Commons, Blair was challenged by one of his own MPs about the teaching of creationism alongside evolutionary science. Asked by Piara Khabra 'whether the national curriculum should be clarified to prevent the two being presented as scientific equivalents', the Prime Minister said, 'We must be careful of exaggerating the issue of creationism in schools,' and that given the 'safeguards' in the national curriculum, 'I am hesitant myself about saying that those particular issues should be dealt with if it is the case, as I believe, that the school in question is a good school, providing a good service for its pupils.'[27] Blunkett was also central to the courting of faith organisations in the wider discussion and formulation of public policy. The Home Office established a Faith Community Unit and a liaison group to involve faith-based organisations in discussion of government policy, to which the Prime Minister attached 'considerable importance'. This brought together ministers and officials from departments, including the Prime Minister's Appointments Secretary, responsible for ecclesiastical matters, and representatives of different faiths and religious organisations and of local government.[28]

When Labour came to power, outrage at the high number of racist murders, most notably that of Stephen Lawrence, and the repeated failure to bring perpetrators to justice, forced the police, the criminal justice system and the wider public sector to examine the way that people from ethnic minorities were treated. The Labour Government was understandably more proactive in encouraging this process, although progress towards extinguishing racism and discrimination continued to be patchy. At the same time, society was starting to acknowledge that the 'ethnic minorities' were already an extremely diverse range of communities, religions, cultures and traditions. In 2001 the real extent of the size and diversity of the non-white population was revealed in the census, which, for the first time, allowed people to register a mixed-race identity. In England and Wales, 660,000 people did so.[29] While this trend necessitated a more sophisticated approach to the needs of different groups by those providing public services including health, education and welfare, it also posed challenges towards the increasingly secular, liberal, human-rights agenda suffusing the law and public life at the same time. Some minority ethnic communities displaying high levels of attachment to 'traditional' values in relation to a whole range of moral issues including sexuality, abortion, women's rights and censorship. Sometimes this provided a fillip to white conservatives who extolled the virtues of authority and morality which they saw professed by such communities. For many liberals, however, there was an opposite tension between their hatred of forced assimilation of immigrants or racism and the challenge cultural practices among some immigrant communities posed. Some politicians representing areas with large non-white communities, such as the Labour MP for Keighley, Ann Cryer, were particularly sensitive to these tensions.

Although strictly prohibited in all major religions which were represented among immigrant communities in Britain, the issue of forced marriages among communities from the Indian sub-continent suddenly became a high-profile issue in the late 1990s. In the two years up to 2001, the Foreign Office received over three hundred calls from people concerned about possible forced marriages. A Home Office working party, set up in response to press reports and concerns among MPs, led to new resources dedicated to assisting those, particularly children, who feared being forced into marriage in the UK or abroad, or those already in such a union. One of the minor provisions of the 1969 Divorce Law Reform Act had been that people who had been the victim of a forced marriage could petition for an annulment, although a time limit of three years restricted its usefulness for some women. A similarly barbaric cultural practice which forced liberals to confront sensitive issues among some African communities was female genital mutilation, sometimes misleadingly known by the sanitising and trivial term 'female circumcision'. The range of mutilating operations which this practice comprised was already covered by the Prohibition of Female Circumcision Act 1985, and enhanced protection for children was afforded under the Children Act 1989. However, as with forced marriages, cultural secrecy and the simple expediency of going abroad to have a procedure performed often evaded the law. Since 1985 only two doctors had been struck off for performing or offering to perform such an operation. Neither had been prosecuted. In this case Parliament took the initiative. The All-Party Group on Population, Development and Reproductive Health investigated the extent of the problem and recommended extending the law. A leading supporter of human rights, Labour MP Ann Clwyd, introduced a bill with government support to make such procedures illegal whether carried out in the UK or abroad, including criminalising parents taking their daughters abroad for such operations, and extending the maximum penalties available from five to fourteen years. Introducing the Bill's second-reading debate, Clwyd said that the latest estimate of the problem was that seventy-four thousand first-generation African immigrant women in the UK had undergone genital mutilation, and as many as seven thousand girls under sixteen within the practising communities were at risk.

> *Respect for other cultures does not mean that we should ignore practices that are so harmful, and that violate the most basic human rights: the right of women not to be discriminated against because of their gender, under the convention on the elimination of all forms of discrimination against women; and, in particular, the right of the child to enjoy their childhood, and to the 'enjoyment of the highest attainable standard of health', as laid down in article 24 of the United Nations convention on the rights of the child.*[30]

More widely, continuing high levels of unemployment and deprivation, as well as low educational attainment, among some non-white communities in London, the Midlands, the north of England and Scotland gave rise to tensions between some black communities and white communities, exploding in 2001 into riots in Bradford and Oldham, the like of which had not been since the early 1980s in Brixton. In many of these areas both white and black communities lived in conditions of severe deprivation following the collapse of traditional industries. These tensions were increasingly linked to concerns about growing immigration and how Britain dealt with people arriving in the country, often characterised in the tabloid press as a 'flood' of 'bogus' asylum seekers, threatening Britain's very way of life. In London, with its large African and Caribbean black communities, the growth of gun violence and poor educational attainment among young black men threw up questions about the values which black youth culture might be instilling.

*

In November 1998 the Government published a Green Paper entitled *Supporting Families*. The document was sponsored by the Home Office under Jack Straw, the chair of the new Ministerial Group on the Family set up by the Prime Minister in September 1997. This was the Blairite version of the Cabinet 'family policy group', an institution beloved of any government afraid that the public might think them anti-family. With the chill ghost of the 'back to basics' fiasco haunting this latest initiative to bolster the family, the consultation paper started from the premise that

> we in government need to approach family policy with a strong dose of humility. We must not preach and we must not give the impression that members of the Government are any better than the rest of the population in meeting the challenge of family life. They are not.

In attempting to face the practical difficulties which lone and unmarried parents and second families faced, Straw conceded that there never had been a golden age for the family. Yet the document clung to the special status of marriage, citing both its inherent greater stability and enduring popularity.[31] The figures, as so often, supported more than one interpretation of the direction of family life. The number of divorces remained high but steady from the mid-1990s onwards. In 2001 there were 143,818 divorces, the first annual rise for five years. However, the rate of divorce was increasing, because of the continuing fall in the number of marriages, to a postwar low of 286,000 in 2001, 114,200 of which were remarriages. This reflected the huge increases in cohabitation and the number of single-person households. However, people's attitudes towards marriage and family life reflected an enduring preference for, even idealisation of marriage, with most people still aspiring to one monogamous lifelong legally recognised union, at the same time as recognising the reality of different outcomes and choices.

Ministerial insecurity about exactly how much support to give to marriage continued. In further details about the Group's proposals in March 2000 Straw appeared to row back from his statement in the Green Paper by saying that the Government was 'committed to supporting families whatever form they take. This Government will not preach about marriage.'[32] *Supporting Families* made modest claims for what governments could achieve and made modest proposals for what the Government would attempt to do, including establishing a national family and parenting institute and a parent helpline, and tinkering with marriage registration and support and information for couples in the hope that this would improve the stability of marriages. The clamour from the right, that the only way marriage could be strengthened was by restoring the fiscal incentives to marry and to stay married, was consistently ignored as reforms to the tax and benefits systems and new welfare-to-work programmes moved more firmly in the direction of helping all parents, whatever their status.

The Ministerial Group on the Family ploughed on in its quest for a credible policy on the family. At the end of 2000 it produced a draft report which continued to try to cover all its bases by balancing 'the family is the basic building block of our society' with 'however, we know that other family structures can also be successful'. The double-speak continued by claiming, 'Children brought up by two birth parents [have] higher levels of life satisfaction, fewer psychological problems,' whilst 'children brought up in restructured families without care experience or early disadvantage did not differ significantly from those brought up by birth parents.'[33] However, other voices added their authority to the debate. The new President of the Family Division of the High Court, Dame Elizabeth Butler-Sloss, just two weeks after becoming the first woman to reach such a high position in the judiciary, held a press conference at which she told candidly how her views on the family had changed in her years as a judge:

I was, when I started, surprised and dubious about the stability of children living in a family with two parents of the same sex. But over the years research has shown that for some children, that is the best that is available for them. Consequently it would be quite wrong when looking at the welfare of the child not to recognise that different children will need different types of parents. We should not close our minds to suitable families who are clearly not within the old-fashioned approach.

Butler-Sloss's comments brought a regretful statement from a leading Conservative family campaigner, Julian Brazier MP, that 'it is very sad that someone in her position should have spoken in this way.' She also criticised the perpetuation of fault-based divorce as a 'hypocritical charade', saying that it encouraged couples to invent a charge of unreasonable behaviour in order to avoid the two-year wait, as before the 1969 Divorce Law Reform Act. She understood, however, why the Government had decided to shelve the plans which it inherited from the Conservatives to implement a no-fault provision.[34] At the same time that Straw and his colleagues were weaving a Blairite narrative on the family, the Lord Chancellor, Lord Irvine, was making a tactical retreat on divorce law reform. Labour had been committed to implementing the 1996 Family Law Act, which would allow no-fault divorce after one year. This capitulation was rounded on by the postwar doyen of divorce reform, Leo Abse, in his psycho-biography of Tony Blair, noting Irvine's own divorced status and blaming a 'consensus-driven' Blair for being scared of the concept of the clean break since they had debated similar proposals back in 1984 during the passage of the Matrimonial Proceedings Bill.[35]

Backing out of further divorce law reform, the Government soon found itself dragged into an even more fraught battle over fathers' rights of access to their children after divorce. Long-standing pressure groups such as Families Need Fathers, which had successfully fostered debate about the importance of fathers to the development of their children, were soon outgunned in the media by a more extreme group – superheroes like Spiderman, Batman and Robin and Superman. Dressed as children's comic heroes, members of Fathers4Justice raged against the unfairness of the family courts towards fathers, saying that 'father-hood is under attack in a way inconceivable thirty years ago,' and finding support from celebrities such as Bob Geldof, who drew on his own experiences to attack the family courts. They adopted tactics of civil disobedience previously unheard of, including affecting roads and railways and harassment of solicitors, barristers and judges at their homes, including on one occasion the house of a judge who was away, but whose teenage sons were present. Women's groups, including the ex-partners of some of the protesting fathers, argued that mothers often had good reason to prevent contact between children and fathers.[36] Despite the fact that in ninety per cent of cases custody was agreed without resort to the courts, fathers' rights became politically highly-charged, particularly when two Fathers4Justice activists threw purple flour bombs at Tony Blair in the House of Commons, causing the chamber to be cleared and security procedures to be tightened.[37]

These developments highlighted an interesting distinction between Labour and Conservative policies on the family. Reshuffling his Shadow Cabinet in June 2004, Michael Howard demoted Teresa May to a newly created portfolio, but one with some social significance – Shadow Secretary of State for the Family. This was in contrast to Labour's recent creation of a Minister for Children in the Department for Education, in the person of Margaret Hodge. Howard was keen

to draw attention to this distinction at a 'family summit' convened shortly afterwards, when he crowed that 'no such position exists in the Government at the
moment. We have created the post because Conservatives understand the key
role that families play in our society.' With such a level of debate, perhaps it was
not surprising that the Tories were seeking to jump aboard the fathers' rights
bandwagon. Howard pledged his party to support 'a strong presumption in
favour of equal rights for parents *to have an influence on the upbringing of their
children*.'[38] This was spun without the italics so that the press reported
Conservative support for equal access, rather than the far less tangible 'influence'.
However, the Government rejected his call for major reform of the Children Act,
arguing that the system could be improved to ensure that 'more non-resident
parents will enjoy meaningful ongoing relationships with their children.'[39]

If Labour was thought to be dragging its feet on fathers' access to their
children after divorce, for those children living with neither parent who found
themselves in care, Tony Blair was far more proactive. Early on in his premiership he took personal charge of a task force established to find ways of reforming
the adoption laws. This followed a growing clamour in the press about the difficulties which couples faced adopting babies and infants in the UK and from
abroad, fuelled by right-wing indignation about the procedural hurdles which
'politically correct' social services departments forced such couples to clear
before approving them for adoption. The implication was that children who
were languishing in institutional or foster care could be found permanant homes
if adoption were made easier. However, the legislative result of this review
process was far from the 1950s utopia of married couples selflessly assuming
permanent guardianship for thousands of extra rosy-cheeked but star-crossed
infants. Apart from anything else, much of the outcry about the existing
adoption system ignored the fact that few couples coming forward to adopt were
interested in, or suited to, the vast majority of children in institutional or foster
care, who were over five and often with severe emotional problems and disturbed
family backgrounds. In 2002 there were only 5,459 adoptions, a small annual
increase, but still twenty-seven per cent lower than ten years earlier.[40] The legislation which the Government brought forward was a classic case of ministers
accepting a backbench amendment to push through more radical reform than
they were prepared to countenance putting into the first draft of the Bill. Existing
rules allowed married couples or single people to adopt. This meant that if step-

parents wanted to adopt children from their spouse's previous marriage, the birth parent also had to 'adopt' their biological children. Non-married couples could not adopt together. However, the perversity in the rules meant that single people could adopt, preventing many children from having two adoptive parents. Extending eligibility to adopt to cohabiting heterosexual and gay couples, providing they met all the normal criteria, spiked the guns of the conservative lobby which had been campaigning for easier adoption. At a stroke, the range of parents avalible to children was vastly widened, without weakening the criteria on which all individuals and couples wanting to adopt would be judged.

Right-wing commentators such as Melanie Phillips called on the Government to loosen the reins of politically correct social workers on married couples wishing to adopt, saying there was no need to extend eligibility to unmarried or gay couples if this was done. Unmarried couples, she argued, were far more likely to split up. Against this the proponents of the new arrangements argued that it was not a question of whether married or unmarried or gay couples were, on average, more likely to stay together, but of assessing and approving those couples from all types of relationship who were most suitable to adopt, and that this would naturally include the stability of their relationship. Statistics themselves told you nothing about individual couples. For many on the right, though, any intrusion into the circumstances of married couples wanting to adopt suggested an antipathy towards marriage itself.

Despite the multiple charges of hypocrisy, callousness and unrealistic nostalgia which Labour levelled at the Conservative Government and party during the 1980s and 1990s, one of the most significant early acts of the new Government in 1997 was to cut lone-parent benefit by ten per cent. This was a result of the flagship policy of Gordon Brown's so-called 'iron chancellorship' to adhere to Conservative spending limits for the first two years of the administration. This necessitated, as Brown interpreted it, implementing Peter Lilley's proposed benefit cuts, though if high enough priority had been accorded to a change, the money could presumably have been found from other budgets without exceeding these spending limits. However, the cut also chimed well with the broader New Labour move towards welfare-to-work policies. Harriet Harman, former Director of the National Council for Civil Liberties and Lilley's successor at Social Security, was made sacrificial lamb for the policy, losing her job and much of her credibility in the process, although she was rehabilitated in both senses after the 2001 general election. The seemingly self-defeating result of imposing the benefit cut was brought home by the fact that as soon as the budgetary straitjacket was relaxed in 1999, lone parents became one of the first and largest beneficiaries, particularly as the new long-term target of eradicating child poverty inevitably helped the disproportionate number of one-parent families in poverty. Under the Government's New Deal for Lone Parents, the proportion of lone parents in work rose from 43.5% to 54.3%. This was justified by research which showed that the majority of lone parents wanted to work. However, concern grew that parents, usually women, who wanted to stay at home and look after young children were being forced into work by the Chancellor's policy – a reaction that was not confined entirely to conservatives.

In July 1998 the Government brought in new rules granting automatic parental responsibility to unmarried parents jointly registering a child's birth. In April 2000 it abolished the married couples allowance (MCA) after a battered seventy-year record of serving changing government attitudes towards the family and women in work. By 1997 its effect was blunted by the existence of the corresponding additional personal allowance, the same as the MCA, but paid to unmarried couples and lone parents with children. These were also abolished in 2000, to be replaced by tax credits targeted at all families with children, regardless of their structure, as well as increases in child benefit, a package which, as Brown and other ministers insisted, was vastly more generous than the MCA. Defending the move when it was announced in 1999 the Paymaster General, Dawn Primarolo, in an acid retort reminiscent of Harold Wilson's withering comment about Britain's 'independent nuclear deterrent', said that the MCA was

restricted neither to marriage nor to couples. Nor, indeed, is it strictly an allowance, as it is a tax credit paid at the same flat rate to married couples, single parents and unmarried parents who live together. Far from recognising marriage ... the allowance is so confused that it can even be paid twice – at the full rate to both partners in the year of separation or divorce. A married couples allowance that can pay more for separation or divorce surely cannot be said to uphold the institution of marriage.[41]

The Conservatives opposed the move, arguing that the MCA should be reformed rather than abolished and in October 2000 William Hague pledged at the Conservative Party conference to restore a married couples allowance. The caveat was later revealed to be the targeting of the new tax credit on married couples with children under five. Explaining his position further he said that 'I do believe it is much the best thing for our society if the vast majority of people are in stable and happy families – and marriage is usually the cornerstone of a stable and successful family.' Unveiling their alternative proposals, the Conservative Shadow Social Security Secretary, David Willetts, argued: 'Something happens when people marry that does not happen when they cohabit. It marks a public commitment.'

As Brown's reform of the tax and benefits system to create integrated tax credits aimed at lifting families with children out of poverty gathered pace, there appeared to be a clear divide between the two main parties about the family and marriage. However, Labour, with one eye on the *Daily Mail* and Middle England, continued to make rhetorical obeisance at the altar of the married two-parent family. Fed by the polling and focus group evidence from Philip Gould and the increasing hostility of the right-wing press, signs of sensitivity about their family policies began to show. In July 2000 a prime-ministerial memo was leaked, written shortly after the abolition of the MCA, which linked it, as well as gay issues, to a perception that the Government was 'weak' on 'family' issues. This fuelled speculation about the influence of the *Daily Mail* because the memo was written by Blair the same day an editorial in the *Mail* harangued the Government on four of the same topics addressed in the memo.

The Government's fiscal policies were directed at reducing poverty among all families with children. This was predicated on the belief that the way to create stable families was to reduce poverty, rather than offer bribes, small in relative terms, which would send a strong social signal about the desirability per se of marriage. The Government's approach was bolstered in 2003 by the publication of research by the Policy Studies Institute which showed that 'work status and income of the family' more clearly accounted for child poverty than whether a child came from a one- or a two-parent family.[42] Meanwhile, the Conservatives, forced to acknowledge that the old MCA unjustifiably benefited wealthy married couples without children, maintained its belief in marriage as the main instrument of creating stable families by proposing to target extra help on married couples with young children. This, they hoped, would act as a further incentive to mothers of young children who wished to stay at home to care for them, rather than go out to work.

*

If campaigners were hopeful that Labour would champion further gay rights measures, there were signs, even before the 1997 election victory, that whatever the past record, present rhetoric or best of intentions of ministers, there were few firm commitments. The 1997 Manifesto pledged the party only to fight 'unjustifiable discrimination wherever it exists', and accepted changes in social attitudes towards sexuality among other areas of individual behaviour and family structure. These *lacunae* would have serious consequences when measures to repeal Section 28 and equalise the age of consent were introduced. But it was not the Labour Government that moved first on the gay-rights agenda in 1997. Yet again, it was the European Court of Human Rights which, in July 1997, found that the UK age of consent for homosexual sex, lowered to eighteen in 1995 rather than the sixteen set for heterosexual sex, breached the Convention. In even greater contrast to the impression of support for gay rights which Labour had given in opposition, in the same month, the MoD announced that it would fight attempts by the Court in Strasbourg to overturn the ban on homosexuals serving in the armed forces. This was less surprising, looking at the new ministerial team at the MoD. John Reid, Minister for the Armed Forces, and John Spellar, his parliamentary under-secretary, had both voted with the Conservative government to retain the ban in 1996. George Robertson, defence secretary until 1999, also made clear his opposition to removing the ban.

Despite this unpromising, start gay-rights campaigners could be rightly confident that Labour's attitude would be substantially different from the Conservatives'. Apart from their opposition to discrimination of minority groups on human rights grounds, it was soon clear, and commented upon, that the Labour Government, and Parliamentary Party, was 'pinker' than in any previous parliament. Whilst the previous Conservative administration had seen its first openly gay MPs, Matthew Parris and Michael Brown, retreat from the Commons chamber to the press gallery, Labour was soon boasting its second openly lesbian MP, Angela Eagle. In contrast to the reception which Maureen

Colquhoun received in 1978, Eagle's announcement caused little stir, and she was promoted rapidly through the junior ministerial ranks, until being culled in a reshuffle in 2002. More insidious were mendacious claims made in some parts of the tabliod press about gay men, notably by Ann Atkins. She was proven guilty of making hysterical, false allegations about the health of homosexual men when she claimed in a column in The Sun in July that the life expectancy of gay men without HIV was a 'shocking' forty-three, and that they were seventeen times more likely than heterosexual men to be paedophiles. Both these claims were refuted by evidence provided to the Press Complaintes Commission, which ruled against Atkins and her paper's 'inadequate' clarification. The first claim was not only bizarre but also obviously wrong as it is impossible to assess, as a person's sexuality has never been recorded at death.[43]

This was in addition to several gay male MPs, who seemed to pass almost unnoticed. Chris Smith, Nick Brown and Peter Mandelson – inside the Cabinet – remained a different matter, however. The right-wing press, which found it difficult to pin any actual crime on any of these ministers as a result of their sexuality, comforted itself with a general paranoid attack on the 'gay' mafia now running Britain. This was bolstered by Norman Tebbit's interesting claim in 2000 that there were too many gay people in the Government, above a nominal two per cent 'quota' which he reckoned to be the homosexual population in the country.[44] This was a curious line of argument for a Conservative to make when the stock response from the right to arguments for greater representation for women and ethnic minorities was that anyone could represent the interests of anyone else among the electorate and that there was no need to reach proportionate 'quotas' for underrepresented groups.[45]

As influential on the progress which the gay-rights agenda made after 1997 as members of the Government itself was the strength and success of the pressure group Stonewall. It had been founded in the wake of the passage of Section 28 when members of the homosexual community came to the conclusion that better organisation was needed to confront anti-gay laws and wider attitudes within society. Although by the time Margaret Thatcher fell the high-water mark of this political atmosphere had perhaps passed, there was little indication that the tide was ebbing quickly under John Major. The lowering of the age of consent in 1995 was in large part a result of Stonewall's work with sympathetic Conservatives such as Edwina Currie, and Major's desire for a less punitive attitude towards minorities than was shown by many in his party. After 1997 Stonewall was able to forge much closer working relationships with personal ministerial contacts. Although it was nearly three years before significant reform began, these relationships paid dividends in terms of cooperation on law reform and changes to public services and employment rights. Stonewall curbed earlier support for some of the more direct moves towards combating discrimination, such as a single equalities bill, attracting criticism for its strategy from more radical gay-rights campaigners such as Peter Tatchell.

In July 1997 the European Commission on Human Rights rejected the British Government's claim that a higher age of consent for homosexual sex was justified to give greater protection to young men uncertain in their sexuality who might otherwise set themselves apart from society at such a young age. Ministers responded by announcing that an agreement had been reached with the individual appellants to defer the case until Parliament had been given an opportunity to decide the issue for itself. If an equal age of consent was agreed, the Government would bring forward its own legislation by the end of the following session. Ministers rejected calls for such an opportunity in the present session through an amendment to its own Crime and Disorder Bill. However, the Government's hand was forced when Labour newcomer Ann Keen tabled an amendment to the Crime and Disorder Bill in June 1998. The amendment was passed by 336 to 129, a majority of 207. Government ministers individually trooped through the 'aye' lobby in droves in support of the amendment, including Tony Blair and nine Cabinet ministers. Ministers who failed to vote included Ann Taylor and David Blunkett, who had both voted against equalisation in 1994. When the Bill reached the Lords, Baroness Young marshalled her troops across the House against the amendment. Denying that opposition to an equal age of consent was 'some religious right-wing plot', she confessed her own Anglican faith, and then pointed to the support of a wide range of religious dignitaries including Roman Catholics, Welsh nonconformists, the Chief Rabbi, the Secretary General of the Moslem Council of Britain, and 'many others who have no religious conviction', though none of these were individually named. In one of Young's other leitmotivs throughout her persistent battles to retain laws discriminating against homosexuals, she implored, 'I speak as a mother and a grandmother; we are family people.' The size of the majority, 290 to 122, larger than later Young victories, partly reflected the strength of her argument that the

Commons' decision had been taken after only a short debate, and other accompanying measures to strengthen protection of teenagers from older men's abuse of positions of trust were still under consideration by the Home Office. In order not to risk losing a valuable criminal justice bill through a game of 'ping-pong' between the two chambers (it had started its passage in the Lords so could not be subject to the Parliament Act), Jack Straw placated MPs by promising to honour the commitment which the Government had made to the European Commission of Human Rights, and would introduce the Bill in the Commons, which would mean that the Parliament Act could be applied if the Lords rejected it twice.

A Sexual Offences (Amendment) Bill duly had its second-reading debate in January 1999. The Bill proposed both to lower the age of homosexual consent to sixteen and implement new protections for all young people under eighteen from abuse by those in positions of trust. Straw sought to allay fears by confirming an earlier written assurance given to Labour traditionalist Stuart Bell that the Bill would not be a slippery slope towards an abyss of an age of consent at fourteen, gay marriage or adoption by gay couples (although, as will be seen below, adoption by single gay men was already legal).[46] By 2003 the Government might justifiably have thought to have reneged on one and a half of these promises, once the Adoption Act was passed and proposals for the civil registration of same-sex partnerships were published. The House gave the new Bill a second reading by 313 to 130 votes. In winding up the debate junior Home Office minister Paul Boateng warned peers that the Government 'did not intend for the will of Parliament [*sic*] to be thwarted again'.[47] Such puny threats, of course, did little to crush the determination of Young and her supporters. In the Lords she tabled an amendment to delay the vote on second reading for six months, which would kill the Bill for that session, arguing that it was not subject to the convention that the Lords do not reject government bills because it was not part of their election manifesto. Nor, she argued, was it a party political matter, because it was not a whipped vote, though this was subject to the opposite reasoning that the Commons majorities of over 180 on free votes made it more compelling that peers should at least consider the Bill.

The Bill was debated for seven and a half hours, with passionate speeches supporting equality on one side, and decrying abnormality and attacks on the family on the other. The most notable speech was the unprecedented intervention by new Labour peer, Lord Alli, who over the next two years became Young's alter ego, subtly helping to organise support of legislation extending gay rights. Unlike any peer before him, he admitted:

> *My Lords, many of your Lordships will know that I am openly gay. I am 34. I was gay when I was 24, when I was 21, when I was 20, when I was 19, when I was 18, when I was 17 and even when I was 16. I have never been confused about my sexuality. I have been confused about the way I am treated as a result of it. The only confusion lies in the prejudice shown, some of it tonight, and much of it enshrined in the law.*
>
> *Many noble Lords probably cannot understand what it is like to be gay and young. It means that one can be called anything: 'sick'; 'abnormal'; 'unnatural'; 'ruined'. Those words were used by colleagues tonight. The noble Earl, Lord Longford, and the noble Lords, Lord Selsdon and Lord Davies of Coity, used them all, and that is supposed to be acceptable.*

Young's amendment was carried by 222 votes to 146, a majority of 76. Of the doomed hereditary peers who voted, a total of seventy-nine voted for the amendment, without which the Bill would have continued its passage.[48] In July Straw had to announce that the Government would reintroduce the Bill in the following session, otherwise the deal struck with the Commission in Strasbourg would have fallen, and the two pending cases reopened.

An identical bill was reintroduced at the beginning of 2000. In the Commons second-reading debate on 10 February, a sense of déjà vu was relieved only by imaginative new attempts by Conservative MPs to embarrass the Government. Christopher Gill, MP for Ludlow, asked Straw:

> *The right hon. gentleman says that he is wholly committed to the Bill and to making buggery legal for people aged over 16. For the benefit of those of us who have led a sheltered life, will he describe the act of buggery so that the House, and the public who are listening to the debate, know exactly what we are talking about?*

Accusing Gill of ignorant prejudice not shared by the majority of people outside the chamber, Straw repeated earlier arguments about the inequality of the law, particularly the historic anomaly between male and female homosexual sex and the lack of protection which the existing law offered to teenage gay men. He also apprised the House of the decision of the Scottish Parliament two weeks earlier, by ninety votes to sixteen, to support the provisions of the Bill as they related to Scotland.

The failure of the Bill in the previous session had left a constitutional hangover for Westminster. Sexual offences had been devolved to Scotland, but the Scotland Bill had provided for the issue of the age of consent to be decided at Westminster before being handed over to the new Parliament. Ann Widdecombe, answering for the opposition, though speaking for herself, suggested not without logic that the real reason that Scotland was still to be included in the Bill, despite competence for sexual offences having moved to Edinburgh, was that in order to invoke the Parliament Act the Government had to introduce a bill identical to the one in the previous session. Challenged by Ben Bradshaw to say whether anyone had a choice over their sexuality, Widdecombe retorted, clearly speaking from experience, that all people, whatever their sexuality, had the choice whether or not to practise it. She acknowledged the previous verdict of MPs but, pointing to the recent Lords vote to retain Section 28, suggested that on these matters peers 'better represent the views of the majority of the people of this country than do the actions of the Government'. Building on this argument, Widdecombe argued that the Government proposal to repeal Section 28 completely changed the issue of the age of consent because now local authorities would be allowed to promote homosexuality, and 'many who are still at school – indeed, some who have not even taken their GCSE examinations – will be able to engage in such acts.' (How passing GSCE examinations would better equip youngsters for sexual activity was not clear.) The Bill was given a second reading by 263 votes to 102.[49]

Back in the Lords in April, Lord Williams, now Attorney General, once again presented the Bill to peers. Baroness Blatch tried to link the Government's handling of gay rights with prime-ministerial patronage and House of Lords reform, saying, 'This House is now to be packed with compliant Labour and Liberal peers who, no doubt, have all been subjected to and passed the Section 28 test.' Lord Carter, Government Chief Whip, responsible for interviewing all new peers taking the Labour whip, angrily demanded a retraction. Accusing the Government of an 'obsession with sex and sexuality', Blatch's central arguments again rested on the protection of sixteen- and seventeen-year-olds, particularly boys, less mature than girls, uncertain in their sexuality and vulnerable to exploitation by older men, making reference to recent child abuse scandals in north Wales. With a shudder she contemplated the buggery of sixteen-year-old girls. Labour peer Baroness Gould, quoting from a Home Office report, *Sexual Offending against Children,* said that opponents of the Bill demonstrated their discrimination against homosexuals by concentrating on the vulnerability of young men whereas, according to Home Office statistics, between sixty and seventy per cent of offences against children were committed against girls.

Lord Waddington, a former Home Secretary, returned to the issue of health and the greater risk of HIV infection for homosexuals, but he also suggested that young men who might be going through a 'passing phase' should be protected because 'we also know that there is little to suggest that those drawn into a homosexual lifestyle find lasting happiness and fulfilment.' He concluded:

> We have to call a halt to this madness. We all know the importance of the traditional family for the bringing up of children and for the stability of society. But the courts and Parliament are allowing its destruction, with completely unpredictable results for both society and civilisation. I will have none of it.

This usual invocation of 'family values' brought a forensic counter-argument from his Conservative colleague Lord Norton, who suggested:

> Homosexuals come from families, usually heterosexual ones, and frequently wish to create their own family relationships. Given that homosexuality is not a matter of choice, it is not a case of people threatening family values by choosing not to marry or by engaging in homosexual activities. Homosexuality is a state of being. Family values are precisely that: values. There is no inherent conflict between these two things. Indeed, if one really believed in the concept of family one would encourage homosexuals to form stable relationships and to be an integral part of wider family relationships, with their parents and so on, not seek to isolate them from society and the opportunity to create such relationships.

Interestingly Gareth Williams, winding up the debate, invoked the sacred family aura surrounding Tony Blair to defend the Government against accusations of having been captured by the 'homosexual lobby': 'To suggest that the Prime Minister – than whom no more devoted family man and father could be found – is in league with any sort of partisan lobby is to be in Cloud-cuckoo-land.'

On this occasion the Bill's opponents had no intention of rejecting the Bill outright again, as to do so would have meant the immediate use of the Parliament Act.[50] In fact the Bill was not considered again by peers until 13 November 2000, making completion of all its stages impossible, given the amendments which peers had tabled to the Bill. These were extensive, as Young had set out compromise proposals to equalise the age of consent at sixteen except for buggery, which would be legalised at 18 for both heterosexuals and homosexuals. Curiously, in Northern Ireland buggery of a woman would remain illegal, but would be legal between men at eighteen, and all other sex at the then existing consenting age of seventeen in Ulster. For Scotland, Young's amendments would tighten the law in respect of girls, where buggery was already legal at sixteen, by raising the age to eighteen, as in the rest of the UK. Lord Alli described these as wrecking amendments, and turning to Young, stated:

> *The noble Baroness does not have a monopoly on concern for children. Does she really believe that all those in another place and in this Chamber who support the Bill and the organisations which welcome this reform are of the view that it will lead to the abuse of children? That suggestion is … offensive.*

Nevertheless peers supported Young's main amendment by 205 votes to 144.[51] The end of the session meant that the Commons Speaker, Michael Martin, invoked the Parliament Act for the first time since the War Crimes Bill had been rejected by the Lords in 1990. The Sexual Offences (Amendment) Act came into force in January 2001.

The meeting of minds between Labour's leading spokesmen on defence and the military establishment on the issue of the ban on gays in the armed forces defied both wider opinion in the Labour Party and the European Court of Human Rights.[51] Labour ministers did not demur from the service chiefs' arguments that to remove the ban would have a detrimental effect on morale. As the case of four sacked personnel at Strasbourg moved nearer a judgment in 1999, John Spellar, clearly sensing the standard blocking response would no longer work, attempted to kick the issue into the long grass by saying any review would have to wait until 2001 when the next armed forces bill was due. Within months this strategy was in tatters. As with the age of consent, the Government faced a pending case at Strasbourg, and in September the Court delivered a blunt rejection of its case. The judgment forced a swift *volte-face* as George Robertson, in consultation with Blair, announced that all pending inquiries into homosexuality in the armed forces, amounting to about sixty, would be suspended while the Government decided its next move.[53]

Conservative and military fury at the news was predictable. What was more difficult to understand was why a government committed to addressing 'unnecessary discrimination', backed by a party overwhelmingly in favour of the change, with a three-figure majority in the Commons and in the sure knowledge that the ban breached the ECHR and would be overturned in Strasbourg, still clung so long to the status quo, meekly parroting the words of the military establishment, despite there being no firm evidence to back claims that the ban was essential to morale. When the ban was eventually lifted in January 2000, the new Defence Secretary, Geoff Hoon, played strongly to the views of the defence establishment by rationalising the move as dictated by the legal constraints of the ECHR, saying, 'We cannot choose the decisions we implement. The status quo was no longer an option.' He refused to be drawn by Labour MPs applauding the move into making a case based on equality or gay rights, or in the words of former Armed Forces Minister Nicholas Soames, these 'lunatic politically correct nostrums'. Iain Duncan Smith, still Tory defence spokesman, blustered about the wisdom of military opinion supporting the ban, but looked constructively on the operation of the new code, which, as one Labour MP observed, a Conservative Government would probably also have instituted faced with the same judgment from Strasbourg.[54]

The transformation from a Canute-like policy to the swift and trouble-free implementation in 2000 of a new code of conduct made the previous position of the Government and military establishment look rather foolish. In the words of one official, 'We are pleased. Generally people have taken a pragmatic view of the change. We had one policy that was right until earlier this year. Now we have another.' That might be seen as the impartial civil service at its best, or the cynical world of Sir Humphrey's descendants. The MoD's own assessment of the first months of the new regime seemed unrelated to the department responsible for the *status quo ante*. The report, leaked to the *Observer*, concluded that

the revised policy on homosexuality had no discernible impact, either positive
or negative, on recruitment ... There is widespread acceptance of the new
policy. It has not been an issue of great debate. In fact, there has been a marked
lack of reaction. Generally there has been a mature, pragmatic approach which
allowed the policy to succeed. The change in policy has been hailed as a solid
achievement.[55]

The Labour Party under Neil Kinnock had pledged itself at the 1992 election to repeal Section 28. Before the 1997 election, Jack Straw, as Shadow Home Secretary, told a public meeting organised by Stonewall that Labour would repeal the section, although such a pledge was absent from the 1997 manifesto. Jack Cunningham, who during the debates on the 1988 Local Government Bill and Section 28 was Labour spokesman, assured the Stonewall tenth-anniversary dinner that the Government was committed to repeal, saying that 'Section 28 was wrong in 1987. It is wrong in 1999.'[56]

Repeal was included as Clause 68 of a long local government Bill in 1999 which reformed the constitution of local councils. Even before any debate, its symbolic significance had been made plain by the sacking and defection of MP, Shaun Woodward in December 1999. Refusing to agree to follow the whip against the repeal of Section 28, he had been sacked by pager when he failed to respond to an ultimatum to fall into line. After secret negotiations with Downing Street through sympathetic Labour MPs, Woodward crossed the floor of the House. Repeal of Section 28 was debated in committee in the Lords on 7 February 2000, the same day that David Blunkett published revised guidelines on sex education, designed to placate those concerned about the protection of children from homosexuals. Cajoled once again by Young, peers rallied to the defence of the Section. Citing correspondence from teenagers who had been bullied because of their sexuality and felt they had no protection, Alli linked the 'morality of hate' of the defenders of the Section to that of the nailbomber who had recently taken three lives in an attack on a gay pub in Soho, as well as attacks against the black and Asian communities in Brixton and Brick Lane. Lord Harris of Haringey, drawing on bitter experience from the 1980s in north London, explained that 'one cannot teach someone to be lesbian or gay by a video, or even by one or two lessons in a classroom. My goodness, how wonderful the maths, English and science results would be in this country if it was that easy to inculcate things into our children.' The Bishop of Blackburn tabled an amendment to substitute a strong duty to promote marriage as the fundamental building block of society and family life, and government minister Lord Whitty agreed to come back with a suitable amendment to the Learning and Skills Bill to deal with revised sex education guidance. Such an amendment was inserted to the effect that children should be taught about 'marriage and stable relationships as key building blocks of community and society'. Nevertheless, Young's amendment passed by 210 to 165 votes.[57] When repeal was later dropped this provision remained in the Bill and read that Section 28 should not 'prevent the headteacher or governing body of a maintained school, or a teacher employed by a maintained school, from taking steps to prevent any form of bullying'.[58]

Following the vote Blair hit back at demands from William Hague to drop the Government's plans by saying that it would listen to concerns about the protection of children from unsuitable materials, but that he intended to 'take on' those who were expressing anti-gay feelings. The Tory leader accused the Government of riding roughshod over the beliefs of the public: '[Section 28] is about tolerance being a two-way thing in this country. It is about the tolerance demanded by the mainstream majority that its views and values be respected.'[59] However, the leaking of a memo by Blair, written in April that year, shortly before Section 28 returned to the Lords, underlined the Government's hesitation. Blair included the Government's treatment of 'gay issues' within the area of family policy where they were considered 'weak' by voters.[60] Another lesson lay north of the border, where the new Scottish Executive had just survived a bruising battle to repeal the Section, against the type of tabloid media onslaught which had New Labour spin doctors in London running for Middle England.

The Scottish Parliament, supporters of repeal, faced down a highly vocal, well-financed minority of religious groups supported by Brian Souter, the millionaire owner of the transport company Stagecoach. The course of the debate in Scotland revealed profound differences of political culture in the post-devolution world, whilst repeating exactly the same arguments as those south of the border. The new Parliament's legislative process was radically different from that at Westminster. Unicameral, there would be no question of the will of elected representatives being frustrated by soi-disant noble guardians of the nation's morals. The first vote on the issue on 10 February 2000 came three days after peers at Westminster rejected repeal for the first time, and on the same day that they threw out the Bill to equalise the age of consent at sixteen.[61] The attitude of the Scottish Executive towards repeal was symptomatic of its wider approach to issues of social reform and showed a willingness, even a determination, to diverge from the Labour Government in London, as a demonstration of the power of devolution. This did not prevent it consulting on the proposal, something which the Government in London had not done. This produced over 2,300 responses, eighty per cent of which supported repeal, including the same range of charities and teaching unions which had done so in England and Wales. Despite the consultation, groups opposed to repeal claimed that 'the Scottish public has been kept completely in ignorance. We don't think that's democratic.'[62] As a result of the consultation and the controversy in the media, the Executive moved to compromise. When the Ethical Standards in Public Life Bill was published it had been amended, and now effectively killed two birds with one stone. It repealed Section 2A (as Section 28 was numbered in the Scottish legislation) and proposed a new duty on local authorities to promote 'the value of stable family life in a child's development' and 'have regard to each child's age, understanding and stage of development'.

The Keep the Clause campaign and its supporters condemned the proposal for putting homosexual relations on the same level as marriage. Even Alex Salmond, the leader of the Scottish Nationalist Party, which supported repeal, warned that the new section was too 'woolly' and would cause problems in the future.[63] The supporters of Section 2A were given a boost when the Conservatives won a by-election to the Scottish Parliament in Ayr, their first by-election win in the country since 1973. Jack Irvine, head of the Keep the Clause campaign, declared that 'Donald Dewar did not listen to the people of Scotland and his party paid the price at Ayr.' Even Labour ministers admitted that the election had been dominated by continual discussion of the issue by Keep the Clause, with UK minister George Foukes accusing them of spending more money than all the other candidates put together.[64] The weekend before the poll both Blair and Dewar made categorical commitments to repeal at the Scottish Labour conference. Wendy Alexander made a staunch defence of the Executive's programme, contrasting a 'a celebrity millionaire's misguided campaign [with] our campaign to lift millions of children out of poverty, Labour's "true moral cause".[65] However, there was no direct evidence that the seat was won by the Tories because of the Section 2A issue. It had been a Tory-held seat for a hundred years until 1997, and the Conservative share of the vote did not increase, while their total vote declined. On the back of what was perceived as a fillip for pro-section campaigners, Souter pledged to fund a national referendum on the issue, saying that it would 'force the Government to fully explain their policy and create the climate for a proper debate, for and against repeal'. The plan was 'commended' by David McLetchie, the Scottish Tory leader.[66]

In April 2000 the Bill came before the Edinburgh Parliament for approval in broad principle. The SNP renewed its calls for statutory protection for children to assuage the concerns about repeal of the section, which it maintained was 'despicable'. The Bill was approved by 103 votes to sixteen.[67] The ballot on Keep the Clause's 'referendum' was held in May, and the results were announced at the end of the month. Of the 3.4 million ballot slips sent out 1.2 million were returned, 86.6 per cent of which supported the Section. Three hundred thousand papers had not been delivered as the 1999 register which was used was out of date. The Scottish Executive condemned the exercise as an abuse of democracy and invalid, given the fact that two thirds of people ignored the poll (though a thirty-four per cent turnout in an official election or referendum was not exactly unheard of at the beginning of the twenty-first century).[68] The day before the result was announced MSPs had rejected an amendment tabled by a Labour supporter of repeal, Michael McMahon, to insert the importance of marriage into the new clause.[69] However, in the wake of the poll result, and with the Scottish tabloid media in full support of retention, the Executive beat a hasty retreat. Their new proposal did indeed insert 'the responsibilities of parenthood and marriage', a compromise which was acceptable to all sides, and which might indeed have been reached months earlier, avoiding the perception, if not the reality, of having been forced into a climb-down by Souter's independent referendum.[70] On 21 June the Parliament took its final vote on the Bill, and the Section was repealed by ninety-nine votes to seventeen. The SNP spokeswoman, Nicola Sturgeon, made much of this achievement for Scotland, saying, 'A discriminatory and shameful piece of legislation that was imposed on Scotland by Westminster will today be repealed by the Scottish Parliament ahead of other parts of the UK. That says something about the state of Scotland that we can all be proud of.'[71] This achievement, not that the SNP would have been too upset at this, came at some political cost to the new Executive, and personally to Alexander, the minister most responsible for the measure.

David Blunkett's new sex education guidelines and the Learning and Skills Bill were far more robust in defence of marriage than the compromise which passed in Edinburgh. However, when Section 28 returned to the House of Lords in July 2000, peers again rejected it by forty-three votes,[72] despite the recent creation of thirty more Labour and Liberal Democrat peers. With the Blair memo leak just before the vote, the Government's commitment was seriously questioned. Ministers decided to drop repeal for the time being to prevent the Local Government Bill holding up legislation into the spill-over session in October.

Following William Hague's resignation, Section 28 loomed large in the battle to succeed him. During the second round of voting among MPs Michael Portillo faced an embarrassing retraction on the issue when, after suggesting he would review the party's position on Section 28, the response forced him to deny that this was part of his campaign. This fumble was seen as an important reason for failing to win over extra MPs.[73] There were also fierce attacks in the *Daily Mail* and other tabloids on Portillo's policy on gay rights, and by implication his own sexuality. One of the two candidates to be put before the whole Conservative membership in the run-off, Iain Duncan Smith, had clearly learned nothing from this episode. At the beginning of September he signalled a possible softening of the Conservatives' position on Section 28, completely against his right-wing credentials and record. In an interview with former Tory MP Gyles Brandreth in the *Sunday Telegraph*, Duncan Smith suggested:

> We as a party have become identified with what we dislike and hate rather than what we like. Clause 28, I accept, has about it a totem which is about saying to a group in the community, 'We actually rather dislike you'... So yes, I'd look at it again.[74]

The outcry from the Tory right at this apostasy, and the hoots of derision from the Tory left at the bungled opportunism, forced a hasty retreat. The following day Duncan Smith reassured members of the Party that he would never repeal Section 28.[75] The row within the party simmered on until the Government's next attempt at repeal along with other 'totemic' issues, which led the new Party Chairman, Teresa May, to describe her party as 'the nasty party'. By the autumn of 2002 it was clear that a decision on what tactics to adopt would soon be necessary.

Two related events unlocked the path to repeal of Section 28 for Labour, both originating in the Conservative Party. The first was Duncan Smith's disastrous decision to impose a three-line whip on a backbench Labour amendment to the Adoption and Children Bill in May 2002, extending eligibility to unmarried couples, whether gay or straight, a vote on which Labour imposed no whip. This was seen as draconian and unprecedented for what was generally treated as a 'conscience' issue. Three Tory frontbenchers failed to vote and Duncan Smith's already weak authority over his party was further damaged. The Lords, once again roused by Baroness Young, defeated the measure, but the Bill did not come before MPs again until the beginning of November, two months after Young had died following a prolonged illness.[76] Conservatives were thus faced with the twin prospect of another damaging split in the Commons, and the mainstay of their moral leadership in the Lords removed. Further rows on gay rights and women at the party's annual conference in Bournemouth heightened the tension. Then, the same day as the Commons vote on adoption was to take place, John Bercow, one of the three shadow ministers who had just intimated that they would once again fail to support a three-line whip on the issue, resigned in protest from the front bench. The vote was lost, and two days later the Lords failed to rally to Baroness O'Caithan, the Tory peer who had picked up the standard of traditional family values, almost literally, from the deathbed of Baroness Young.[77]

Labour's less confrontational approach, which had worked so well over adoption, was now deployed over Section 28. Repeal was not included in the Queen's Speech, but when the Local Government Bill received its second-reading debate in the new year, Labour MP Kali Mountford announced that she would table an amendment to that effect. In a characteristic piece of staging, Bercow's denunciation of Section 28 was visibly supported by Portillo and other Tory modernisers.[78] Party spokesmen immediately sounded a retreat. It was announced that Tory MPs would have a free vote on this amendment, but that the Deputy Leader, David Davis, would table the party's own amendment based on an alternative to Section 28, which an internal working group had been devising, to give more protection to children by offering parents a veto on any materials to be used in schools.[79] Mountford's amendment was approved in committee, and when the Bill came back to the House in March, Tory divisions were laid bare. Portillo, Bercow and the modernisers supported Mountford. The official party compromise was duly voted down, though it was supported by Ann

Widdecombe, Duncan Smith and a large group of frontbenchers. David Wilshire, the Conservative MP for Spelthorne, who had tabled the original amendment which became Section 28, defended his footnote in history, saying, 'I tabled Section 28 because there were various councils that were wasting huge sums of public money to achieve social change that the overwhelming number of people in this country did not want.'[80]

In July retentionists continued to feel the loss of Young keenly. Despite Baroness Blatch's attempt to amend the Bill by using the Tory proposal for parental ballots on sex education material, peers rejected this by 180 to 130 votes.[81]

In 1998 Jack Straw set up a Home Office committee under Betty Moxon to review the sexual offences laws. Two years later the Committee produced a seminal document, *Setting the Boundaries*, which for the first time proposed that sexual offences legislation should no longer distinguish between heterosexual and homosexual offences in terms of what was deemed appropriate and inappropriate, and therefore criminal, either in public or in private. This was a major departure from previous practice, including the Wolfenden Report, which had sought to identify and criminalise only that behaviour which was considered harmful, whilst still giving public protection from certain homosexual practices which it was thought were widely abhorred. *Setting the Boundaries* thus achieved the comprehensive reform of sexual offences legislation which had been discussed within government since the 1960s under a Labour Party committed to equality and non-discrimination between gay and straight sex. Ministers still acknowledged that many people might not approve of certain sexual acts or lifestyles, on religious or other grounds, but that the law should no longer criminalise these. Whilst most of the Government and its supporters, though not all of them, strongly believed in this philosophy, the wider legal context in which the UK was finally being forced to honour its obligations under the European Convention was still key. If successive administrations had been relatively relaxed about decisions in Strasbourg overturning law and policy at home, Labour's incorporation of the convention into UK law as the Human Rights Act meant that all new laws had to be certified as compatible with them. Though judges could not strike down laws which were ruled to be in conflict with the Act, some ministers, notably David Blunkett, were unhappy with the challenges which the Act posed to the political discretion of ministers.

Shortly after *Setting the Boundaries* was published in 2000, Blunkett took over stewardship of the Home Office following the general election. Unexpectedly, given his reputation for illiberalism and opposition to an equal age of consent, Blunkett moved within eighteen months to implement the new framework for sexual offences which the report recommended. In November 2002 he published a White Paper with the even more reassuring title *Protecting the Public*. These proposals comprised three main themes – child protection, rape (including the definition of consent) and eliminating discrimination on grounds of sex or sexuality. Although the rape and consent provisions caused much controversy when a bill was eventually introduced, by far the most contentious section was that which dealt with sex in public places, or the 'cottaging' laws under the 1956 Sexual Offences Act. This Act specifically criminalised buggery or gross indecency between men 'in a lavatory to which the public have, or are permitted to have access, whether on payment or otherwise'.[82] When the Bill was published, the junior Home Office minister Hilary Benn attempted to allay the fears of those who thought this would legalise sex in public. Writing to the *Daily Telegraph*, he insisted that the Bill would not 'permit people to have sex in public lavatories. The offence of outraging public decency will continue to protect the public from activity that causes or is likely to cause alarm, distress or harassment, including obtrusive sexual behaviour in lavatories.'[83] What it was attempting to decriminalise was unobtrusive sexual behaviour in public lavatories. In another press report, Benn was quoted as saying, 'If the cubicle door was open then clearly an offence had taken place. If it's closed that's different.'[84] During second reading in the Lords, Lord Falconer, the government minister in charge of the Bill, agreed to look at the clause again. Baroness Noakes, the Conservative spokeswoman, welcomed this move, saying that what people heard might offend them as much as what they might see. She added that the implication in the Bill that sexual activity in a private garden would be an offence, whilst the same activity inside a private house with 'the windows wide open and the lights on' would not be, might open up 'a whole new dimension to disputes between neighbours'.[85] Such legal absurdities, and fears that cottaging would become more difficult to prosecute under the Bill, forced the Government to drop the proposal, instead relying on existing public-order offences, including outraging public decency, and allowing prosecutions to take place in magistrates' courts. This approach was condemned by gay-rights groups and some lawyers, who said that relying on an eighteenth-century legal concept would cause problems in interpretation, including as it did 'all open lewdness, grossly scandalous behaviour, and whatever openly outrages decency'.[86] Peers were not satisfied with the Government's assurances on this point and voted in June for a Conservative amendment banning all sex in public toilets, whether heterosexual or homosexual. Proposing the restriction, Noakes said:

> *Sexual offences in a public lavatory can never ever be permitted. I believe the vast majority of the public agree with that. Public lavatories have become no-go areas. Parents are afraid to send their children in alone, many public lavatories have had to be closed, and the time has come that the public get the protection it deserves and which the Government promised.*[87]

While the Government said the Conservative amendment was unworkable, Lord Alli complained that outlawing such consensual sex was a mistake when cultural pressures forced some men to seek sex in such a way. However, peers were given an important boost before the Bill came before MPs, when the Commons Home Affairs Select Committee also recommended that sex in public toilets be outlawed.[88]

If the main external pressure on the British Government to extend equality came from Strasbourg and the obligations under the ECHR, employment law was governed by the European Union. Not that one would have noticed the difference from the coverage of human rights and Europe in the right-wing press, particularly the *Daily Mail*. An EU directive published in 2000 by the European Commission, known as the 'Article 13 Directive', covered, in addition to sexuality, religious discrimination, age and disability. The first two came into force in December 2003, the latter two would do so in 2006. Despite the accusation in some parts of the media that this was another politically correct imposition by Brussels, the provisions had been agreed by ministers, including the fresh-faced Labour Government, in June 1997 at the Amsterdam Summit.

Once the European Commission's directive was accepted, the Government published draft regulations to implement it in October 2002. They covered gay men, lesbians and bisexuals. Transsexual people's employment protection had been strengthened by new regulations under the Sex Discrimination Act in 1999, which was forced on the Government after a successful application to the

European Court of Justice in 1996,[89] although groups representing transsexuals remained concerned about the coverage and operation of the new rules.[90] The new proposals put discrimination on grounds of sexual orientation on the same footing as for gender and race in most areas. However, two strands of policy remained particularly contentious. The first related to rights under occupational pension schemes. The Government argued that the directive was 'without prejudice to national laws on marital status and the benefits dependent thereon'. However, as will be seen with the Government's proposals for partnership rights, by 2003 it was arguing that same-sex couples should not be treated in the same way as unmarried opposite-sex couples, because they were not in a position to marry. Trade unions and gay rights campaigners suggested that fears over the cost of implementing the change, rather than a moral objection, were the real reason for resisting granting full pension rights under the regulations. However, as the TUC argued, the gradual fall over several decades in the proportion of married pension-holders resulted in funds having to pay out much less than was budgeted for, despite the fact that all contributors paid in exactly the same, regardless of their marital status. In a spectacular case of 'do as I say and not as I do', MPs voted to grant pension rights to their own unmarried partners, same sex and opposite sex.

One of the areas of persistent discrimination which the implementation of Article 13 highlighted, against couples with respect to pension rights, was a central part of the Government's next step towards equality of treatment between heterosexuals and homosexuals. In June 2003 it published a White Paper on the registration of civil partnerships of same-sex couples. This was in large part the result of the work of one minister, Barbara Roche, who announced plans for a scheme in December 2002, encouraged by parliamentarians across the political spectrum, and supported by the work of Stonewall. Its director, Angela Mason, became director of the Government's Women and Equality Unit at the Department of Trade and Industry in 2002, shortly before Roche was sacked in the 2003 reshuffle. The issue of partnership rights had been rising up the agenda, following two cases in which gay men were barred from succeeding to their dead partner's tenancy. In the first, in October 1999, the House of Lords upheld an appeal by Michael Fitzpatrick against a private housing association, granting him succession to the assured tenancy,[91] and in 2002 the Appeal Court ruled a resident spouse could include a same-sex partner under the Rent Act

1977. Mr Mendoza had lived with his partner for thirty years, but when he died, his landlord refused to grant him tenancy. The court ruled that the Act's wording should be interpreted to include Mr Mendoza's partner.

A bill introduced by Lord Lester, a human-rights barrister and former special adviser to Roy Jenkins, in the Lords proposed creating such a system both for gay couples and cohabiting heterosexual couples. The Government was not prepared to concede a new status for the latter category, fearing, as did conservatives, that this would weaken the attractions of marriage. Conservatives were not, however, exclusively hostile to partnership rights for gay couples. In a mark of how far even they had travelled, Baroness Buscombe revealed that she had already produced a policy paper advocating this.[92] Other conservatives claimed the rights proposed could be achieved through piecemeal reform of welfare systems and other laws, and creating civil partnership rights would somehow pollute hetero-sexual marriage or, in Melanie Phillips' words, 'would bring marriage into disrepute by the promiscuity which gay people themselves concede is a signifi-cant element of homosexuality'[93]

A number of local schemes for civil registration of same-sex partnerships had recently been established. The highest profile, not surprisingly, was that initiated by the new Mayor of London, Ken Livingstone. Similar schemes were soon operated across the country by councils including Swansea, Leeds, Bournemouth, Manchester, Liverpool, Brighton and Hove, Bath, Devon, Somerset and Caerphilly. The media inevitably portrayed these as 'gay marriages', though they conferred no legal rights (nor, as New Labour would insist, responsibilities) on couples. However, they could be used to encourage employers and landlords to recognise a couple's status.[94] The Government was at pains to point out that their new proposals did not represent a form of gay marriage, something which Jack Straw had given categorical assurance that the Government would not introduce. The civil partnership consultation document suggested that the scheme

would encourage stable relationships, which are an important asset to the community as a whole. It would reduce the likelihood of relationship breakdown, which has a proven link to both physical and mental health ... Strengthening adult couple relationships not only benefits the couples themselves, but also other relatives they support and care for and, in particular, their children, as they grow up and become the couples, parents and carers of tomorrow.[95]

Interestingly it linked the scheme with *Supporting Families*, which in 1998 had shied away from any inclusion of same-sex couples as a form of family unit. One motive for the change of heart was a possible reduction in social security payments. More widely, the Government hoped that such a partnership scheme would have an effect on social attitudes, 'increasing the social acceptance of same-sex relationships, reducing homophobia and discrimination and building a safer, more tolerant society'. Ministers also hoped it would also encourage, countering Phillips and others, long-term committed relationships among same-sex couples.

The effect on Conservatives of the introduction of the Civil Partnerships Bill in 2004 was profound. While Baroness O'Cathain climbed the barricades against this further extension of gay rights, Michael Howard – the ministerial midwife to Section 28 – announced a free vote, and his personal support, for the Bill with a significant softening of his party's attitude towards the family:

> *The family remains the most immediate and important group within which people share responsibility for one another's well-being. But families are changing. Not all conform to the traditional pattern. I continue to believe that the conventional marriage and family is the best environment within which to bring up children. But many couples now choose not to marry. And more and more same-sex couples want to take on the shared responsibilities of a committed relationship. It is in all our interests to encourage the voluntary acceptance of such shared responsibilities. But in some instances the State actively discourages it. That should change, and I will support the Government's Civil Partnerships Bill that makes some important reforms.*[96]

However, O'Cathain was not ready to lie down because of her new leader's moral apostasy. She tabled an amendment in the Lords to include other relationships such as carers. Stonewall was livid at what was seen as a wrecking amendment, although Peter Tatchell of OutRage! saw it as a step towards giving partnership rights to unmarried heterosexual couples – not how Conservative peers viewed it. The Government vowed to reverse the decision in the Commons, but gay-rights campaigners managed to exact swifter revenge on O'Cathain. In what its director, Ben Summerskill, described as 21st-century ethical consumerism, Stonewall organised a 'Boycott BA' campaign to oust O'Cathain from the board of British Airways, well known for its large number of gay employees and gay-friendly employment practices. In Summerskill's words, 'just as black people wouldn't visit a restaurant where staff are known for their racist attitudes, gay people aren't keen on using businesses where staff or senior figures hold offensive views.' Just days after O'Cathain had been re-elected to the board for her last year, British Airways announced her early departure before the end of the year. O'Cathain claimed the move was unconnected to the campaign.[97] Once again, however, the power of consumer pressure was seen to have reaped a reward, just as commercial freedom to open gay businesses had, over the years, proved as powerful in forging a gay community and changing attitudes as changes in the legal status of homosexuals. Interestingly the Scottish Parliament, following its own consultation on the plans voted over whelmingly to allow Westminster to take the legislative lead, provided any amendments with significant implications for Scotland could be brought back to Edinburgh for approval.

One small group of people whose right to marry was also being recognised by government for the first time was Britain's 5,000 transsexuals. In not conceding this right, Britain yet again found itself effectively isolated in Europe, this time with only Ireland, Albania and Andorra for company. Although employment protection had been extended to transsexuals in 1999, the right to change the sex on their birth certificate, which would be necessary for someone to marry legally under their reassigned sex, posed both moral and practical difficulties which the Government found more difficult to overcome. The corollary of refusing transsexuals this right was, of course, that such people could, unlike everyone else, actually marry people of their own sex, or be sent to a prison for the opposite sex, where medical treatment could even be refused, having damaging physical and psychological consequences.

Over three years from 2000 the Government gradually caved in to pressure from campaigners and their parliamentary supporters, but more particularly with the result of one case, that of Elizabeth Bellinger, a woman transsexual married for twenty years, who began a campaign to have the relationship officially recognised. When government proposals were eventually announced at the end of 2003, the Home Office was clearly aware of the sensitivities of pursuing this policy for benefit to a relatively small group of people. One official was quoted as saying, 'Obviously it is not exactly mainstream, but it shows that when we talk about equality, we mean it.'[98] However, transsexuals faced continuing difficulties and discrimination in society, due partly to attitudes, but fundamentally because of the absence of a clear cut-off point when they could be considered to have changed sex. This was highlighted the same month that the Government published its draft Bill, when a court ruled that a pub landlord was entitled to bar a group of women transsexuals because one of them tried to use the toilet and they were upsetting his customers. The publican was reported as saying, 'You shouldn't have male genitalia in the ladies' lavatories. It's as simple as that.' Given the tendency for women's toilets to use cubicles rather than urinals, how he could be sure male genitalia had been taken into the ladies was not clear.[99] However, the Government soon introduced legislation which reached the statute book as the Gender Recognition Act in July 2004.

*

By the end of the 1990s it was becoming clear that the legislative framework which had been constructed on the principles in the Warnock Report was being outstripped by the pace of technological advance in genetics, embryology and fertility treatment. In 2000 the first sequence of the human genome was published, and the complete genome was released in 2003. Political responses to these developments showed a remarkable capacity and willingness to grasp the nettle of even the most controversial ethical dilemmas where the speed of change demanded it, in startling contrast to the tendency over many generations to avoid most issues of morality if at all possible. In May 2002 Tony Blair delivered a speech to the Royal Society entitled, profoundly, 'Science Matters'. Calling for an 'evidence-based approach', the Prime Minister exhorted both scientists and the public to develop a 'mature compact' over debates about the ethics of scientific advance:

> *The fundamental distinction is between a process where science tells us the facts and we make a judgement, and a process where* a priori *judgements effectively constrain scientific research. We have the right to judge but we also have a right to know. A priori judgement branded Darwin a heretic; science proved his tremendous insight. So let us know the facts; then make the judgement as to how we use or act on them.*

The choice of Darwin to illustrate this point was ironic, given the Department for Education's continuing funding for a school in the north-east of England where creationist teaching meant that public money was being used essentially to brand Darwin a heretic. Nonetheless, Blair made a strong defence of stem cell research despite his Catholic leanings, which chimed with polling evidence suggesting that Catholics were only marginally less likely than others to support stem cell research.[100] This underlined the main difference with the other issue which Blair was keen to pursue, GM technology. On stem cell research he was preaching to the converted. Only a small minority, albeit a vocal and influential one, wanted it outlawed. Similarly, the recent violence against facilities conducting medical research on animals prompted Blair strongly to defend such therapeutic research. Again, the public agreed, given the potential medical benefits. But on genetically modified foods, no matter how much he talked the Blairite language of reason and partnership, the public continued stubbornly to reject the technology. The advent of the use of stem cells, unspecialised cells at an early stage of development which are capable of dividing into many different types of cell, with the potential to develop new treatments for disease, was a particularly controversial development. Within government there was widespread concern that to hamper scientific research in this area would mean lessening the chances of finding important new medical cures for diseases like Parkinson's, Alzheimer's and muscular dystrophy. As in the GM debate there was a fear that if Britain were to impose overly tight restrictions on research, cutting-edge scientists and their work would simply relocate elsewhere. However, unlike the GM debate, the human ethical implications raised by genetic research were recognised to touch people at a more visceral, if no more rational, level.

Although the 1990 Human Fertilisation and Embryology Act had clearly outlawed human reproductive cloning which involved the nuclear substitution of a cell in an embryo, and permitted embryo research in strictly limited circumstances for therapeutic purposes, the technique of complete nuclear replacement (CNR) had not then been developed. This technique, pioneered in Scotland by scientists at the Roslin Institute, led to the birth in January 1997 of Dolly the Sheep, the first cloned mammal. Fears that human reproductive cloning were just around the corner were fuelled by claims from Italian and American scientists about their intentions and progress towards this goal.

The Blair Government reaffirmed its complete opposition to human reproductive cloning and committed itself to giving this the force of primary legislation, while wanting to allow therapeutic cloning. At the end of 1996 the Conservative Government had set up the Human Genetics Advisory Commission (HGAC) along with a similar body on genetic testing, which were subsumed into the single Human Genetics Commission in 1999 under the chairmanship of Helena Kennedy QC, the leading human-rights barrister and Labour peer who was rapidly developing a reputation as a leading critic of the Home Office under Jack Straw and David Blunkett. Such permanent commissions were one important response to the increasing pace of technological change. The traditional government response since the nineteenth century of establishing Royal Commissions or other ad hoc inquiries was no longer responsive enough. In the case of embryology research, a Warnock Committee every twenty years would no longer do. Harnessed to this move for greater capacity for investigation of science and technology was an urgent need to restore public confidence in government action in this area following the BSE disaster and other food-related failures of public policy. Greater openness in government had begun under the Major Government, but after 1997 new rules were introduced, and public bodies began to develop a culture of greater and more meaningful consultation either with users or with the wider public.

It was a report from the House of Lords Science and Technology Committee in March 1997 on the implications of Dolly the Sheep that led to the Government's reaffirmation of its opposition to human reproductive cloning. A joint report by the Human Fertilisation and Embryology Authority (HFEA) and the HGAC considered that the 1990 Act was sufficiently robust to prevent human reproductive cloning and covered CNR. However, it suggested the Government might introduce primary legislation specifically to outlaw human reproductive cloning, as well as consider extending the regulations under the 1990 Act to cover new techniques like CNR not envisaged when the legislation was passed. To this end Sir Liam Donaldson, the Chief Medical Officer, chaired another committee to investigate the potential for new techniques. Their report, *Stem Cell Research: Medical Progress with Responsibility*, concurred with the previous inquiries' support for stem cell research, perhaps not surprisingly given the close working relationships between all the regulatory bodies and other professionals involved. The Government accepted its recommendations.

This led to an application for a judicial review by the Pro-Life Alliance, led by the irrepressible Bruno and Josephine Quintavalle. They argued that because CNR had not been developed when the 1990 Act was passed, this Act and any regulations under it could not be considered to cover, or later extended to cover, the new technique. In November 2001 the High Court accepted this view, which, if upheld, would have meant that all human cloning, whether reproductive or therapeutic, was outside the regulation of the law.[101] In response the Government introduced an emergency two-clause bill to ban human reproductive cloning which was rushed through Parliament effectively in two days and became law at the beginning of December. The legislation was supported across both chambers, though with serious misgivings about the speed with which the Government had moved, guillotining debate to one afternoon in the Commons. Liberal Democrat MP Paul Tyler, invoking memories of the Dangerous Dogs Act and Football Disorder Act, warned:

We must all face the fact that Parliament has a bad reputation for legislating in haste and repenting at leisure. In successive governments, Home Office Ministers especially have bamboozled the House into thinking that speed is more important than security of outcome. Each time we are told that it is an emergency.

There was no indication that any scientists would, or could, exploit the theoretical legal loophole within days or weeks, making such frenzied parliamentary scrutiny unnecessary. This was caricatured by Ann Widdecombe (who opposed therapeutic cloning as well as reproductive cloning): 'The Government are not genuinely afraid that, as we race against the clock to debate the Bill in the next five hours, a scientist will carry out a specific procedure unless we have decided by 7 p.m. that he cannot.'

Hazel Blears, Junior Health Minister, admitted that media coverage of recent events had contributed towards their precipitate response.[102] In the Lords, peers were particularly peeved because the Government was not only second-guessing the Court of Appeal, but acting in advance of a report from the House of Lords Science and Technology Committee on stem cell research, which was eventually published in February 2002.[103] In January 2002 the High Court decision was overturned by the Court of Appeal, but in June the Pro-Life Alliance was given leave to appeal to the House of Lords. In March 2003 five Law Lords unanimously ruled against them, Lord Bingham stating that Parliament could not rationally have been thought to have excluded CNR techniques from the 1990 Act 'had it known of them as a scientific possibility'. In view of the eventual outcome of the case, the passage emergency legislation could perhaps be seen as unnecessary.[104]

Of course, one argument for Parliament taking the initiative in areas where controversial moral questions are involved is that confidence in the criminal law rests on public acceptance of its provisions. This had been a major reason for accepting abortion law reform in the 1960s and the Warnock Committee's recommendation that artificial insemination by donor should be regulated, despite ethical concerns – because they would continue whether or not they were legal. The Human Rights Act established principles of higher law by which judges must interpret legislation and the common law, and with which legislation passed by Parliament should be compatible, but the centrality of parliamentary scrutiny of moral issues, and Parliament's ability to legislate for them, had not been totally eroded. However, it if was desirable for Parliament to rule specifically on human reproductive cloning, given the uncertainty introduced by the High Court ruling in November 2001, this was undermined by the cursory examination of the proposals which the Government allowed. While there was broad support for the ban, there were widespread concerns about whether the scope of the Bill was wide enough, and motivation for support of the Bill obviously ranged between those who wanted to ban all cloning and those who wanted to permit and encourage it for therapeutic purposes.

Baroness Warnock was coming to similar conclusions herself about the continuing validity of much of her original report, displaying a characteristic lack of embarrassment about changing her mind as the evidence changed.[105] She thought that the surrogacy prohibitions were not working, that the restrictions on who should be eligible for IVF treatment reflected the social outlook of the 1980s not the twenty-first century, and that Parliament, acting on her Committee's recommendation, had been wrong to prevent children born from donor insemination from tracing their donor parent, something for which the Government began to legislate in 2004. However, the principles on which the report had been based remained valid. They were concerned to prevent harm to potential children from new treatments, exploitation of those seeking treatment and, in the case of embryology, the use of embryos which would be generally unacceptable or which would cause them pain. When the possibility of 'harvesting' eggs from discarded embryos to implant in infertile women arose, Warnock saw no fundamental moral objection, saying that providing there was consent from the mother of the aborted embryo, 'I suppose the question is whether that woman, the hopeful mother, would object to the thought that this is where the egg came from, I don't see why she should.'[106] Others ranged from the predictable response of 'grotesque' from a SPUC spokeswoman to other ethical objections from non-religious people who thought that the whole debate about fertility and child-rearing had been distorted to focus on solving fertility problems at any cost.

The law and regulations relating to fertility treatment were becoming obsolete at an even faster pace. This was hardly surprising. Whereas genetics and embryology research has been essentially a conversation between legislators, regulators and the science community, fertility treatment has always been given greater publicity with more of a tangible, emotive resonance for ordinary people. The permeability of national law governing ethical behaviour, keenly felt over abortion legislation, became even more palpable in the field of fertility treatment. Surrogacy, which the Warnock Report had condemned and the Human Fertilisation and Embryology Act had heavily circumscribed, flourished abroad, with many British couples taking advantage of laxer regulations in other countries. Such 'reproductive tourism' came to greatest prominence with the case of Diane Blood, whose dying husband had fallen into a coma before having had a chance to give the written consent to use his frozen sperm as the couple had agreed. The HFEA refused her permission for insemination because of lack of consent. Blood was given treatment in Belgium.

An even more vexing question increased the scrutiny of the HFEA's decisions when the possibility of screening embryos for particular genetic traits, known as pre-implantation genetic diagnosis, became possible. The Authority divided cases into two groups, symbolised by two equally distressing and media-friendly families, one where there was a risk for the baby of inherited disease, the other where the couple wanted to have a second baby with cord blood cells which could treat their existing child, who suffered from an incurable condition. The second family, the Whitakers, were refused permission to screen their embryos in the UK on the grounds that the invasive treatment did not benefit the potential child and was unnecessary because of the minute risk of the child itself having the same condition. The couple travelled to the USA for treatment. The HFEA chairwoman conceded that the law might have to be reviewed, although their case rested on the fundamental principles of resisting the commodification of babies and protecting future children from possible psychological problems associated with their artificial origins. The sense of regulating in a moral vacuum was heightened by splits even within the pro-IVF medical profession. The BMA supported the Whitakers but the leading IVF specialist and Labour peer Lord Winston strongly opposed the treatment, saying, 'Can you think of any other medical treatment which you would expect anybody to undergo without informed consent for somebody else's benefit? This child has the spectre of being born for somebody else's benefit throughout his whole life. I find it incredible that the law might be changed.'[107]

Despite such eminent opposition, the HFEA did relax the rules on this technique in July 2004, although the statement from Suzi Leather, the HFEA chairwoman, seemed not to address Winston's fundamental ethical, as opposed to medical, concerns: 'Our job is also to consider the welfare of the tissue-matched child which will be born. Our review of the evidence available does not indicate that the embryo biopsy procedure disadvantages resulting babies compared to other IVF babies.'[108]

The plethora of new treatments and potential treatments for infertility also raised concerns about their effect on women and men, as well as children born through such treatment. The Blood case and the growth of fertility treatment for single women and lesbian couples amply demonstrated that a man's utility could be reduced to his gametes. As Ruth Deech suggested in 2000,

there is a grave danger that men's bodies are not treated with the same respect as women's. The danger is not just with the Blood case but with some other modern developments that men are treated simply as a bundle of useful tissues. I think we have a problem now not so much with respect for women's bodies – that particular aim I think has been won [something not all women might agree with] – but with respect to men's bodies – men's necessity. The danger for women is that they are treated only as beings who want babies at all costs. The danger for men is they are treated just as the source of the gamete and no more.[109]

Greater demand for infertility treatment among heterosexual couples, the result
of a mixture of women waiting longer to have babies and a rise in infertility,
particularly among men, focused attention on the newly termed 'postcode
lottery' within the NHS which operated as unequally with access to IVF
treatment as with abortion. Criticism of this led the Health Secretary, Alan
Milburn, to ask the Government's new watchdog on the licensing of medical
treatments, the National Institute for Clinical Excellence (NICE), to devise a
scheme for ironing out these inequalities. NICE's recommendation that all
women satisfying existing criteria should be entitled to up to six cycles of IVF
treatment was not uncontroversial. The estimated cost of £400m led some within
the NHS to fear that this would lead to cuts in other services of higher priority
such as cancer treatment. Fertility campaigners welcomed these developments,
presaged by Milburn in December 2000, by saying, 'this comes at a particularly
good time. Christmas is devastating for infertile couples who desperately want a
baby.'[110] Of course, those dying of cancer, or their families, might also have
considered Christmas a particularly difficult time.

*

A pledge to give fast access to NHS abortions across the country was just one
small part of the Government's wider strategy on sexual health and HIV, which
it published in 2001. If rates of teenage pregnancy were beginning to decline,
rates of infection of STDs were soaring. HIV infection, following the effective
emergency campaign which the Conservative Government had launched under
Norman Fowler in the mid-1980s, was worryingly high, even among high-risk
groups such as the gay community which had responded quickly to the earlier
exhortation to change behaviour and follow safer-sex guidelines. Just as
disturbing was the explosion in rates of chlamydia among young women, a
disease which could remain asymptomatic but cause infertility. Clearly messages
about the importance of using condoms, or avoiding high-risk behaviour or
promiscuity, were not being heard by many young people. The 2001 strategy was
the first time a government had comprehensively tackled the issue, and targets to
improve rates of infection became part of the NHS's Public Service Agreement,
by which performance would be judged and future funding decided. The pace of
change was not fast enough, though, for the committee of MPs which monitored

the work of the Department of Health. In 2003 it produced a damning report on the state of sexual health and services in England and Wales. It condemned the state of clinic services within the NHS and demanded greater action on this and better promotion of sexual health through sex education and campaigns. This problem presented a dilemma for liberals. In the words of one, 'it is not consenting sex between adults we need to discourage but certain outcomes.' However, poor sexual health, and its causes and consequences, were discussed far less on the left than on the right, where conclusions were easy – the message to young people should be 'just say no'. On the other hand, liberals seemed to find it difficult to discuss the failure of young people to use responsibly the freedom which had gradually been conceded since the 1960s, first to their generation, and then to their children and their children's children.

Turning its attention to some of the intractable problems which compounded social inequalities, the new Social Exclusion Unit in the Cabinet Office produced a report on teenage pregnancy in 1998 acknowledging that Britain had the highest rate in Europe (though lower than some countries, including the USA), which the Government aimed to halve within ten years. More pertinent to its wider remit, the report highlighted the fact that a girl from social class V (unskilled manual) was more than ten times more likely to become a teenage mother than a girl from social class I (professional). In discussing why UK rates were comparatively high, the report argued that countries with high rates shared high levels of income inequality, low educational attainment, high percentages of lone parents and benefit systems that did not require parents to work before their children left school. It went on to describe how rates of teenage conception in the 1970s and 1980s fell by up to half in countries ranging from Sweden, Denmark and the Netherlands to Germany, Switzerland and Italy. In these cases this trend coincided with greater access to contraception and widespread publicity encouraging its use and later, concern about the possible spread of AIDS. On the other hand, a twelve per cent drop in the teenage conception rate in the United States was attributed to a range of possible factors from the health of the economy and better job prospects to fear of AIDS, the popularity of long-lasting contraceptive methods such as implants and injectables and more conservative attitudes towards sex. The report, and teenagers quoted in it, also complained about the mixed messages which were sent out – on the one hand the media encouraged sex, whilst the Government, health system and schools often failed to provide contraceptive help necessary for young people to protect themselves.[111] Adverse influence from cultural messages on the sexual activity of teenagers worried both liberals and conservatives, with the Chief Inspector of Schools, Chris Woodhead, blaming the fashion and pop industries, rather than poor teaching in schools for the inculcation of 'negative values'. Woodhead's intervention on this subject was controversial in itself following earlier revelations that as Head of English at a school in the 1970s he had had a relationship with a former pupil for whom he left his wife.[112]

Controversy continued over whether the most effective strategy lay in encouraging sexual abstinence or in providing thorough sex education and access to contraceptive advice and services, including emergency contraception and abortion. Despite other evidence from abroad, two studies in Canada and Scotland added fuel to this debate by suggesting that sex education programmes did not increase use of contraception or reduce levels of pregnancy.[113] The Family Planning Association (FPA) reacted by agreeing that such programmes alone were not enough, and that wider social, economic and cultural factors also needed to be addressed, as well as access to services.[114] Other commentators insisted that the solution lay partly in increasing the age of consent to eighteen.[115] Mixed signals from within government itself in 1999 suggested not all departments were in agreement. David Blunkett was reported to have redrafted sex education guidelines in response to outrage from the *Daily Mail* about the lack of reference to marriage. The Department for Education and Employment's press release on the Government's teenage pregnancy strategy launch in June 1999 made noticeably less reference to the provision of sex education than sexual abstinence and support for marriage. One department official was quoted as saying, 'Essentially we don't see what you would regard as sex education starting until the last year of primary school. That is the guidance now and that is not going to change.' In secondary schools, the new guidance would stress the importance of involving parents in drawing up the sex education syllabus and place a new emphasis on encouraging sexual abstinence. The importance of marriage would be central to all sex education. This was little different from demands from the veteran family-values campaigner Valerie Riches, of Family and Youth Concern, who said that only biological details were necessary for primary schoolchildren: 'I don't think they should go into anything sexual like contraception and abortion. They should keep it nice and pure and clean … in secondary schools they should teach moral concepts of right and wrong and stress they don't have to have sex.'[116] In stark contrast the Public Health Minister, Tessa Jowell, championed the provision of better contraceptive advice and services.[117] Tony Blair also emphasised the importance of sex education, although he couldn't resist the temptation to exhort the nation to a 'new moral purpose' later that year in response to the news that two twelve-year-old girls in Rotherham had become pregnant, declaring himself to be 'appalled' at the news.[118] This seemed closely to echo the reaction of the *Daily Mail* to the news the previous week, when it described teenage sex as having become 'a way of life' in Rotherham.[119] Added to concern for the sexual health and life opportunities of children was an underlying concern in government about the short- and long-term cost to the Exchequer of supporting teenage mothers and their children, who were more likely to need support from the state. In the words of one government spokesman, 'We have got to get the message across to teenagers that an evening's fun could mean having to pay up for 16 years.'[120]

Accepting recommendations from the Independent Advisory Group on Teenage Pregnancy (IAG), the Government agreed to extend the provision of health advice and services in schools through additional clinic and nursing services, and to raise the importance of sex education within the national curriculum. By 2003 conception rates among under-eighteens had fallen by ten per cent and among under-sixteens by eleven per cent although, as the IAG commented, progress was slow among hard-to-reach groups including children in care and some black and minority ethnic communities. The Government's other main aim was to increase the proportion of teenage parents in full-time education, a problem which was compounded by the habit among some schools of excluding girls who became pregnant. Of course it was difficult to subject boys to a similar sanction, but this was a practice which the Government banned in 1999.[121]

At the same time that pro-life campaigners were challenging the extension of embryo and stem cell research, they also returned to the fray over teenage contraception. In 2000 the Government made the morning-after pill available from pharmacists without a prescription. The order giving effect to this was challenged in the House of Lords by Baroness Young, who claimed it would lead to greater promiscuity and a rise in STDs, and to girls under sixteen obtaining the pill easily. She was supported as usual by Lord Longford, who considered a rise in teenage pregnancy to be a lesser evil than a rise in adultery or fornication, although quite how teenage pregnancy could be seperated from fornication the noble Earl didn't make clear. Lord Moran, son of Winston Churchill's doctor, identified wider access to the morning-after pill with a collapse in morality which the father of the murdered ten-year-old Damilola Taylor had blamed for his son's death on a run-down estate in Peckham. The Government and supporters of the move among medical professionals and family-planning advisers and the media claimed that it would reduce rates of unwanted pregnancy which were the result of failed contraception, and would not lead to greater promiscuity and higher rates of STDs, given low rates of use by women.[122]

Despite a major split within the SPUC in 1999, which saw Phyllis Bowman and half the executive leave the organisation, by 2002 it was back at the forefront of attempts to restrict access to family-planning services by banning such over-the-counter sales of the morning-after pill. Using similar tactics to those which Mary Whitehouse regularly deployed to combat obscenity, the SPUC's case invoked a piece of Victorian legislation, the 1861 Offences against the Person Act, which outlaws the supply of any poison 'or noxious thing' with intent to cause a miscarriage. However, SPUC cannily linked the claim that this was abortion by other means to concerns about sexual health among young women, arguing that 'when you have chlamydia rising at a rate of twenty-eight per cent per year, it would be quite irresponsible to allow this government policy to go unchallenged.'[123] In reality, the basis of their legal argument, that in 1861 Parliament intended that pregnancy be understood to begin at the point of fertilisation, was a thinly disguised attack on abortion as well as other contraceptives such as the mini-pill and interuterine devices. Mr Justice Munby's decision at the High Court not only dismissed the application, but also undermined such attempts to invoke centuries-old legislation which had fallen into desuetude or been superseded by modern practice. He ruled that there was nothing in the 1861 Act to demonstrate a parliamentary intention to protect life from the point of fertilisation, only to criminalise the procurement of miscarriages. Crucially, he said that

the content of that parliamentary intention had, as a matter of law, to be assessed by reference to current, and not nineteenth-century, understanding of what that word meant. It had to be interpreted in the light of the best current scientific and medical knowledge that was available to the court. Applying those principles, miscarriage was the termination of post-implantation pregnancy.

The judge went further, including current lay and popular understanding of 'miscarriage' in interpreting the law, which 'plainly' excluded the Pill, the mini-pill and the morning-after pill.[124]

While some pro-life groups still hoped to undermine the 1967 Act in any way possible, even some of those opposed to abortion on religious grounds, such as Shirley Williams, conceded that on principle, all women in the UK should have equal access to abortion, in the same way as with other health services or comprehensive education. 'Limiting access to the least well off is not an acceptable way of controlling the issue. You have to take it head on.'[125]

Prompted by the anti-abortion pressure group LIFE, and long-standing concerns among many disabled people about their own status in an age of legal abortion, the new Disability Rights Commission (DRC) suggested that the foetal abnormality provision in the Abortion Act 'reinforced negative stereotypes' of disabled people, and the provision for such abortions to take place after the twenty-four-week limit for other grounds compounded this. While claiming that it did not want to undermine the Act itself, the Commission argued 'that priority should be given to making major progress [on disability as a reason for abortion] before any consideration is given to adjusting the provisions of the Abortion Act itself.' This raised the question, of which Polly Toynbee had warned, of whether the DRC was effectively conceding anti-abortionist arguments about moral and legal equivalence between the embryo and the living, and all for the sake of a very small number, fewer than one hundred, of foetuses aborted annually. This problem made even bigger headlines in 2003 when a telegenic Anglican curate, Joanna Jepson, was granted a judicial review of a decision by doctors to abort a foetus which had a cleft palate. Jepson, who had herself been born with the condition, argued that it could not merit the description of severe abnormality in the Abortion Act. However, some doctors argued that a cleft palate was often a symptom of more serious cranial deformity. Ms Jepson's campaign had early success when the police pre-empted the courts by announcing they were reopening their inquiry.

By this time, however, the abortion law was under much wider scrutiny. In June 2004 the *Daily Mail* ran pictures of a foetus in the womb, showing that it was 'walking' and 'yawning' at twelve or thirteen weeks, and cooing that 'at twelve weeks they look like they are enjoying jumping off the womb like a trampoline.' Anti-abortion campaigners claimed the pictures proved the 'reality of the unborn child', with LIFE's spokeswoman predicting that 'after this, everyone will see that abortion is as barbaric as killing a born baby.' As doctors pointed out, such evidence of physiological development did not change the reality of the point at which viability was reached.[126] However, this grey area was also becoming controversial again, as further claims were made about the reluctance of some doctors to resuscitate babies born alive following failed late abortions, and the number of terminations carried out on social grounds close to the twenty-four-week limit. One tabloid commentator raged that 'we seem to kid ourselves that abortion at twenty-four weeks is just another form of contraception. It is far closer to cold-blooded murder.' Defenders of the Abortion Act, such as Ann Furedi of the British Pregnancy Advisory Service, found holding the line increasingly difficult. Despite the evidence that late abortions on social grounds were often the result of social pressures preventing women seeking help earlier, political support for revisiting the law was growing rapidly. Alongside predictable calls from conservatives such as William Hague, David Steel himself questioned the operation of his own Act, admitting that medical advances meant that the upper limit should be reduced to about twenty-two weeks, and that the continental practice of making abortion easier up to twelve weeks, and more difficult thereafter, should be adopted. He denied press reports that he now thought abortion on social grounds should be restricted to the first trimester.[127] Although the *Times* columnist Mary Ann Sieghart was probably right that most people agreed with Steel's support for moderate amendment of the law, her prediction that hysterical debate was unlikely seemed rather misplaced when anti-abortionists like Anne Atkins regularly compared abortion to the Holocaust – condemning millions of women to moral equivalence with the Nazis whilst implying that the extermination of Jews might be acceptable in certain circumstances. The same week as Steel's re-entry into the debate, Tony Blair, in answer to a question in the Commons, gave a cautious approval to re-examining the law if the scientific evidence had changed.[128] Though generally felt to be of a piece with Blair's personal instincts, this new statement makes an interesting comparison with his comments sixteen years earlier when David Alton made his failed attempt to restrict the time limit for abortions. On that occasion, Blair penned an article in *The Times* warning MPs that, in common with Margaret Thatcher, Alton's Bill was a first step towards outlawing all abortion, not a minor tightening of the law to reflect scientific advances. In a thorough defence of a woman's right to choose abortion until the foetus becomes viable outside the womb, Blair argued:

It is the abortions after eighteen weeks which are precisely the most sympathetic: where the foetus is found to have serious disability; young girls too are afraid or ignorant to acknowledge pregnancy; those delayed by the NHS; women who for one reason or another have come late, and so usually in circumstances of great anguish, to want an abortion.

Any sensible person is against abortion. The real question is whether, outside of the obvious protection given to a foetus capable of surviving without the mother, and the requirement to show minimal cause to obtain an abortion, the law should make criminal those who face the acute moral and personal dilemma of carrying an unwanted child and decide to abort; in other words, to force where we have failed to persuade.

When we reject this proposition, we do not in any sense deny the rights of the foetus or affirm a belief in abortion. We merely reject the law as the best instrument to resolve the conflicts between the rights of the foetus or child and those of the woman.

The inescapable consequence of the Alton Bill is that a woman will be made, under threat of criminal penalties, to carry and give birth to a child, perhaps severely disabled, that she does not want. I do not say she is right, in those circumstances, to have an abortion. But I cannot in conscience, as a legislator, say that I can take that decision for her.[129]

Although the abortion law remained unchanged after 1990, pro-choice MPs pressed hard during the first three years of the new Labour Government to equalise access to free NHS abortion. With a ministerial team led by Frank Dobson, Tessa Jowell and Yvette Cooper, the Department of Health was not unreceptive, and when the Government produced its Sexual Health and HIV Strategy in 2001 it made improving abortion services a high priority, saying that health authorities should follow the guidelines drawn up by the Royal College of Obstetricians and Gynaecologists the previous year, which the department had commissioned to inform its sexual health strategy. The strategy promised that 'from 2005 Commissioners should ensure that women who meet the legal requirements have access to abortion within three weeks of the first appointment with their GP or other referring doctor.'[130]

While the postcode lottery continued, abortion in Britain, under New Labour, those with a Northern Irish postcode remained governed by nineteenth-century criminal and common law on abortion. Fewer than one hundred legal abortions each year were carried out in the province, though more than 1,500 women travelled to Britain annually to pay for private abortions. Public opinion in the 1960s had not supported Ulster's inclusion within the Act, but by the mid-1990s there was majority support for widening access to the present standard in the rest of the UK.[131] Despite this the UK Government and the devolved Department of Health resisted a legal challenge by the FPA to force a clarification of the abortion rules. This claimed that many women were being unfairly denied an abortion because of uncertainty among doctors. In July 2003 the High Court in Belfast ruled that the Government was not obliged to issue such guidance, but that it would be 'prudent' for it to do so.[132] Underlying this case was the continuing unwillingness of successive governments to tackle the abortion issue in Northern Ireland. John Major had promised that the law would not be changed until a majority of Northern Irish MPs supported such a move. Given his government's need to pander to their special claims as its Commons majority ebbed away this is not surprising. But the new Labour Government also resiled from dealing with the anomaly, declaring it had no plans to extend the 1967 Act to Northern Ireland.

As bills to devolve power to Edinburgh and Belfast progressed through the Commons in 1998, abortion was a frequently raised issue among Conservatives to illustrate the illogicality of devolution. Confusion seemed to be widespread about the discrepancy in responsibility for abortion law. Blair responded to a Conservative question about the differences between Scotland and Northern Ireland by saying it was sensible for the differences between parts of the UK to be reflected in their devolved powers, clearly chary of discussing, or unaware of, the actual position and history of abortion law.[133] The Scotland Act reserved responsibility for a range of ethical issues – abortion, human fertilisation and embryology, genetics and xenotransplantation – to Westminster. Some of these exceptions caused great controversy during debate on the Bill because the Government's case, particularly over abortion, was so clearly contradicted by the existing anomalies between Northern Ireland and Britain. In addition, as Liam Fox pointed out, human transplantation was devolved while xenotransplantation was reserved. Even more fundamentally, euthanasia and capital punishment were both devolved, while abortion, human fertilisation and embryology were reserved, although the issue of capital punishment was effectively decided by the

Europe-wide ban under both the ECHR and a European Union agreement to which the UK was already party. As well as declaring that 'cross-border traffic' for abortion would be undesirable, despite no move to equalise the law between Britain and Northern Ireland, the Government also made the bizarre case that such issues 'require expertise to be pooled' across the UK, with no explanation of how this applied to those ethical issues which were to be reserved as opposed to those which were devolved.

Scottish Catholic MPs, supported by their bishops and Cardinal Winning, led protests at the failure to devolve abortion to the new Parliament, sensing political advantage and a chance to tighten the abortion law in Edinburgh. In fact pro-choice and anti-abortion politicians from all parties united in declaring this an issue which Scotland should be allowed to decide. The Scottish Nationalist leader, Alex Salmond, condemned Westminster's negligent handling of abortion in the same terms as wider social policy, saying:

> Whatever the moral arguments and the efforts that hon. members on both sides of the Chamber put into these debates in trying to settle the position with their consciences, the issue would be treated in a better fashion by the Scottish Parliament than it has been in the past eleven years by the House. It is a question not of whether people were satisfied with the outcome but of whether people were satisfied that their position had been exercised in a debate that matched the importance of the issue. Whatever else we may say, none of us can put our hand on our heart and say that the House has dealt properly with one of the supreme moral and social issues of our time.
>
> ... I am not convinced that the legislation would be substantially changed [by Edinburgh]. I am certain that, among other factors, a Scottish Parliament would bear in mind the experience of the legislation in England and Wales – it would be sensible and important to do so – but I am convinced that the Scottish Parliament is entitled to express what it believes is the conscience and view of the Scottish people on this supremely important topic.

As the Liberal Democrat Menzies Campbell and Labour's Tam Dalyell, veteran of the 1966 parliamentary debates on abortion, pointed out, even before the 1967 Act Scottish doctors and prosecutors had taken a much more liberal view of existing abortion law than those south of the border, with places such as Aberdeen renowned for access to abortion which might be illegal in England. Donald Dewar's adherence to the case against 'cross-border traffic' was particularly peculiar. He claimed that 'the fact that, even now, there are differences in social approach and medical practice in different parts of the country is not a justification for having different criteria and different tests within the legislative framework.' But that was one of the central arguments for devolution, and from 1999 he and successive First Ministers in Edinburgh would develop a Scottish legislative framework in social policy increasingly at odds with that in England. Perhaps more tellingly, Dewar admitted that the decision to exclude abortion had been made only after 'considerable debate' within the Scottish Office.[134] More fuel was added to the fire by the handling of the issue by the Government whips. The vote on a Conservative amendment to the Scotland Bill to devolve abortion law to the new Parliament ignited a fierce row within the Labour Party. While one Labour MP, Ian Davidson, accused the Tories of a 'crude attempt to manipulate religious feeling' in Scotland with their amendment, four of his Catholic colleagues defied a three-line whip to vote with the opposition. Two of these were whips themselves, John McFall and Tommy McAvoy, who had obtained permission to exercise their conscience from Nick Brown, the Chief Whip. This caused indignation among Labour MPs who had either voted with the Government or abstained, and were not aware that the PLP standing order which allowed the exercise of conscience on such issues applied to this vote.[135]

The wider importance and controversial nature of the abortion issue throughout the world also stimulated pro- and anti-abortionists within Parliament to press the Government. When the new Bush administration in the USA pulled the plug on funding programmes in the developing world which advocated abortion, pro-choice MPs condemned the move, and sought agreement from ministers normally anxious to avoid appearing divided from Washington.[136] This also provided an opportunity for anti-abortion parliamentarians to press the Government on which pro-choice organisations in Britain and around the world it was funding.

*

If government policy on sex education and sexual health under Labour was a contradictory mess, the fight against drug use was little more coherent. The clear evidence was that the drugs trade was linked to organised crime and that drug use among young people was sky-rocketing. Equally, the social acceptability of soft drugs was increasing, blunting the deterrent effect of legal and penal sanctions. A drugs 'czar', Keith Hellawell, former Chief Constable of West Yorkshire Police, was appointed to coordinate drugs policy. He attempted to push forward a strategy of increasing treatment and rehabilitation of drug-users in the criminal justice system, to prevent recidivism and tackle the underlying causes of drug addiction. However, the continuing contradictory pressure on resources, and conflict with the Home Office, led to him being sidelined, and eventually leaving his post. Caught in the traditional dilemma between a more liberal, pragmatic approach to drug use, typified by Mo Mowlam, who held the drugs brief in the Cabinet Office for two years, and conservative fear of admitting defeat in the 'war on drugs', government policy failed to satisfy either camp, or to demonstrate whether either a 'zero tolerance' approach or a radical decriminalisation and therapeutic approach could in reality work.

However, new voices brought weight to bear in favour of a more liberal approach. Senior police officers, including the Chief Constable of Cleveland, called for 'the legalisation and subsequent regulation of some or all drugs'. This was followed in 2000 by a similar conclusion from the Police Foundation on cannabis. The Home Office under David Blunkett once again showed its unusual combination of intolerance and pragmatic liberalism in drugs policy after 2001. Although severely challenged by its critics, Blunkett proposed the reclassification of cannabis from class B to class C. This dramatic move followed the experiment conducted in Lambeth by Commander Brian Paddick, where cannabis offenders were not arrested or charged, which, Paddick claimed, resulted in a large number of man hours being saved and redirected towards tackling hard drugs. Allegations that Paddick had allowed his former (male) lover to keep cannabis at their home led to his removal from Lambeth and a suspension of the experiment. Paddick was cleared, but the episode demonstrated that those in the police and the wider community who opposed a relaxation on the part of the criminal justice system towards cannabis use would take advantage of any perceived moral weakness on the part of advocates of a more liberal approach.

Conservative policy towards drugs also shifted after 2000. A significant, if rather farcical moment, came in 2000 when Shadow Home Secretary Ann Widdecombe announced a new policy of on-the-spot fines for those caught possessing cannabis. The policy immediately unravelled as, besides a complete lack of consultation with colleagues, most of the Shadow Cabinet suddenly admitted to youthful experimentation with the drug, prompting the *Daily Mirror* to dub Widdecombe 'Doris the Dope' (after her existing soubriquet Doris Karloff). Public attitudes reflected this uncertainty amongst politicians about how to combat drug use and its links to crime. Support for legalising cannabis increased from twelve per cent in 1983 to forty-one per cent in 2001, by which time the public was roughly evenly divided on the issue, though attitudes towards other drugs including ecstasy and heroin remained firmly opposed to relaxation.[137]

This was not the only area of the criminal law where changes proposed by the Government led many people, including some on the left, to question whether harmful effects would outweigh any benefits from greater individual freedom. The draft Gambling Bill, based on an independent review in 2001, proposed to relax restrictions to allow American-style casinos, particularly in run-down resorts such as Blackpool. Critics feared it would make enormous profits for developers and businessmen and encourage gambling addiction, much as relaxation under Harold Macmillan had had unfortunate social effects. The Government's policy on licensing, enshrined in the Licensing Act 2003, proposed to relax opening hours to discourage binge drinking towards closing times and encourage the entertainment industry. Once again, critics feared that, with the explosion of Britain's traditional problem with alcohol, this would actually make matters even worse.

*

The tension between the two principles underlying New Labour's policies towards individual morality, the protection of children and the promotion of equality, revealed itself nowhere more colourfully than in the regulation and censorship of television, film and the internet. In film, by the beginning of the twenty-first century, the British Board of Film Classification (BBFC) had reached a postwar low in the number and proportion of films which it cut annually, standing at around two per cent, compared to around ten per cent in the late 1940s, up to twenty-five per cent in the 1950s, and a staggering one in three in 1974.[138] However, as Alan Travis details in *Bound and Gagged*, the election of New Labour came just as the BBFC began implementing the principle that only that which could be said to produce lasting harm in an audience should be cut or banned. One corollary of the this was the decision to grant R18 certificates to hard-core porn films which included non-violent, consensual oral sex and anal intercourse. A further justification for this was that the licensed sex shops were restricted to such soft material that it encouraged a thriving black market in films which contained unregulated violent and exploitative sex. Jack Straw was outraged, and hauled Lord Birkett at the BBFC over the coals, demanding, 'Do you really mean that you are going to allow oral sex and buggery and I don't know what else?' Apart from the Home Secretary's moral objection, despite the fact that such acts were perfectly legal for those who were allowed access to them in licensed sex shops, his other point of concern, which carried greater weight, was that the BBFC had made the decision with little or no reference to the police or other law enforcement agencies, elected politicians or the public. Straw brought in Andreas Whittam Smith, founding editor of the *Independent*, as the new president of the BBFC with a remit to reverse the decision on the new R18 videos and pursue a more open and consultative strategy which, Straw calculated, would lead to a tighter rein on sex and violence. Whittam Smith and the new chairman, Robert Duval, enthusiastically ran a more open operation at the BBFC. Duval published guidelines which, for the first time, set out clearly to the industry and public exactly what would be permissible in terms of sex, violence and anti-social behaviour including drug-taking and crime, at different levels of classification.[139] Although clearly a response to political pressure from the Home Office, this also represented another anticipation of the effects of the implementation of the ECHR. When the Human Rights Act came into force the following year, all public bodies would have to give detailed reasons for restrictions to the right under Article 10 to freedom of speech.[140]

The decision on the R18 films was also reversed. However, this was the last victory Straw would see. Under the Video Recordings Act, because the regulation of certificates is statutory, there had to be a mechanism for repeal against the BBFC's decisions, unlike film, where the classification system is a voluntary one, delegated by local authorities. The Video Appeals Committee, appointed by the BBFC, was the body designated by the Home Secretary to do this, and at this time included figures such as Biddy Baxter, Fay Weldon and Claire Rayner. It failed to fall into line, and continued to apply a stricter 'harm' test, upholding the original BBFC verdict. This decision was also upheld in the High Court by Mr

Justice Hooper.[141] Following this defeat, Straw vowed 'to improve the protection of children in this area [and] bring the Video Appeals Committee into line with other, similar appeals bodies fulfilling an important public function, in terms of their recruitment and appointments system'. Along with structural reform, Straw considered the options of higher fines and bypassing the legal judgment that the films passed R18 would cause little harm by insisting the BBFC must take more account of the likelihood that children might be exposed to them. Before Straw had any chance to follow through with these plans, the 2001 general election intervened. Straw moved to the Foreign Office, to be replaced by David Blunkett, who might have been expected to take a similar line, but responsibility for film and video classification moved as well, as the Home Office continued to shed some of its postwar empire, to the Department for Culture, Media and Sport. For the first time, the political oversight of censorship was divorced from the operation of the obscenity laws and the criminal justice system. In 2002, when Whittam Smith stepped down from the BBFC to take over the finances of the Church of England, Tessa Jowell replaced him with Sir Quentin Thomas, a recently retired mandarin with an impeccable Home Office CV including long periods responsible for various regulatory responsibilities ranging from street offences, through film and broadcasting, to gambling. The row over video classification fell into abeyance, along with the Home Office's plans to tighten the system. The Video Appeals Committee was reinvigorated with new members appointed by the BBFC, but still took a noticeably more relaxed approach.

The downside of Straw's dismantling of a board which, under James Ferman, had been described as a 'personal fiefdom', was that when the new regime at the board began to consult the public systematically about where they felt boundaries should be set, they endorsed the more liberal attitude towards sex which Straw was trying to reverse. This also applied to violence, to a lesser degree, with a stricter attitude towards drugs and bad language in front of young audiences. Paying little heed to the clear wishes of Straw and his supporters, Whittam Smith and Duval approached film and video in a pragmatic way, generally applying a strict harm test, liberalising on sex, but reflecting on earlier decisions on drugs, for example with Quentin Tarantino's *Pulp Fiction*, where they felt a blurred distinction between accurate portrayal of drug-taking and its promotion and glamorisation had perhaps led to the wrong decision. A number of European art-house films challenged, and breached, the existing prohibitions on erections and penetrative sex, including the French film *Romance* and Lars von Trier's controversial *The Idiots*, about a group of people pretending to be mentally ill. Then a British film broke another taboo. In the words of philosopher A. C. Grayling:

> *Frank representation of sex in serious films [had] until now been left to foreign-language cinema, doubtless because former censors thought their provenance gave a kind of zoological respectability to their sexual content. They also doubtless thought that since such films attract mainly small numbers of intellectuals, their depiction of foreign goings-on would not damage the nation's morals.*[142]

Hanif Kureishi's *Intimacy*, starring Mark Rylance, was the first film to include oral sex to be passed uncut by the board.

At the same time that film censorship was stuttering towards a more liberal era, much to the chagrin of Labour Home Secretaries, regulation of taste and decency on television was also setting new standards and facing new challenges. Just as cinema-goers were expressing more relaxed attitudes towards sex and film censorship, television viewers were giving researchers similar responses, indicating that they preferred information and warning to cuts in films shown on television. Interestingly, such views were even more prevalent among households with children (ninety-eight per cent) than those without (eighty-two per cent).[143] Some notable television landmarks were reached, though not without controversy. In 1999 Channel 4 broadcast the first high-profile drama centring on gay life, *Queer as Folk*. From the very first scene, depicting a thirty-year old man seducing and rimming a fifteen-year-old schoolboy, it tested public attitudes and those of the Broadcasting Standards Commission (BSC) in a new way. More generally, the BSC operated a new policy, reflecting what it considered to be changes in public attitudes, that judgments about sex in programmes should no longer distinguish between heterosexual and homosexual acts. If something was acceptable at a certain time between a straight couple, it would now be acceptable for a same-sex couple. Such judgments were applied, for instance, when complaints about a gay kiss in the peak-time hospital drama *Casualty* were dismissed.[144] However, research into public attitudes revealed a rather different picture. The widely respected British Social Attitudes survey in 1999 showed that people still judged straight and gay sex on television, cinema and video very differently. Attitudes changed markedly between 1995 and 1999, but, for example, forty-eight per cent thought male homosexual sex scenes should not be allowed to be shown at all on television, compared to only twenty-three per cent who thought the equivalent heterosexual sex scene should be similarly proscribed. However, when the responses were analysed by age, younger people were predictably more permissive. Only twenty-seven per cent of those between twenty-six and thirty-three thought a gay sex scene should be banned, compared to seventy-nine per cent of those over seventy-four.[145] Channel 4 also broke new ground in 1999 by deciding to broadcast an ejaculation, though this came as part of a late-night documentary on the history of pornography in a clip from the notorious 1970s film *Behind the Green Door*, giving it the cover of academic respectability. Sensational and trivialisation of sex in reality TV shows became increasingly pervasive, though often concentrated in a small number of individual programmes. However, as was being demonstrated by research carried out by all the regulators, sex was no longer the public's main concern. Violence, drug-taking, bad language and anti-social behaviour, where they might be seen by children, were all higher priorities, and those programmes which did cause an outcry about sex were often those relating to sexual exploitation of children, rather than consensual sex between adults.

One television programme in July 2001 encapsulated almost every argument about censorship in a liberal society – different audience taste and under-standing, the political response of ministers, the reaction of the press and the job of the regulators. When the Channel 4 satire *Brass Eye* broadcast a spoof on the media's treatment of paedophilia, it provoked the largest public reaction to a single programme ever. The context was the recent explosion in media coverage of paedophilia and the way in which released sex offenders were resettled in the community by the criminal justice system. A 'name and shame' campaign by the *News of the World* against paedophiles encouraged parents and others in the community to take action against suspected paedophiles. A number of instances of mistaken identity occurred where people unconnected to these ex-offenders were forced from their homes, injured or even killed. There was even a case where the house of a paediatrician was targeted by the baying mob. Television broadcast distressing scenes from the Paulsgrove Estate in Portsmouth where mobs of local people vented their anger at the perceived threat in their community and the failure of politicians and officials to respond to their fears. *Brass Eye* set out to parody these attitudes and the more general media sensationalisation of the issue and its sexualisation of children. Celebrities and MPs were hoodwinked into giving interviews to endorse spoof campaigns against paedophiles, as well as acting out sketches about child abuse.

The reaction of the right-wing press was predictable – the *Daily Mail*, the *Sun* and the *News of the World* all piled in to condemn it as the sickest thing ever to be broadcast, calling for Channel 4 to lose its licence and the programme-makers never to work in television again. Right-wing broadsheets were split with the *Sunday Telegraph* firmly against, whilst its sister *Daily Telegraph* supported the programme on the grounds that it broached a taboo subject which liberals were keen to avoid, like racism. Ministers, supposedly with no direct responsibility for broadcasting standards, demonstrated a complete inability to resist temptation to comment on a programme which some had not even watched. It managed to unite two ministers normally seen as being from different sides of the Government: Beverley Hughes, the granite-faced junior minister at the Home Office, and Tessa Jowell, Secretary of State for Culture, Media and Sport, with a reputation for liberal nannying, normally loathed by the right-wing press. Hughes, who carried the child protection portfolio, condemned the programme as 'appalling' and 'unhelpful', though it was confirmed that she had not actually watched it. Jowell initially condemned the programme, saying, 'As a viewer and a parent, I think it is a great shame that a public service broadcaster has chosen to transmit this programme. If this is considered acceptable material, we are tearing down the boundaries of decency on TV.'[146] It was suggested that she might want to give regulators extra powers, something which had disappeared under Margaret Thatcher. Having broken off her holiday to speak to Channel 4's chairman, Jowell was in less confrontational mood, merely commenting that 'I've made it absolutely clear that programme content and regulatory issues that arise from this are a matter for broadcasters and regulators, not government.' What was common to most of the reaction from left and right was that almost every commentator decided that there was a black-and-white answer: either its content was all trivial and degrading, or all cutting and provocative. Some child abuse experts, who understood the satirical idea behind the programme, felt it had failed to distinguish between the media's treatment of the issue and the horror of paedophilia itself. Yet even this does not account for the large number of viewers who felt that the programme had done exactly that. Whilst there were 2,500 complaints, Channel 4 claimed that there had also been seven hundred calls of support.

The liberal left were divided on the programme. Some took the opposite knee-jerk response to the *Daily Mail* – if the tabloid right condemned it, the broadcast must be serving a purpose. A few sided with those who thought it trivialised the subject of paedophilia, particularly as it used the specific case of Sidney Cooke, whose horrific abuse, torture and murder of Jason Swift had only recently been brought to justice. Some admitted that the programme pandered to middle-class liberal disdain for genuine working-class concerns about paedophiles. One thought that editorial judgement should have kept it off the airwaves without actually censoring it.[147] The adjudication of the regulators vindicated the broad lines of its content whilst upholding some of the complaints made about the programme. The Independent Television Commission ruled that the warnings before the broadcast, and the opening scenes, did not prepare the audience adequately or make clear the satirical nature of the programme. The BSC, adjudicating on three complaints about an earlier trailer for the programme, also criticised Channel 4 on the grounds that the trailer was too brief for the satirical nature to be conveyed. It also upheld complaints about the programme itself, partly because of the use of child actors who would not have understood the context (although parental consent had been given). However, when the programme was repeated in 2002, the BSC ruled that enhanced warnings before transmission met their earlier concerns. The complaints to which both regulators gave unequivocal dismissals were those from celebrities and MPs who complained about their treatment by the programme. Both noted that had they taken the time to think about the content of the interviews they gave, the spoof would have been obvious.

Channel 4 was again at the forefront of debates about decency on television in November 2002 when it broadcast the first public autopsy in over 170 years. The dissection of an old man, who had given consent to the use of his body for the unprecedented display, provoked an avalanche of complaints and anguished discussion about whether it constituted a breach of taste in terms of broadcasting or offence to the sanctity of the dead. Gunter von Hagens, whose taste for rather bizarre dress and self-publicity blunted the enthusiasm of some for the idea of breaking taboos about death and the dead body, made a comment after the autopsy which was a telling signal of how familiarity breeds ennui:

I achieved what I wanted to, which was to get a proper discussion in this country about anatomy and what the public are permitted to know and see. The audience were splendid. I have performed many post mortems in front of medical students and there is always much more disrespect of the body among them, more laughing and shouting. But the atmosphere at ours was very peaceful, people tried to cope with it and learn.[148]

Although police officers attended the autopsy and filed a report, no charges were brought. In terms of the television broadcast, the regulators ruled that Channel 4 had taken adequate precautions in warning the audience about the content. Regulators did show they were prepared to rein Channel 4 in over such programmes when it was admonished for showing a Chinese man cannibalising a baby in a documentary.[149]

The death in 2002 of Mary Whitehouse, leader and spokeswoman for the National Viewers and Listeners Association or 'Valour', as its supporters knew it, marked not only the demise of a tireless campaigner, but also the burial of the tactics and style which had sustained Whitehouse's campaigns for much of the previous forty years, but which had become increasingly shrill and anachronistic at the beginning of the twenty-first century. The organisation, reborn as Mediawatch UK, continued, bereaved but unbowed, and was in high demand as the representative of grassroots conservative opposition to the liberal media. Coincidentally, just after Whitehouse's death, one of her most famous cases returned to haunt, when Joan Bakewell read an excerpt from James Kirkup's gay poem, 'The Love that Dares to Speak Its Name', during a BBC series on censorship, *Taboo*. The original illustration for the poem of a naked, aroused, Christ crucified, was also shown on screen. Whitehouse's successor, John Beyer, complained to the Director of Public Prosecutions, David Calvert-Smith, and the BSC. Neither considered any action should be taken. Beyer also complained to Gavyn Davies, BBC Chairman, pointing that *Producer Guidelines*, the bible of programme-makers, states on religious sensibilities that

deep offence will be caused by profane references or disrespect, whether verbal or visual at deities, scriptures, holy days and rituals which are at the heart of various religions – for example the Crucifixion ...

Blasphemy is a criminal offence in the UK and advice should be sought,

through Heads of Department or Commissioning Executives, from Editorial
Policy and lawyers in any instance where the possibility of blasphemy may arise.

In a reply, the BBC's Head of Programme Complaints, claiming that public attitudes had changed considerably since 1977, explained that Bakewell had identified within the Church a 'tacit tolerance of blasphemy' but Kirkup's poem had pushed this tolerance 'too far':

The court action merited examination and it would have been difficult to do
this adequately without providing an example of the poem's content which ...
would have the potential to cause offence ... The documentary was shown late
in the evening on a channel whose remit includes the examination of serious
social issues such as this, and gave ample indication that sexual and other
taboos were to be examined openly.[150]

Not that the regulators had completely given up on defending the Lord from televisual assault. One BBC children's programme was upbraided when a chef let out a 'Jesus' in a fit of kitchen rage.[151]

Broadcasting's self-regulation of its standards of taste and decency was severely tested in an unprecedented way after 1997 when the Pro-Life Alliance took the BBC to court over its refusal in the 1997 general election to show a Welsh party political broadcast with pictures of abortion operations because they would offend viewers. The European Court of Human Rights had refused to hear the case, and the High Court in England had also rejected it, but at the Court of Appeal in March 2002, three judges ruled that the BBC had acted in the wrong, operating, in the words of one judge, 'political censorship'. Mr Justice Laws, in a particularly crushing statement, said: 'I have well in mind that the broadcasters do not at all accept that their decision should be so categorised. Maybe the feathers of their liberal credentials are ruffled at the word's overtones; maybe there is an implicit plea for the comfort of a euphemism.'[152] In May 2003 the House of Lords ruled in the BBC's favour. Though the BBC's position was portrayed by anti-abortionists as a desperate attempt by politically correct liberals to prevent the reality of abortion being shown to the public, the BBC's defence rested on the wider question of what distressing or violent images should be broadcast and at what times, given the likely audience. This was the judgement which regulators at the BSC had to make.

Broadcasters were also mindful of the cumulative effect of repeatedly showing such images. However, by the following year Channel 4, who had also refused to show the abortion images in the party election broadcast, screened *My Foetus*, a documentary showing an abortion operation at four weeks, and terminated foetuses at later stages. The few complaints which OfCom received about the programme were dismissed.

Increasingly, what concerned politicians and the public more than film or broadcasting was control of the internet. Just one example of how broadcasters could subvert taste and decency regulations was when Channel 4 webcast sex scenes which were cut from *The Idiots* for broadcast on its digital film channel. The crudity of filtering systems was amply demonstrated in the corridors of power when a new parliamentary network system not only prevented MPs and their constituents from corresponding on matters including sex or sexual words, but also prevented staff accessing their emails because they happened to have the surnames 'Gay' and 'Butt'. However, more serious concern centred on the use of the internet by child-abusers to groom victims by using the anonymity which the net provided to gain the trust of children before meeting them. This led the Government to take new legislative powers against 'grooming' in 2003. Whatever the success of measures taken by governments against exploitation and child pornography on the internet, evidence began to appear that showed that the number of people regularly using internet pornography was growing rapidly.

*

The increasing focus of public and political concern on the dangers posed by the internet to children from pornographers, paedophiles and political extremists is just the latest threat in a long line of moral panics about the corrupting influence of obscene publications of one sort or another since the Second World War – from American comics in the 1950s, the underground magazines of the late 1960s and early 1970s and video nasties from the 1980s to the time of the Bulger murder. There are undoubtedly others whose malign influence we are yet to witness. Efforts to ban such purveyors of depravity and corruption have been found to be increasingly hollow, particularly in a globalised, wired world. But censorship itself, along with other Victorian attempts to control individual behaviour, has collapsed under the pressure for social and commercial freedom.

If some of the liberal reformers of the 1960s did not reckon for the extent to which the moderation of their intentions would be overtaken by events, it is hard to argue that their moderate steps were the only or even the major cause of the profound social changes which continue to this day. The economic and cultural pressures which encouraged people to argue for reforms to reduce the injustices of the law and tailor it more to modern circumstances and mores were, and continue to be, largely autonomous of government and the criminal law. Conservatives have been wilfully in thrall to market-led purveyors of immorality and the 'structures of sin', picking off the more vulnerable advocates of permissiveness in the public realm. Liberals have been equally apt to ignore some of the undesirable consequences of liberalisation, or to act where possible to address them. As Shirley Williams observes, society has not been preparing young people well enough for the freedoms and pressures which they now face: 'The losers from most of the permissive legislation have been children. We know that the effect of divorce on children is worse than we once thought. People thinking of divorcing need to know that as well as that the law will allow them to divorce.'[153]

However, to use Baroness Warnock's phrase, for people who think the slope too slippery, they shouldn't have got on it in the first place. Where the slippery slope began remains contentious – the introduction of the Pill in 1961, the spread of progressive education, the partial decriminalisation in 1967 of homosexuality? The introduction of legal aid in 1949, giving the working class similar access to divorce as middle-class couples, presaged the success of the argument that rich women already had abortion on demand, and only working-class women were left to mutilate themselves or be mutilated in the back streets. The Pill may have heralded a fundamental disjuncture between sex and reproduction, but it received a warm welcome because birth control and contraception, if only for married couples initially, was seen as increasingly acceptable and desirable from the late 1940s onwards. However, it was the very depth of the abyss down which Clement Attlee and his colleagues stared in 1950 when considering whether to relax the divorce law which made them resist even a modest concession lest it lead to divorce after only a year of marriage – something which did indeed arrive by the 1980s. How slippery the slope really could be was amply demonstrated by the Conservatives' relaxation of gambling laws in the early 1960s. 'Rab' Butler and his colleagues were genuinely shocked by the spread of bingo, casinos and less savoury associated businesses. The fear of losing control over a potent social addiction was equally prevalent when debating drugs policy, and particularly whether to relax the law on cannabis, from Jim Callaghan's halting of the permissive tide to David Blunkett's insistence thirty years later that reclassification was an attempt to focus on the greater evil of hard drugs and the criminality which accompanies them.

The degree and rate of the evaporation of social stigma from previously deviant social and sexual behaviour has varied enormously across the nations, regions and communities of the UK. Morality can, indeed, be a geographical expression. But it is also a cultural one, which is now more complex than ever in our multi-cultural society – something which many liberals have yet to come to terms with. Secular as well as religious Britons in 2004 may baulk at the massive public support in France for its Government's determination to outlaw the wearing of visible religious symbols in schools, but we are also still learning how to accommodate the more traditional social structures within some immigrant communities. While conservatives have long bemoaned the disappearance of previously important social stigmas from premarital sex, divorce, abortion, single parenthood and homosexuality, stigma has been increasingly attached to behaviour which was often traditionally kept behind the sacred walls of the family. Domestic violence carries increasingly heavy cultural and legal penalties. Child abuse, most often committed by men known to the child despite the 'stranger danger' hysteria among the tabloids, is now a greater priority than at any time since the morality campaigns of Josephine Butler and W. T. Stead which led to the Criminal Law Amendment Act in 1885.

However, as the Education Minister, Edward Boyle, said in that momentous year of 1963, morality cannot simply be equated with sexual morality. Many people are more concerned with the morality of international relations, the arms trade, the tobacco industry, animal rights, civil liberties; the list is pretty well endless as political action inevitably involves attempting to divine right from wrong, and its moral significance depends in part on the level of importance attached to the subject in hand. Whether or not one agreed with his prescriptions, the Gladstonian reach of the new moral world order, which Tony Blair called post-9/11, attempted to tap into this enduring understanding people have of the conduct of nation states and diplomacy in moral terms.[154]

How shared moral values should continue to be communicated within society by politicians, the law and individuals has once again become extremely contentious. After a long period of certainty that Christian doctrine was the basis of the criminal law, from the 1950s onwards uncertainty and obfuscation grew about the extent to which these ethics should be restricted by utilitarian principles. Even by the late 1940s, politicians were conceding that religion's influence had waned since the beginning of the twentieth century, and could therefore no longer claim the same position of authority in formulating responses to moral problems. The religious renaissance in the 1950s was only ever superficial and by the late 1950s its hold on society had begun to wane rapidly. If Margaret Thatcher were right that only Christianity could 'resupply the virtues necessary to remoralise society' the next few decades would have been perilous indeed. Blair may draw his own moral compass from his Christian beliefs, but his Government has embraced the secular language of human rights, shackled implicitly or explicitly with responsibilities, albeit with reticence and ambiguity. Whether conservatives like it or not, the reciprocal values underpinning the Human Rights Act will increasingly reach into the 'nooks and crannies' of individual lives in the UK. How quickly this happens depends on the extent to which politicians and the public view human-rights principles as being the language with which to communicate the values by which we relate to each other and to the state.

Politicians invoke public opinion as blithely and partially as they do statistics in relation to moral issues as much as any other. However, because 'conscience' issues are seen to cut across party lines and discipline, the relationship is more delicate. It is the area where the legitimacy of a representative, as opposed to a popular, democracy is most keenly tested. How far politicians can get out of kilter with public opinion is not a precise science. In Lena Jeger's words, politicians cannot govern, despite über-pollster Philip Gould's best efforts, 'by the counting of correspondence'. As staunch parliamentarians such as Baroness Boothroyd emphasise, MPs are representatives, not delegates.[155] The law has to be seen to be credible and enforceable as well as providing the right blend of carrots and sticks. Whether you choose carrots or sticks pretty well defines your view of public morality.

In the wake of Blair's call for a new moral purpose in 1999, hard on the heels of the *Daily Mail* reports from Rotherham about the pregnancy of twelve-year-old girls, the veteran family values campaigner Valerie Riches condemned Labour's record since the 1970s:

It was under a Labour Government that the policy was introduced in 1974 that parents should not be told about the provision of contraception to their underage daughters. This has been extended to include abortion and his own government has said that parents should not be told if their children in schools are involved in underage sex, homosexual sex and drugs.

On the one hand the Government wants parents to be responsible for their children's behaviour but on the other hand makes it virtually impossible for them to be so. Tony Blair can't have it both ways.[156]

Whatever the accuracy of this, for Riches and others, the record of Conservative governments, even under Thatcher, has not been much better. For these girls and others like them, perhaps the final verdict, on which Blair, the media and the rest of us should ponder, might go to Macauley and his verdict on the fall from public grace of Lord Byron:

We know no spectacle so ridiculous as the British public in one of its periodical fits of morality. In general, elopements, divorces, and family quarrels, pass with little notice. We read the scandal, talk about it for a day, and forget it. But once in six or seven years our virtue becomes outrageous. We cannot suffer the laws of religion and decency to be violated. We must make a stand against vice. We must teach libertines that the English people appreciate the importance of domestic ties. Accordingly some unfortunate man, in no respect more depraved than hundreds whose offences have been treated with lenity, is singled out as an expiatory sacrifice. If he has children, they are to be taken from him. If he has a profession, he is to be driven from it. He is cut by the higher orders, and hissed by the lower. He is, in truth, a sort of whipping-boy, by whose vicarious agonies all the other transgressors of the same class are, it is supposed, sufficiently chastised. We reflect very complacently on our own severity, and compare with great pride the high standard of morals established in England with the Parisian laxity. At length our anger is satiated. Our victim is ruined and heart-broken. And our virtue goes quietly to sleep for seven years more.

It is clear that those vices which destroy domestic happiness ought to be as much as possible repressed. It is equally clear that they cannot be repressed by penal legislation. It is therefore right and desirable that public opinion should be directed against them. But it should be directed against them uniformly, steadily, and temperately, not by sudden fits and starts. There should be one weight and one measure. It is the resource of judges too indolent and hasty to investigate facts and to discriminate nicely between shades of guilt. It is an irrational practice, even when adopted by military tribunals. When adopted by the tribunal of public opinion, it is infinitely more irrational. It is good that a certain portion of disgrace should constantly attend on certain bad actions. But it is not good that the offenders should merely have to stand the risks of a lottery of infamy, that ninety-nine out of every hundred should escape, and that the hundredth, perhaps the most innocent of the hundred, should pay for all ... But such is the justice of mankind.[157]

Notes

Chapter 1

1.   H. L. A. Hart, *Law, Liberty and Morality* (OUP, Oxford, 1963), Preface.

2.   J. S. Mill, *On Liberty* (Everyman's Library, London, 1992), pp. 12–13

3.   Sir Edmund Leach, *A Runaway World? The Reith Lectures 1967* (BBC, London, 1968), p. 49.

4.   Quoted in Kenneth Tynan, *A View of the English Stage, 1944–63* (Davis Poynter, London, 1975) p. 357. An English translation of *Oedipus Rex* by Gilbert Murray was eventually licensed in 1910, British Library (BL), LCP/814.

5.   Tony Blair, 'A new consensus on law and order', speech at launch of the Home Office and Criminal Justice system strategic plans, 19 July 2004.

6.   A. H. Halsey, *Change in British Society* (OUP, Oxford, 1995), p. 23.

7.   Anthony Browne, 'Why a woman's place is behind the fridge', *The Times*, 21 July 2004.

8.   Peter G. Richards, *Parliament and Conscience* (George Allen & Unwin, London, 1970), p. 199.

9.   Ibid., pp. 197–8.

10.   Ivor Jennings, *Parliament*, 2nd ed. (Cambridge University Press, Cambridge, 1957), p. 373.

11.   David Steel, *Against Goliath: David Steel's Story* (Weidenfeld and Nicolson, London, 1989) pp. 60–66.

12.   Donald Shell, *The House of Lords* (Phillip Allan, Deddington, 1988), p. 31. The Conservative Government created a further forty-eight hereditary peerages between 1958 and 1964.

13.   I am grateful to Lord Dubs for showing me a copy of the Bill and suggesting this particular recreational use for it.

14.   HL Deb., vol. 602, col. 1133, 27 May 1999.

15.   James Callaghan, 'Cumber and Variableness', in *The Home Office: Perspectives on Policy and Administration* (Royal Institute of Public Administration, London, 1982), p. 12.

16.   Interview with Sir Brian Cubbon, 21 July 2003.

17.   Lord Allen of Abbeydale, 'Reflections of a bureaucrat' in *Home Office*, p. 30.

18.   Hugo Young, 'The Department of Civil Liberties', in *Home Office*, p. 87.

19.   Interview with Lord Jenkins of Hillhead, 25 November 1999.

20.   Alan Travis, *Bound and Gagged: A Secret History of Obscenity in Britain* (Profile, London, 2000), p. 196.

21.   Roy Jenkins, *A Life at the Centre* (Macmillan, London. 1991), pp. 181–4. 'Rab' Butler concurred with this view of the Home Office under Cunningham in his own memoirs.

22.   Interview with Sir Brian Cubbon, 21 July 2003.

23.   Callaghan, 'Cumber and Variableness', pp. 13–14.

24.   Andrew Martin and Gerald Gardiner, *Law Reform Now* (Victor Gollancz, London, 1963), pp. 8–10.

25.   Law Commission, *The Field of Choice* (Cmnd. 3123, 1967).

26.   Interview with Sir Brian Cubbon, 21 July 2003.

27.   PRO, T 171/803, 'Teenage Compulsory Saving Scheme'.

28. David Willetts, *Old Europe? Demographic Change and Pension Reform* (Centre for European Reform, London, 2003).

29. C. A. R. Crosland, *The Future of Socialism* (Jonathan Cape, London, 1956), p. 522.

30. Peter Thompson, 'Labour's "Gannex Conscience"? Politics and Popular Attitudes in the "Permissive Society"', in R. Coopey, S. Fielding and N. Tiratsoo (eds), *The Wilson Governments 1964–1970* (Pinter, London, 1993), p. 139.

31. Interview with Lord Jenkins of Hillhead, 25 November 1999.

32. For example HC Deb, vol. 625, col. 1510, 29 June 1960.

33. Barbara Castle, *The Castle Diaries 1964–1970* (Weidenfeld and Nicolson, London, 1984), p. 103, 11 February 1966.

34. Sunday Express, 27 November 1960.

35. Margaret Thatcher, *The Path to Power* (HarperCollins, London, 1994) pp. 150–53.

36. Barbara Castle, *The Castle Diaries 1974–1976* (Weidenfeld and Nicolson, London, 1980) p. 278, 15 January 1975.

37. Andrew Rawnsley, interview with Tony Blair, 'My moral manifesto for the 21st century', *Observer*, 5 September 1999.

38. 'Carey warns on moral crusading', *Guardian*, 9 September 1999.

39. Shirley Williams, *God and Caesar: Personal Reflections on Politics and Religion* (Continuum, London, 2003), pp. 16, 77–8.

40. Amanda Plattell, 'Blunkett's affair: love or sleaze?' *Evening Standard*, 17 August 2004; 'The new moral correctness; I have an oppinion about the Blunkett affair. And why shouldn't I?' *Independent on Sunday*, 22 August 2004.

41. Melvyn D. Read, and David Marsh, 'Homosexuality', in Philip Cowley (ed.), *Conscience and Parliament* (Frank Cass, London, 1998), p. 25.

42. Private information.

43. Conversation with Anne Perkins, May 2003.

44. PRO, PREM 15/437, Carr to Heath, 15 December 1970; P. L. Gregson to Heath, 28 April 1971, note by Heath.

45. Paul O'Higgins, *Censorship in Britain* (Nelson, London, 1972), pp. 78–90.

46. Ibid., p. 102.

47. *Report of the Departmental Committee on Homosexuality and Prostitution* (Cmnd. 247, 1957), para. 13.

48. Lord Devlin, *The Enforcement of Morals* (Oxford University Press, London, 1959), p. 23.

49. Ibid., pp. 14–15.

50. Ibid., pp. 8–9.

51. H. L. A. Hart, *Law, Liberty and Morality* (Oxford University Press, London, 1963), p. 51 (emphasis added).

52. Interview with Lord Fowler, 7 July 2003.

53. Mary Warnock, *A Question of Life: The Warnock Report on Human Fertilisation and Embryology* (Blackwell, Oxford, 1985), pp. vi–vii.

54. Ibid., p. ix.

55. PRO, HO 291/127, Brian Cubbon to Sir Norman Skelhorn (Director of Public Prosecutions), 17 November 1965.

56. Quoted in Francesca Klug, *Values for a Godless Age: The Story of the New Bill of Rights* (Penguin, London, 2000), p. 122.

57. PRO, LCO 2/5570.

58. Earl of Kilmuir, *Political Adventure: The Memoirs of the Earl of Kilmuir* (Weidenfeld and Nicolson, London, 1964), pp. 182–3.

59. PRO, HO 291/1536, Soskice to Chuter Ede, 17 November 1949.

60. K. D. Ewing, and C. A. Gearty, *Freedom under Thatcher: Civil Liberties in Modern Britain* (Clarendon Press, Oxford, 1984), p. 14.

61. Legislation on Human Rights: With Particular Reference to the European Convention (Home Office, 1976); interview with Sir Brian Cubbon, 20 July 2003.

62. Klug, *Values for a Godless Age*, pp. 154–7.

63. Devlin, *Enforcement of Morals*, p. 25.

64. HL Deb, vol. 573, col. 1692, 15 July 1996, quoted in Klug, *Values for a Godless Age*, p. 139.

65. Klug, *Values for a Godless Age*, pp. 55–66; Joan Smith, *Moralities: Sex, Money and Power in the Twenty-first Century* (Allen Lane, London, 2001).

66. Mary Warnock, *An Intelligent Person's Guide to Ethics* (Duckworth, London, 1998).

67. Gorer, *Exploring English Character*, pp. 94–124.

68. John Selwyn Gummer, The Permissive Society: Fact or Fantasy? (Cassell, London, 1971), pp. 5–6.

69. Klug, *Values for a Godless Age*, p. 148.

70. Gorer, *Exploring English Character*, p. 95.

71. Peter Hitchens, *The Abolition of Britain: the British Cultural Revolution from Lady Chatterley to Tony Blair*, rev. ed. (Quartet, London, 2000), pp. 292–3.

72. Lara Marks, *Sexual Chemistry: A History of the Contraceptive Pill* (Yale University Press, New Haven and London, 2001), pp. 202–3.

73. Melanie Phillips, *All Must Have Prizes* (Little, Brown, London, 1996), particularly pp. 241–260

74. Philip Cowley, 'Divorce', in *Conscience and Parliament*, p. 75.

75. Sir Edmund Leach, *A Runaway World? The Reith Lectures 1967*, (BBC, London, 1968), p. 44.

76. Alison Park and Ceridwen Hughes, 'The Ties that Bind', in Alison Park, John Curtice, Katarina Thomson, Lindsey Jarvis and Catherine Bromley (eds), *British Social Attitudes: The 19th Report* (Sage, London, 2002), p. 205.

77. Sandra Vegeris and Jane Perry, *Families and Children 2001: Living Standards and the Children* (Department for Work and Pensions, 2003).

78. Jonathan Freedland, 'The moral majority', *Guardian*, 10 October 2002.

Chapter 2

1. Aldous Huxley, *Brave New World* quoted in Philip Cowley (ed.), *Conscience and Parliament* (Frank Cass, London, 1998), p. 75.

2. Introducing her Bill to give known prostitutes the same legal protection as other women. HC Deb, vol. 482, cols 1175–8, 13 December 1950.

3. Following the Government's defeat on capital punishment, quoted in 'Unity to retain freedom', *The Times*, 22 April 1948.

4. Debating the Report of the Royal Commission on Marriage and Divorce, HL Deb, vol. 199, cols 972–1066, 24 October 1956.

5. John Newsom, *The Education of Girls* (Faber and Faber, London, 1948), pp. 146, 102.

6. Jeffrey Weeks, *Sex, Politics and Society: The Regulation of Sexuality since 1800* (Longman, London,

1989), pp. 232–9.

7. *Report of the Royal Commission on Population*, Cmnd. 7695 (HMSO: 1949), p. 227.

8. PRO, CAB 124/1037, note by Morrison, undated, presumably summer 1949.

9. Audrey Leathard, *The Fight for Family Planning: The Development of Family Planning Services in Britain 1921–74* (Macmillan, London, 1980), pp. 78–85.

10. PRO, PREM 8/1061.

11. HC Deb, vol. 468, cols 747–9, 20 October 1949; 'Compulsory measures discussed', *The Times*, 16 November 1949.

12. Quoted in Weeks, *Sex, Politics and Society*, p. 233.

13. 'Today's families', *The Times*, 30 November 1955.

14. Leathard, *Fight for Family Planning*, pp. 93–4.

15. Robert Chester, 'Divorce in England and Wales', in Robert Chester (ed.), *Divorce in Europe* (Martinus Nijhoff, Leiden, 1977), pp. 72–3.

16. Leo Abse, *Private Member* (Macdonald, London, 1973), p. 165.

17. National Museum of Labour History, R.D.100, *Memorandum on Divorce*, anonymous, April 1948; R.D.104, *Marriage and Divorce Law Reform*, Robert Pollard, May 1948.

18. PRO, PREM 8/1386, Jowitt to Attlee, 6 July 1949; Jowitt to Morrison, 2 July 1949.

19. PRO, CAB 128/16 CC (49) 44th conclusions, 7 July 1949.

20. PRO, CAB 128/16 CC (49) 45th conclusions, 11 July 1949.

21. PRO, CAB 128/17 CC(50) 11th conclusions, 16 March 1950.

22. PRO, PREM 8/1386, A. Johnston to Attlee, 8 March 1951.

23. PRO, CAB 128/19 CC (51) 18th conclusions, 8 March 1951.

24. Shawcross's own marital history was scarred by tragedy and drama. His first wife, who had suffered terrible illness throughout her life, committed suicide after nineteen years of marriage in 1943. His second wife, the mother of his children, died in a horse-riding accident in 1974. When he decided to marry his new companion at the age of ninety-five, his children won a court ruling, after the humiliation of medical and psychological tests, that Shawcross was incapable of rational decision. The following month, the couple eloped to Gibraltar, where the courts ruled the opposite. His wife survived him when he died in 2003 at the age of 101. (Dan van der Vat, obituary, *Guardian*, 11 July 2003.)

25. HC Deb, vol. 485, cols 926–1020, 9 March 1951.

26. PRO, PREM 8/1386, Shawcross to Attlee, 13 March 1951.

27. HC Deb, vol. 485, cols 1547–9, 14 March 1951.

28. PRO, CAB 129/45 CP (51) 119, 27 April 1951.

29. PRO, PREM 8/1386, Brook to Attlee, 1 May 1951.

30. PRO, CAB 128/19 CC (51) 33rd conclusions, 3 May 1951.

31. Anne Perkins, *Red Queen: The Authorised Biography of Barbara Castle* (Macmillan, London, 2003), pp. 94–5.

32. HO 45/25339.

33. HC Deb, vol. 482, cols 1175–8, 13 December 1950.

34. HO 45/25339.

35. HL Deb, vol. 171, cols 1198–1206, 6 June 1951.

36. Anne Perkins to the author.

37. Kevin Jefferys (ed.), *Labour and the Wartime Coalition: From the Diary of James Chuter Ede 1941–1945* (Historians' Press, London, 1987), pp. 15–16.

38. Bernard Donoughue and George Jones, *Herbert Morrison: Portrait of a Politician* (Weidenfeld and

Nicolson, London, 1973), pp. 309–10.

39.   Ibid., pp. 430–1, 545.

40.   J. B. Christoph, *Capital Punishment and British Politics: The British Movement to Abolish the Death Penalty 1945–57* (George Allen and Unwin, London, 1962) p.

41.   HC Deb, vol. 449, cols 979–1098, 14 April 48. Interestingly, at the end of the debate the Labour MP Reginald Paget announced that he had been informed that Paterson had made a deathbed conversion to abolition, and joined the National Council for the Abolition of the Death Penalty. This was later disproved, causing Paget to be scorned by retentionist colleagues, though it is doubtful that at this late stage many minds would have been swayed by his erroneous claim.

42.   'Unity to retain freedom', *The Times*, 22 April 1948.

43.   HL Deb, vol. 156, cols 19–75, 102–216, 1–2 June 1948.

44.   HC Deb, vol. 453, cols 1411–1545, 15 July 1948.

45.   Christoph, *Capital Punishment and British Politics*, p. 63.

46.   HL Deb, vol. 157, cols 1002–72, 20 July 1948.

47.   HC Deb, vol. 454, cols 707–56, 22 July 1948.

48.   PRO, PREM 5/435, Brook to Attlee, 6 November 1948.

49.   PRO, PREM 5/435, Attlee to Chuter Ede, 19 January 1949; 21 January 1949.

50.   Tynan, Kenneth, *A View of the English Stage* (Davis Poynter, London, 1975), p. 366.

51.   John Johnston, *The Lord Chamberlain's Blue Pencil* (Hodder and Stoughton, London, 1990), p. 7.

52.   Johnston, *Lord Chamberlain's Blue Pencil*, pp. 119–25.

53.   Roger Wilmut, *Kindly Leave the Stage! The Story of Variety 1919–1960* (Methuen, London, 1985).

54.   John Elsom, *Post-war British Theatre* rev. ed. (Routledge and Kegan Paul, London, 1979), p. 204.

55.   Johnston, *Lord Chamberlain's Blue Pencil*, p. 173.

56.   PRO, LCO 2/4705, Clarendon to Jowitt, 6 February 1951; Jowitt to Clarendon, 7 February 1951.

57.   BL, LCP/1452, comment by Lord Scarbrough on reader's report, presumably mid-May 1957. *The Catalyst* was eventually licensed on 13 November 1958, though no correspondence relating to this decision survives in the file.

58.   HC Deb, vol. 463, cols 713–98, 25 March 1949.

59.   John Parker, *Father of the House: Fifty Years in Politics* (Routledge and Kegan Paul, London, 1982), p. 118.

60.   Peter Hennessy, *Never Again: Britain 1945–51* (Jonathan Cape, London, 1992) p. 316.

61.   Parker, *Father of the House*, pp. 218–125.

62.   *The Economist*, 23 December 1950, letter from Phillip Williams and David Butler, quoted in Peter Richards, *Parliament and Conscience* (Allen and Unwin, London, 1970), p. 163.

63.   PRO, HO 300/2, J.S., No. 10, to Maxwell-Fyfe, 22 January 1953.

64.   PRO, CAB 134/998 LC(53), 1st meeting, 20 January 1953.

65.   HC Deb., vol. 510, cols 1350 & 1343, 30 January 1953.

66.   Parker, *Father of the House*, p. 120.

67.   'Scots critic of Duke's Sunday polo', *Sunday Times*, 4 September 1955.

68.   LPL, GFP/182, Fisher to Edinburgh, 9 September 1955.

69.   LPL, GFP/182, Edinburgh to Fisher, 27 September 1955.

70.   PRO, HO 291/123, Kilmuir to Butler, 3 March 1958.

71.   Weeks, *Sex, Politics and Society*, pp. 160–61; Hyde, H. Montgomery, *The Other Love: An Historical and Contemporary Survey of Homosexuality in Britain* (Heinemann, London, 1970), pp. 216–28.

72.   Weeks, *Sex, Politics and Society*, pp. 158–9.

73. Hyde, *Other Love*, p. 215.

74. J. F. Wolfenden, *Turning Points: The Memoirs of Lord Wolfenden* (Bodley Head, London, 1976), p. 131.

75. CEMWC, *The Problem of Homosexuality* (Church Information Board, London, 1952).

76. NMLH, RD/109, May 1948.

77. Interview with Peter Hennessy for Channel 4 series *What Has Become of Us?*, 31 May 1994.

78. Interview with Lord Deedes, 23 September 1997.

79. Quoted in Weeks, *Sex, Politics and Society*.

80. HC Deb, vol. 523, col. w229, 18 February 1954.

81. PRO, CAB 128/27 part 2 CM (54) 11th conclusions, 24 February 1954.

82. PRO, CAB 128/27 part 2 CM (54) 20th conclusions, 17 March 1954.

83. PRO, CAB 128/27 part 2 CM (54) 29th conclusions, 15 April 1954.

84. PRO, PREM 11/1241, Brook to Churchill, 30 July 1954; C (54) 264, 'Royal Commissions', note by the Prime Minister, 1 August 1954.

85. PRO, CAB 128/28 CP (55) 10th conclusions, 9 February 1955.

86. Nicolson, Nigel, *People and Parliament* (Weidenfeld and Nicolson, London, 1958) p. 87.

87. HC Deb, vol. 536, cols 2064–2184, 10 February 1955.

88. PRO, PREM 11/1241.

89. PRO, PREM 11/1241.

90. HC Deb, vol. 548, cols 2536–2656, 16 February 1956.

91. PRO, PREM 11/1241, Heath to Eden, 21 February 1956. Carr had by then moved to a junior ministerial post at the Ministry of Labour and National Service.

92. Anthony Howard, *Rab: The Life of R. A. Butler* (Jonathan Cape, London, 1987), pp. 225–6. According to Howard, two caveats should be entered. Butler now maintained a silence on capital punishment, perhaps partly through unhappiness at being isolated from his natural allies in the party. He also supported Peter Kirk to succeed him as MP for Saffron Walden, who staunchly resisted pressure from the whips and his local association to desist from leading Conservative support for Silverman's Bill in 1965.

93. 'Eden stops Cabinet crisis', *Daily Mail*, 24 February 1956; PRO, PREM 11/1241, F.A.B. to Ian Bancroft, Lord Privy Seal's Office, 3 March 1956.

94. PRO, PREM 11/1241.

95. HC Deb, vol. 550, cols 58–146, 12 March 1956.

96. Quoted in Richards, *Parliament and Conscience*, p. 47.

97. HL Deb, vol. 198, cols 564–842, 9–10 July 1956.

98. Christoph, *Capital Punishment and British Politics*, p. 154.

99. HC Deb, vol. 560, cols 1144–1259, 15 November 1956.

100. O. R. McGregor, *Divorce in England: A Centenary Study* (Heinemann, London, 1957), pp. 134–47.

101. McGregor, *Divorce in England*, pp. 177–89.

102. LPL, GFP/128, Morton to Fisher, 20 July 1953; 'note of conversation between Fisher and Morton', 28 July 1953.

103. Lawrence Stone, *The Road to Divorce: England 1530–1987* (Oxford University Press, Oxford, 1990), pp. 401–9.

104. HL Deb, vol. 199, cols 972–1066, 24 October 1956.

105. PRO, CAB 134/1253 HP(56) 17th meeting, 22 October 1956; CAB 134/1968, HA(57) 15th meeting, 28 June 1957.

Chapter 3

1.   Report of the Departmental Committee on Homosexual Offences and Prostitution, Cmnd. 247 (HMSO, 1957), paras 12–13, pp. 9–10.
2.   Bernard Fergusson, 'Higher Motive' in *Hubble Bubble* (Collins, London, 1978).
3.   John Osborne, Look *Back in Anger* in A II.ii (Faber and Faber, London, 1954), p. 94
4.   BBC1, 26 September 1973, quoted in Alistair Horne, Macmillan, vol. 2: 1957–1986 (Macmillan, London, 1988), pp. 495–6.
5.   Quoted in Christine Keeler, *The Truth at Last: My Story* (Pan, London, 2002).
6.   Mark Abrams, *The Teenage Consumer* (Routledge and Kegan Paul, London, 1959), p. 9.
7.   Arthur Marwick, *British Society since 1945* (Allen Lane, London, 1982), p. 117.
8.   Bernard Sendall, *Independent Television in Britain, vol. 1: Origin and Foundation* (Macmillan, London, 1982), p. 371.
9.   Callum G. Brown, *The Death of Christian Britain: understanding secularisation 1800–2000* (Routledge, London, 2000), p. 188.
10.   See, for example, Raymond Williams, *Communications* 3rd ed. (Pelican, Harmondsworth, 1976), pp. 82–116 for a contemporary discussion of the effects of commercial television and advertising.
11.   John Selwyn Gummer, *The Permissive Society: Fact or Fantasy?* (Cassell, London, 1971), p. 14.
12.   Richard Hoggart, *The Uses of Literacy* (Penguin, London, 1958), pp. 171–223.
13.   Frank Parkin, *Middle Class Radicalism – The Social Bases of the British Campaign for Nuclear Disarmament* (Manchester University Press, Manchester, 1968), chapter 7.
14.   Michelene Wandor, *Look Back in Gender: Sexuality and the Family in Post-war British Drama* (Methuen, London, 1987), p. 40.
15.   Anthony Aldgate, *Censorship and the Permissive Society: British Cinema and Theatre 1955–1965* (Oxford University Press, Oxford, 1995), p. 41.
16.   Marwick, *British Society since 1945*, p. 133.
17.   Betty Friedan, *The Feminine Mystique* (Victor Gollancz, London, 1963).
18.   Carol Smart, *The Ties that Bind* (Routledge and Kegan Paul, London, 1984), p. 52.
19.   Interview with Lord Deedes, 23 September 1997.
20.   Hugo Young, *This Blessed Plot: Britain and Europe from Churchill to Blair* (Macmillan, London, 1998), p. 95.
21.   *The Next Five Years* (Conservative Central Office, London, 1959).
22.   Lord Butler, *The Art of the Possible: The Memoirs of Lord Butler* (Hamish Hamilton, London, 1971), pp. 197–8.
23.   Butler, *Art of the Possible*, pp. 199–200.
24.   James Margach, *The Anatomy of Power: An Enquiry into the Personality of Leadership* (W. H. Allen, London, 1979) pp. 116–17.
25.   Quoted in Horne, *Macmillan*, vol. 2, p. 80.
26.   Taped conversation between Horne and Macmillan, quoted in Alistair Horne, Macmillan, vol. 1: 1894–1956 (Macmillan, London, 1988), p. 80.
27.   Peter Hennessy, *The Prime Minister: The Office and Its Holders since 1945* (Allen Lane, London, 2000), pp. 255–6.
28.   Quoted in Mark Jarvis, *Conservative Governments, Morality and Social Change in Affluent Britain, 1957–1975* (Manchester University Press, forthcoming); Ramsden, John, *Winds of Change:*

Macmillan to Heath 1957–1975 (Longman, London, 1996), p. 54.

29. J. F Wolfenden,. *Turning Points: The Memoirs of Lord Wolfenden* (Bodley Head, London, 1976), pp. 141–2.

30. LPL, GFP/193, Wolfenden to Fisher, 24 September 1957.

31. PRO, HO 45/25306, minutes of committee, 14th meeting, 4 October 1955.

32. Lord Allen of Abbeydale, interview with Peter Hennessy for Channel 4 series *What Has Become of Us?*, 31 May 1994.

33. LPL, GFP/193, Fisher to Wolfenden, 14 September 1957, 18 November 1957.

34. Wolfenden, *Turning Points*, pp. 140–41.

35. 'Homosexual acts: call to reform law', Letters to the Editor, *The Times*, 7 March 1958.

36. 'Homosexual acts', Letters to the Editor, *The Times*, 19 April 1958.

37. PRO, CAB 134/1968 H(57) 26th meeting, 29 November 1957; PRO, CAB 134/1972 H(58) 20th meeting, 24 October 1958.

38. PRO, HO 291/123, Cunningham to Butler, 21 October 1957; W. S. Murrie, Scottish Home Department, to Butler, 30 October 1957.

39. For example Desmond Donnelly, Labour MP for Pembroke, HC Deb, vol. 588, cols 1475–6, 16 May 1958.

40. PRO, HO 291/123, Theobald Matthew to F. L. T. Graham-Harrison, Police Division, Home Office, 4 November 1957.

41. PRO, CAB 134/1968 HA(57) 26th meeting, 21 November 1957.

42. PRO, HO 291/124, Sir Charles Cunningham to Butler, January 1958.

43. PRO, HO 291/124, J. H. Walker, Secretary, Prison Commission, to Conwy Roberts, Criminal Department, Home Office, 11 November 1957.

44. PRO, HO 291/124, Cunningham to Butler, January 1958; HC Deb, vol. 596, cols 503–4, 26 November 1958.

45. HC Deb, vol. 596, col. 365, 26 November 1958; interview with Lord Deedes, 23 September 1997.

46. Peter Richards, *Parliament and Conscience* (Allen & Unwin, London, 1970), pp. 73 & 75; Anthony Grey, 'Homosexual Law Reform', in Brian Frost (ed.), *The Tactics of Pressure: A Critical Review of Six British Pressure Groups* (Stainer and Bell, London, 1975), p. 43; *Homosexuals and the Law* (Homosexual Law Reform Society, London, 1959); Peter Wildeblood, *Against the Law* (Weidenfeld and Nicolson, London, 1955); Eustace Chesser, *Live and Let Live: The Moral of the Wolfenden Report* (Heinemann, London, 1958).

47. Jeffrey Weeks, *Sex, Politics and Society: The Regulation of Sexuality since 1800* (Longman, London, 1989), p. 170.

48. Kenneth Walker, *Sexual Behaviour: Creative and Destructive* (William Kimber, London, 1966), p. 244.

49. Grey, 'Homosexual Law Reform', p. 46.

50. *Daily Mirror*, 5 September 1965.

51. Richards, *Parliament and Conscience*, p. 73.

52. 'Vice', leader, *The Times*, 26 November 1958.

53. 'Gallup poll on the Vice Report', *News Chronicle*, 10 September 1957.

54. PRO, LCO 2/5762, J. W. Bourne, Lord Chancellor's Department, to R. R. Pittam, 12 December 1957.

55. Quoted in Jeffrey Weeks, *Coming Out: Homosexual Politics in Britain from the Nineteenth Century to the Present* (Quartet, London, 1977), p. 168.

56. B. A. Young, Letters to the Editor, *Spectator*, 26 October 1956; BL, LCP 1459 Nugent to Scarbrough, 25 October 1956.

57. PRO, HO 300/12, note by Scarbrough of meeting with Butler, 4 June 1957.

58. PRO, HO 300/12, note for the record, 4 June 1957.

59. *Daily Mail*, 30 January 1958.

60. *Daily Express*, 31 January 1958. It should be remembered that this comment was made before the Obscene Publications Act 1959 introduced a defence of 'literary merit', so was hardly advocating a free-for-all.

61. PRO, HO 300/12, note by Scarbrough of meeting with Butler, 4 June 1957.

62. PRO, HO 300/12, Amendment of the Theatres Act 1843, memorandum by the Secretary for the Home Department and Lord Privy Seal, February 1958.

63. PRO, CAB 134/1972 H(58) 12th meeting, 17 June 1958.

64. PRO, CAB 134/1972 H(58) 16th meeting, 25 July 1958.

65. BL, LCP/WB 23, minute by Scarbrough, 31 October 1958.

66. BL, LCP/1017, reader's report by C. D. Heriot, 5 May 1958.

67. BL, LCP/1017, comment by Gwatkin, undated but presumably 5 or 6 June 1958; PRO, HO 300/12, note of meeting between Scarbrough and Butler, 4 June 1957.

68. John Johnston, *The Lord Chamberlain's Blue Pencil* (Hodder and Stoughton, London, 1990), p. 278. Thirty plays out of 10,219 under Scarbrough between 1952 and 1963, and 11 out of 4,405 under Cobbold between 1963 and 1968, were refused a licence.

69. Anthony Howard, *Rab: The Life of R. A. Butler* (Jonathan Cape, London, 1987), p. 266.

70. Alan Travis, *Bound and Gagged: A Secret History of Obscenity in Britain* (Profile, London, 2000), pp. 92–127.

71. Howard, *Rab* p. 266.

72. Travis, *Bound and Gagged*, pp. 128–65.

73. Ibid., p. 162.

74. BBC IR/62/58, 'Alfie Elkins and His Little Life', 30 January 1962.

75. *Daily Telegraph*, 30 May 1960.

76. Asa Briggs, *The History of Broadcasting in the United Kingdom, vol 5: Competition* (Oxford University Press, Oxford, 1995), pp. 395–6; BBC T16/543, 'Control over the subject matter of programmes in BBC television', note by Huw Wheldon, Controller of Programming (Television), 28 September 1966.

77. Anthony Aldgate, *Censorship and the Permissive Society: British Cinema and Theatre 1955–65* (Oxford University Press, Oxford, 1995), pp. 7–8.

78. Johnston, *Lord Chamberlain's Blue Pencil*, p. 183.

79. BL, LCP/4112, reader's report, 14 March 1964.

80. Richards, *Parliament and Conscience*, p. 120.

81. Ibid., p. 119.

82. Johnston, *Lord Chamberlain's Blue Pencil*, p. 210.

83. PRO, HO 300/12, Scarbrough's note of meeting with Butler, 4 June 1957.

84. 'Theatre on thin ice', leader, *The Times*, 1 February 1958.

85. HC Deb, vol. 570, cols 33–4, 13 May 1957.

86. Johnston, *Lord Chamberlain's Blue Pencil*, p. 212.

87. *Manchester Guardian*, 1 February 1958.

88. PRO, HO 300/12, note by Miss M. Hornsby, General Department, 17 February 1958.

89. PRO, HO 300/12, Hornsby to N. D. Walker, Scottish Home Department, 29 October 1957.

90. PRO, CAB 134/1972 H(58) 12th meeting, 17 June 1958.

91. PRO, HO 300/12, S. A. Gywnn, Children's Department, to Walker, 19 November 1957; H. W. Stotesbury, Home Office, to Walker, 6 February 1958.

92. PRO, HO 300/2, Butler to Cunningham, 16 January 1959.

93. Quoted in Jarvis, *Conservative Governments*.

94. Quoted in Ramsden, *Winds of Change*, p. 54.

95. Jarvis, *Conservative Governments*.

96. W. F. Deedes, *Dear Bill: W. F. Deedes Reports* (Macmillan, London, 1997), p. 137.

97. PRO, T 233/1369, Macmillan to Peter Thorneycroft, 28 May 1957. Quoted in Jarvis, *Conservative Governments*.

98. PRO, HO 295/1, Cyril Black to Macmillan, 2 July 1959. Quoted in Jarvis, *Conservative Governments*.

99. CPA, CRD 2/44/1, Home Office Affairs Committee, 11 November 1959.

100. Bernard Levin, *The Pendulum Years: Britain and the Sixties* (Jonathan Cape, London, 1970), pp. 14–15.

101. Jarvis, *Conservative Governments*.

102. 'On the threshold of victory', *The Times*, 2 October 1962.

103. MS.RAB/K51, notes for a lecture to the Law Society, 'The Home Office in Modern Times', October 1967. Quoted in Jarvis, *Conservative Governments*.

104. PRO, PREM 11/3686, 4960.

105. HC Deb, vol. 584, cols 777–876, 14 March 1958.

106. John Parker, *Father of the House: Fifty Years in Politics* (Routledge and Kegan Paul, London, 1982), p. 120.

107. PRO, HO 300/2, Cunningham to Butler, 2 March 1959.

108. Jarvis, *Conservative Governments*.

109. PRO, HO 300/2, note of meeting between Butler, Cunningham, David Renton and Austin Strutt, 14 December 1959.

110. PRO, HO 300/13, Vosper to Butler, 25 November 1960.

111. PRO, HO 300/13, Cunningham to Butler, 26 November 1960.

112. PRO, HO 300/13, Vosper to Butler, 19 December 1960; Cunningham to Butler, 26 January 1961; note by Vosper, 29 January 1961.

113. HC Deb., vol. 644, col. w69, 13 July 1961. Dugdale had been forced to resign as a minister under Churchill over the Crichel Down affair, hounded from office by his own backbenchers. He was rewarded for what Churchill described as his chivalry 'in the extreme' with a hereditary peerage. (See Peter Hennessy, *Whitehall* rev. ed. [Pimlico, London, 2001], pp. 502–4.)

114. PRO, HO 300/13, C. M. Woodhouse to Brooke, 5 September 1962.

115. PRO, HO 300/13, Cunningham to Butler, 7 April 1961.

116. PRO, HO 300/14, Cunningham to Brooke and Charles Woodhouse, 1 May 1964.

117. Jarvis, *Conservative Governments*.

118. HC Deb, vol. 625, col. 1510, 29 June 1960.

119. Norman St John Stevas, 'Wolfenden Reconsidered – I', *Crossbow*, vol. 2, no. 2, pp. 12–14.

120. Richards, *Parliament and Conscience*, p. 75.

121. Interview with Lord Deedes, 23 September 1997.

122. HC Deb, vol. 625, col. 1489, 29 June 1960.

123. HC Deb., vol. 615, cols w215–16, 17 December 1959; HL Deb, vol. 228, col. w1008.

124. Butler, *Art of the Possible*, pp. 203–4.

125. HC Deb, vol. 625, cols 1480–9, 29 June 1960; LPL, GFP/193, 182, Fisher to Canon J. S. Bezzant, St John's College, Cambridge, 21 November 1957.

126. PRO, HO 291/125, 'Draft Analysis…', unsigned, 26 July 1960.

127. HC Deb, vol. 625, cols 1453–1514, 29 June 1960.

128. HC Deb, vol. 655, cols 858–9, 9 March 1962.

129. PRO, CAB 134/2173 LC(62) 6th meeting, 27 February 1962.

130. PRO, HO 291/125, note of meeting held 15 March 1962.

131. PRO, HO 291/125, F. L. T. Graham-Harrison, Criminal Department, to Cunningham, 18 April 1962.

132. PRO, HO 291/125, Cunningham to Butler, 14 March 1962.

133. BLPES, HC/AG 1/2a, minutes of meeting of HLRS, 21 March 1962, 23 March 1964; HC Deb, vol. 693, cols 586–7; BLPES, HC/AG 1/5, Arran to Grey, 28 April 1964.

134. HC Deb, vol. 682, col. w242, 24 October 1962.

135. PRO, HO 291/125, Brooke to Cunningham, 1 December 1962; Cunningham to Brooke, 28 December 1962, note by Brooke, 1 January 1963.

136. PRO, HO 291/125, Astor to Brooke, 26 April 1963; Wright to Jellicoe, 8 May 1963.

137. PRO, HO 291/125, Hobson to Cunningham, 19 March 1963.

138. PRO, HO 291/125, Cunningham to Brooke, 4 January 1963 and comments by Jellicoe, 11 January 1963, Fletcher-Cooke, 14 January 1963.

139. Rebecca West, *The Vassall Affair* (*Sunday Telegraph*, London, 1963), p. 16.

140. HL Deb, vol. 249, cols 752–4; BLPES, HC/AG 1/5, Grey to Arran, 14 May 1963.

141. PRO, HO 291/125, Hobson to Cunningham, 19 March 1963.

142. Matthew Parris, *Great Parliamentary Scandals: Four Centuries of Calumny, Smear and Innuendo* (Robson, London, 1995), pp. 159–75.

143. HC Deb, vol. 674, col. 727.

144. Ramsden, *Winds of Change*, p. 183.

145. 'It is a moral issue', *The Times*, 11 June 1963.

146. Ramsden, *Winds of Change*, p. 187.

147. HC Deb, vol. 679, cols 34–176, 17 June 1963.

148. John Turner, *Macmillan* (Longman, London, 1994), pp. 262–3; Ramsden, *Winds of Change*, pp. 189–230.

149. PRO, PREM 11/4689, Derek Mitchell, PPS to Chancellor of the Exchequer, to Douglas-Home, 19 July 1964.

150. PRO, PREM 11/4689, Sir Timothy Bligh, PPS to Prime Minister, to Douglas-Home, 21 July 1964.

151. PRO, PREM 11/4689, Redmayne to Brooke, 30 July 1964.

152. Richards, *Parliament and Conscience*, pp. 74–5.

153. PRO, PREM/11/4689, Timothy Bligh to Douglas-Home, 21 July 1964.

154. Interview with Lord Deedes, 23 September 1997.

155. Andrew Roth, 'Top of the Tory form', Obituaries, *Guardian*, 27 February 1999.

156. PRO, FO 1109/277, Eccles to Macmillan, 6 July 1959.

157. PRO, T 18/169, Eccles to Macmillan, 'Leisure in our affluent age', 23 December 1959; *Patronage and the Arts*; Timothy Raison, 'Patronage, Prestige and Principles', *Crossbow*, vol. 3, no.9, pp. 58–9.

158. PRO, T 18/169, R. C. Griffiths to Burke Trend, 8 January 1960.

159. PRO, T 18/169, Trend to Griffiths, 29 February 1960.

160. PRO, T 18/169, Heathcoat-Amory to Macmillan, 9 February 1960.

161. PRO, ED 86/356, 'Teacher training, morality and religion'.

162. 'Chastity speech storm for Boyle', *Daily Mail*, 31 July 1963.

163. Editorial, *Daily Express*, 24 August 1963.

164. 'Youth and chastity', *Daily Mail*, 30 July 1963.

165. 'The man with your children's future in his hands', *Daily Express*, 25 August 1963.

166. 'BMA man lashes at Boyle over sex', *Evening Standard* (London), 27 August 1963.

167. 'Chastity rebuff to doctor', *Sunday Telegraph*, 25 August 1963.

168. 'Whose job to teach morals', *News of the World*, 1 September 1963.

169. 'Nature's intention for sex', *Guardian*, September 1963.

170. PRO, ED 50/862, correspondence between Fisher, Macmillan and Boyle.

171. Leo Abse, *Private Member* (Macdonald, London, 1973), p. 164.

172. Interview with Leo Abse, 5 December 1997.

173. PRO, CAB 134/1993 HA(63) 3rd meeting, 22 February 1963.

174. HC Deb, Standing Committee C, 1962/1963, vol. 2, 1st to 4th sittings, 6–27 March 1963.

175. *The Times*, 3 April 1963. According to Abse he was called by the editor of *The Times*, who said, 'A rather interesting event is taking place which will rather disturb you. For the first time in ecclesiastical history all the Churches have come together … to make a statement condemning your Bill.' Interview with Leo Abse, 5 December 1997.

176. Abse, *Private Member*, pp. 170–71.

177. PRO, PREM 11/4745, TJB to Douglas-Home, 16 March 1964; Trend to Douglas-Home, 16 March 1964.

178. LPL, RP/43, Eric Fletcher to Ramsey, 16 April 1963; Beloe to Ramsey, 2 May 1963; note of meeting with Robert Brooke, Ramsey's private secretary; Charles Woodhouse, Parliamentary Under-Secretary; Guppy, a Home Office official; and Beloe, 7 October 1963; press release, 'Archbishop of Canterbury appoints group to consider divorce law', 10 April 1964; LPL, RP/82, note of telephone conversation between Beloe and Fletcher, 18 March 1965.

179. Lawrence Stone, *The Road to Divorce: England 1530–1987* (Oxford University Press, Oxford, 1990), p. 406.

180. J. A. T. Robinson, *Honest to God* (SCM Press, London, 1963); A. Heron, (ed.), *Towards a Quaker View of Sex: An Essay by a Group of Friends* (Friends Home Service Committee, London, 1963); Tony Benn, *Out of the Wilderness: Diaries 1963–1967* (Hutchinson, London, 1987), 13 May 1963, pp. 17–19.

181. Tim Newburn, *Permission and Regulation: Law and Morals in Post-war Britain* (Routledge, London, 1992), p. 175.

182. Quoted in Paul A. Welsby *A History of the Church of England 1945–1980* (Oxford University Press, Oxford, 1984), p. 113.

183. Heron, *Towards a Quaker View of Sex*, p. 39.

184. Christopher Booker, *The Neophiliacs* (Collins, London, 1969), pp. 194–5.

Chapter 4

1.   Tribute on the death of Harold Wilson, HC Deb, vol. 260, col. 909, 24 May 1995

2. HC Deb, vol. 750, col. 1372, 13 July 1967.
3. Second-reading debate on Lord Willis' Sunday entertainments Bill, HL Deb, vol. 278, col. 64, 21 November 1966.
4. 'Patron of the Arts', BBC2, 14 January 1988.
5. Interview with Gwyneth Dunwoody, 27 March 2000.
6. PRO, PREM 5/1965, '1965 Ministerial Appointments', notes by Derek Mitchell (Wilson's PPS), 2 August 1965, 21 September 1965, 13 December 1965.
7. Interview with Lord Jenkins, 25 November 1999.
8. Roy Jenkins, *A Life at the Centre* (Macmillan, London, 1991), pp. 176–7.
9. Barbara Castle, *The Castle Diaries 1964–1970* (Weidenfeld and Nicolson, London, 1974), p. 103, 11 February 1966.
10. Joe Haines, *Glimmers of Twilight: Murder, Intrigue and Passion at the Court of Harold Wilson* (Politico's, London, 2003); Bernard Donoughue, *The Heat of the Kitchen* (Politico's, London, 2003).
11. Alan Travis, 'How Wilson hounded the colonel', *Guardian*, 13 April 1999.
12. CMAC, SA/ALR A.16/7, note of meeting between Soskice and abortion law reform deputation, 2 February 1965.
13. PRO, HO 291/126, Sir Charles Cunningham to Soskice, 4 December 1964; comment by Soskice, 12 December 1964.
14. PRO, HO 291/125, note by Soskice, 19 December 1964.
15. PRO, CAB 129/126 part 1 C(65)68, 4 May 1965.
16. PRO, CAB 128/39 CC(64) 15th conclusions, 15 December 1964.
17. HC Deb, vol. 707, cols. 1701–2.
18. PRO, CAB 128/39 part 2 CC(65) 15th conclusions, 11 March 1965.
19. PRO, CAB 128/40 part 1 CC(65) 28th conclusions, 6 May 1965.
20. Leo Abse, *Private Member* (Macdonald, London, 1973), p. 149.
21. HL Deb, vol. 266, cols. 631–712, 24 May 1965.
22. LPL, RP/78, Ramsey to Arran, 18 May 1965.
23. BLPES, HC/AG 1/5, Queensberry to Grey, 25 May 1965.
24. *Daily Mail*, 1 November 1965; PRO, HO 291/127, 'NOP Poll on Wolfenden', November 1965.
25. Lord Arran, 'A Personal Memoir', *Encounter*, March 1972, p. 3.
26. Abse, *Private Member*, p. 150.
27. PRO, HO 291/126, Cunningham to Soskice, 24 June 1965.
28. PRO, HO 291/127, Stonham to Arran, 11 November 1965.
29. This result was despite the less than candid assistance given by some of the crustier Tory MPs to their colleagues. Shirley Williams recalls rushing in to the Commons just before a vote on the Sexual Offences Bill and asking one such knight of the shires what the issue at stake was – to which he replied, 'Don't trouble your pretty little head about it.' (Interview with Baroness Williams, 13 September 2003).
30. LPL, RP/98, Berkeley to Ramsey, 23 February 1966.
31. Stanley Henig to the author, 5 January 2004; Michael Steed, 'Lancaster's choice', Letters, *Independent*, 2 October 1991.
32. Hindell Keith and Madeleine Simms, *Abortion Law Reformed* (Peter Owen, London, 1971), p. 134.
33. *Sun*, 19 May 1966.
34. CMAC, SA/ALR A.15/3, Steel Papers.
35. 'Pressure on MPs', *Guardian*, 18 November 1966.

36. David Steel, *Against Goliath* (Weidenfeld and Nicolson, London, 1989), pp. 60–66; Hindell and Simms, *Abortion Law Reformed*, pp. 155–6.

37. LPL, RP/98, 242, Arran to Beloe, 3 June 1966.

38. BLPES, HC/AT, Henderson to Arran, 3 November 1965.

39. Interview with Jenkins, 25 November 1999. This comment looks surprisingly generous alongside the analysis in Abse's 1973 memoir, *Private Member*, of Jenkins' behaviour and the important influence of his socially pretentious mother (Abse, *Private Member*, pp. 34–6).

40. PRO, HO 291/128, 'Legislation Committee, Sexual Offences Bill (to be raised orally)', 24 June 1966.

41. Anthony Howard, *Crossman: The Pursuit of Power* (Jonathan Cape, London, 1990), pp. 24–5.

42. Richard Crossman, *The Diaries of a Cabinet Minister, vol. ii: Lord President of the Council and Leader of the House of Commons 1966–68* (Hamish Hamilton/Jonathan Cape, London, 1976), p. 407, 3 July 1967.

43. PRO, CAB 128/41 part 3 CC(66) 52nd conclusions, 27 October 1966.

44. Crossman, *Diaries of a Cabinet Minister, vol. ii*, p. 538, 27 October 1966.

45. Crossman, *Diaries of a Cabinet Minister, vol. ii*, p. 610, 19 December 1966.

46. David Butler, 'Electors and Elected', in A. H. Halsey (ed.), *British Social Trends since 1900: A Guide to the Changing Social Structure of Britain*, 2nd ed. (Macmillan, Basingstoke, 1988), p. 318.

47. Crossman, *Diaries of a Cabinet Minister, vol. ii*, p. 401, 29 June 1967.

48. 'Labour attacked for depravity', *The Times*, 2 July 1967.

49. HL Deb, vol. 285, col. 523, 21 July 1967.

50. Hindell and Simms, *Abortion Law Reformed*, pp. 112–24.

51. CMAC, SA/ALR A.13/1/1–5, surveys on abortion 1965–7.

52. CMAC, SA/ALR A.15.18, 'Survey of clergymen's opinions about abortion', 22 November 1966.

53. CMAC, SA/ALR A.15.18, 'NOP press release: Survey on abortion', 14 July 1966.

54. Survey of GPs' Opinions of the Medical Termination of Pregnancy Bill (NOP, 1967).

55. CMAC, SA/ALR A.15.18, 'NOP press release: Survey on abortion', 14 July 1966.

56. CMAC, SA/ALR A.15.18, 'NOP survey on abortion', 7 March 1967.

57. Hindell and Simms, *Abortion Law Reformed*, p. 102.

58. John Grigg, *History of The Times, vol. 6: The Thomson years 1966–1981* (Times, London, 1993), p. 60.

59. Hindell and Simms, *Abortion Law Reformed*, p. 128; 'Unclear and uncertain', *The Times*, 7 February 1967; 'Neutrality out of place', *The Times*, 13 December 1967.

60. Hindell and Simms, *Abortion Law Reformed*, p. 90.

61. LPL, RP/70, note by Robert Beloe of conversations in House of Lords, 25 November 1965.

62. PRO, CAB 128/41 part 1 CC(66) 5th conclusions, 3 February 1966.

63. HC Deb, vol. 725, cols 837–56, 25 February 1966.

64. Steel, *Against Goliath*, pp. 80–81.

65. Hindell and Simms, *Abortion Law Reformed*, p. 95.

66. CMAC, SA/ALR A.15.19, 'Mr Macleod supports Mr Steel's Bill', press release by David Steel, 7 December 1966.

67. Phone conversation with Paul Tulley, SPUC, 8 February 2000.

68. Interview with Gwyneth Dunwoody, 27 March 2000.

69. HL Deb, vol.285, cols 1068–70, 26 July 1967.

70. HL Deb, vol.285, col. 1069, 26 July 1967.

71. *Catholic Herald*, 21 August 1970, quoted in Hindell and Simms, *Abortion Law Reformed*, p. 149.

72. Interview with Baroness Williams, 13 September 2003.

73. Abse, *Private Member*, p. 218.

74. CMAC, SA/ALR A.13/3/1, January 1965, full figures of survey of London doctors.

75. 'The Royal Medico-Psychological Association's Memorandum on Therapeutic Abortion', *British Journal of Psychology*, 1966, vol. 112, p. 1071; 'Therapeutic Abortion: Report by BMA Special Committee', *British Medical Journal*, 2 July 1966, pp. 40–44; 'Legalised Abortion: Report by the Council of the RCOG', *British Medical Journal*, 2 April 1966, pp. 850–52.

76. CMAC, SA/ALR A.16/7, notes for speakers, 3 November 1965.

77. Interview with Gwyneth Dunwoody, 27 March 2000.

78. PRO, CAB 134/2854 H(67) 14th meeting, 12 May 1967.

79. John Keown, *Abortion, Doctors and the Law: Some Aspects of the Legal Regulation of Abortion in England from 1803 to 1982* (Cambridge University Press, Cambridge, 1988), p. 97.

80. CMAC, SA/ALR A.16/7, note of meeting between Silkin and Drs Stevenson and Gullick, 14 December 1965.

81. *British Medical Journal*, 31 December 1966.

82. HC Deb Standing Committee, vol. x, 3rd to 5th sittings, cols. 107–260, 1 February 1967, 8 February 1967, 15 February 1967.

83. Hindell and Simms, *Abortion Law Reformed*, pp. 192–3; *The Times*, 1 June 1967; PRO, CAB 128/42 part 2 CC(67) 35th conclusions, 1 June 1967.

84. PRO, CAB 134/2854 H(67) 14th meeting, 12 May 1967.

85. David Owen, *Time to Declare* (Michael Joseph, London, 1991) p. 55. Owen also felt a stronger backlash in his constituency about his support for homosexual law reform than abortion. He recounts that in his local party 'an older engine driver and stalwart in ASLEF got up after hearing my parliamentary report and said, "David, I accept that you're all in favour of abortion and that you support family allowances for unmarried mothers, but I do draw the line at buggery." He was rather upset when the entire committee burst into uncontrollable laughter. They were decent, tolerant people in my CLP and they never tried to inhibit me from exercising my judgement on such questions even if on occasions they felt the backlash in Plymouth pubs or even the Labour club.'

86. Steel, *Against Goliath*, p. 357.

87. PRO, CAB 128/42 part 2 CC (67) 30th conclusions, 11 May 1967.

88. Hindell and Simms, *Abortion Law Reformed*, p. 196.

89. Amy Baker, *Prime Ministers and the Rule Book* (Politico's, London, 2000), p. 30.

90. Crossman, *Diaries of a Cabinet Minister*, vol. ii, p. 410, 5 July 1967.

91. Ibid., p. 357, 30 May 1967.

92. Ibid., p. 403, 30 June 1967.

93. PRO, CAB 134/2956 LG(67) 15th meeting, 30 May 1967.

94. PRO, CAB 128/42 part 2 CC(67) 35th conclusions, 1 June 1967. At one point Steel had had to reject the idea put forward by the Earl of Dalkeith, Secretary of State for Scotland from 1962–64, that Scotland should be omitted from the Bill, because of both the anomaly that would be created and the absurdity of a Scottish MP introducing a bill which would apply only to England and Wales (HC Deb, Standing Committee F, vol. x, 9th sitting, 15 March 1967, cols 441–59).

95. PRO, CAB 128/42 part 2 CC(67) 35th conclusions, 1 June 1967.

96. HC Deb, vol. 748, col. 1964, 22 June 1967.

97. Crossman, *Diaries of a Cabinet Minister*, vol. ii, pp. 292–4, 22 June 1967.

98. PRO, CAB 128/42 part 2 CC(67) 45th conclusions, 6 July 1967; NMLH, PLP, 4 July 1967.

99. Crossman, *Diaries of a Cabinet Minister*, vol. ii, pp. 408–9, 4 July 1967.

100. Castle, *Castle Diaries 1964–1970*, p. 274, 6 July 1967.

101. HC Deb, vol. 749, col. 1996, 6 July 1967; Crossman, *Diaries of a Cabinet Minister*, vol. ii, p. 412, 6 July 1967.

102. HC Deb, vol. 732, col. 1166, 22 July 1966; vol. 750, cols 1385–6, 13 July 1967.

103. *Daily Telegraph*, 5 August 1967.

104. *Daily Telegraph*, 11 August 1967.

105. Crossman, *Diaries of a Cabinet Minister*, vol. ii, p. 522, 17 October 1967; p. 444, 26 July 1967.

106. Ibid., p. 522, 17 October 1967.

107. Ibid., p. 532, 24 October 1967.

108. Ibid., p. 539, 29 October 1967.

109. Abortion Act 1967, 1(1)(a).

110. HL Deb, vol. 285, cols. 1471–2, 23 October 1967.

111. LPL, RP/110, Robert Beloe to Michael Ramsey, 10 August 1967.

112. BLPES, HC/AT 7/28a, Abse to Antony Grey, 10 March 1967.

113. Interview with Alistair Service, 12 April 2000.

114. Anthony Crossman, *The Diaries of a Cabinet Minister, vol. iii: Secretary of State for Social Services, 1968–70* (Hamish Hamilton/Jonathan Cape, London, 1977), pp. 549–50, 4 July 1969.

115. Crossman, *Diaries of a Cabinet Minister*, vol. iii, pp. 569–70, 15 July 1969.

116. Ibid., pp. 806–7, 4 February 1970.

117. Ibid., p. 854, 10 March 1970.

118. 'Ministry aids MP with birth control Bill', *The Times*, 4 January 1967.

119. 'Warm welcome to family bill', *The Times*, 18 February 1967.

120. HC Deb, vol.741, cols 935–1020, 17 February 1967.

121. Crossman, *Diaries of a Cabinet Minister*, vol. iii, pp. 693–4, 22 October 1969.

122. Ibid., p. 749, 7 December 1969.

123. 'Questions about the Pill', *The Times*, 6 February 1967.

124. Crossman, *Diaries of a Cabinet Minister*, vol. iii, pp. 877–8, 2 April 1970; p. 886, 13 April 1970.

125. Lara Marks, *Sexual Chemistry: A History of the Contraceptive Pill* (Yale University Press, New Haven and London, 2001), pp. 148–50.

126. PRO, ED 50/862.

127. Lord Goodman's tribute to Lee on her retirement, London *Evening Standard*, 25 June 1970; Martin Priestman, 'A Critical Stage: drama in the 1960s', in Bart Moore-Gilbert and John Seed (eds), *Cultural Revolution? The Challenge of the Arts in the 1960s* (Routledge, London, 1992), pp. 122–3.

128. Brian Brivati, *Lord Goodman* (Metro, London, 1999).

129. PRO, PREM 129/ C(65) 22, 'A Policy for the Arts: the first steps', 15 February 1965.

130. Paul O'Higgins, *Censorship in Britain* (Nelson, London, 1972), p. 90.

131. John Elsom, *Post-war British Theatre* (Routledge and Kegan Paul, London, 1976), p. 129.

132. John Johnston, *The Lord Chancellor's Blue Pencil* (Hodder and Stoughton, London, 1990), p. 217.

133. Ronald Hayman, *British Theatre since 1955: A Reassessment* (Oxford University Press, Oxford, 1979), p. 34.

134. BL, LCP/WB 26, Tynan to Johnston, 10 April 1967.

135. BL, LCP/WB 23, Johnston to Christine Smith, Royal Court Theatre; 'Osborne play bar by Lord Chamberlain', *Daily Telegraph*, 17 September 1964.

136. BL, LCP/WB 23, minute by Scarbrough, 31 October 1958.

137. BL, LCP/WB 23, Johnston to Skelhorn, 2 July 1965; PRO, HO 300/56, note of meeting, 22 November 1965.

138. PRO, PREM 13/2152, 'Theatre Censorship', Jones to Sir Frank Soskice, 22 October 1965.

139. PRO, PREM 13/2152, Jones to Soskice, 22 October 1965.

140. BL, LCP/WB 29(B), Cobbold to Skelhorn, 6 October 1965.

141. PRO, HO 300/56, K. P. Witney to Guppy, 28 October 1965.

142. PRO, HO 300/56, note of meeting, 22 November 1965.

143. William Gaskill, *A Sense of Direction* (Faber and Faber, London, 1988), p. 70.

144. BL, LCP/WB 29(A), Penn to Nugent, 25 July 1965; Nugent to Cobbold, 27 July 1965.

145. BL, LCP/WB 29(A), Johnston to Cobbold, 3 August 1965, comment by Cobbold.

146. BL, LCP/WB 26, Goodman to Cobbold, 23 October 1967.

147. HC Deb, vol. 716, cols 1335–6, 20 July 1965.

148. HC Deb, vol. 721, col. 1229, 30 November 1965; PRO, HO 300/56, note by Sir Charles Cunningham to Soskice, 2 December 1965.

149. PRO, PREM 13/2152, Douglas Houghton to Wilson, 14 December 1965.

150. PRO, HO 300/56, Ross to Soskice, 1 December 1965 (emphasis added).

151. PRO, CAB 134/2850 H(65) 28th meeting, 3 December 1965.

152. Alan Travis, *Bound and Gagged: A Secret History of Obscenity in Britain* (Profile, London, 2000), pp. 190–215.

153. PRO, HO 300/56, note of conversation between Jenkins and Victor Stonham, 7 January 1966.

154. PRO, CAB 134/2852 H(66) 1st meeting, 12 January 1966; H(66) 2nd meeting, 26 January 1966.

155. PRO, PREM 13/2152, Derek Mitchell to Shuffrey, Home Office, 7 January 1966; note by Cobbold to Wilson, 11 January 1966; LPL, RP/93, 68, Donald Coggan, Archbishop of York, to Ramsey, 28 March 1966; 63, Eric Barker, secretary to the Methodist Conference, to Ramsey, 21 March 1966.

156. PRO, CAB 134/2852 H(66) 2nd meeting, 26 January 1966; PRO, PREM 13/2152, T. S. Legg (private secretary to Lord Chancellor) to Shuffrey, 19 January 1966.

157. PRO, PREM 13/2152, note by Cobbold to Wilson, 11 January 1966.

158. HL Deb, vol. 272, cols 1151–1248, 17 February 1966.

159. Report of the Joint Select Committee on Censorship of the Theatre, pp. 87–102, 147–52.

160. LPL, RP/93, 147, draft evidence to the Joint Select Committee, Pauline Claisse, Board for Social Responsibility, 21 November 1966.

161. Report of the Joint Select Committee, pp. 38, 45.

162. Ibid., para. 39.

163. Richard Findlater, *Banned! A Review of Theatrical Censorship in Britain* (Panther, London, 1968), p. 201.

164. O'Higgins, *Censorship in Britain*, p. 95.

165. Johnston, op.cit. p. 217.

166. Report of the Joint Select Committee, p. 36.

167. BL, LCP/1758, Reader's report by Heriot, 24 April 1967.

168. Richard Ingrams, and John Wells, *Mrs Wilson's Diary* (Private Eye, London, 1966); BL, LCP/1758.

169. Johnston, op.cit., p. 117.

170. PRO, PREM 13/1395, A. N. Halls, PPS to Prime Minister, to Miss E. M. Fisher, LCO, 18 May 1967.

171. BL, LCP/1758, John Johnston to Cobbold, 8 May 1967.

172. Alan Travis, 'How Harold censored diary spoof', *Observer*, 17 September 2000.

173. BL, LCP/1758, Note by Cobbold, 15 August 1967.

174. BL, LCP/WB 26, reader's report by Fletcher, 18 January 1967.

175. PRO, PREM 13/2152, Le Cheminant to Wilson, 24 July 1967; CAB 134/2154 H(67) 23rd meeting, 19 July 1967.

176. PRO, CAB 128/42 part 3 CC(67) 53rd conclusions, 27 July 1967.

177. BL, LCP/1748, reader's report by Heriot, 6 August 1967; Clark to Cobbold, 15 August 1967.

178. BL, LCP/1748, reader's report by Heriot, 6 August 1967.

179. PRO, PREM 13/2152, Cobbold to Wilson, 29 November 1967; Goodman to Wilson, 30 November 1967.

180. PRO, PREM 13/2152, Jenkins to Wilson, 26 July 1967.

181. Ben Pimlott, *Harold Wilson* (HarperCollins, London,: 1992) p. 485.

182. PRO, CAB 128/42 part 3 CC(67) 74th conclusions, 21 December 1967.

183. PRO, PREM 13/2152, Culf to Le Cheminant, 12 March 1968.

184. HL Deb, vol. 295, cols 594–624, 19 July 1968.

185. Gerald Gardiner, and Andrew Martin, (eds), *Law Reform Now* (Victor Gollancz, London, 1963).

186. Byung Hak Lee *Divorce Law Reform in England* (Peter Allen, London, 1974), pp. 61–2.

187. Quoted in Gavin Drewry, 'The Legislative Implementation of Law Reform Proposals', in Graham Zellick (ed.), *The Law Commission and Law Reform* (Sweet and Maxwell, London, 1988) p. 36.

188. Interview with Sir Brian Cubbon, 20 July 2003.

189. Law Commission, *First Annual Report 1965–1966* (HMSO, London, 1966), p. 15.

190. Archbishop of Canterbury's Group, *Putting Asunder: A Divorce Law for Contemporary Society* (SPCK, London, 1966), pp. 10, 37.

191. Ibid., pp. 38–9.

192. Law Commission, *Reform of the Grounds of Divorce: The Field of Choice*, Cmnd. 3123 (HMSO, London, 1966).

193. PRO, CAB 134/2851 H(66) 25th meeting, 18 November 1966.

194. HL Deb, vol. 278, cols 239–62, 264–348, 23 November 1966.

195. Law Commission, *Third Annual Report 1967–1968* (HMSO, London, 1968), appendix III, pp. 30–32.

196. PRO, BC 3/377, Lord Chancellor's speech to annual conference of NMGC, 5 May 1967.

197. Law Commission, *Field of Choice*, para. 84, p. 42.

198. LPL, RP/102, Robert Beloe to Duncan Sandys, 13 May 1966.

199. HL Deb, vol. 303, col. 310, 30 June 1969.

200. PRO, CAB 128/42 part 3 CC(67) 59th conclusions, 12 October 1967; PRO, CAB 129/133 C(67) 154, 'Divorce Law Reform', memorandum by Gardiner, 5 October 1967.

201. PRO, CAB 134/2956 LG(67) 27th meeting, 19 December 1967.

202. Abse, *Private Member*, p. 174.

203. Interview with Lord Jenkins, 25 November 1999.

204. James Callaghan, *Time and Chance* (Collins, London, 1987).

205. Kenneth O. Morgan, *Callaghan: A Life* (Oxford University Press, Oxford, 1997), pp. 290–322.

206. PRO, FCO 13/193, J. S. Champion to Cosmo Stewart, 4 June 1968, paper commissioned for Cabinet's Anti-Communism (Home) Official Working Group (AC(H)), 'Student Protest', 22 May 1968.

207. PRO, FCO 13/193, Stewart to J. H. Peck, 28 May 1968; *Guardian*, 31 May 2000.

208. PRO, FCO 13/193, speech by Shirley Williams, Minister of State, Department of Education and

Science, at Chatham House, 27 May 1968, quoted in Stewart to Peck, 28 May 1968.

209. Report of the Committee on the Age of Majority, Cmnd. 3342 (HMSO, London, 1967), para. 518, p. 125.

210. Interview with Baroness Serota, 18 January 2000.

211. HC Deb, vol. 773, cols 1019–29, 18 November 1968.

212. HC Deb, vol. 779, cols 958–68, 27 January 1969.

213. David Butler, and Michael Pinto-Duschinsky, *The British General Election of 1970* (Macmillan, London, 1971), pp. 27–8 and n.

214. Crossman, *Diaries of a Cabinet Minister*, vol. ii, p. 764, 6 April 1968; Interview with Lord Jenkins, 25 November 1999.

215. Lee, *Divorce Law Reform in England*, p. 114.

216. PRO, PREM 5/500, press notice, 29 April 1969; Crossman, *Diaries of a Cabinet Minister*, vol. iii, p. 463, 29 April 1969.

217. LPL, RP/82, Irvine to Ramsey, 17 November 1965.

218. HC Deb, vol. 758, col. 840, 9 February 1968.

219. Crossman, *Diaries of a Cabinet Minister*, vol. iii, p. 610, 19 December 1966.

220. Interview with Baroness Williams, 13 September 2003. Contentiously, when discussing this episode and the threat of resignation, Williams suggested that 'women are consistently more principled in public life [than men]. Women ministers put their principles ahead of status [more often].'

221. Lee, Divorce *Law Reform in England*, p. 89.

222. 'Service: he puts the ball in the MPs' courts', *The Times*, 21 April 1968.

223. Abse, *Private Member*, p. 174.

224. Service Papers, Service to William Wilson, 12 December 1967.

225. PRO, BC 2/381, Service to J. M. Cartwright-Sharp, 1 July 1968.

226. Edith Summerskill, *A Woman's World* (Heinemann, London, 1967), p. 237.

227. Service Papers, Abse to Service, 23 January 1968.

228. Summerskill, *A Woman's World*, pp. 233–43.

229. Abse, *Private Member*, p. 169.

230. 'Women vote on marriage breakdown', *Guardian*, 2 February 1968.

231. LPL, RP/103, 125, Robert Beloe to Geoffrey Derby, 24 June 1966; *Methodist Recorder*, 20 July 1967; HL Deb, vol. 278, cols 319–24, 313–15, 23 November 1966.

232. HL Deb, vol. 303, col. 370, 30 June 1969; 'Catholics keep eye on new divorce bill', *Catholic Herald*, 19 January 1968.

233. 'Eye-to-eye on divorce: Leo and the Archbishop', *Daily Mirror*, 27 July 1967.

234. LPL, RP/102, Bentley to Ramsey, 6 November 1966.

235. PRO, CAB 134/3031 P(68) 8th meeting, 20 June 1968.

236. Peter Richards, *Parliament and Conscience* (Allen and Unwin, London, 1970), p. 149; 'Divorce Bill is blocked', *The Times*, 6 July 1968.

237. 'Parliament's 70 wasted hours', *Sunday Telegraph*, 28 July 1968.

238. Abse, *Private Member*, p. 185.

239. PRO, BC 3/381, J. W. Bourne, LCD, to Cartwright-Sharp, Law Commission, 25.10.68; PRO, CAB 134/3031 P(68) 12th meeting, 7 November 1968; PRO, CAB 134/3031 P(68) 12, 'Divorce Law Reform Bill', memorandum by Gardiner, 4 November 1968.

240. PRO, CAB 134/2964 LG(69) 8, 'Matrimonial Property Bill', memo by Gardiner, 9 January 1969; Richards, op.cit., pp. 151–2.

241. PRO, CAB 134/2964 LG(69) 1st meeting, 14 January 1969.

242. PRO, CAB 128/44 part 1 CC(69) 5th conclusions, 23 January 1969.

243. NMLH, PLP minutes, 23 January 1969; 'Ministers give way to revolt on divorce vote', *The Times*, 24 January 1969; Abse, *Private Member*, p. 200.

244. HC Deb, vol. 776, cols 801–896, 24 January 1969; 'Wilson's whip in trouble', *Evening Standard*, 25 January 1969.

245. PRO, PREM 13/2710, Wilson to Williams, 30 January 1969; Williams to Wilson, 14 February 1969.

246. PRO, PREM 13/2710, Michael Blair, private secretary to Lord Chancellor, to P. L. Gregson, No. 10, 25 February 1969.

247. Abse, *Private Member*, pp. 199–200; HC Deb, Standing Committee C, 1968–1969, vol. ii, 10th sitting, cols. 434–6, 19 March 1969.

248. Service Papers, sponsors of Bill to MPs, 5 February 1968, 'list of MPs' intentions'; Richards, op.cit., p. 153.

249. PRO, CAB 129/142 C(69) 51 'Divorce law reform', memo by Gardiner, 13 May 1969.

250. PRO, CAB 128/44 part 1 CC(69) 23rd conclusions, 15 May 1969.

251. Abse, *Private Member*, p. 187.

252. PRO, PREM 13/2754, Peter Gregson to Wilson, 9 May 1969; HC Deb, vol. 784, col. 1797, 12 June 1969.

253. PRO, CAB 134/3118 PM(69) 7th meeting, 12 June 1969.

254. PRO, CAB 128/44 part 1 CC(69) 27th conclusions, 12 June 1969.

255. HC Deb, vol. 784, cols. 1789–1852, 12 June 1969.

256. Abse, *Private Member*, p. 201; HL Deb, vols 303, 304, 30 June–13 October 1969.

257. 'Freedom on Sundays', *Sun*, 15 February 1965.

258. Report of the Departmental Committee on Sunday Observance, Cmnd. 2528 (HMSO, London, 1964).

259. HL Deb, vol. 278, col. 13, 21 November 1966.

260. Crossman, *Diaries of a Cabinet Minister*, vol. ii, p. 373, 9 June 1967.

261. PRO, HO 300/53, Alice Bacon to Jenkins, 16 June 1967; Crossman, *Diaries of a Cabinet Minister*, vol. ii, p. 382, 13 June 1967.

262. PRO, HO 300/53, Bacon to Jenkins, 16 June 1967; Howell to Jenkins, 24 July 1967.

263. HC Deb, vol. 755, cols 1910, 1916, 8 December 1967.

264. HC Deb, vol. 755, col. 1918, 8 December 1967.

265. Richards., op.cit., p. 167; HC Deb, vol. 755, cols 1931–2, 8 December 1967.

266. John Parker, *Father of the House: Fifty Years in Politics* (Routledge and Kegan Paul, London, 1982), p. 122.

267. HC Deb, Standing Committee C, 1967–1968, vol. iv, 1st to 4th sittings, cols 1–190, 31 January–21 February 1968.

268. HC Deb, vol. 673, col. 689, 26 April 1968.

269. Parker, *Father of the House*, p. 123.

270. HC Deb, vol. 778, cols 2069–2174, 28 February 1969.

271. PRO, CAB 134/2964 LG(69) 5th meeting, 11 February 1969.

272. HC Deb, vol. 778, cols 2069–79, 28 February 1969.

273. HC Deb, vol. 778, col. 2083, 28 February 1969.

274. HC Deb, vol. 778, cols 2113–4, 28 February 1969.

275. HC Deb, Standing Committee B, 1968–1969, vol. ii, 1st to 19th sittings, 8 May–15 July 1969.

276. PRO, CAB 134/2964 LG(69) 22nd meeting, 9 December 1969.

277. Parker, *Father of the House*, p. 125.

278. Morgan, *Callaghan* p. 321.

279. PRO, HO 291/1551, 1552.

280. PRO, CAB 128/48 part 1 CC (69) 24th conclusions, 22 May 1969; CAB 134/3032 P(69) 15, 29 April 1969.

281. PRO, CAB 128/48 part 2 CC(69) 45th conclusions, 25 September 1969.

282. 'Tories strive to delay hanging vote', *The Times*, 27 November 1969.

283. PRO, PREM 13/2552, note of meeting between Callaghan and Hogg, 26 November 1969.

284. HC Deb, vol. 793, cols 1148–1298, 16 December 1969.

285. HL Deb, vol. 306, cols 1106–1258, 1264–1322, 17 December 1969.

Chapter 5

1. Edward Heath, *The Course of My Life* (Hodder and Stoughton, London, 1998), p. 453.

2. 'Mrs Castle plans state-owned sector for drugs industry and free medicine', *The Times,* 6 October 1972.

3. Mary Whitehouse, *Quite Contrary* (Sidgwick and Jackson, London, 1993), p. 41.

4. *Sunday Times*, 14 November 1971.

5. 'The Bishop's Gambit', BBC2, 20 February 1986.

6. 'Child benefit plan will be rescued from dustbin', *The Times*, 13 October 1977.

7. 'Action on permissiveness not a matter for Government, Mr Maudling says', *The Times*, 3 May 1971.

8. HC Deb, vol. 857, cols 672–3, 25 May 1973.

9. David Wood, 'Assurance is given that no other minister is involved', *The Times*, 25 May 1973.

10. PRO, Prem 15/1733, Correspondence between Armstrong and Tony Hetherington, 27 September to 18 October 1973.

11. The files relating to this episode at the Public Record Office can be found at PREM 15/1904–1906. However, there are many documents which have been retained and long passages blanked out, presumably including the identity of the other individuals who were named.

12. Quoted in Alan Travis, 'Call girls shook Government', *Guardian*, 1 January 2004.

13. PRO, BN 13/223; PREM 15/864, note for the record by Robert Armstrong, 4 January 1971.

14. PRO, PREM 15/864, note for the record by Robert Armstrong, 4 January 1971. (One can imagine the letter beginning, 'Dear Marje, I'm the Prime Minister's Principal Private Secretary, and I've got a terrible personal problem. I can't find any suitable women...')

15. PRO, BN 13/223.

16. John Roper, 'Woman judge to head Abortion Act Inquiry: more money for family planning', *The Times*, 24 February 1971; Anthea Hatt, 'Family planning as preventive medicine', *The Times*, 28 April 1971.

17. Interview with Baroness Williams, 10 September 2003.

18. LPL, Ramsey Papers, vol. 197, Gummer to Ramsey, 22 April 1971; Ramsey to Gummer, 1 May 1971; Ramsey to Gardiner, 13 May 1971; Whitworth to Ramsey, 30 April 1971.

19. Audrey Leathard, *The Fight for Family Planning: The Development of Family Planning Services in Britain 1921–74* (Macmillan, London, 1980), p. 188.

20. HC Deb, vol. 829, cols 855–64, 21 January 1972.

21. Leo Abse, *Private Member* (Macdonald, London, 1973), pp. 213–16.

22. HC Deb, vol. 838, cols 2051–88, 16 June 1972.

23. HC Deb, vol. 839, cols 237–8, 20 June 1972; 'Rule on time broken for vasectomy bill', *The Times*, 18 October 1972; HC Deb, vol. 843, cols 944–6, 23 October 1972.

24. Pat Heely, 'Minister launches campaign to save doomed children from "cycle of deprivation"', *The Times*, 30 June 1972.

25. PRO, PREM 15/433, Joseph to Heath, 18 May 1971; P. L. Gregson (No. 10) to R. G. Wendt (DHSS), 20 May 1971.

26. John Roper, 'Duke accused of knocking the poor in his "tax for having children" comment', *The Times*, 29 December 1971.

27. John Groser, 'Commons Committee recommends free contraception on Health Service', *The Times*, 10 August 1972.

28. 'Minister launches campaign to save doomed children from "cycle of deprivation"', *The Times*, 30 June 1972.

29. 'Mrs Castle plans state-owned sector for drugs industry and free medicine', *The Times*, 6 October 1972.

30. HC Deb, vol. 848, col. 234, 12 December 1972. Interestingly, Joseph was misreported in *The Times* as saying that it was abortion, rather than unplanned pregnancy, that caused unhappiness and ill-health. Though Joseph might well have been considered to be against abortion, he was scrupulous about not condemning it publicly, particularly while the Lane Inquiry was in progress.

31. HC Deb, vol. 848, col. 239, 12 December 1972.

32. Leathard, *Fight for Family Planning*, pp. 199–200.

33. HL Deb, vol. 337, cols 950–69, 987–1014, 19 December 1972.

34. 'Fifty four Tories call for NHS birth control', *The Times*, 14 February 1973.

35. HC Deb, vol. 853, cols 1101–1232, 27 March 1973.

36. HC Deb, vol. 859, cols 173–210, 25 June 1973.

37. HL Deb, 25 June 1973.

38. HC Deb, vol. 859, cols 173–210, 2 July 1973.

39. HL Deb, vol. 344, cols 387–432, 5 July 1973.

40. HC Deb, vol. 871, cols 657–68, 28 March 1974.

41. *Putting Britain First*, Conservative general election manifesto, September 1974.

42. Andrew Denham and Mark Garnett, *Keith Joseph* (Acumen, Chesham, 2001), p. 265.

43. 'Sir Keith Joseph denies bid for Tory leadership as critics mount attack', *The Times*, 21 October 1974.

44. 'MP's warning on Tory lurch to the Right', *The Times*, 22 October 1974.

45. Letters, *The Times*, 23 October 1974.

46. *Sunday Times*, 20 October 1974.

47. Ronald Butt, 'The link between public money and public morality', *The Times*, 24 October 1974.

48. Denham and Garnett, *Keith Joseph*, p. 269.

49. 'Mrs Castle challenges Sir Keith Joseph's "irresponsible views"', *The Times*, 26 October 1974.

50. Denham and Garnett, *Keith Joseph*, p. 269.

51. 'Birth facts refute Sir Keith's idea', *Guardian*, 21 November 1974, quoted in Leathard, *Fight for*

Family Planning, p. 203.

52. 'Sir Keith says letters "back me fourteen to one"', *The Times*, 28 October 1974.

53. Denham and Garnett, *Keith Joseph*, p. 270.

54. Ibid., pp. 272–3.

55. HC Deb, vol. 880, cols 544–51, 1 November 1974.

56. Leathard, *Fight for Family Planning*, pp. 201–4.

57. 'Profit rule shrinks Durex margins', *Guardian*, 17 October 1975.

58. Report of the Committee on the Working of the Abortion Act (HMSO, London, 1974).

59. 'Walk-out by MPs kills abortion amendment bill', *The Times*, 25 July 1974.

60. David Owen, *Time to Declare* (Michael Joseph, London, 1991), p. 229.

61. HC Deb, vol. 887, cols 506–38, 26 February 1975.

62. Michael Hatfield, 'Women MPs in revolt on abortion Bill', *The Times*, 14 March 1975.

63. 'BMA attack on abortion bill ends sit-in', *The Times*, 24 May 1975.

64. Neville Hodgkinson, 'MPs reject radical abortion law change', *The Times*, 6 August 1975.

65. See Anne Perkins, *Red Queen: the authorised biography of Barbara Castle* (Macmillan, London, 2003) for an account of the deterioration of their relationship.

66. Barbara Castle, *The Castle Diaries 1974–76* (Weidenfeld and Nicolson, London, 1980), pp. 628–9, 21 January 1976.

67. Ibid., p. 629, 22 January 1976.

68. 'Six MPs leave Committee on Abortion Bill', *The Times*, 17 February 1976.

69. Frances Gibb, 'MPs call for stricter control of abortion agencies and 20 week limit on operations', *The Times*, 29 July 1976.

70. 'Duchess of Kent speaks up for abortion controls', *The Times*, 7 July 1977.

71. 'Government wants to defeat abortion measure', *The Times*, 30 June 1977.

72. HC Deb, vol. 926, cols 1783–1896, 25 February 1977.

73. 'Prosecute makers of sex film, says MP', *The Times*, 19 April 1971.

74. 'Full city council to see sex education film courtesy of Dr Cole', *The Times*, 27 April 1971.

75. HC Deb, vol. 816, cols 1633–4, 6 May 1971.

76. Travis, *Bound and Gagged: a Secret History of Obscenity in Britain* (Profile, London, 2000), pp. 242–4.

77. PRO, PREM 15/1198, P. Halsey (DES) to Armstrong, undated 1971.

78. Quoted in Martin Durham, *Sex and Politics: The Family and Morality in the Thatcher Years* (Macmillan Education, Basingstoke, 1991), p. 40.

79. HL Deb, vol. 367, cols 134–270, 14 January 1976.

80. Interview with Baroness Williams, 13 September 2003.

81. Durham, *Sex and Politics*, p. 41.

82. LPL, Ramsey Papers, unfoliated files for 1971–2, Hugh Whitworth to Edwin Barker, 15 June 1971.

83. 'Jesus fleet sails to deliverance', *Guardian*, 1 September 1972.

84. Dallas Cliff, 'Religion, Morality and the Middle Class', in Roger King and Neill Nugent (eds), *Respectable Rebels: Middle Class Campaigns in Britain in the 1970s* (Hodder and Stoughton, London, 1979), p. 139.

85. Bridget Pym, *Pressure Groups and the Permissive Society* (David and Charles, Newton Abbot, 1974), p. 148.

86. Travis, *Bound and Gagged*, pp. 251–2.

87. Cliff, 'Religion, Morality and the Middle Class', p. 139.
88. *Guardian*, 12 October 1977.
89. LPL, Ramsey Papers, vol. 198, statement by Ramsey to British Council of Churches, 28 April 1971.
90. LPL, Ramsey Papers, vol. 202, Whitworth to Ramsey, 8 July 1971.
91. LPL, Ramsey Papers, vol. 202, Ramsey to Muggeridge, 30 September 1971.
92. Campbell Page, 'Demonstrators dim Festival of Light', *Guardian*, 10 September 1971.
93. LPL, Ramsey Papers, vol. 202, Whitworth to Floyd Ewin (St Paul's Chapter House), 24 November 1971.
94. Some of these samples are indeed hardcore, even to 21st-century eyes, as surprised scholars at Lambeth Palace Library will soon discover.
95. Sample from 'Who's Who think Britain's prestige is fading', *The Times*, 1 October 1971.
96. Norman Shrapnel, 'Dirt flies in Lords', *Guardian*, 22 April 1971.
97. HC Deb, vol. 336, cols 1256–1400, 29 November 1972.
98. LPL, Ramsey Papers, unfoliated files 1971–2, Whitworth to Ramsey, 31 October 1972.
99. LPL, Ramsey Papers, unfoliated files 1971–2, Whitworth to Ramsey, 1 November 1972.
100. LPL, Ramsey Papers, unfoliated files 1971–2, note by Whitworth of meeting in Longford's office, 16 November 1972.
101. Jeffrey Weeks, *Sex, Politics and Society: The Regulation of Sexuality since 1800*, 2nd ed. (Longman, London, 1989) pp. 280–81.
102. Travis, *Bound and Gagged*, p. 260.
103. 'Philosopher for inquiry on obscenity', *The Times*, 17 June 1977.
104. 'The law and child pornography', *The Times*, 6 September 1977.
105. 'Mrs Thatcher urges action over child pornography', *The Times*, 6 September 1977.
106. *Daily Telegraph*, 15 May 1978.
107. 'Mrs Thatcher urges action over child pornography', *The Times*, 6 September 1977.
108. HC Deb, vol. 939, cols 737–9, 17 November 1977.
109. 'Campaign to end use of children in sex films', *The Times*, 10 October 1977.
110. Whitehouse, *Quite Contrary*, pp. 108–9.
111. HC Deb, vol. 943, col. 1844, 10 February 1978.
112. Travis, *Bound and Gagged*, p. 261.
113. 'Pornography Bill to go ahead', *The Times*, 19 April 1978.
114. 'Child porn Bill goes through the Commons', *The Times*, 20 April 1978.
115. O. R. McGregor, *Social History and Law Reform* (Stevens, London, 1981), p. 43.
116. Matthew Parris, *Great Parliamentary Scandals: Four Centuries of Calumny, Smear and Innuendo* (Robson, London, 1995), pp. 144–52.
117. HC Deb, vol. 906, cols 767–819, 27 February 1976.
118. Jeffrey Weeks, *Coming Out: Homosexual Politics in Britain from the Nineteenth Century to the Present* (Quartet, London, 1977).
119. HL Deb, vol. 384, cols 13–15, 14 June 1977.
120. 'Reprimand for judge from Lord Chancellor', *The Times*, 6 July 1978.
121. Hugh Noyes, 'MP clerics protest at Mass in Palace of Westminster', *The Times*, 7 July 1978.
122. Christopher Walker, 'Paisley Party condemns "The Sound of Music"', *The Times*, 17 December 1977.
123. HC Deb, vol. 952, cols 313–66, 20 June 1978.

Chapter 6

1. Margaret Thatcher, *The Path to Power* (HarperCollins, London, 1995), p. 554.

2. Quoted in Mary Warnock, *Nature and Mortality, Recollections of a Philosopher in Public Life* (Continuum, London, 2003), p. 129.

3. Quoted in John Carvel, 'Prime Minister derides "Gannex conscience"', *Guardian*, 20 March 1989.

4. Victoria Gillick, *A Mother's Tale* (Hodder and Stoughton, London, 1989), p. 210.

5. Ferdinand Mount, *The Subversive Family: an alternative history of love and marriage* (Free Press, New York, 1992).

6. George Clark, 'Ministers want to create responsible families', *The Times*, 18 February 1983.

7. Margaret Thatcher, *The Downing Street Years* (HarperCollins, London, 1993), p. 279.

8. Ibid., pp. 630-1.

9. Hugo Young, *One of Us: A Biography of Margaret Thatcher* (Macmillan, London, 1989), pp. 343–5.

10. Tony Benn, *The End of an Era: Diaries 1980–1990* (Hutchinson, London, 1992), p. 227, 9 June 1982.

11. NMLH, NEC, 16 June 1982.

12. Interestingly, there is no reference to the elder postwar Labour stateswoman, Barbara Castle, in either volume of Thatcher memoirs.

13. Michael Durham, *Sex and Politics: the Family and Morality in the Thatcher Years* (Macmillan Education, Basingstoke, 1991), p. 131.

14. *Financial Times*, 14 May 1983, quoted in Durham, *Sex and Politics*, p. 131.

15. 'Unlikely local boy makes good', *The Times*, 23 February 1983.

16. Peter Riddell, 'Kinnock aide warns on London loony left', *Financial Times*, 6 March 1987.

17. Benn, End of an Era, p. 496, 6 & 7 March 1987.

18. 'Gays have been betrayed by Party leadership', *The Times*, 6 October 1989

19. Paul Routledge, *Mandy: the Unofficial Biography of Peter Mandelson* (Simon and Schuster, London, 1999), pp. 98–109. Considering the unbearable snideness with which the rest of this biography is written, managing to make even the most hardened Mandelson critic feel sorry for him, this particular part is written relatively sympathetically.

20. Andrew Grice, and John Furbisher, 'Labour planning free vote on gay sex at 16', *Sunday Times*, 11 February 1990.

21. Thatcher, *Path to Power*, p. 556

22. Thatcher, *Downing Street Years*, p. 628 (emphasis added).

23. Gillick, *Mother's Tale*, pp. 210, 251.

24. *The Next Moves Forward* (Conservative Central Office, London, 1987).

25. William Whitelaw, *The Whitelaw Memoirs* (Headline, London, 1990), p. 231.

26. HC Deb, vol. 34, cols 637–8, 17 December 1982.

27. Philip Cowley, 'Divorce', in Philip Cowley (ed.), *Conscience and Parliament* (Frank Cass, London, 1998).

28. Report of the Committee on Obscenity and Film Censorship, Cmnd. 7772 (HMSO, London, 1979).

29. Peter Hennessy, 'Some inquiries meant to achieve nothing', *The Times*, 11 April 1981.

30. Alan Travis, *Bound and Gagged: A Secret History of Obscenity in Britain* (Profile, London, 2000), pp. 266–7.

31. David Nicholson-Lord, 'Romans prosecution is withdrawn', *The Times*, 19 March 1982.

32. Private information.

33. 'DPP rejects obscenity complaint against play', *The Times*, 29 October 1980.

34. 'GLC grant to national arts groups up 9%', *The Times*, 25 March 1982.

35. Michael Durham, 'Obscenity' in Cowley, *Conscience and Parliament*.

36. Dennis Barker, 'TV-makers denounce Churchill for obscenity bill "laundry list"', *Guardian*, 21 February 1986.

37. *Next Moves Forward*.

38. Travis, *Bound and Gagged*, pp. 269–70.

39. Lesley A. Hall, *Sex, Gender and Social Change in Britain since 1880* (Macmillan, Basingstoke, 2000), p. 182.

40. HC Deb, vol. 5, col. 748, 2 June 1981.

41. Quoted in Durham, *Sex and Politics*, p. 109.

42. Frances Gibb, 'Campaign to combat teenage pregnancy', *The Times*, 28 April 1981.

43. CARE pamphlet, quoted in Durham, *Sex and Politics*, p. 109.

44. Lucy Hodges, 'Europe rules against Ulster "gays" law', *The Times*, 23 October 1981.

45. Virginia Berridge, *AIDS in the UK: The Making of Policy 1981–1994* (Oxford University Press, Oxford, 1996).

46. Quoted in Berridge, *AIDS in the UK*, p. 66.

47. Margaret Thatcher makes no mention of the AIDS crisis – perhaps the most significant health issue during her premiership – in her memoirs.

48. HC Deb, vol. 105, cols 799–864, 21 November 1986.

49. The most recent and convincing biography of Kinsey is Jonathan Gathorne-Hardy, *Alfred C. Kinsey: Sex the Measure of All Things – A Biography* (Chatto and Windus, London, 1998).

50. Interview with Lord Fowler, 27 May 2003.

51. Kenneth Baker, *The Turbulent Years: My Life in Politics* (Faber and Faber, London, 1993), p. 251.

52. Berridge, *AIDS in the UK*, p. 253.

53. For example Liz Stanley, *Sex Surveyed 1949–94: From Mass-Observation's Little Kinsey to the National Survey and the Hite Reports* (Taylor and Francis, London, 1995), pp. 49–53.

54. Berridge, *AIDS in the UK*, p. 254.

55. Interview with Gillian Shephard, 19 January 2004

56. *Daily Mail*, 24 January 1987.

57. Sue O'Sullivan, in 'Section 28 and the revival of Gay, Lesbian and Queer Politics in Britain' seminar held on 24 November 1999 (Institute of Contemporary British History), 28 pp. 27–8

58. Interview with Lord Dubs, 23 July 2003.

59. HL Deb, vol. 483, col. 336, 18 December 1986.

60. HC Deb, vol. 133, col. 413, 14 May 1987.

61. Quoted in Durham, *Sex and Politics*, p. 116.

62. Durham, *Sex and Politics*.

63. 'Thatcher tells party it is a staging post on a much longer journey', *The Times*, 10 October 1987.

64. Allan Horsfall, in 'Section 28', pp. 34–5.

65. Nicholas de Jongh, 'Thatcher pushed to keep section 28', *Guardian*, 8 April 1988.

66. HC Standing Committee A, vol. ii, cols 1199–1231, 29th sitting, 8 December 1987.

67. HC Deb, vol. 124, cols 987–1039, 15 December 1987.

68. NMLH, NEC/LGSC, 25 January 1988.

69. Lisa Power, in 'Section 28', p. 42.

70. 'Commons suspended after "gay protest"', *Financial Times*, 16 December 1987; HC Deb, vol. 124, cols 932–1038.

71. 'Family-smashing poll-tax will be dismembered in Lords, says Kinnock', *Guardian*, 30 January 1988.

72. HC Deb, vol. 129, col. 423, 9 March 1988.

73. 'Women protestors disrupt Lords', *Financial Times*, 3 February 1988.

74. HC Deb, vol. 127, cols 192–286, 9 February 1988. Experimental televising of the Commons was approved with a majority of fifty-four, despite Thatcher's reservations.

75. Durham, *Sex and Politics*, p. 116.

76. For example, Peter Tatchell in 'Section 28', pp. 29–33.

77. Durham, *Sex and Politics*, p. 114.

78. Ibid., p. 21.

79. Patrick Wintour and Andrew Veitch, 'Thatcher speaks out against Abortion Bill', *Guardian*, 22 January 1988.

80. Given the opprobrium which was subsequently heaped upon Warnock, not least over the consequences of her recommendations for disabled babies and 'human vivisection', these two previous experiences seem peculiarly useful and fitting.

81. Mary Warnock, *A Memoir: People and Places* (Duckbacks, London, 2002), pp. 158–83.

82. Warnock, *Nature and Mortality*, pp. 81–6.

83. Mary Warnock, *A Question of Life, The Warnock Report on Human Fertilisation and Embryology* (Blackwell, Oxford, 1985), p. 3.

84. Warnock, *Nature and Mortality* pp. 91–9.

85. Durham, *Sex and Politics*, p. 60.

86. Leo Abse, *Tony Blair: The Man behind the Smile* (Robson, London, 2001), p. 6.

87. Joan Isaac, 'Britain: the politics of morality', *Parliamentary Affairs*, 1994, vol. 47, p. 177.

88. HC Deb, vol. 146, cols 424–6, 2 February 1989.

89. HL Deb, vol. 515, cols 950–90, 8 February 1990.

90. HC Deb, vol. 171, cols 28–133, 23 April 1990.

91. HC Deb, vol. 171, cols 166–305, 24 April 1990.

92. Carvel, 'Prime Minister derides "Gannex Conscience"'.

93. Anthony Bevins, 'Marriage break-ups putting children at peril, says Thatcher', *Independent*, 18 January 1990.

94. Nicholas Wood, 'Baker rounds on runaway fathers', *The Times*, 31 January 1990.

95. Martin Linton, 'Gays and deviants "undermine family"', *Guardian*, 10 October 1990.

96. Melanie Phillips, 'The stressful state of family life', *Guardian*, 12 October 1990.

Chapter 7

1. Speech to Conservative Party conference, 1993, quoted in *John Major, The Autobiography*, (HarperCollins, London, 1998) p. 553.

2. Major, *Autobiography*, p. 388.

3. Major, *Autobiography*, p. 554.

4.   Speaking after the revelations about his four-year affair with Edwina Currie. Tracey McVeigh, and Gaby Hinsliff, 'I was used as a decoy for Major's affair', *Observer*, 29 September 2002.

5.   Major, *Autobiography*, p. 212.

6.   HC Deb, vol. 235, col. 38, 11 January 1994.

7.   HC Deb, vol. 235, col. 81, 11 January 1994.

8.   Roy Jenkins, 'Tory Nasties have got the upper hand', *Observer*, 10 October 1993.

9.   Leo Abse, *Tony Blair: The Man behind the Smile*, rev. ed. (Robson Books, London, 2001), pp. 6–7.

10. Tony Blair, The sporting metaphor is also reminiscent of the *soi-disant* 'centre forward/centre half' Wilson style in 1964 and 1974.

11. Quoted in Francesca Klug, *Values for a Godless Age: The Story of the UK's new Bill of Rights* (Penguin, London, 2000), p. 61.

12. HC Deb, vol. 225, cols 1029–34, 27 May 1993.

13. Major, *Autobiography*, p. 551.

14. Melanie Phillips, *All Must Have Prizes* (Little Brown, London, 1996), p. 340. The comparison with the Church has become particularly sensitive since this was written. As the Churches, particularly the Roman Catholic Church, have been hit by child abuse scandals their authority has indeed been damaged, and some of their doctrines, notably sacerdotal celibacy and the marriage ban, have been increasingly challenged.

15. Private information.

16. 'Back to Basics ends with trip to back benches', *The Times*, 6 January 1994.

17. Philip Webster, 'Major defies critics over Back to Basics', *The Times*, 14 February 1994.

18. Major, *Autobiography*, p. 553.

19. Simon Hoggart, 'Why insiders trade in tittle-tattle', *Observer*, 31 January 1993.

20. Michael Leapman, 'Major accused of "Maxwellian libel tactics"', *Independent*, 6 February 1993.

21. 'Caterer settles libel action', *Independent*, 16 July 1993.

22. Vicki Orvice, 'Premier "not too happy" as caterer talks of those rumours', *Daily Mail*, 16 August 1993.

23. 'Major reaches libel agreement', *Independent*, 30 September 1993.

24. McVeigh and Hinsliff, 'I was used as a decoy for Major's affair'.

25. Major, *Autobiography*, p. 554.

26. 'The secret passion that rocked Westminster', *Observer*, 29 September 2002.

27. Nicholas Wood, 'Major switches "basics" emphasis off family values', *The Times*, 15 November 1993.

28. *The Times*, 28 September 2002.

29. Matthew Parris, *Great Parliamentary Scandals: Four Centuries of Calumny, Smear and Innuendo* (Robson, London, 1995), p. 329.

30. Michael Jones, 'Wedded to welfare', *Sunday Times*, 11 July 1993.

31. Richard Cracknell, 'Children and Families', House of Commons Library Standard Note SG/1698, January 2002.

32. Michael Prescott, 'Tory Right urges radical welfare cuts', *Sunday Times*, 1 August 1993.

33. *News of the World*, 8 August 1993.

34. Nicholas Wood, 'Portillo fuels debate on benefits for single parents', *The Times*, 16 September 1993.

35. Philip Webster and Nicholas Wood, 'Clarke rejects Tory Right's welfare threat', *The Times*, 3 December 1993.

36. HC Deb, vol. 241, col. 457, 14 April 1994.

37. HC Deb, vol. 241, cols 459–62, 14 April 1994.

38. Philip Cowley, 'Divorce Reform', in Philip Cowley (ed.), *Conscience and Parliament* (Frank Cass, London, 1998), pp. 74–5.

39. Cowley, 'Divorce Reform', pp. 71–2.

40. HC Deb, vol. 278, cols 582–4, 25 April 1996.

41. Phil Webster, 'Blair puts the family at heart of his policies', *The Times*, 4 November 1996.

42. Sir Matthew Hale, *Historia Placitorum Coronæ: The History of the Pleas of the Crown* (Professional Books, London, [1736] 1971).

43. Kim Stevenson, 'Observations on the Law Relating to Sexual Offences: The Historic Scandal of Women's Silence' in *Web Journal of Current Legal Issues*, 1999, no. 4.

44. Quoted in Stevenson, 'Observations on the Law Relating to Sexual Offences'.

45. R v. R [1992] 1 A.C. 599, House of Lords.

46. S.W. c. Royaume-Uni/v. United Kingdom, Ser. A 335-B, 1995; C.R. c. Royaume-Uni/v. United Kingdom, Ser. A 335-C, 1995.

47. Alexandra Frean, 'Viewers protest at Bulger trial coverage', *The Times*, 9 December 1993.

48. Martin Durham, 'Censorship', in Cowley, *Conscience and Parliament*, pp. 139–40.

49. Alan Travis, *Bound and Gagged: A Secret History of Obscenity in Britain* (Profile, London, 2000), pp. 282–4.

50. Durham, 'Censorship', pp. 138–9.

51. Alexandra Frean, 'Drama ruling tests role of watchdog', *The Times*, 6 December 1993.

52. Jamie Dettmer, 'BBC rebuked over Lady Chatterley', 13 August 1993.

53. Interview with Lord Dubs, 23 July 2003.

54. 'Head's widow appeals for moral revival', *The Times*, 21 October 1996.

55. 'Major and Blair back crusade', *The Times*, 23 October 1996.

56. 'Labour accuses Howard of playing party politics', *The Times*, 23 October 1996.

57. HC Deb, vol. 284, col. 22, 23 October 1996.

58. 'Blair winning political battle to gain moral high ground', *The Times*, 1 November 1996.

59. 'Blair puts the family at the heart of his policies', *The Times*, 4 November 1996.

60. Alice Thompson, 'Blair admits smacking his children – and feeling remorse', *The Times*, 6 June 1996.

61. Nick Varley, 'Ashdown admits he smacked his own children "with regrets"', *Independent*, 2 November 1996.

62. Gillian Shephard, *Shephard's Watch: Illusions of Power in British Politics* (Politico's, London, 2000), pp. 84–5.

63. HC Deb, vol. 289, cols 212–40, 28 January 1997; Pierce, Andrew, '90 Tory MPs defy Government line in caning vote', *The Times*, 29 January 1997.

64. The Health of the Nation, Cm. 1968 (HMSO; London, 1992) pp. 92–101.

65. HC Deb, vol. 228, col. 338, 8 July 1993.

66. HC Deb, vol. 230, col. 608, 22 October 1993.

67. HC Deb, vol. 230, col. 640, 22 October 1993.

68. HL Deb, vol. 545, cols 1090–1119, 10 May 1993.

69. HL Deb, vol. 228, cols 1290–1324, 6 July 1993.

70. Howarth defected to Labour in 1995, finding a new seat in Newport East to fight at the 1997 election. He went on to serve as a junior minister for education and then the arts.

71. HC Deb, vol. 229, cols 31–4, 19 July 1993.

72. HC Deb, vol. 241, cols 456–7, 14 April 1994.

73. Nicola Douglas, Ian Warwick, Sophie Kemp and Geoff Whitty, *Playing It Safe: Responses of Secondary School Teachers to Lesbian, Gay and Bisexual Pupils, Bullying, HIV and AIDS Education and Section 28* (Health Education Research Unit, Institute of Education, University of London, 1997).

74. Major, *Autobiography*, p. 212.

75. HL Deb, vol. 556, cols 16–18, 20 June 1994.

76. HL Deb, vol. 556, cols 1770–79, 12 July 1994.

77. 'Police to enforce new law on age of consent', *The Times*, 23 February 1994.

78. Michael Evans, 'Ban on gays in armed forces survives appeal', *The Times*, 4 November 1995.

79. HC Deb, vol. 271, col. 123, 6 February 1996.

80. Special Report from the Select Committee on the Armed Forces Bill, Session 1995–1996, HC 143, Minutes of Evidence, 19 March 1996, pp. 99–109.

81. Parris, *Great Parliamentary Scandals*, pp. 343–50

82. HC Deb, vol. 276, cols 913–1052, 30 April 1996.

83. NickWood and Sheila Gunn, 'MPs reject the return of hanging by big majorities', *The Times*, 18 December 1990.

84. HC Deb, vol. 238, cols 24–74, 21 February 1994.

85. Steve Boggan, 'Protest crawl over rights for the disabled', *Independent*, 24 May 1994.

86. HC Deb, vol. 244, cols. 759–60, 16 June 1994.

87. Scott's career suffered further blows and humiliations. In 1995 he was involved in an incident in which he reversed his car into a child's pushchair and left the scene of the accident, resulting in a year's driving ban. The child was luckily unharmed. At the Conservative Party Conference in 1996 he was found face down in the street after a reception. He claimed a small amount of alcohol reacted adversely with painkillers. He was then deselected by his Kensington and Chelsea constituency association.

88. Matthew Bailey and Kevin Shinkwin, 'Disability Rights', in Cowley, *Conscience and Parliament*, pp. 99–106.

89. Melvyn R. Read, 'Sunday Trading', in Cowley, *Conscience and Parliament*, pp. 79–98.

90. Ibid., pp. 79–98.

91. HL Deb, vol. 573, cols 1691–1778, 5 July 1996.

Chapter 8

1. Tony Blair, Interview with the *Observer*, 5 September 1999.

2. Report stage, Matrimonial and Family Proceedings Bill. HC Deb, vol. 61, col. 973, 13 June 1984.

3. 'The Whisky Priest', BBC2, 16 December 1982.

4. Alison Park, 'The Generation Game', in *British Social Attitudes – the 17th Report: Focusing on Diversity* (Sage, London, 2000), pp. 1–21.

5. In 2001 Parliament passed the Sex Discrimination (Election Candidates) Act, which changed the law to ensure that positive discrimination, including all-women shortlists, was legal, leaving it up to the political parties whether to use such mechanisms in the future.

6. Tony Blair, 'Climate of violence', *The Times*, 12 April 1988.

7.   Tony Blair, 'Licence to print anything', *The Times*, 13 October 1987.

8.   Roy Hattersley, 'Not only doomed, but dotty too', *Guardian*, 20 March 2000.

9.   Norman Tebbit, quoted in Lucy Ward, 'Too many gay ministers and Hague's small, bald with odd voice', *Guardian*, 2 June 2000. Adoption has never been the responsibility of the Home Office.

10.   Shaun Woodward, 'Rebuilding John Bull', *Guardian*, 18 December 1999.

11.   Quoted in Peter Preston, 'Tories show themselves, in adversity, to be a nasty lot', *Guardian*, 20 December 1999.

12.   Michael White, 'Woodward deflects Tory flak', *Guardian*, 20 December 1999.

13.   *New Statesman*, 2 June 2000.

14.   Michael White, 'A Tory of his time, or just a chancer?', *Guardian*, 30 July 2002. Princess Margaret once exclaimed to a fellow guest at a party at St John Stevas' London flat, 'Have you seen this extraordinary place? It's full of pictures of the Pope and my family!' Jonathan Altaras to the author.

15.   Jasper Gerrard, 'If politics be the food of love', *Sunday Times*, 30 November 2003.

16.   Francesca Klug, *Values for a Godless Age: The Story of the UK's New Bill of Rights* (Penguin, London, 2000), p. 163.

17.   HC Deb, vol. 317, cols 1361–2, 21 October 1998.

18.   HC Deb, vol. 306, cols 1296–1300, 16 February 1998.

19.   Law Report, *The Times*, 23 February 1998.

20.   'Human Rights: Have the Public Benefited?', Lecture to the British Academy, 15 October 2002.

21.   Yvette Cooper, 'Threatened by reaction', *Guardian*, 15 March 2003.

22.   Interview with Baroness Williams, 13 September 2003.

23.   *The Case for a Human Rights Commission*, Sixth Report of the Joint Select Committee on Human Rights, 2002–2003, HC 489-1.

24.   Andy McSmith and Liz Lightfoot, 'Speech at school rebounds on Blair', *Daily Telegraph*, 10 May 2001.

25.   Matthew Tempest, 'Blair sticks to his guns under Paxman fire', *Guardian*, 16 May 2002.

26.   Polly Toynbee, 'We don't need the Church to educate our children', *Guardian*, 15 June 2001.

27.   HC Deb, vol. 386 part 1, col. 291, 22 May 2002.

28.   HC Deb, vol. 408, col. 13W, 30 June 2003.

29.   Census 2001, Office for National Statistics.

30.   HC Deb, vol. 410, cols 1190–1211, 21 March 2003.

31.   *Supporting Families* (Home Office, 1998).

32.   Quoted in Will Woodward, 'Are we turning into a nation of loners?', *Guardian*, 27 March 2000.

33.   Polly Toynbee, 'Forget the hot air on family values and think positive', *Guardian*, 1 November 2000.

34.   Clare Dyer, 'Gays can bring up children – judge', *Guardian*, 16 October 1999.

35.   Leo Abse, *Tony Blair: The Man behind the Smile* (Robson, London, 2000).

36.   Sandra Laville, 'Partners condemn protest fathers', *Guardian*, 22 May 2004.

37.   George Jones, 'Purple flour bomb hits Blair', *Daily Telegraph*, 20 May 2004.

38.   Michael Howard, 'Speech to a Families Summit, addressing the problems affecting today's families', Conservative Party website, 12 July 2004. Emphasis added.

39.   Department for Constitutional Affairs and others, *Parental Separation: Children's Needs and Parents' Responsibilities*, Cm. 6273, July 2004.

40.   Office for National Statistics, 5 November 2003.

41.   HC Deb, vol. 330, cols 395–6, 28 April 1999.

42.   Sandra Vegeris and Jane Perry, *Families and Children 2001: Living Standards and the Children*

(Department for Work and Pensions: 2003).

43. The fatal but admirable political death-wish exhibited by Maureen Colquhoun, Labour MP for Northampton North, after she left her husband for another woman and became the first openly gay MP in the 1970's, is sympathetically told by Matthew Parris in *Great Parliamentary Scandals*, pp. 234–9

44. *New Statesman*, 2 June 2000.

45. Anne Atkins, 'It is cruel to let gay kids try sex at 16' *Sun*, 15 July 1997: PCC Report 41 (1998). I am greatful to Simon Fanshaw for drawing my attention to this gem.

46. HC Deb, vol. 324, col. 22, 25 January 1999.

47. HC Deb, vol. 326, col. 87, 1 March 1999

48. HL Deb, vol. 599, cols 647–760, 13 April 1999.

49. HC Deb, vol. 344, cols 432–500, 10 February 2000.

50. HL Deb, vol. 611, cols 91–167, 11 April 2000.

51. HL Deb, vol. 619, cols 18–121, 13 November 2000.

52. Richard Reeves, 'Portillo backed gay ban to cut payouts', *Observer*, 26 September 1999.

53. Alexander Nicoll, 'Gays win case against armed services ban', *Financial Times*, 28 September 1999.

54. HC Deb, vol. 342, cols 287–302, 12 January 2000.

55. Ben Summerskill, 'It's official: gays do not harm armed forces', *Observer*, 19 November 2000.

56. Local Government Chronicle website, 10 June 1999.

57. HL Deb, vol. 609, cols 396–486, 7 February 2000.

58. Local Government Act 2000, Chapter 22, Section 104.

59. HC Deb, vol. 344, cols 240–41, 9 February 2000.

60. Paul Waugh and Andrew Grice, 'Series of leaks linked to office of Blair pollster', *Independent*, 18 July 2000.

61. SPOR, cols 936–70, 10 February 2000.

62. Kirsty Scott, 'Media protest fuels Section 28 row', *Guardian*, 19 January 2000.

63. Jason Allerdyce, 'Dewar is betraying family life, says Winning', *The Times*, 25 February 2000.

64. 'Tories humiliate Labour in Ayr by-election', *Guardian* Unlimited, 17 March 2000.

65. Alex Bell, 'Dewar barrage on Section 28', *Observer*, 12 March 2000.

66. Jason Allerdyce, '£1m private poll is savaged', *The Times*, 29 March 2000.

67. SPOR, cols 84–130, 27 April 2000.

68. Kirsty Scott, 'Edinburgh rejects private Section 28 poll', *Guardian*, 31 May 2000.

69. SPOR, Local Government Committee, 18th meeting (2000), Session 1, 30 May 2000.

70. Harris, Gillian, 'Galbraith gives way on marriage in Section 28 row', *The Times*, 17 June 2000.

71. SPOR, cols 480–600, 21 June 2000.

72. HL Deb, vol. 616, cols 97–130, 24 July 2000.

73. Nick Watt, 'Portillo backtracks after rival's strong showing', *Guardian*, 12 July 2001.

74. Gyles Brandreth, 'You share William's strengths, and you're bald and look what happened to him: why should it be different for you?', *Sunday Telegraph*, 2 September 2001.

75. Brian Groom, 'Tory leadership rivals clash over Section 28', *Financial Times*, 4 September 2001.

76. Julia Langdon, obituary, Lady Young of Farnworth, *Guardian*, 7 September 2002.

77. HL Deb, vol. 640, cols 567–624, 5 November 2002.

78. Benedict Brogan, 'Portillo adds support to abolish Section 28', *Daily Telegraph*, 8 January 2003.

79. Anne Perkins, 'Tories get free vote on Section 28', *Guardian*, 16 January 2003.

80. Nick Watt, 'Tory split in vote to scrap Section 28', *Guardian*, 11 March 2003.

81. HL Deb, cols. 496–527, 10 July 2003.

82. Sexual Offences Act 1956, Section 12; amended Sexual Offences Act 1967, Section 1.

83. 'Sex and society', Letters, *Daily Telegraph*, 1 February 2003.

84. 'Blunkett unveils sex crime overhaul', *Guardian*, 29 January 2003.

85. HL Deb, vol. 644, cols 775–6, 13 February 2003.

86. Alan Travis, 'Government backs down on sex law', *Guardian*, 16 April 2003.

87. HL Deb, vol. 649, cols 47–80, 9 June 2003.

88. The Sexual Offences Bill, House of Commons Home Affairs Select Committee, 2002–2003, 5th Report.

89. P v. S and Cornwall County Council, [1996] IRLR 347 ECJ; Sex Discrimination (Gender Reassignment) Regulations 1999 SI no. 1102.

90. 'Transsexuals unhappy with new job rules', Gay Times, June 1999.

91. Fitzpatrick v. Sterling Housing Association, *The Times*, 2 November 1999, [2001] 1 AC 27.

92. HL Deb, vol. 630, cols 1691–1746, 25 January 2002.

93. Evan Davis and Melanie Phillips, *A Fruitless Marriage: Same-sex Couples and Partnership Rights* (Social Market Foundation, London, 1999)

94. 'Gay couples rush to register at town halls', *Observer*, 9 February 2003.

95. *Civil Partnerships: A Framework for the Legal Recognition of Same-sex Partnerships* (Department of Trade and Industry, 2003).

96. Michael Howard, 'Everyone should live the British Dream', *Daily Telegraph*, 10 February 2004.

97. Tania Branagan, 'Peer in gay rights row quits BA board', *Guardian*, 3 August 2004.

98. Kamal Ahmed, 'Transsexuals win right to marry', *Observer*, 6 July 2003.

99. Sam Coates, 'Transsexuals lose fight over ejection from ladies', *The Times*, 15 August 2003.

100. Harris poll in the USA. This is also consistent with the historic level of support among Catholics for abortion in Britain.

101. 'Emergency laws to ban human cloning', *The Times*, 16 November 2001.

102. HC Deb, vol. 375, cols 1122–6, 29 November 2001.

103. Stem Cell Research, House of Lords Science and Technology Committee.

104. Kate O'Hanlon, 'Act regulates creation of live human embryos by CNR', *Independent*, 18 March 2003.

105. Catherine Bennett, 'Why Warnock's law no longer delivers', *Guardian*, 25 July 2002.

106. Quoted in Jeevan Vasagar, 'Use of foetal eggs grotesque, say campaigners', *Guardian*, 2 July 2003.

107. Sarah Boseley, 'As saviour sibling dawns, pressure mounts inexorably to change embryo rules', *Guardian*, 20 June 2003.

108. David Derbyshire and Jonathan Petrie, 'Parents win right to have donor babies', *Daily Telegraph*, 22 July 2004.

109. Quoted in Sarah Boseley, 'Cracking fertility's ethics code', *Guardian*, 14 February 2000.

110. Sarah Boseley, 'End in sight for fertility treatment lottery', *Guardian*, 1 December 2000.

111. Social Exclusion Unit, *Teenage Pregnancy*, Cm. 4342, June 1999.

112. Rebecca Smithers, 'Teenage culture harming pupils says Woodhead', *Guardian*, 12 February 2000.

113. 'Interventions to reduce unintended pregnancies among adolescents: systematic review of randomised controlled trials', *British Medical Journal*, 15 June 2002, vol. 324, no. 7351, p. 1426.

114. 'Sex education fails to cut pregnancies', BBC Online, 13 June 2002.

115. For example, Melanie Phillips, *All Must Have Prizes* (Little, Brown, London, 1996), p. 341.

116. Quoted in Rosie Waterhouse, 'Too much too young?', *Guardian*, 14 September 1999.

117. Polly Toynbee, 'Mixed up teenagers need more than this botched job', *Guardian*, 16 June 1999.

118. Tony Blair interview in the *Observer*, 5 September 1999.

119. Paul Eastham, 'Blair's moral crusade to cut teenage pregnancy', *Daily Mail*, 6 September 1999.

120. Joan Smith, 'Down with marriage', *Guardian*, 8 September 1999.

121. Government Response to the First Annual Report of the Independent Advisory Group on Teenage Pregnancy, (Teenage Pregnancy Unit, 2002), p. 40; Patrick Wintour, 'Blair to stop schools from expelling teenage mothers', *Guardian*, 13 June 1999.

122. HL Deb, vol. 621, cols 512–46, 29 January 2001.

123. Quoted in 'Court challenge to morning-after pill', *Guardian* Unlimited, 12 February 2002.

124. R (on the application of Smeaton) v. Secretary of State for Health, 18 April 2002, 193 QBD (Butterworths Family Court Reports: 2 FCR 193–288, 8 June 2002).

125. Interview with Baroness Williams, 13 September 2003.

126. Beezy Marsh, 'Room in the womb for those first few steps', *Daily Mail*, 29 June 2004.

127. David Steel, 'We need to rethink my abortion law', *Guardian*, 6 July 2004.

128. HC Deb, col. 836, 7 July 2004.

129. Tony Blair, 'Alton: tactics and principles', *The Times*, 19 January 1988.

130. Sexual Health and HIV Strategy (Department of Health, 2001), p. 28.

131. Ulster Marketing Surveys Ltd, 'Birth Control and Abortion – a Northern Ireland Opinion Survey', August 1994.

132. Clare Dyer, 'Court rejects call to clarify Ulster abortion law', *Guardian*, 8 July 2003.

133. HC Deb, vol. 326, col. 1056, 4 March 1998.

134. HC Deb, vol. 328, cols 1093–1111, 31 March 1998.

135. David Thompson, 'Abortion stitch up sparks Labour revolt', *Herald*, 2 April 1998.

136. 'Bush in foreign policy shift', *Financial Times*, 23 January 2001.

137. Arthur Gould and Nina Stratford, 'Illegal Drugs: Highs and Lows' in British Social Attitudes – the 19th Report (Sage, London, 2002) pp. 119–40.

138. Source: BBFC website statistics.

139. Alan Travis, *Bound and Gagged: A Secret History of Obscenity in Britain*, (Profile, London, 2000), pp. 283–9.

140. 'BBFC to consult filmgoers on censorship', *Guardian*, 18 October 1999.

141. Travis, *Bound and Gagged*, p. 288.

142. A. C. Grayling, 'Close encounters of the rude kind', *Guardian*, 17 May 2001.

143. Quoted in Jason Deans, 'TV film viewers want information not censorship', *Guardian*, 10 November 2000.

144. Interview with Lord Dubs, 23 July 2003.

145. Annette Hill and Katarina Thomson, 'Sex and the Media: A Shifting Landscape', in British Social Attitudes – the 17th Survey, pp. 71–99.

146. Lisa O'Carroll and Jason Deans, 'Jowell changes tack over Brass Eye', *Guardian*, 30 July 2001.

147. Jonathan Freedland, 'Censure not censor', *Guardian*, 1 August 2001.

148. Fiachra Gibbons, 'Anatomist will escape charges', *Guardian*, 22 November 2002.

149. Jason Deans, 'Channel 4 rapped over dead baby broadcast', *Guardian*, 10 March 2003.

150. Quoted in Mediawatch UK newsletter, Spring 2002.

151. John Sutherland, 'I say it's funny, you say it's filth', *Guardian*, 10 January 2000.

152. Joshua Rozenberg, 'Pro-life victory over BBC "censorship"', *Daily Telegraph*, 15 March 2002.

153. Interview with Baroness Williams, 13 September 2003.

154. Richard Shannon, 'History lessons', *Guardian*, 4 October 2001.
155. Interview with Baroness Boothroyd, 21 January 2004.
156. Paul Eastham, 'Blair's moral crusade to cut teen pregnancy', *Daily Mail*, 6 September 1999.
157. Thomas Babington Macaulay, 'Moore's Life of Byron', in *Critical and Historical Essays, Contributed to The Edinburgh Review* (Bernhard Tauchnitz, Leipzig, 1850), vol. 1, pp. 311–3.

Index